ALL W

PEOPLE ARE RACIST! (WELL, 75-80% OF THEM ARE)

WRITTEN BY

SOME WHITE WOMAN FROM L.A.

IN LOVING MEMORY OF DEACON GREY, THE FUNNIEST MAN I KNEW.

R.I.P. DAVID.

Table of Contents

ACKNOWLEDGMENTS

To Eliza McClaine, the child we lost whose death triggered all of these memories. I would also like to dedicate this to any pricks that didn't give a shit about his death, or the death of many black men at the hands of white men with badges. Enjoy the read, the truth hurts, huh?

ABOUT THE AUTHOR

I'm an old, skinny, out of work actor, teacher, chef, comedian, adult entertainer and smartass. That's about it. Run with it.

INTRODUCTION

I think all white people should be treated like they are in the military court; they are guilty until proven innocent. Why? Because that's how they treat black people. It's only fair. Don't you think? HELLO! Did I get your attention, Whitey? I hope so because I don't think many white people will want to be around me after this comes out. Well, not all of them, just 75-80% of them.

Now I'll start right off the bat! You are going to think I'm making all this up but I'm not. Since white people need a disclaimer for everything, here you go. I'm a writer, a comedian, and a smartass. All of this may be fiction. I would like the readers to guess what part is fiction, and which isn't.

Here comes a warning! If you are a white male cop, or very sensitive, a hippie, a midget, a Karen, a Boogaloo boy, a pedophile, or into Hitler, the Klan, or any hate group, or worse, if you are in A.A, part of a sorority, the royal family, have bipolar disorder, are a Mormon, nun, a born again Christian, Katelyn Jenner, Taylor Swift, Tekashi 69, Megan McCain, Jon Elway, Donald Trump, David Duke, Mayor Hancock, Mr. Wonderful, Madonna Janice Dickinson, My ex-girlfriend, or to be precise, easily offended, this information is not for you.

Some people, read 'white people, are used to everything being sugar-coated. But tough shit, the truth hurts! So, I do not want any complaining from Whiteys. I am fully aware of the potential trouble I'm going to get when this comes out. I couldn't share any of this until my dad was dead and Trump was out of office. I have never told anyone any of this except my friend Deacon Grey, a fellow comedian who has passed away, so I don't know how you will take it. But it is the truth, and we have freedom of speech!

I'm just a privileged white woman from L.A., and I have to get this out. White people don't tell the truth much, so you better pay attention to this. I have left out some names of certain people on purpose, but if the ones I left in have a problem with the truth, don't blame me for telling everyone about the stupid shit you did. Anyone who doesn't like what I'm going to say, you can't get blood from the truth. That's why you give yourself a disclaimer and hire a lawyer before you get into deep shit. I have nothing to hide or lose.

CHAPTER ONE: WHITEYS FAMILY TREE

I'll start right from the beginning. My parents' names are Dick and Jane, Richard and Jane Williams. Yep, that's how white we are. They named me Jan in the 70s. MARSHA, MARSHA, MARSHA, I heard that my whole life growing up. Mom and dad got engaged on their first date. Not kidding. They met at a college grad party. My mom got her degree in fine art and education from Pacific University in Oregon. Something about P.U. sounds funny to me. Dad just became a dentist. He went to U.S.C. – University of Spoiled Children, perfect for that stuck-up asshole. Dad asked her out at the Big Sky drive-in theater in L.A. No, Dad didn't bang her on the first date.

Mom was a virgin, a twenty-six-year-old virgin. No pressure, though! To talk about myself, I lost my virginity at eighteen. When mom found out, I said, "I wanted to see what I was missing. Oh, and also, I think I might be lesbian." Her reply was not something that surprised me. "You are not one of those! Now, no man will ever want you. You have ruined yourself for the rest of your life," she said with utter disgust in her voice. It was evident that I really disappointed her. That was the way it was in her family. You had to be a virgin until you were married, so you could wear white.

Clearly, mom was very old school. She was perfectly aligned with dad's criteria for a wife. She hit all the right points for him. She was a virgin, educated, white, a breeder, would stay home with the kids, and she spoke German fluently. That had to give dad a hard-on. Mom taught ballet in Germany for two years, and that's how she learned the language. Dad had an affinity towards Hitler. Mom did not know this at the time. She was a looker too; she looked like a blond Rita Hayworth. I asked her once. "Mom, did dad have a ring? Did he get down on one knee?" I mean, that is how one envisions their parents' proposal. She replied, "Nope. He looked at me in the front seat and said, 'Jane, I think you and I both want the same things, so when your parents come home from Europe, tell them we are getting married'." She simply accepted it. Three months later, they got married. They said their vows at this beautiful church on the corner of San Gabriel Boulevard and Huntington Drive, right by where we grew up in L.A.

If you ever saw the movie, "Father of the Bride," starring Steve Martin, it was shot in the same neighborhood I grew up in. The church in the movie where she gets married is at the end of our street. My mom played piano in that church for quite a while. The truth is, it was very middle class for L.A. Nobody locked their doors as everyone knew each other or they went to your church. There were no signs of crimes or anything illegal. People only got nervous when the Night Stalker was out in the 80s. It was the only time everyone was on high alert, but other than that, life back then was monotonous, really boring.

I always remembered my parents' anniversary. They got married on November 23rd, 1963. Any guesses on what happened on the 22nd? J.F.K.'s assassination! They got married the day after JFK was assassinated. What a shit way to remember your anniversary! We would see stuff on the T.V. about it and go, "Oh yea, mom and dad's anniversary is coming up." Isn't that awful?

Since we are on this topic, I'll tell you another really bad omen for a wedding. I was on a wedding cruise in the Pacific Ocean when Columbine happened. Everyone at the wedding was from Colorado. I get a knock on my door at 8:00 AM in the morning. I get told to turn on my T.V. Almost instantly, our jaws dropped. The guy I was watching it with said, "You see where they are doing triage in that apartment building parking lot? I live there." All I could think was that this was no joke. What a thing to go home to. That afternoon, they got married on the ship. I don't know if they're married anymore as we lost touch. All I can say is that this was like watching the twin tower fall in New York and go, "That is too bad. Let's go to the Plaza and get married now." But there is one thing I can say for sure; they will never forget their anniversary, a classic marital bliss in other words.

After pulling off quite a few stunts throughout my life, I do have some advice to pass on to anyone going to a wedding. Don't get drunk at the reception and go, "Hey, I give it two years!" Yes, I did that, and to make it worse, I was the maid of honor. But get this, her name was Karen! And believe me when I say that she did full justice to her name. White, pretty, spoiled, and I called it. She didn't make it two years before she started cheating on him. Some women are like that. They cheat and they're forgiven, I don't understand it.

If you have seen Sex and the City, and know Carrie, read "Chapter Sixteen: O.K. Karen", you will know what I am trying to say here. She is a spoiled little bitch who can't stay faithful. For the record, I like Sara Jessica as an actor. If they do Sex and the City 3, I hope Samantha goes into politics, becomes the next mayor of New York City, and legalizes prostitution. Samantha will move into Trump Towers and make it New York's next Bunny Ranch. Miranda can do all her press and keep her out of jail. Charlotte and Harry live happily ever after and her kid Lilly becomes a tattoo artist, who is very successful. She works with top clients and everybody loves her. Rose, her little sister becomes an attorney like her daddy. I like Harry as a character as well. It is the right amount of sweet. It took me time, but I finally figured out who the actor who plays Harry is. He was in TAPPS with Sean Penn and Timothy Hutton. He had hair back then, which explains why it took me time to figure out who he was. He's a terrific actor!

Coming back to the point, Carrie doesn't deserve to have a happy ending. She's nothing but a spoiled brat. I hope Mr. Big dumps her on her ass and steals all her shoes just to fuck with her. The best part of Sex and the City 1 was when Carrie gets dumped at the altar. I truly loved it! This time after Mr. Big dumps her again, she can move in with Stanford and Anthony until she becomes too much with her constant, "WHAAA STANFORD?! GET ME SOME MORE. I NEED I NEED I NEED," attitude. Eventually, they get sick of that shit and lock her out. In my opinion, Carrie represents all the Karens in the world. White, spoiled pretty, rich but never with her own money, and always out for herself. I hope girls don't really look up to her character. It's a bad example of the way women should behave. *GIMMIE, GIMMIE, GIMMIE, BAD CARRIE, BAD KAREN, BAD!*

My mom's family, they're interesting, not bad, just different. We went to a family reunion in Oregon at a Christian church camp when I was about thirty-five. My mother had to pull us aside, only to say, "Now girls, I have to warn you, we have Mormon relatives." We tried but we just couldn't stop ourselves from bursting with laughter. They were our second and third cousins, and we had never met them before. Now, I love Donny and Marie. They were good, clean, white, geeky, and fun but we didn't know we were related to them back then. Mormons are very "holier-than-thou" and have the "we are superior" mindset. I met them and said, “Hi, I am your cousin from Colorado.” They didn’t say anything in response but this is what I got out of their body language. “Hi! You are not Mormon? Okay well, we are. You know heavenly father loves us more than anything, right? Could you stay over there? We know you’re here but you’re not one of us. We are better than everyone, so we’ll be up here on this pedestal and you can stay over there. It’s more comfortable for us and I’m sure you understand. God loves us more than you.” They said all that without uttering a single word.

Yeah, Mormons are fun. Now, don’t get them all together and have them smile at you. Lay off the toothpaste! Did you know that Ethiopians won’t let them adopt? They don’t want them to become Mormons. Ethiopians are smart! I don’t know how they trick blacks to become Mormons as there is no reference to black people in the Book of Mormon. It’s like putting a poppy seed in a bowl of rice. Mormons are trying to make it look more even and it’s not working. My mom was clear to me, not to use any profanity or do anything “out-there” in front of the Mormons, so all I did was ask one of them to pop open a bottle of champagne for me, just to fuck with him. My sister thought it was funny. I have to commend my sister on her behavior that day. Since she’s an atheist and watching her bite her lip while we sang and prayed for four days, I thought she was going to explode when she met the Mormons. To our surprise, she handled herself really well, and the Mormons can consider themselves truly lucky!

To be very honest, I think the Book of Mormon was written on acid. I know they don’t drink but God damn, if you ever try to read that piece of shit, it’s really funny on acid! I have read Dianetics, and even though I didn’t get all of it, at least it was interesting. If you ask me, I don’t like the way people attack Scientologists. If a Scientologist has gone directly after you or someone you know then sure, it is justified. But would you go up to a Jewish person and say some anti-Semitic racist thing to them and walk away thinking that's acceptable? I don't think so. Now, Judaism is a beautiful and deeply profound religion. We don't do that because they have been through enough misfortune, we just know better than to cause them pain by barking some hurtful words. Be clear that I'm not comparing Judaism to Scientology. I am well aware that it is almost equivalent to comparing apples and oranges. All I am saying is, when it comes to religious beliefs, we should just know better. Just because you don't follow their religion doesn't mean it is okay to dump on it. I go after my Mormon cousins because they deserve it. Not all of them, just 75-80% of them.

I knew two people who lived close by and were Scientologists. They were always polite enough to say a courteous hello whenever we crossed paths. They didn't go after me as they knew that I'm Catholic. We just never talked about religion. They never threw accusations at my face about priests and pedophilia in the Catholic Church unlike Lea Remy, who is busy throwing dirt against Scientology.

I see no point in doing so because I know their beliefs have nothing to do with me. What do we know about the truth of their religion, after all? We were just civil to one another. I like Jenna Elfman, Tom Cruise, Jon Travolta; they're Scientologists and they're very good at their craft. Why can't all of us follow whatever makes us a better person? Don't be dicks! I'm talking about all of us who think our religion is better than others. It's not! Just enjoy your spiritual side any way you want to as long as it doesn't hurt anyone. Even if you don't follow or understand it, just be comfortable with whatever makes you spiritually happy and floats your boat. I don't think my Mormon cousins will like this, but I'm not worried if they get mad at me. I'll bet if they get a load of this, they will deny even knowing me. I can see their friends coming out of the temple going, "Hey! Don't you have a cousin in Colorado? Isn't her name Jan?" With hysteria in their eyes, they would reply back with, "Oh no! We don't know her at all. Who is that? Go burn all of her pictures. Destroy any evidence! We don't know her at all!" Yep, I wasn't one of their favorite cousins at the reunion. Oh, well.

We have Amish relatives as well. They don't give me any shit for my beliefs, so I would claim that they're really nice people. I shook their hand once. They said something very faintly under their breath, and I think it was Swedish. I'm not really sure but they walked away after that, miles down the road by foot to their little cabin in the middle of nowhere. There's no electricity there but it's warm in the winter, I am not sure how. They are the kind of folks who make apple butter and quilt. Then they tell all their family members that they shook the hand of a relative they never knew they had, and that lasts them a year. They're not very exciting people but very nice. At least they're not dicks to me like my Mormon relatives, so it's fair to give them some credit for their understanding nature.

Who doesn't have embarrassing relatives, right? Everyone does! Let me introduce Walt as we talk about that. He is a man who doesn't have both oars in the water. He's a third cousin and married into the family. It's kind of where the family tree stops branching. Walt is a Bible banging Baptist, a minister from Kentucky. He always has a leather-bound copy of "The King James Bible" in his hand at all times. Walt kind of looks like the monopoly man but white trash. He doesn't look like anyone else in the family. He is short, considering I have third cousins, who are 6'6 or 6'8, and skinny. When I met him, I said, "Hi Walter, I am your cousin from Colorado." Looking at me with slightly questioning eyes, he said, "Hello, do you follow God?" I could see him drifting away and the next thing I know, he is over there talking to God. *Walter, God's this way, over here. Oh, Jesus is this way, Walt, and yup, he is gone.*

In all seriousness, Walt is a sweet guy. He has daughters, and one of them is called Laura. And oh boy, she is big. You ever watched the movie, Willy Wonka? If you have, I am sure you remember the Blueberry? Yep, that is her but just paint her white. She is 5'2 and over three hundred pounds. On top of that, she is schizophrenic. I don't know the plan in the head of old Christian therapist Walt, but he thinks it's a good idea to put headphones on her and have her listen to religious music and sermons all day to drown out the other voices in her head. GO WALT!

Then there is Sarah. I have four cousins named Sarah. No shit Whitey, big surprise! Sarah is severely autistic-like Rain Man. I know that raised questions in your head but I can explain. She's shy, timid and is under full-time special care. Her hair is always pulled back with thick glasses shielding her eyes from too much light. Sarah doesn't really look at you when she speaks. If you ask her how she's doing, she won't answer you but if you ask her, "Hey, Sarah. When was the White House built?" She will start with its history and how it came to exist and will go on and on until you touch her and she stops. The weirdest thing, I'd say. She has a degree with honors in lineage and history. She's brilliant but has zero social skills. I described her to some people and some stupid dickhead said to me, "You have a cousin like Rain Man? You should take her to Vegas." Confused, I said, "She is afraid of bright lights and loud noises." That was a fucking dick! Nobody in our family, not even the Mormons, would expose her to that. It would freak her out, you drunk white guy prick, go figure your own sad life first! They are family and we love them. I love the Mormons too, I just don't like them very much.

The thing with me is, I am religious but I refrain from comparing my faith with anyone else's. I am pretty sure God doesn't love me more because I go to church. That is utterly stupid. My cousin might be retarded, but she knows better than to do that. Do you know why? Because she is not a Mormon! Speaking of comparatively tolerable relatives, I do have some nice ones who are not Mormons. Our Charlie's Angel's cousins. They are three girls with blond, red, and brown hair, and with voices of spun gold. They saw me at my worst when I was drinking myself to death, but they prayed for me. Well, girls, it worked! I have been sober for over a decade. Thanks. I love you very much.

My dad's family is much different. They were all K.K.K. Elite in Los Angeles. They were doctors, like dad, and real estate guys like grandpa. His dad had his fair share of connections with politicians, clergy, police, military, with a secret handshake pat on the shoulder, wink and a nod, and little K.K.K. pins under their lapel. The guys with power who make things really disappear, if you know what I mean. The guys who don't get caught, not like those retards in the south skinheads, Hitler Youth, sheet-wearing hillbilly clansmen with confederate flags in their trucks, who fuck their sisters and burn crosses on people's lawns with their torches and have low I.Q.s. Let them take a fall if something bad happens, they like the attention. Do you think those guys my grandfather was friends with are going to get their hands dirty if they don't have to? Those guys were old school rich clan, they didn't give one fuck about any of those lower-class haters and let them do all the dirty work. My dad's klan would be like the kind Donald Trump would hang out with, you know the type; socially awkward, needy, lonely, sexually confused, and fashionably challenged, white guys with money who slouch and have no common sense. Mom knew nothing about it, and I didn't know for sure as well until high school. I don't discuss it with my sister, but I think she may know more about it than I do. At home, we don't discuss it and she's going to be really pissed at me for telling everyone this but I have to! We don't talk about it as if it's a taboo subject. We used to joke about it when we were younger. "You know, it's a good thing mom raised us instead of dad or we would be in the Klan, huh?" One of us would giggle and say, "I know!" It got less funny as we got older.

My grandparents retired to Palm Springs. I mean, whose white grandparents don't? They go there or Florida and play golf with Bob Hope. I met him once. They had a place in Yucca valley, that place was fun when we were teenagers. We would ride our dirt bikes around and would mess around in the dirt. But when we were little, we hated going out there. Always felt like a museum. Don't touch anything, don't talk too loud, and don't run anywhere. It wasn't very kid-friendly. My grandma had this lovely garden with gravel around it. If we ran around, messing up the gravel, she would give us a long rake to smooth it all out. Now I understand that the woman had O.C.D. My grandma would go on long walks with her dog Hobo, the ugliest dog you ever saw. He had a wicked under-bite, but they loved each other.

Once, grandma caught scorpions, put them in mason jars, and showed them to us. She gave us both big flat rocks, dumped them out, and said, "Okay, now kill them." My sister rocked them to push them back and said, "Are you okay?" with a shaky voice. Back then, I didn't know why she did that. I do now. She was a twisted old bitch, and it's not a surprise my dad was so screwed up.

I always wanted to have the kind of grandma who didn't scare me or make me feel uncomfortable. I know my mom didn't get any of her wonderful traits from her mother. That woman was scary; six feet tall, played the saxophone and was a big band leader. No shit, right? She was an unhappy woman most of the time, but mom wasn't like her at all. Thank God for that. The other grandma, the racist one, anal-retentive, a nurse, and the coldest woman was no fun as well. I always wanted a grandma I could cuddle up with whenever I needed comfort but she wasn't close to one. The best grandma I can think of right off the bat is the actress in Good Times. You could see her cuddling up with her grandchildren, singing or telling them a story. My grandmothers were nothing like that. Again, thank God, my mom wasn't anything like her. Instead, she got all her sweetness from my Pops, who was a very sweet and kind person.

My paternal grandmother was the perfect visual representation of a racist. She would say stuff to me when I was little like, "Jan, I don't know why your mom won't let you watch Birth of a Nation with us. It's a classic like The Wizard of Oz." She would say, "Don't tell your mom."

I got that a lot from dad when I was growing up, "Don't tell mom." My mom is the most P.C. person on the planet. Grandma would say, "Back in the day, men used to ride their horses down Orange Grove and it was lovely. We would leave the daughters of the American Revolutionary Party meetings, and if a black man came down the street, he would get off the sidewalk to let us by. I don't know why they don't do that anymore."

My dad's side of the family never apologized for any kind of rude remark or racist slander. His father would have no problem walking up to a man of color and saying, "Get out of my way, Nigger." Yes, he was that awful. This is the only time I will use the "N" word because I don't think any white person should ever use it, not even as a joke because when we do use it as a joke, we get reprimanded for it. They would keep it quiet around mom most of the time, so I don't spill their racist tea. The only good thing about going to Palm Springs was Hadley's date shakes! This place on the way, Hadley's, had the best shakes with dried dates in it. Sounds weird but it was so good! Try it; take some dates, cook them down, make a puree, add it to French vanilla ice cream with milk, and Viola! So good! If you ever make the trip from L.A. to Palm Springs, hit it for their date shakes. I hope they didn't close after COVID, fingers crossed.

Once, we were at grandma's in the desert. We were having dinner. Dad was at one end and grandma at the other. She said something, assuming racist, and mom obviously didn't like it. Mom with a chilly tone said, "Ruth, may I have a word with you in the other room, please?" After a while, they came back. I don't know what kind of conversation was exchanged between them but they surely shut the hell up. It was at Christmas or Easter, and I was only six but I still remember it. Grandma didn't say a word after that and it was a show to see this happening in her own house. Mom didn't care. She was fierce in the sense that she wasn't going to let her talk that way in front of us even in her own home.

We started to have Christmas together at one point, with the Williams on one side, the Marsh family on the other. When we were really young, they couldn't stand each other enough to get along during the holidays, so after a while, we had to have them separately. I remember, the last time we had dinner together was when I was four. Mom's family tried to just ignore dad's family entirely. They would go outside to smoke and dad's family would tear them to shreds behind mom's back, right in front of us girls. Cowards. When they would come back in, they tried to "pretend to behave." Who gives a fuck who you know, where your family is from, what tax bracket you live in, or if you went to school, anyway? Your name is not what makes you a good person. Your actions play a part here. Put lipstick on a pig. It is still a pig, get it?

Boy, am I glad dad's family is entirely gone for the long slumber. Yes, I mean, they all died. I mean, I wouldn't be able to make this book happen if they were alive. I'm not so worried about the klan coming after me. They're just pissed that I'm not one of them. Jesus, I should have been their poster girl! Lucky for me, my mom would never let that happen.

My mom was a teacher in the Los Angeles Public School System for twenty-five years. She was a professional pianist as well. Mom always played for all of our plays and shows at school. Once, she also came to the rescue at a wedding when they forgot to hire a piano player for the event. So mom jumped in like the savior she is, and said, "I am okay with doing it. No problem," with the most genuine smile on her face. She played for them for free. Mom was at a rough school in L.A. All of the music and art were eliminated from the school syllabus. She brought in her laptop piano one day and incremented music into all of her curricula. Half her kids didn't speak English but they learned. Mom taught every kid how to sing their name, address, and phone number in case they get lost. It's brilliant; she did it with us before we could read.

Let me be clear, mom went back to work after she divorced dad. She renewed her teaching credentials taught from 50 to 75. Now, don't you think that's a strong woman? Hell yes! Dad didn't believe women should work. They should be barefoot, pregnant, and in the kitchen all the time. Well, I call that bullshit. He was all talk, but no game. Mom, with a resilient mind of her own, always had a say in everything, and half the time, she ignored him. She was always the smartest woman in the room when I was growing up, saying the most wisest and impactful things! With a very high tolerance for a big jackass like my dad and his fucked up family, they were married for almost thirty years. I've heard of prisoners of war that had a better time for thirty years than mom did. Conclusively, let's agree on the fact that my mom is a saint with balls of steel.

My mother is not only a woman of caliber but grace as well. She has those white blue eyes that can pierce right through you. She had such control over those kids that if she walks into the room, they would be on their seats with their hands on their lap in mere seconds. Can you do that? Yes, she's that good. I think I got a lot of my patience from her with my own kids. "Don't rush them, they want to know something, take the time to explain things to them," she would always tell me. I like to believe that kids have a sixth sense or something. They know when to cry or be sad if you are someone who's not nice or a mean person. They can sense a negative aura, and so they will avoid you if you offer them that. But if they know you will read them a book, play a game or go swimming again for the tenth day in a row, they naturally like you a lot. It's hard to turn down a kid who just wants attention. Would it kill you to break down and have fun? Not in the least. I know you look silly, playing ball, swimming, bending on a "twister," or dancing with a kid, but who cares? Go run through the sprinklers! A kid will remember the good times, no matter how silly you might look. Get them in the kitchen with you, teach them how to cook, show them how to play ball, go fishing, teach them how to tie their own flies, and make learning fun for them. It is more than fun and larger than just spending time with a kid. Thank the lords, but we never sat still.

If we had the American Ninja Warrior when I was a kid, you don't even want to know the consequences. But I am still going to tell you. We would have made dad build us a Ninja course in the backyard! All I would have to say to dad was, "Dad, if you build this, you won't have to see us at all!" He would have had that done in a day and we never would have gone inside. Mom would have had to pull us off it during dinner time. We would scream, "No mom! We're not done yet! The sun's still up, and we don't want any dinner."

As kids, we weren't afraid to get dirty. Our school had metal slides and there was no cushioned pavement, so every time, we would just hit the rock-hard pavement whenever we played. We would take Tootsie Pop wrappers and put them under our butts to slide down in the summers, so we wouldn't scald the shit out of our little asses. The wax paper wrapper would melt, and that's how you knew you had a good slide! Pussy kids of this age couldn't have handled it. It's kind of funny, our butts were so tiny that we could fit them on an entire tootsie wrapper.

Too many kids don't get up and out as we did. I think that's why there is so much child obesity in this country. Kids aren't as driven to play and do sports as much as they used to and that is sad. However, if one thinks about it, the fault is not of the kids, but the parents. I know some of it is genetic but maybe if we put our electronics down for ten minutes and go run around, it might help. Our mom was always doing stuff with us. If we went swimming, so did mom. If we played volleyball, so did mom. I was lucky that way. We had a hands-on mom!

I worked in a restaurant in Colorado where a lot of white people came on vacation in the summer and winter. It was a seasonal town. There were families that would come in sometimes twice a week and order enough food to feed an army. I would pick up their glass to refill it and the glass would be all greasy from their hands. I know you're on vacation, but you're already fat as it is. These fat kids can barely fit into a life vest for river runs and really don't like to ski, but they love to eat! I think we are going way too far with how Hollywood is embracing obesity. "My Big Fat Fabulous Life," "My Six Hundred Pound Life," "Thousand Pound Friends," I mean, come on. I'm all for a little meat on your bones but when you get to be over five hundred pounds, have a fucking salad. Get off your ass and go running, walking, skiing or go have a swim.

My first real job was teaching swimming. I think I got a lot of inspiration from my mom, even in my career. I know the kid's mom I taught will look back on their life and go, "My favorite teacher was Mrs. Williams. She taught me how to sing my name, address, and phone number when I was six. She was the kind of teacher who would keep little containers for the kids in her class who lose a tooth, so they don't misplace it to take home for the tooth fairy. Now, that's a great teacher!"

Mom was always thinking outside the box. She would go on trips all the time and dad hated to travel. I swear she would take a globe, spin it, land, and go, "Oh, China?! Always wanted to see that wall!" Poof, she would be off with her bags packed. She would come back to the kitchen table after her travel to show us about her trip and explain whatever she did there. After a while, she would do the same and the cycle never ended. Poland, Alaska, Africa and on and on.

Mom always traveled alone and didn't speak the language of the country she was going to. She traveled a lot all her life and she loved it. So did my sister. She and my mom have been all over the world. I've only been to twelve countries, big deal! Can you believe that she went on a covered wagon trip at seventy! Mom wanted to put a streak in her hair, and I told her to do blue for her eyes. I thought she was kidding, but she wasn't.

I think she has kind of become more open-minded and really embraced life after dad died. Mom got a tattoo at sixty-five for her birthday, a flower on her ankle but if she gets a tongue ring, I think I might have to have her committed! The idea of thong shopping with mom may kill me. I got sober to live, and I can't risk losing it over seeing something like that. "How did she die? Well, she was thong shopping with her elderly mother and she just keeled over," are words that will make me turn in my grave. Clearly, not the way I want to be remembered. It fills my heart when I say that mom's in better health than I am. Definitely has a better liver, but she's a three-time over-cancer survivor. She's got me beat with that too. I only had cancer once.

We were very lucky to have a woman like her as our mother. She always did fun stuff with us, even when we aged. Mom and I would go to brunch, and I would use all my best manners. She would have a mimosa, the only time I ever saw her drink alcohol. I would have a seven-up with a peach in it. I think it's a good idea to do "special stuff" with your kids like that; mom always went out of her way to show us that she loved us. My birthday was in August, and I never had a birthday party, so mom told my friends in Junior High that she was throwing a belated birthday party for me at a Mexican restaurant and surprised me. They all came and gave me presents too. That's a good-spirited mother!

Once, we wanted to see a real farm with chickens and cows, so mom took us to a farm for vacation in Illinois, and it was the most fun I have ever had in a smelly and muddy place! She took us to go cherry-picking where they give you a basket and you pick them by yourself and eat them until you puke. All in all, it was a great experience. We went to Oregon to visit mom's side of the family once, and she took us to a zoo where we got to pick up and pet a two-month-old baby lion. Now, I am in no favor of caging wild animals, but he was so soft. The baby lion would suck on our fingers until we put a bottle in his mouth, so he could drink up his food. Sigh, what a wonderful experience.

Mom also took me to the dinner theater at college and I loved it! Dad would go with us to Knott's Berry Farm, Disneyland, and Sea World, but never did anything with us that he didn't want to do. That meant for us going to the car, gun, and train shows. How boring is that for six-year-olds? My dad did have his office modeled in a way that it looked like you are entering an old-time train station. The architect was really cool and it was photographed for a dental magazine as well. He only did it to inflate his ego that was already massive. We had guns, trains, and car shit all over the house. *TOOT-TOOT, HERE COMES THE RACIST EXPRESS!*

My first memories were from church when I was the littlest bell in the choir of bells at church for Christmas. The same year, I think I had to go across the stage, give a flower to the minister and he sang a song. I was four years old back then. The reason why I am sure of my age is that it was before I cut off my hair and had to get a "pixie-cut." I think all little girls will do that at least once. Well, white girls anyway. I can also remember screaming for my mom through the gate at church because I didn't want her to go to the big church without me.

Other first memories weren't so great. I remember playing hide and seek, though. I was four, and my sister was six. She was counting and I had to hide. I didn't like to play this game as I was afraid of the dark. She started to count and with a racy heart, I thought to myself, "Okay, where can I go? Where she won't find me? Oh, the closet. She knows I'm afraid of the dark; better yet Grandpa's closet, she'll never look there." I ran into the closet. I had to leave it open about four inches. I scooted back and there is dry-cleaning in there. You aren't supposed to touch that film around it. I looked back, there was a red robe in there and it had a cross on it. Our robes for the choir were blue. It freaked me out so I left. I'm pretty sure that wasn't a choir robe. If someone calls your grandpa a Grand Wizard, I don't think it's a Harry Potter thing. Sorry, bad joke.

A while ago, I saw something that triggered these memories that was one of them. A lot of what I wrote was really hidden, deep down for a long time. I also remembered other things, such as pins that Grandpa showed me and other stuff that dad brought. The famous "Don't tell moms." You know when you remember stuff you saw as a kid and think that's normal. Dad showed me a German luger he had with a swastika on it and told me I'd inherit it someday. If I had any of that shit, I'd burn it and bury it. My grandpa showed me pins with symbols. I didn't know what they meant as a kid, but I do now. It was all Nazi and Klan stuff. Some white guys are really into that garbage; this tells you a lot about them if they are into that stuff. Usually, it's not just a hobby or a collection. If they show you any interest in any of it, run!

My dad would go on and on about our family name and how important the "Williams" family name was. We did come over on the mayflower, our ancestor William Williams signed the Declaration of Independence, and for some reason, our name is in really small print on the back of the ten or five-dollar bill. I don't know who they bribed to get that done. Dad said, "You know why so many blacks are named Williams? It is because we owned them all!"

What a prick of a human he was! He even went as far to say we were related to the Queen of England. I know we are seventy percent English but really? I don't want to be related to that fucked-up family! Henry the eighth beheaded five of his wives and killed his best friend because he was in a bad mood. Fuck the Royal Family. I'm not a big fan of Prince Charles. He brought his mistress to his wedding. That's some tacky shit! Megan Markel was smart to get out of that.

At the end of the day, we have Walt and the Mormons. Isn't that enough? Can you see Walt in the Royals waving his bible around, while Sarah, the autistic one, she would know everything about them but would refuse to talk because she can't lie. I don't think the Royals would really want the public to know the truth about their lives? Sarah may be disabled, but she has morals. The question is, when are people going to understand that? How many times do I need to say that your name is not what makes you a good person. Your actions do! Position and power don't come first; what is this, the sixteenth century? That's what the Royals want it to be. God, I hope I'm not related to them.

They would be so embarrassed if I was. I would of course laugh my ass off!

My mom went to Africa when I was eight, only to piss off dad. Just kidding! It did piss him off big time, but she went because her roommate from college was from there, and she promised she would visit after she got married or not. Her friend didn't know she married one of the biggest racist dicks on the planet. I can't imagine what dad had to tell the guys at the Klan meetings. "She's in England, visiting our relatives." Mom made dad a list of the dos and don'ts. He was awful. He didn't even give us our vitamins. Mom did everything for us. When she left us for the trip, she even did a little treasure hunt so she could tell us she loved us every day.

Mom didn't go to South Africa. She went to Liberia, Monrovia, West Africa, where there is still civil war going on. She was very open and honest about her trip. They had twelve-foot walls around their house with armed guards and broken bottles over the top, so if anyone tried to climb over, they would get cut. She opened her luggage on the kitchen table and told us all about it, showing us some beautiful fabric she brought back and art. She said even though her friends were rich, at any time, her son could get a rifle put in his hand, and they would say, "You're in the army now!" It killed her that there was nothing she could do about it. Mom kept it real. Dad however came in the middle of it and said, "You know, this is the best country in the world?" Mom ignored him, of course and continued to tell us about her trip. Dad wanted us, especially me, to stay in his little "Pasadena bubble" forever. He hated to travel outside of California. He felt really uncomfortable around anyone who wasn't white, republican or from a certain family or outside anything that wasn't too waspy for his taste.

I'm not telling you this story because my mom's friend was black. It was an important part of her life. She just happened to be black. She and mom just connected as women and became friends. I hate it when white people say, "Oh, we have black friends," just to hide their deeply hidden racism. The most, they only have one black friend. They just don't want you to think they're still stuck up in their racist thought process. I will tell you this that there was a lot of Klan in Portland in the late 50s when mom was going to college. She ignored them or she would guilt-trip them, and that's worse! I can just see mom laughing right in their faces. That would be a real slap in the face coming from the whitest woman on the planet. They would be pissed off because she wasn't one of them and mom had a black friend too. Ouch!

Mom and dad took us to see family, and my sister and I were collecting acorns and I fell down. Dad took pictures of me falling down, crying. He thought it was funny. Mom picked me up and cleaned me off. "Are you okay, sweetie?" She asked me. Dad didn't know how to parent at all! I know some people are really good with kids naturally, but if you don't have any maternal instincts and don't like kids, don't just have them to pass on the family name because they are not going to turn out well if you're a shitty parent, for God's sake. I remember dad trying to do our Halloween project for school and mom wouldn't let him help us. Dad said, "I'll help them do it right," but mom interjected with her, "it is their responsibility, not yours Richard." We went to school and thought we did a pretty good job carving our pumpkins but the other white dads did their kid's projects for them, so ours looked terrible next to theirs. Their dads were like, "Yeah, he did this all by himself." Bullshit! They did all the work and my dad got mad at me because I didn't win anything. Yeah, my dad was a super supportive parent.

When we went to Disneyland, dad wouldn't let us get balloons. I don't know why, but this time mom said we could. We got to pick a balloon and keep it all day! When we got to the car, dad took both of our balloons and popped them in front of us. "Get in the car," he demanded. I started to cry, and mom said, "Richard, that's not nice" All my dad had to say was, "I don't want them in the car. It blocks my view of the traffic!"

Mom made our trip fun, she actually let us have candy. She got me a big purple and white swirly lollipop. I wouldn't stop eating it, which got her mad. She took it. "You can't have all of this, no way," and she threw it away. I really think it's not a good idea to keep all candy and sweets from kids, a little now and then is okay, but we didn't have any sugar in almost anything on a daily basis. Mom wasn't very smart to throw that candy away from me where I could see it. I went into the backyard, dug it out of the trash, and rinsed it off with the hose and thought, "Fuck, it looks clean to me," and started to eat it on the patio floor so she couldn't see me. I wasn't out there very long, and this little endeavor of mine ended with a "Mom, not the metal fly swatter! Ouch!"

I remember going to the museum when we were kids to see the "King Tut Uncommon" exhibition. It was the only time mom let us have soda pop and a Twinkie in our lunch! The other kids always had treats in their lunches on a daily basis, but we weren't allowed except on special occasions. The kids were taking their soda, shaking it up, and opening it to watch it explode. I thought, what a waste! I wasn't going to waste my pop like that but those kids got to eat whatever they wanted. My mom made sure we had balanced meals always! I do have to compliment her, she made the best thanksgiving dinner ever! Mom would get ready for thanksgiving at three in the morning and cook all day. She would make a twenty-five-pound turkey, and her leftovers were the best!

When we were kids, my sister was the "perfect sister" while I was the "black sheep" but I kept it interesting. I can remember as a really little kid, my sister was always looking out for me even when I didn't know it, she was. I was really spazzy and got picked on a lot. My teacher Mrs. Powell told me, "Kill them with kindness," but you can't always do that easily, so I became a smart-ass as my defense. I had to learn how to run really fast! Laugh and Run! Sometimes I don't know how funny I'm being until someone points it out to me, and sometimes they point out that I'm being too honest. I am never blatantly rude but when you're a kid, and you want information that you're not getting, that will make you ask an honest question, and they can't get that mad if you're being honest. "Why are his eyebrows so thick, doesn't he know how silly he looks?" Or, "Mom, why doesn't she have a bra on? Everyone can see her nipples!" Yeah, I have really embarrassed my mom a lot over the years. It's payback for her being so strict and conservative.

Mom came to our school to help with a special lunch we had in my class. She went around to every kid to give them their treat and she wouldn't give it to them until they said, "thank you, or please." She wouldn't give us anything unless we said please or thank you too, but some of the white kids I went to school with had parents who didn't make them use their manners for anything. I can remember mom saying to them, "If you don't do what I say, sorry but you don't get your way. This isn't your house and I'm not your mother. If I was, we wouldn't be having this problem. You either say, 'Please, may I have my treat and thank you Mrs. Williams,' or you don't get your treat. That's it." Like I didn't have a hard enough time with kids as it was. Mom was strict, but the kids made sure it was my fault that they didn't get their way.

Mom was a looker. We went to this restaurant for lunch and some guy my dad was friends with stopped us to say hello. I think he was drunk because he grabbed my mother and kissed her on the lips! She pushed him off her and she turned all red. He turned to sit down and I punched him in the knee caps because I didn't know to punch him in the dick. He sat down, "Hey honey, just saying hello." I said, "You are not my daddy! Don't you touch her like that!" Mom interjected, "She's just not used to anyone but her father being like that." We left and I realized my mother had never been affectionate with anyone but my dad. Mom thought, you should only be that way if you are married to the person and public displays of affection were really frowned upon.

First grade was hell. I got really sick, had severe diarrhea and we heard the bell. We are supposed to freeze when you hear the bell. I couldn't wait as I was holding my runny shit in and it was not working. It started to run down my legs and there were no recess ladies around to help me. Everyone was going to laugh at me. All the kids started to line up to go back to class and I had poop running down my legs, I started crying. Mrs. Jim, that bitch, yelled at me, "Jan, come get in line now." I couldn't go; I was covered in poop. I looked around and one lady saw me, thank God! She came over to me, "Honey, it's okay. We will get you cleaned us." She took me to the nurse's office and called my mom to get me. I remember Mrs. Jim coming into the nurse's office to see me. She said to the lady who helped me, "Don't call her father, he doesn't like me." She was yelling at me and I was crying, covered in poop and she didn't care; the worst teacher ever!

When I was in kindergarten, my teacher Mrs. Westfall was on "Family Feud." I knew a lot of people who did shows and were in the business, so it wasn't unusual to be around people who were on T.V., in special choirs or dance studios for events. I grew up in the business to an extent, but I never wanted to direct! I see a lot of actors who think, "I know how the business works, I can direct too." No, you can't, jackass. It's a real skill to direct. Just because you can act, doesn't mean you can direct stupid! I am not saying all actors who are directors are bad, just not as well informed on that avenue of the business.

Some actors, not all, think that directing is just another ego booster for them. "Oh, I'm a director too!" Really? If you want to impress me, try set design, or working in the costume department, or give a shot at production first. Get your feet wet with something that can't ruin everyone's day with a bad film you can brag about, and come up with sayings such as, "I know the film wasn't my best, but my next one will be better!" Ed Wood was great, but his films sucked and he reveled in it! Ed Wood never made excuses for his film being bad because he liked them. Ed didn't care about what everyone else thought. He was just having fun, kind of like me in the business. I was just having fun, I didn't care what people thought of my work as long as I made people laugh. I was enjoying myself for the most part. Too many people take the business too seriously. Everybody's a critic!

We always went to church, but dad didn't go. He stayed at home and worked on his car collection. I remember asking grandma, "Why doesn't daddy go to church with us?" Grandma said to me, "We don't go to that church anymore, they let the homos go there." Grandma was an Episcopalian and I remember dad saying to us at the dinner table, "There is no good homo like a dead one." We were sitting at the table and mom said, "Richard, that's not nice." That's it. I think my dad was molested as a child or something because he hated homosexuality, and he thought oral sex was a mortal sin. Now you understand why I never came out to my parents when I was young? They wouldn't understand. My mother didn't have any experience with her own sexuality. Mom just did what she was told. I think she deserved so much more than what she got!

When I was little, my mom made me special shoes that had a high arch in them because my feet were really fucked up. Not from ballet, my feet were small and really narrow so she made me wear saddle shoes to school when everyone else got to wear Mary Jane's and cool tennis shoes, and my hair was all fucked up from me cutting it when I was four. So I looked like a fucking retard! I got picked on a lot, but hey, what doesn't kill you makes you stronger, right? Bullshit, try explaining that to a first grader when everyone is making fun of her. I also got the added pleasure of wearing my sister's hand-me-downs too.

I remember, we would get clothes to give to the poor for Church and once while going through the bags of clothes, I found a pair of neon pink bell bottoms that fit me! I tried them on and it looked great. Mom came into the room, "You can't have those as they are for someone else, not you." I said, "Mom, let's give them some of my old clothes instead and I can keep these." She told me," No, that's too grown-up for you to wear. Put it back," and when mom wasn't around, I got them out, put them back on, and went for a bike ride to show them off. I guess I should have thought about it a little more, the pant legs got stuck in the bike spokes and I couldn't get it out, so I had to walk home and explain to mom why I was wearing them. Another beating! My mom wouldn't let me get my hair cut like Farrah Fawcett either. She said, "You're not mature enough to have that kind of haircut, it's too adult for you." Strict! I think that's why I went a little nut when I turned eighteen.

We had a hobby shop when we were little. Dad wanted it because he was really into trains and cars, so it was perfect for him but he made mom run it sometimes. She didn't like it but did it anyway. If you asked my dad anything about trains or cars from this country, he could tell you anything about it. He had a photographic memory. We always went to gun and car shows, but he did tell me a little about the military too. Dad said that he designed camps where they would make bombs for chemical warfare. He showed me some maps when I was a kid, I don't think he was supposed to do that, but he was nuts so who cares, right? Military Intelligence, what a joke! Now that's an oxymoron for sure! How our military could let someone like my dad and others like him have the position, power, and authority like he did? Don't you think we should have some kind of background check on the people we have in our military who have the most influence? God, what was I thinking? White men who are in those positions make the rules so unless we start to get more women in the military, I guess we have to put up with it.

When I was a kid, we went to Disneyland with our youth group from Church. A couple of the teenage girls who were white got caught trying to shoplift. The youth advisors talked to the people at Disneyland and asked them to let them go and they will punish them, so they let them all go. I seriously think the only reason they let them go was that they were white. Do you think for one second if they were black, they would let them go? Hell no! White privilege!

I remember as a kid, my dad hated the people who would come over to tell us about religion. Have you heard of the Book of Mormon? Dad thought it would be funny to scare them. Dad came to the door and started to yell at them in German, or he would show them his weapon; that usually got them off our porch pretty fast.

My sister was one of those kids who skipped second grade. Her birthday was in December and she was an advanced kid. I don't know who does the testing for kids, who they think are smart enough to skip, but I didn't get to skip. I remember them taking us to the test and I got the answers correct but put it in a way they didn't understand.

Fucking Dyslexia! I had a reading problem as most dyslexic people do, that's why my mom put me in a tutored class for me to be able to read better. It wasn't that I couldn't read, it's that the material was bad. I can still remember the entire book cover to cover because they never changed the book. They had a bookmobile that came to our school, and I got to choose what I wanted to read, so I was actually interested in what I was reading. Mom wasted her money. She should have just given me more fun stuff to read! I did get a hold of a dirty book, don't know how, but my friends in Junior High read it with me, and we thought it was really funny! Maybe mom should have gotten me some porn. I would have been able to pick up on reading faster! I'm kidding! Kids shouldn't read that stuff, they won't get it! We didn't. Someone look up the word 'orgasm'!

When I was about eight, my sister was ten and she went to a birthday party and won a pink plastic skateboard to play on. My sister took it home and mom said it was okay to ride it because she was the responsible one, and my mother didn't think she would do anything dangerous on it. My perfect sister was holding onto the back of one of the Davis boy's cars. Jimmy asked, "Are you holding on or not?" My sister said, "Nope!" He peeled off and my sister was still holding on. The car didn't make it two houses when they realized she was still on her skateboard behind them. The skateboard whooshed out from under her and drug her about twenty feet. My sister was wearing a T-shirt and shorts. When the car stopped, she got off the pavement and was a bloody mess. My sister came home, and my mom threw a fit! "What happened?" she screamed. My sister told her what had happened and she wasn't happy. I was supposed to be the daughter who should be doing something that stupid. She missed about a week of school and had to cover herself in Neosporin. My dad came home, took the pink plastic skateboard, and went into the garage and split it in half. No more skateboarding from now on! That's why I never learned how to ride a skateboard. My sister fucked it up for me.

We lived in the same house our whole life. We had some interesting neighbors. The Davis boys were always getting into trouble in some way. They were both P.K.s and really funny. Jimmy got married to a lovely woman who had two kids and went to Hawaii for their honeymoon. Jimmy loved waterfalls, so he was getting a picture of himself by his new wife at their favorite waterfall. Jimmy slipped, fell, broke his neck, and died on their honeymoon. His wife saw him fall and tried to help, but failed. She fell badly too but lived. The people at their wedding were the same people who were at his funeral. The people from their church helped with all of the arrangements in Hawaii with a sister church. My dad and I went down to their house to say our condolences, and my dad put his hand on Jimmy's dad's shoulder and said, "We are so sorry for all of this, let us know if we can help." Dad almost cried. I never saw my dad like that ever! Jimmy's new wife was in a hospital in Hawaii and didn't get to go to her own husband's funeral. When she got back, my dad did free dental work on her because she lost a few teeth in her fall. My dad had his moments. The Davis boys were white, if they weren't, dad wouldn't have lifted a finger to help them. White privilege

In our backyard, we had a California fig tree, yummy! It bloomed twice a year, and mom would trim it down to practically nothing and the fruit was wonderful. We would trade for other fruit in the neighborhood. Some people would put out a stand with a jar for money or a sign that said, "Trade for your fruit." It was nice when I moved to Colorado. I almost had a heart attack when they wanted to charge a dollar for a lemon. All of San Gabriel Valley was citrus orchards before it became homes. We had about thirty types of fruit and veggies grown year-round.

We remodeled our house when I was about eight, a total nightmare! My dad wouldn't hire anyone that was Mexican or Black, so he hired two rednecks with no experience to do it because he thought," These guys are white, they will do a better job than some Mexicans." Bullshit! I came home from school and the white guys my stupid father hired kept asking me to fetch them beers. They did such a bad job. We had a flooding problem in the house when it rained. Mom said, "Richard hire someone with experience. Who cares if they are Mexican?" So dad hired a man who was half Mexican, not completely Mexican, so he met mom halfway. He didn't trust him and the guy knew it too, so the guy said to my dad, "I tell you what, I will pay for all of the construction costs and when it's finished, you can re-pay me." My dad took him up on it and he did a good job. He is so lucky that guy was so nice to him. He had no idea who he was working for, thank God.

I had a teacher who was gay in the fourth grade and he and his boyfriend went to my dad's office for dental work. Dad kicked them out and said, "I don't want those fairies in my office ever again." Dad said that they were trying to hold hands in the lobby. I don't believe that for a second. That was in the 70s and in a conservative white neighborhood, no way would he hold hands in public. Dad hated faggots of any kind or any man who was feminine at all. That teacher was supposed to be my fourth-grade teacher, but dad wouldn't have it. So I got transferred to Mrs. Powel's class.

My mom was in the P.T.A. and was always involved with the school in some way. Being a professional pianist, she, of course, played for all of our school plays, at church, and other stuff too such as weddings, and funerals. Yeah, people don't like to sit in a quiet room when everyone is mourning, so mom would get them riled up with church music. Not the kind where you stand up and cheer, nope! That's fun. Mom would play for whitey boring shit that makes you want to get drunk or really high. The stuff they play during the church procession, nobody really knows what to make of it. Just melodies that don't make you want to slit your wrists. Speaking of slitting your wrists, yes, I'm going there with all of the suicide that's been going on. Why don't they make a "Sorry, you didn't succeed" or "Thank God, you're still with us" card? I think Hallmark is really missing out on a big market! I don't know what to say to someone who's stupid enough to try it and fail at it. "Well better luck next time" or "Please don't do that again" comfortably for them. What do you say? We need a card to say that. I'm pretty sure that's what cards are for. I'm not saying the card should be funny or anything, but it would make a pretty fun pop-up book or porno, actually no. That's sick. I just don't know how to make suicide funny. I'm really trying, I am but it's not funny, not at all, especially when someone treats suicide like it's a game.

CHAPTER TWO: KID TALK, WOODPECKER, BIG GUN

When I was three, my mom took me to her bank. As usual, everyone knew mom. “Hello, Mrs. Williams. Is that your daughter? Hi Jan!” That was Miss Davis, a woman with a smile plastered on her face at all times. Mom always told us to use our best manner when we meet people and say words like “Please” and “Thank you.” “She looked at me with comforting eyes that said, “Jan, say hello sweetie and use your inside voice so they can hear you.” I replied, “Hello, Miss Davis. How are you today?” The lady looked at me with a big grin. She told mom, “She is so cute. Hello, Jan!”

We go to the teller and he is black. I mean, really black. Now imagine a three-year-old who has lived all her life in an all-white neighborhood and sees a black man standing in front of her for the first time. I was in awe. Mom always told me, “Honey, it’s okay to ask questions or say anything, as long as you are polite and don’t interrupt. Always be articulate with your words and use you’re inside voice so everybody can hear you.” In my opinion, that is the worst advice you can give to a three-year-old. I couldn’t stop looking at him because he was so beautiful. The minute my mother saw my face, she started praying harder than ever. “She is going to say something. Oh, God! Please don’t let her speak. I’ll become a nun, but please don’t let her speak, God!” Well, He did not answer. Nope. Because the next thing I did was like her worst nightmare coming true.

I looked at the beautiful man in front of me and said, “Sir, excuse me,” making sure I don’t interrupt him. He replied with a sweet curve of his lips, “Yes?” Mirroring his smile, I said, "You have such neat purple lips. They're so pretty." He threw his head back and laughed. "Thank you! You have pretty hair too, young lady." I could only muster up a "Thank you," as mom dragged me away. That was the end of it for us, but my mother was mortified. How many shades of red can you turn? Mom got them all! She kept saying, "I'm sorry. She has never seen a black person ever." He was polite enough to reply, "She is a little girl. She gave me a compliment."

He was nice about it for sure, but when mom turned around, everyone was laughing because I used my "inside voice." She didn't get mad at me. Instead, she took me home and showed me pictures of how other people looked. My mom was so good at teaching us about different cultures but dad wanted us all to be just "White." That's something I learned from my mom; don't get mad at a kid for asking questions or being honest. My mom told me this story as I didn't remember it. I mean, I was only three but it shows you this; my mom has a great sense of humor! For the record, it gets worse than the "purple lips" thing was just the beginning.

Now we all know that kids will just say anything. I babysat a lot in L.A., and my dad got me a Mercury Station Wagon back then. It was great I could fit eight kids in it safely. I babysat this kid called Emily, an extremely smart one! She was about two and a half and she was reading her book in her car seat. This was before airbags were mandatory, so she was in the front seat in her booster seat with her legs crossed like a princess. Emily used to do that when she was in a swing set too, it was super cute! Emily wasn't really reading it word for word. She was making up her own words, in her cute little two-year-old voice. "There is the apple on this page, so I will turn the page. Oh, look!

There's the apple. Hehe. And look at this! There is a tree. Where did the boy go over on this page?" She would mumble to herself with her innocent little giggles adorable, right? Now keep in mind that I was diving in L.A. traffic when I got cut off. Instinctively, I exclaimed, "Shit! Shoot! Ugh!" I realized it pretty late that I just cursed in front of a child. I hoped that she didn't notice, but my lucky stars were busy somewhere else. She dropped her book and said, "Janny, you said shit!" Nervous, I replied, "No, I didn't. I said shoot!" Adamant on what she heard, she pressed, "No, Janny! You said 'shoot' the second time. The first time, it was 'shit'." Oops, I was caught, and there was no way around it but to accept it. "I am sorry, Emily. Please don't say that word. It's not very nice, okay? Say 'shoot' instead?" With an innocent nod, she said, "Okay, Janny," and went back to reading her book.

In my head, I knew I was fucked. Emily's mom was friends with my mother, and she hates cussing, mainly from me. "It's a bad reflection on me as a parent, Jan!" She would always say this whenever I would mutter curse words in front of her. Especially, when I did that in front of the kid I've known since I was fourteen.

Emily's mom is a devout Catholic, strong emphasis on devout. She knows the archbishop in L.A. by his first name. She sponsors a woman who is completely blind in Africa and goes over there to meet her with the Archbishop's approval and comes back to give a presentation to everyone about her visit, yeah, that kind of Catholic. "I am royally fucked," that was all I could think of as I drove the smart little kid home. We had to drive five minutes to get home, but it felt like an hour.

I thought if her dad was home, it wouldn't be that bad. He is a little more easy-going than her mother, and hopefully, he won't be that mad. We get to the house and they are both home! Emily got out of the car and I was just waiting for her to go "SHIT, SHOOT, SHIT, SHOOT." I couldn't lie to them, so I thought I should come clean myself before my profanities are exposed. "I'm so sorry. I said 'shit' right in front of Emily in a moment of weakness, I got cut off and it just came out. I promise it will never happen again." I said it all in a breath.

Her mom was standing there with her hand over her mouth. I waited for her to backhand me, but from the corner of my eye, I saw the dad smiling. "Now, don't worry, Janny. You won't believe what she said last week," he said. Emily, her older sister, and her dad were down the street from our house at the San Marino Book Store. She made a little cubby of books to read as she was learning how to read. The dad came around the corner and said, "Emily, wrap it up.s Time to go, honey." Emily looked at him and went, "Jesus Christ! I'm not fucking finished yet."

Imagine a two and a half-year-old saying that! The horror! Utterly embarrassed, I said, "I never said that in front of her! I swear!" In an amusing tone, the dad replied, "Not you," and pointed his fingers towards her mom. She took her hand off her mouth and said, "I was on the phone with someone from the church in the other room and she picked it up!" She looked quite embarrassed and I, shocked. I thought of her as a saint, and my mind was blown away. Then later on, I realized that she is only human, like the rest of us. I looked at her and said, "You said that to someone from church?"

The dad, enjoying the scene, said, “Well, I guess you both earned your lessons,” and walked away, chuckling. I looked at the mom and said, “I’ll never say that again.” In a reassuring tone, she replied, “Neither will I.” We dropped it and she never told my mom. Thank God! I definitely had a good guardian angel on my side for that one! I thought they would judge me harshly for doing that, but they were both very forgiving.

This made me think that if we could judge a little less harshly and be more forgiving, the world would be a better place. As the saying goes, “Don’t judge a book by its cover,” you never know who’s a really talented or intelligent person just by how they look. My boyfriend has a daughter and she is beautiful. Her name is Jamey. She’s 6’1, and I never know what color her hair will be next month. She’s got scary tattoos with zombies and horror movie stuff all over her body. Honestly, she has to explain them to me because I hate scary movies and I don’t know what half of the creatures are. To think of it, Jamey is very patient with me about it. I love to see the wicked outfits she puts on. They dress so much better than we did in the 80s for sure.

Jamey does burlesque dancing, and her moves are simply neat! She is twenty-five years old and a walking piece of art, a good kid as well. I truly adore her and anyone would be lucky to have her as a daughter. If I had my own kids, I would wish they would be half as responsible, sweet, smart, outgoing, hardworking, determined, kind, honest, thoughtful, loyal, fearless, funny, Intelligent, and amazing as Jamey. When I say “fearless,” I mean it! Jamey broke her nose twice in a mosh pit, believe me now?

I do think she’s a little nut, but so was I at that age. Jamey is also the kind of girl who tells her friends, “Don’t get fucked up and drive. I will come to get you if you need a ride." She does it all the time for her friends and when I was a kid, I did it too for my friends. So the next time you see someone with tattoos and piercings, don't judge too harshly just because she looks like that. It doesn't mean she's not smart or responsible. I went to school with a bunch of kids who looked like they were right out of an L.L. Bean Catalogue. If those kids got in trouble with the law, they would get out of it because they were white, looked nice, and probably knew or owned the police like my dad did.

Just because a kid looks a certain way doesn't mean they are bad or good. Judge them for who they are as a person, and not for what they wear on their skin. It has been my experience and I say it with no doubt that rich kids get away with everything because of their looks and connections. We trust them because they are not a kid with a couple of tattoos and piercings, nor are they black. I would trust a kid like Jamey over any of the rich white kids I grew up with any day. To quote David Bowie, "Turn and face the strange!"

I had a run-in with someone you might judge right off the bat! I babysat for this kid who was three. We were at the pharmacy in line to get my inhalers. Now the three-year-old looks like Cinderella, and the guy in front of us looked like Marilyn Manson and Rob Zombie had a baby. The baby was staring at him and smiling. Nostalgia hit me hard and I was thinking, "Oh God! Here it comes, purple lips!" She gently looked at him and she said, "What happened to your hair?" Amused, he replied, "What happened to your hair?" She went on and mumbled. "I have a brush. You can borrow it if you want to." He laughed and got down on one knee for her so she could touch his hair. He had a mohawk. The entire scene filled up my heart with so much happiness and was hands down the cutest interaction I have ever witnessed between a baby and an adult. If only I had a camera to document it. After they said their goodbyes, I gave her the most basic piece of advice. "Don't judge a book by its cover, little one."

My mom always told us. "You should always treat others the way you want to be treated, with kindness. Be polite to everyone, no matter where they are from or what they look like." Mom would say stuff like that at the dinner table in front of dad and he would never say a word. She had him by the balls when they were alone. Trust me, dad never said racist comments at the dinner table or in front of mom but he did behind her back. I can't remember all of the dinner talks we had but when I look back, they are always a source of humor for me.

I was a little 'PYRO' when I was a kid. Don't worry, I didn't ever set someone on fire or a building, I just liked the look of fire, that's all, but I got caught lighting a campfire by my dad's office. My parents thought it would be a good idea to have me talk to the Fire Chief about how dangerous it is to play with fire, YHAWN! My dad thought I'm stupid because I'm dyslexic and a spaz, so if they were thinking that I can't outfox some old guy who was friends with dad, they must've been kidding me, right? I'm going to fuck this guy up. He had no idea this is where playing dumb was not going to work.

They must have thought I would go in with pleading eyes and tell him, "I didn't know it was so dangerous. God, forgive me. I'm so sorry and I will never do that again. I promise. Thank you, Captain. You're a wise man." Fuck that, too easy. He was friends with my dad, so he probably had a big ego too. My dad wouldn't be friends with just some grunt fireman but the captain, oh yea, they are old buddies.

My dad probably did his family's teeth. He would trade his "services" for dental work.

I know there are some cops who knew my dad was out there going, "Don't tell them about your dad stitching up people without any records. Also, don't tell them about all the so-called favors he did for his buddies at the department." I wish I could say, I won't do that but, fuck them if they don't like it. If anyone asks, dad's dead, after all. I have nothing to hide.

Anyways, we got to the fire department and my dad introduced me to the Fire Chief, "So, I hear we need to talk about setting fires." I looked at him and with confidence, I said, "Yes, I think we do right in here." I went into his office, sat down, and left him in the hall with my parents. I know for a fact that my mom was out there convincing them and saying, "This is never going to work, Richard. I'm telling you, she is a very smart little girl but you can have it your way. Let her talk to the Fire Chief." And what can I say? Mom was right as always.

The Fire Chief came in, sat down, and started to lecture me about fire and how dangerous what I did was. I looked at him and said, "I completely agree with you that what I did was stupid. It was really stupid of me to do that. I won't do it again and I think you made your point; not to set fires. Thank you. Is there anything else you think we should discuss, or is that it?" The look on his face was hilarious. This fucker didn't know what hit him. Of course, he was expecting me to cry, but I gave him something else, which I am sure he will remember all his life. I heard him and my stupid father talking, and I knew the route he was going to take with me. The moron was standing right in front of me while talking to my dad about what he was going to do.

I hope this fucking guy was never in the military because I could imagine him saying, "Hey, guys! Let's go to this bar. The enemy hangs out there. We can go over our strategy there, but we will keep it low. Okay, my boys?" what a dumb shit!

Anyone who thinks children are stupid, you're a fucking idiot. This guy came out of the little talk we had and said to my mom, "After talking to your daughter, I forgot who the adult was, and who was the child. She is so smart. Don't worry, she won't do it again." My mom looked at my broken father and proudly said to the chief, "What did you say about my daughter? I don't think her father got all of that. Do you mind repeating that?"

My mom always wins when it comes to the smarts! I always got in trouble and got caught by her for everything but my sister did fuck up once or twice when she was about eight. We had a foul-mouthed little kid, Chris, next door to us, who said to my sister, "You're a fucker!" My sister didn't know what it meant, so she went home. That day, my parents were in the living room with a banker with whom my dad did business. My sister walked in and said, "Excuse me." She was polite like mom told us to be. The next thing she said made my mom's ears ring with embarrassment. "Mom, what does a fucker mean?" She was so mad at dad for using that kind of language all the time with his pals. The people who were visiting us for business with dad laughed, but can you imagine them thinking, "Yeah, we were going to give them the loan but their kid was a foul-mouthed little bastard."

I don't know the details of the aftermath of my sister's innocent blunder, but mom went over to Chris's house and he was in so much trouble. Once, he was playing with a basketball, throwing it back and forth to my sister over the fence and it came right through my bedroom window while I was in bed, missed me but scared the shit out of me. He came over after his dad beat him to say he was sorry. He was crying, and to assure him, I said, "Look, I am okay. I didn't get hurt. It's okay." I felt bad for him, we all were aware of his father's temperament.

We all knew whose dads were in the "not to mess with" and "who to laugh at behind their back" category. Now, my dad wasn't the tough kind, but he was smart, with a touch of crazy in him and always armed – a pretty bad combination most of the time.

He always had a boot gun and a gun in the car, so to me, that's normal. But he couldn't fight or do anything athletic because of his asthma. However, once when I was in first grade, Woah! He really stood up for me and I would've never believed it if I never witnessed it with my own eyes. I was the kid who got picked on a lot; a spaz, with A.D.D., misunderstood, you know the drill. BOO-HOO I got over it. I was painting with the other kids and the teacher was Mrs. Jim, bitch. She went to our church when I was little. In class, she ordered all of us to paint the house we live in.

I asked her, "Can I paint my dream house?" All the kids started laughing, and I had no clue why. Mrs. Jim replied in her bored tone, "Jan, just paint a house." It didn't help me when even the teachers didn't like me for some reason, and experiencing that only in the first fucking grade was too harsh. Artistic people see things differently. Anyways I started to paint and some kid interrupted, "That not her house. She is doing it wrong." Mrs. Jim came over and said, "Jesus, Jan. You have paint in your hair. Go wash it out now!" I couldn't understand what did I do so wrong to be treated like this? I dropped my brush and said, "Okay." I could hear a couple of the kids snickering behind my back. I went down the hall to the bathroom and I realized I have never washed my own hair before. My mom always did it in the bathtub. Ignoring my racing heart, I dunked my head under the sink and tried to wash my hair to get the paint out.

I looked in the mirror to check if I got all the color out, and to my horror, there was no towel to dry out my hair. The hand towel refused to come off the wall even after my few failed attempts. So, I brushed my fingers through my hair and went back to class. I walked in all wet and the kids burst out laughing. Ignoring them, I picked up my brush and started to paint again. Mrs. Jim walked towards me and said, "Jan Williams, what do you think you are doing?" I was honest and said, "I washed my hair. I got all the paint out but there was no towel. So, I just brushed my hair with my hands." She stopped me by grabbing my hair hard and yanked me over to my seat in class. "You will not do any more painting and when we have recess, you will sit in a chair under the sun until you are dried," she screamed at my face. I naturally started to cry and all the kids went back to painting.

Mrs. Jim took my painting and threw it in the garbage right in front of me. She was a wicked woman who should have never been allowed to work with kids in the first place. The bell rang and everyone rushed to recess except me. Mrs. Jim waited until everyone was outside. Then, she turned to me and said, "You will obey me. I don't care who your father is! Now get up!" Even after hearing that, I went on with my only defense as a kid, "I'm going to tell my daddy on you."

We went out the door after she grabbed a chair for me. She went to the very middle of the schoolyard and opened the chair, making me sit in it. "You sit there for the entire recess!" She scolded. I felt like a lamb tied to the steak! I could see that the majority of the kids were making fun of me, and teasing me by calling me names and throwing stuff at me. Nobody came to help me as the school recess attendants were told by my teacher, "You leave her there." So I knew I was fucked, but I wasn't going to let myself go through this torture for nothing. I thought, "Fuck this! I am out," and got up from the chair. I walked to the office, looked in, and nobody was around. I thought I'll walk instead, and so I did. I marched my little six-year-old ass home.

I walked in and mom was in the kitchen. The moment she turned around I blurted, "Mom, I'm not going to school anymore, starting now." I went straight to my room and shut the door behind my back. Mom was dumbfounded. She wasn't expecting her six-year-old daughter to walk in like that. She dropped what she was doing and knocked on my door. "Honey, can we talk about this? What happened?" She slowly opened my door. I looked at her and started telling her everything that happened. "Mrs. Jim grabbed me by the hair after she told me to wash it. We were painting and I got some on my hair by mistake. She sat me in a chair under the sun because I didn't have a towel."

Mom dried me off and called the principal who she knew as a friend. He came to get me and take me back to school. He picked me up in his porches speedster and we hit the road. He went on and on about how we all have bad days and how it always gets better. All I replied was, "You wanna bet." Once we reached the school, I went back to my class. All the kids were shocked. I heard them whispering, "She walked back home. She is in trouble."

Mrs. Jim didn't say a word to me and pretended like nothing ever happened. She did give me a little wink that I assumed meant, "Yeah, you think you can just run away from me? I don't think so." I knew better so I kept my mouth shut. This day, I realized how teachers can be evil too.

Another joy was the bus ride home where Ricky Gillette would kick me in the shins every day until I showed my mom about six months later, when she saw me limping as I walked into the house. Dad was home. I think it was Friday as he always took a half-day. He looked at me and went, "Come with me now, honey. Tell me what did she do to you?" We got in his car and I told him the truth, this time with no lies. He was fuming mad. "How dare someone touch his royal seed? God forbid, they hurt a Williams's child? Do they know how important she is to our race?" That would be my guess on what he was thinking at that time. We got to the school and dad marched into the teacher's lounge with me, all wet. I was trying hard not to cry.

Mrs. Jim was sitting on a couch. She looked up, and all the color drained off her face. She froze. Dad went up to her in front of about ten other teachers and growled, "If you ever lay a hand on my kid again, I'll have you fired and arrested. Do you understand me?" It was the first time I saw dad like this, but I liked it. He was yelling at the woman who I can't stand and it was satisfying, so you go, dad! She tried to justify her behavior and said, "I'm sorry, but she is making this out to be worse than it really. Other people were there."

They weren't in the room with us when she yanked my hair and threatened me. I didn't even tell dad about that. He grunted, "I don't care what your excuse is. You touch her again and I find out about it. You're done. You understand me?" Some male teacher was there and he started to pull some hippie shit with dad, "Hey, we don't need to be yelling at each other now. Come on!" He didn't get far until dad shut him up with a simple, "Fuck off or I'll shoot you, fairy." I didn't know what it meant back then, but now I do. We went home, and mom and dad had a little talk behind closed doors. I don't know what happened, but Mrs. Jim laid off of me.

My dad took me to a car show when I was six. It was boring but I wouldn't miss a chance to spend time with my daddy. As I mentioned earlier, he only did stuff with us that he wanted to do. Dad only collected American cars. He had a collection of some of the coolest cars in the country. He had a 1965 silver Corvette Stingray. Mom made him get rid of it; she said it was too dangerous. We only had one foreign car. A 1955 navy blue Rolls Royce with a tan interior and jump seats in the back, no seatbelts. Dad would take us to church in it, sit outside in the parking lot and brush it with a diaper to show off.

Dad's friends all dressed alike at the car shows. They all looked like cowboys, but none of them had a horse. It was very confusing for a 6-year-old's mind. You know those white guys with cowboy hats, blue jeans, cowboy boots, glasses from the range, standing together with their arms crossed, looking around and acting superior. The Europeans, dad called them "Queers." They had the Austin Martins and Porsches. They always looked like they were going to the beach, all stuck up and all smoked. Keep in mind that this was the 70's. They were very "Oh, these Americans. We piss on them with their stupid cars." The car shows were very segregated.

I was clearly not having fun, but when I heard music, and it wasn't like anything I have heard before, I was intrigued. We always had music in the house because of mom playing the piano all the time. I knew big band music and church music, but this was different. It was Latin music for the low riders!

I remember thinking, "Why don't we have cars like that?" My dad wasn't paying attention to me anyway, so I went over where they were all standing together, drinking beer. I walked up to this big cholo. He was about six-three tall and three hundred pounds heavy, with tattoos, gold chains, a wife-beater, and a beer in his hand. I tugged on his shirt, so he could notice my existence. He turned around and said, "Are you lost?" I can't imagine what went through his mind when he saw this little white girl with a pixie cut and a smile on her face standing at his feet. He was genuinely concerned about me.

I said, "No." With a frown, he inquired, "Where are your parents?" I lied my ass off and said, "My dad's in the bathroom. May I please get in that car with those kids? It looks like so much fun. I don't know why my daddy doesn't have any cars like yours. Is it okay if I play with your kids in your car, please? I won't be a pest." He looked around to think while his friends started laughing, mainly at me. "When your dad comes back, you go find him and tell him that you aren't lost. Okay?" I nodded with excitement. He picked me up and put me in the car. The kids in the car had a "What's with the white girl" look on their faces. He said something to them in Spanish, after he turned up the hydraulics and the music. Oh lord, it was fun. The guy would look from the window at me to see if I was okay every now and then, proving to be a nice man after all. I was having the most fun I have ever had in a car show until dad realized I was missing.

All I felt was dad's hand on my arm through the window. He yelled something at me and yanked me out through the window, he didn't want to touch their car and get Mexican on him. He planted me on my feet in front of him and said, "Which one of these spicks let you in this car?" I didn't know what a spick meant, but I wasn't supposed to get into a car with a stranger. I was in big trouble.

He roared again. "Which one of these wet-backs put you in this car?" The music stopped and everyone was looking at us. The silence was deafening; you could have heard a pin drop. Looking bad at the severity of the situation, this was more than bad. My dad's all-white klan against the Mexicans, even as a six-year-old, I know the consequences of this face-off would end up treacherous.

Sure, my dad was six feet tall, but he was frail and small as compared to the guy who put me in his car. Now he was standing behind my dad and was double the size of him. He looked at me and barely shook his head, no. I knew exactly what he meant without saying a word. I looked at my dad and said, "I got in all by myself. Please don't tell mom." When he turned his gaze towards me, my stomach dropped. Dad said, "You're so stupid!" I wet my pants. My daddy had never yelled at me like that and it scared the hell out of me. He grabbed my hand and started to drag me away. I looked back and mumbled a thank you to the nice man. My dad snarled, "Don't talk to those spicks!" The look the nice big guy gave me is still etched in my mind. It said, "I feel so sorry for that little girl with a father like that."

My dad took a piece of cardboard and made me sit on the floor of the backseat all the way home because he didn't want to get his car dirty. I held my hands over my ears while he yelled at me. I can't even get into the stuff he said. We got home and he told me to change. Mom was cooking in the kitchen and I ran inside my room. Mom with a concerned voice asked, "Richard, what is wrong?" He replied, "She wet her pants." She shot back. "Well, go help her maybe?" As expected, his only reply was, "She can do it herself." Mom dropped everything like the good parent she was and came to help me out. She kept saying, "Honey, it's okay. We'll work on it." I wet my pants a lot as a kid. "Wash up and come to dinner, sweetie."

I washed up and started praying. "Dear God, do not let dad tell her that I got into a car that I wasn't supposed to be in." As I sat for dinner, I just waited for dad to explode the bomb on my mother so I could assume the position. She looked at me as we said our prayers and asked, "So, did you have fun at the car show? What did you do today?" I was too hurt and confused to tell her what went down there. I remember how mom always used to encourage us to ask questions, and so I did. "Mom, what's a spick?"

My mom with those cold blue eyes shot a look at dad. Of course, she knew where I got it from. Shocked to the core, she said, "Excuse me?" I, like the trouble maker I was, didn't stop with my questions. "And what's a wet-back?" My sister, who was two years older than me, was smiling ear to ear. She knew what it meant. Are you thinking she was going to help? No fucking way. Instead, she going to make a big bowl of popcorn and enjoy the show. Mom looked at dad, and I could see that she was really mad. Whenever, she would talk through her teeth, which meant she was extremely mad.

"Richard, I'd like to have a word with you in the other room, right now!" She slowly folded up her napkin, pushed back her seat, and without taking her eyes off him, she went down the hall to the bedroom.

I have to thank my mom for the fact that she never argued in front of us. If you are mad at your partner and you think you may have an adult conversation with grown-up words, take it outside or do it behind closed doors. Kids get traumatized when they go through shit like that; being a kid is hard enough. Send them to college to get exposed to yelling screaming and bad language, get your money's worth. You should never fight an adult fight in front of a kid ever! Mom and dad went to the bedroom and came back after a while.

With an unbelievable calmness on her face, she nudged dad and said, "Richard, isn't there something you would like to tell the girls?" He goes, "Girls, you can't use those words anymore from now on. You can say 'Mexican.'" He threw an annoyed look at mom and continued, "Happy?" That was dad's way of apologizing. I loved how mom always had the upper hand. I didn't hear any creaking from their bedroom for a while, if you know what I mean. Mom was always trying to get dad out of his element. She would take us to Olvera Street for Mexican food. It is the oldest street in Los Angeles. Adorned with cobblestones, the street has open shops, a really fun place. Once, when we left the restaurant after having dinner, my sister realized she has to go to the bathroom. I didn't want to any further as mom told us that we are going to go for ice cream after we are done with food. In my head, all I could think of was the cold and delicious feeling of ice cream melting in my mouth. I mean, who can blame me? Ice cream is my favorite thing!

All of a sudden, dad stopped in front of this hat shop with a stupid look on his face. He was smiling ear to ear like the

Cheshire cat. My mom was clearly annoyed and pried, "Richard, what are you doing? Your daughter has to go to the bathroom and the other won't stop about her ice cream?" She followed his gaze and whispers, "Well, my goodness!" Curious, I peek into the shop and all I see is two old people.

My mom instructed, "Jan, go get that woman's autograph for your sister, and then we'll get your ice cream."

I looked in again and went, "Who is she?" I am six and if you aren't Snow White or Cinderella, who gives a shit? My mom said with an exasperated expression, "That's Fay Dunnaway. Go with your dad. Feeling more annoyed by the minutes, I asked her with pleading eyes, "Do I have to?" Understanding my discomfort, she said warmly, "Yes, you do. Now, take your dad."

I grabbed my dad's hand and went to the shop. He pushed me towards her and stood in the doorway. Only then did I realize what that stupid look on dad was about. He was infatuated with her. I went up to her and tugged on her blouse. She was wearing a see-through blouse with no bra, my mom never dressed like that, but she was the most beautiful woman I have ever seen. She turns around to look down and said, "Hi, there. May I help you?" I replied, "Are you, Miss Fay Dunnaway?" She nodded with a smile growing on her face. "Yes, I am Fay Dunnaway."

"Well, my name is Jan and that's my dad. He is afraid of you. My mom and sister went to the bathroom. Mom said I couldn't go get my ice cream at Thrity One Flavors until I get your autograph. So, will you sign this so I can get my ice cream?" I told her honestly. She kind of laughed and said, "Of course, I will." She got on one knee and started to make small talk. "What do you want to be when you grow up?" I said, "Ballerina."

I had no idea I would go to a performing arts school later, but she started to sign it. I think she didn't understand that all I wanted was my ice cream, she was moving too slowly. Hurry it up, lady! Then the old guy she was with got down on his knees and said to me, "Would you like my autograph too?" Clearly annoyed, I told him, "No. Didn't you hear me? I just need Miss Dunnaway's autograph so I can go get my ice cream?" The guy stood up and shook my dad's hand. He said, "Well, she knows what she wants, doesn't she?" My dad replied with a shy look on his face, "Yes, she does. She is not aware of who you are."

They chatted a bit and then finally, mom and my sister came back. As I saw them from the window, I looked at the woman and said, "Miss Dunnaway, thank you!" She politely replied, "You're welcome, honey." I went to my dad, who was still shaking this old guy's hand and dragged him out of the store. We, at last, went to get my ice cream, pralines, and cream, from my favorite ice cream parlor Thirty One Flavors. Yummy.

Later I found out that the old guy who I mouthed off to was Steve McQueen. Oh well, live and learn. Something else also happened to me at Olvera Street. I was going to see a friend who did the Mexican dancing with her family there and I didn't want to see her perform on Cinco De Mayo; the spectators for that are awful, so I went to see her rehearsal. I was standing there by myself when some guy came up to me and asked, "Are you Jan?" I said, "Good guess. How did you know?" I will never forget what he said next. He pointed at the stage and said, "My cousin's up there. She asked me to look out for you. She told me to look out for the whitest woman in the world." I laughed hard and was surprisingly not offended. It's a good thing my mom wasn't standing next to me or he would have been really confused. "Which one do you mean they are both white as fuck?"

I've met a lot of famous people just from growing up in L.A. It's no big deal. We were coming back from Portland and Gene Simmons was on our plane. Mom told me to get his autograph. I told her, "I'm not six anymore. He's in first-class because he doesn't want to be bothered, mom." Growing up in L.A., you see a lot of celebrities. I think that's why I'm not generally taken back when someone famous is around. I find that there is no need to get their autograph. It's actually an unwritten rule in L.A. Let them have their privacy. Don't go up to someone when they're eating in a restaurant, it's rude. I waited on Pat Bolan and Mike Shannahan in Denver at a place I worked at, called Little Ollie's, in Cherry Creek. Charlie, God, I love him, would always want to do a tableside service to them of the Crispy Sea Bass, and they hated it. Not that the dish was bad, it was just not according to their taste palette. I tried to tell Charlie, "Just let them drink their bud lites, and say hello. I don't think they want the Crispy Sea Bass tonight." Mike even told me once, "Tell Charlie, we don't need the fish tonight, okay?" They were always really nice about it. Charlie wouldn't listen; he took it to them anyway. You should have seen Mike's face as I looked at him and shrugged my shoulders. "Sorry, dude. He's the boss." They would ask people not to bother them until they are done with dinner. Most people were really good about it. Others are rude dicks. For the record, Mike is a good tipper, a nice guy, and so was Pat. R.I.P. Pat.

I have never told this to anyone but now that dad's dead, I can talk about it. There was a girl who moved in down the street from us. She was about my age, so I played with her a few times. Her dad drank and my parents never drank. For the record, my dad's father was an alcoholic. I had to go home for dinner and I ran through her house. Her dad was in a big leather swivel chair and he grabbed me by my arm really hard. It startled me. He said, "Where are you going in such a hurry?" I said, "Home for dinner." He checked me out in the creepiest way and everything about it still grosses me out. He licked his lips like he wanted to take a bit of me. With filth laced in his voice, he said, "You can play down here anytime." I said, "Thank you," pulled my arm away, and started to run home. Halfway I realized, I wet my pants. I ran into my room to get changed. I sat on the floor and wanted everything to shut off! You may think I was overreacting, but I have had faced sexual trauma before as well, and it all came flooding in. A year prior, a man in a V. W. Bug tried to get me in his car to help him find the racetrack, which was nowhere near our house. He was naked from the waist down, jerking off. I did what my mom told me to; I walked into the first house I saw and called for help. Mom called the police. I had to look at pictures of men and describe what he looked like. It was a mess. I didn't want to go through that again.

Dad came into my room and said, "Dinner." I said something that caught his attention. I can't remember what it was but he shut the door behind him, which was something very unusual. He came over and sat down next to me. "What's wrong?" I think dad was a little more on his game from the whole "Male-genital exposure" incident I had to face back then. Have you ever been so scared you can't think of a lie? I just told him the truth.

"Dad, the girl down the street, I play with her. Her dad grabbed me and told me I could play down there anytime. I wet my pants. I'm sorry, but I got all cleaned up. He scared me a little and I don't want to play down there anytime." I could see my dad's hands start to fist and his face getting all red. I instantly started thinking he was mad at me for wetting my pants; I'm too old to be doing that. He looked at my arm where I had a visible mark. He said, "Did you tell your mother about this?" I shook my head and said, "Don't call her. She'll call the police again." He replied, "No. I'm not going to tell your mother. I'm just going to have a little talk with him."

I was only about ten, but my first reaction was, "Dad, are you going to kill him?" He said, "No, just talk to him. Don't tell your mother where I'm going. I'll be right back." He kissed me on the forehead, weird. He wasn't an affectionate person at all. I went to dinner; dad went to gear up.

"Richard, where do you think you're going?" My mom called back to him. He simply replied, "Be right back." She hated it when we weren't all sitting at the same table, praying and eating together. Mom said, "Do you know where your dad went?" I lied and said, "Nope."

He went and came back about twenty minutes later. He rushed to the bedroom to disarm himself. God forbid, if dad came to the dinner table with his sidearm on, mom would have had a fit! Dad winked at me as he seated himself. We finished dinner and got up to resort to our bedrooms. As he was shutting his door, he said to me, "You're not to go down there to play again, and they're going to move."

I couldn't believe it. "How do you know they're going to move?" Dad said, "Well, don't tell your mom. You know the big gun you like? I put it in his mouth, and told him, 'If he ever touches you again, I would pull the trigger, and if they didn't move, I'd burn their house to the ground."

Overwhelmed, I whispered, "Dad, I liked that girl. Don't do that." He, with a calm voice, said, "I'm not going to do that. I was just kidding, but he bought it now. Don't tell your mom about this, and don't go down there to play anymore. All I could say was, "Thank you," and gave him a hug.

The 'big gun' dad was referring to was a three fifty-seven magnum; try having that in your mouth. Dad wasn't protecting his little girl, really. What dad was doing was protecting his seed, the family name. I don't think dad would have killed him, but honestly, he could have blown his head off and gotten away with it. Since he owned the police. They moved shortly after that. I never told anybody this either but in the sixth grade once again, this time on the way to school, another man, a white guy in his sixties in a Cadillac was naked from the waist down, jerking off. "Hey, honey. What do you think of that?" He barked as I was walking by. I froze and he drove off. I ran to school and didn't tell a soul. There was nothing the police could do. I was confronted with perverts who were always white and not black men. I'm not afraid to get into an elevator alone with a black man, but I would be more worried about getting into an elevator alone with a middle-aged white guy. They're a lot scarier!

Do you know hunting guns? My dad does, and he didn't even hunt but he had them. Dad collected all types of guns, to the extent that we had weapons in every room of the house! When I was eight, we had a woodpecker problem. I was watching T. V and this comedian, Tom Segura, was on. He did this show called, "Disgraceful" in Denver. If you haven't watched it yet, I would recommend you do it right now. You'd thank me later. He was talking about how his dad woke him up to kill this woodpecker that was fucking up their house. My jaw dropped. Tom, I got you beat. We had a woodpecker alright, but it didn't live in our house. It was 100 yards away on top of a wooden telephone pole, and this little bastard wouldn't stop!

It's echoed thru the entire neighborhood! Nobody could do anything about it, city problems. Dad had an idea and he called me into the bedroom. It was one of those "Don't tell your mom" moments. I could hear it but I couldn't see it. Dad said, "Do you hear that woodpecker?" I replied, "Yes, dad. Where is it?" He pulled out these "Something about Mary goggles," the really big ones. He had popped out the screen door to their window and got under the bed. He unzipped the case and pulled out his thirty-out rifle. This weapon is used for big long-range game hunting, a little overkill for a woodpecker. It's kind of like taking an elephant gun to kill a squirrel. He lined up the shot and "poof." Nothing but feathers with one shot.

Dad was an excellent marksman. Honestly, dad could have hit that bird with a higher-powered weapon from a thousand yards. Yes, he was that good. Now, he couldn't ride a bike or play ball. Dad couldn't even swim. His lungs were so underdeveloped he was given last rites three times before the age of five. They didn't think he'd make it. Dad surely had his moments. For us, that was one of the good memories. It's kind of fucked up, but it's true that I enjoyed these few intimate moments with him. So if Tom Segura hears about this, all I have to say is that I loved your story. So I'm telling you Tom, "Thank you motherfucker. I appreciate it!" Hehe. He'll know what I mean. Oh, by the way, don't say that phrase to a cop while he gives you a ticket. "What did you just say to me, Ma'am?"

Dad and I were home alone on the weekend my sister and mom were out. To get rid of my boredom, I went to do a puzzle on the kitchen table. I was wearing my purple Fonzie T-shirt from happy days that said "AAAYYYYY" across the front of my favorite shirt. I can remember it because that was the year we did a "drill team" show and used the music from Happy Days and Laverne and Shirley. I loved those shows. We would sit on the floor, I would sit in the splits for flexibility, and we would eat peanuts from a barrel bowl because mom wouldn't let us have candy or sweets, but we could have nuts and raisins. Mom put our Easter Bunny baskets together and we always thought the Easter Bunny was a dick! She would give us carob-covered nuts and fruit leather but no chocolate, peeps, or jelly beans. We didn't get that stuff. Mom was strict with our diets, and she didn't think it was a good idea to have sugar at all, if possible.

Anyway, I dumped out the puzzle and when I looked down, there was something under the table. Dad had put a loaded 45 in a holster under the table. It wasn't pointed at me, so I ignored it and started to do my puzzle. I have to mention here that my dad is the worst actor. He came down the hall with a smile on his face. Like you know already, he was never interested in what we were doing but he goes, "Well, honey. How is that puzzle going on? Are you enjoying it? Do you notice something different about this room?"

He started to look around. I said, "Dad, there is a 45 under the table." It's kind of sad that an eight-year-old knew what kind of weapon that was but I did. It was the first gun I ever fired. Dad thoughtfully said, "Do you think mom will notice?" I was looking at him with a "You're an idiot" face. Yes, Dad, I think she will. If I can see it, so can mom. He takes it out and puts it in my closet because that's much safer for an eight-year-old. He was nuts! Mom insisted that we were trained to use weapons, so now I feel comfortable around weapons. I just don't feel the need to have one with me all the time. If you feel the need to carry a weapon, do it. But know how to store it, clean it, and above all, fire it properly. Don't let a kid get to it but if you do have a firearm in your house, legal or not, and a child lives there, make the kid understand that this is not a toy! That goes for anybody who owns a gun. I'm sure every mom in the country would agree with that; if you have a gun around, keep it out of reach or anywhere a child can't get to it. They don't know how dangerous it is. You should treat your kids like you would treat a drug addict living in your house. If you think a drug addict can get to something, you don't want them to get their hands on, put it under lock, and even then, keep in mind that they still might get to it and it can kill them.

CHAPTER THREE: OLD SCHOOL, MY POPS, CARIBEAN

It was the 70s. L.A. public schools and some of the kids from the "inner city" would get "bussed to school" in the nicer areas. My dad hated it. He liked things that were more white and exclusive; prick mindset. I thought it was great, new kids to play with, you know? There was a little black girl who came to our school. The kids were calling her the 'N' word. I heard my dad use it but didn't know what it meant, so I joined in as well. Of course, the teacher told us not to use that word. She ordered us, "Please use her name." We did but some of the boys kept on and the teacher didn't scold them again. The teacher didn't explain what the "N" word was, she just told us not to say it and I went home. Jesus, take the time to explain things to kids!

I had the regular routine, out of your school clothes, get in your grubbiest, and out of the house until dinner. It was the 70s and that's how it was back then. I went into the house and mom said over her shoulder in the kitchen, "How was school?" I replied casually, "there was some little "N" girl at school today." I said the entire word in front of here without realizing its grave consequences. The next thing I know, I'm flat on my back and I can't breathe. Mom took that shit from the floor and BOOM! She hit me so hard she knocked me right off my feet. I couldn't breathe. Mom pulled up a chair and told me why I would never use that word again, or she would kill me. Fuck the time-out chair. Can you imagine doing something like that to a white kid? I deserved that hit. I never said it again. I can't tell you how many kids I wanted to slap but couldn't. I have never hit anyone, much less a kid, but I thought about it. Think right now how many kids you would love to give one really good hit to, just once for fun? I am sure many would come to mind.

Kids today go with their helmets, safety pads and all that stuff just to take a shit!! We broke bones! I broke my tailbone doing an inverted dive at a swim meet. Yep, hurts as much as you think it does. I didn't land the dive and everyone saw it. They all huddled around me in the pool asking. "Are you okay?" I remember nodding a polite "Yes" and coming out of the water utterly embarrassed. As soon as I set my foot on land, I heard a crunch. I knew it right away that's not good.

Mom was talking to one of her other mommy friends. "Mom, I think I broke my tailbone." She thought I was kidding. She turned around and just said, "You aren't getting out of the five hundred," and jumped right back in her conversation. I had to swim the five hundred and did twenty laps freestyle with a broken tailbone. OUCH! It freaks out every doctor that I see. If I wasn't allergic to pain killers, I'd be set. "Oh Doctor, I am in real pain. Can I have some pain pills?" They would say, "Oh, you think you broke your tailbone huh?" The moment they'd place their hand on my back, I'd hear, "Oh God!"

When we were kids, we would just rub some dirt on it and get back in the game. I saw my sister's best friend get whacked in the head with a baseball at a game and her mom gave her a cold compress for it and kept talking to the other mom's simultaneously as if she scratched her hand. Today, if a kid gets hit, they call the National Guard for help and try to sue everyone for pain and suffering. Just so you know, I'm referring to all of the white Karens of the world. The parents who want their kid to be number one and the only way the children can achieve that is if their drunk or drug-induced

Karen Moms wine about how "my kid got hurt. Give him a medal for trying!" Get the fuck out of here with that pussy shit. My mom didn't buy the whole "I'm hurt! I can't! I'm hurt! You do it, Mommy!" I don't think so! If we bitched to our mom about a little scrape, she would just laugh and say, "Well, don't do that again," and continue with whatever she was doing. Suck it up! Sometimes you get hurt when you play. It's a part of life.

I got spanked many times when I was a kid. I probably deserved every beating I ever got! My mother didn't torture us or lock us in a closet or anything. Jesus, do not take it too far. Look what happened to Kemper. He turned out really well regardless of the fact that his mom really fucked him up. Once, I saw a woman who was drunk in the market hit her kid twice. I looked her dead in the eye and said, "You hit him again, and I'll call the Police." She obviously told me to mind my own business. I didn't. Instead, I informed the manager and he called the cops, poor kid. You don't have to hit a kid to get them to do what you want. Just get in their head. Find out what scares them or makes them flinch. You don't need a baseball bat to do that. Although some kids today deserve a good beating, if you ask me. I sound so old when I say that. My grandfather used to beat my father relentlessly as a kid, but he never touched us. Dad left the punishment up to mom.

Anyway, in the restaurant business, you see a lot of families from different places all over the world, so you need to be well versed in manners and grace. Mind your P's and Q's, I know that sounds hokey, but it is true. I've worked in fine dining with white gloves and in some real shit holes. It really bothers me to see children with no manners; it is like nails down a chalkboard for me. You're not supposed to correct a kid you're waiting on, but fuck it, I did that more than once. It sucks when these "white dickheads" need a server to correct their kids because they're too busy "being them." That's some bullshit! It's no wonder their kids turn to drugs. No, it's not their environment, take blame where it is due. When I see an unruly child, the first thing that comes to mind is, "Wow, their mom and dad must be really fucked up." It's not his fault he has no manners and doesn't even hear the word "No!" He's a spoiled little tyrant that bad behavior starts in the home. They didn't get that shit from watching too much cable. It comes from good old mom and dad. Please do us all a favor, you want to get them something for their sweet sixteen? Get them spayed or neutered. For the rest of us who don't want to be around kids will become adults with no manners.

Please, tell your kids to have basic manners; napkin on the lap, no chewing with food in your mouth, don't speak when you have a mouth full of food, elbows off the table, don't slouch, sit up straight, pass to the left, say "Please," when asking for something from the table, ask politely to be excused, have pleasant conversations, be articulate when you speak and don't interrupt. Wash up before dinner, pray before dinner, you will finish everything I have got on the plate for you, if you want seconds, finish your plate first, then I will portion out a serving for you, those were mom's rules and we didn't fuck with them! I can't stand kids who won't eat what they are served because they don't like it and their stupid white parents let them get away with being a spoiled brat who gets whatever they want. My mom was more like, "Eat it, wear it, or starve to death." Those were our options. If I ever looked at my mom and said, "Mom, could you cut the crust off for me?" or "Mom, I want my apples sliced a different way than this?" My mother would laugh and say, "Why don't you go live somewhere where they do it like that? You will eat whatever I make you." That was it.

If you are a rich white parent and you want mom's advice, I'd give it to you, but if mom met you, she would probably say, "I'd like to help, but I'm retired." That would be mom's polite way of saying to me, "No way am I going to work with those weenies." The word weenie would be cussing for her. She would give you advice and you would ignore it like most well-off white people who are too involved with themselves. "I know he needs something but I'm busy with my yoga and spin class. Now, that is really important to me, so you go teach him what he needs to know. My nails are wet, okay?" Typical Karen mindset.

I think kids and animals have a weird sixth sense. They know when they're in danger to grovel or whimper. I had a friend whose dog, Geanie, would jump up and down in excitement to see me every time I was around, and I get the same reaction with kids as well. I would go to some of the kids I babysat for, and the moment I was in their sight, they would go bonkers. "Yay, Janny's here to play!" The little monsters would surround me with their infectious giggles. What my point is; kids are really smart, so are some animals. They can always gauge how sympathetic one is; if they can read a book or play with them until they're out of breath or yeah, let's go swimming for the tenth day in a row.

The bottom line is: if you are good to a kid, they don't care who you are, where you are from, what you do for a living, or what tax bracket you live in. They just want to have fun, learn new stuff, and play. However, take a nap first and bring a lot of coffee if you need it because kids, especially little ones, never run out of steam! You have to keep the kids going all the time but it can be exhausting, specifically if your kid is A.D.D. I have A.D.D. and I still behaved. As I mentioned earlier, mom was the piano player at our church when we were little. We would go from the nursery school to the big church at the end of the services. She would play the procession. Even when everyone would leave the church as the service would come close to its ending, my sister and I stayed in the front pew for mom to finish. We didn't have iPads, coloring books, or crayons. We would just sit there in our seats politely. Because if we didn't, we'd get it at home that we behaved without drugs. Mom's rules! Don't break them or else God forbid, you act out in church! Did you see that little spoiled white kid on the plane? That little shit got her parents kicked off the plane because she wouldn't put on her mask. "Oh, she won't wear a mask. It isn't her fault." Oh c'mon! Yes, it is actually your fault because she's a brat who does whatever she wants. Is her name Karen? It wouldn't surprise me at all. That shit would not fly with my mom!

When I was in the fourth grade, my grandfather taught me how to play poker very well. He had a gambling problem, but I don't know how bad it was. All I know is that he was a good poker player. Learning from him is like sharing a family recipe, so I'm going to keep that information to myself for now, but I loved to play.

My Pops, my mother's father was wonderful. He looked like a cross between Fred Astair and Danny Kay. Strawberry blond red hair, big blue eyes, bald but still handsome Pops was an amazing artist, a professional cartoonist. I don't remember much, but I think I heard something about Hanna-Barbera from him. He also did a golf strip. Pops was a marine in WWII, but before that, he was in Texas Mounted Police in 1938. This man didn't have a racist bone in his body. I know I rip on white cops now; they deserve it but not all of them, just 75-80% of them. He would be proud of me for telling the truth. He had these big Popeye arms, which he would wrap around me like a security blanket.

Pops had tattoos on his arms as well. One was from WWII and one was a memorial tattoo for a friend that was killed in Korea. I remember him explaining them to me in his calming sound. My dad used to say, "Tattoos are for cheap uneducated people." What a stuck-up prick. Pops was also a teacher and he was impeccable at explaining things. So was mom. Dad was more like, "Here are five bucks. Go play someplace else, I am busy." My pops drew clowns and ballerinas all over my bedroom for me when I was little. My dad retaliated with, "This will lower the resale value of the house." Mom ignored him and Pops did it anyways.

Pops didn't like dad but he was a good provider. If dad ever got out of line with his daughter, he would have killed him with one punch. He was a chain-smoker; two packs a day unfiltered! He wasn't allowed to smoke in front of us, though. We had asthma and dad wouldn't go in his house because he couldn't breathe. Pops had this big beanbag ashtray next to his recliner. I would empty it, climb up into his arms and we'd talk. He had a pacemaker fixed under his skin and he would let me touch it. EEWWWEEEYY! Pops once said, "Do you know what a Marine is?" I replied, "No, Pops. What is it?" He chuckled and said, "That means, I work for a living." I told him daddy was in the army but he only signs papers, which was true. He made a face and said. "Your dad's a pencil pusher. Why don't you tell him that?" I did and dad didn't like it. "Kid tricks." You tell a kid to say something "out there" and see what happens. Dad could never take a joke; it was Pop's way of razzing him. I'd say something to dad Pops told me to just for shits and giggles. I would say, "Dad, you know some people think Nixon was a crook?" There was nothing dad could do about it. Pops liked a good razzing!

Pops came to my school in the fifth grade to give a presentation for the class on the chalkboard. He was really good. I was at recess and Pops was outside the classroom, smoking. I ran over to him and hysterically told him, "Pops, you can't smoke at school!" He just took one last long drag and put it out. We entered the classroom and Mr. Stephenson introduced Pops to the students. He said, "Okay, this is Jan's grandpa and he is an artist. He can draw anything. You just have to ask him." This kid, Johnny, asked him to draw a boy riding a skateboard on one hand upside down. Pops looked at him and said, "Is that all?" He took his sweet time with everything, keeping the kid and everyone else hooked to the board. They didn't think he could do it. As always, Pops knocked it out of the park. He was surely a wonderful man. I wish Pops was around to see all the wonderful art today. I could just see him smoking a cigarette with his big bean bag ashtray, hanging out with Mr. Cartoon or any other artist who shares the same love for the "Art of Drawing," like him. That would be Pop's idea of heaven. It is important to keep an open mind, especially when it comes to art. The best part about it is that even though it is ever-changing, anyone can fit in their creativity and end up creating something extraordinary. There is a reason why there are all types of art; acting, painting, photography, dancing, or music of any kind. Don't miss any of it!

Pops and mom were both artists and teachers. They just had that spark that made them work well with kids. I do too although my method of disciplining would be different from theirs. On the first day in school, I'd tell the kids in first grade this, "Okay, I'm Miss Janny, kids. Do you know who Houdini was? He could get out of all kinds of things, such as a straitjacket, like this one here. So, let's all try it on. Try to get out of it, okay?" I'd have them all try it on. When I see them struggling, wanting to get out, I will tell them, "Well, you know that time-out chair that your mom likes? It doesn't work for me. So, if you're bad and don't listen to me, I'm going to put you in the straitjacket and make you stand in the corner, facing the wall." The kids will pay attention to that. I'd also go with, "If you wet your pants or need to get up at all, I won't let you until your mom or dad come to get you. So, you will sit in your wet pants, until your parents come to pick you up and all the kids will tell your mom how bad you were." The kids will all listen up when I'd continue, "When you get home, your parents will probably spank you too. You don't want that, do you? No right? So, pay attention. Also, I have an extra jacket for your mom if she needs one at your house. So everybody read to learn? Yay!" That's how I'd start my year, get straight to the point. Just to scare them a little, instilling some fear is necessary to get them into shape. I wish I had sky-blue eyes like mom; I can't just give a look and scare someone. I love my mom out of fear! Just kidding, I know if I'm going to say something that might issue a slap, I stay at arm's length. Mom won't hit me, not in public. We are white and that's tacky. White people keep that shit behind closed doors.

When my sister and I were little, we weren't allowed to have any sugar. No sugar in our cereal, no sugar in our tea, no soda pop, no chewing gum except on the weekend, and only one piece of candy, even at Halloween. Mom would take our candy and dump it out on the kitchen table after we went trick or treating and she would say, "Now girls, you can pick five pieces and the rest goes to the hospital for kids who can't go trick or treating. Let's think about them." My sister and I figured out pretty quickly if we wanted our candy, we had to shove them in our socks or eat as much as possible without mom knowing. That's why I have a sweet tooth now.

Mom was very diligent about our diets not being full of crap. Dad was a dentist and we weren't allowed to have gum that was full of sugar, but once he brought home a box of sugarless Trident gum. They were giving it to dentists for a trial run with their patients. My father's an idiot. Instead of giving the whole box to mom, that stupid ass gave it to us. Well, to my sister, she was the 'responsible' one. We take it in mom and dad's bedroom, where they have a full-length mirror. We wanted to practice blowing bubbles, so we opened the pack and started to chew. I blew bubbles really well, but the gum was getting stuck in our hair. To save our asses from mom's wrath, we thought it was a good idea to take off our shirts and pull our hair back. But that was not enough because the gum was really sticky so we decided to put shower caps on. Moreover, we took out a big jar of Vaseline and rubbed it all over our faces and neck, so we can pull off the gum easily. Pretty smart! My sister and I were blowing bubbles like crazy, but the Vaseline kept mixing with the gum, so we had to spit it out a lot and start over. I don't know how long we did this but we did it for a long time, over and over again. Mom came into the bedroom and saw us doing this, two little girls covered in Vaseline with an empty box of chewing gum. Dad was in big trouble now. I can't remember what happened but I know mom had a good laugh about it.

Mom always had a good sense of humor. We were at church when I was little and the minister said to the congregation when the services were over, "Now Jane Williams will 'tinkle' on the keys for us." My mom fell over off the piano bench, laughing. Mom couldn't hold it together. The whole congregation laughed.

We did some really stupid stuff as kids. There was a time when we took packaging tape from dad's office along with some bubble wrap and put it in the middle of the street. Whenever a car came by and hit our creation, it sounded like they blew a tire. They would stop and hysterically get out of the car, thinking they were in trouble. They would look around in confusion and reality would sink in slowly. "Goddamn it, you kids!" They would scream in frustration. Talk about bored white kids, but we were creative. We never did anything really bad like toilet papering a house that was "bad" for us, but there was one kid who did something really bad when we were little. I will never forget Chris, our next-door neighbor's kid, who got drunk and peeled out across the house lawn because the guy was a dick and wouldn't let us go back into his backyard to get his Pomegranates. He was the only one with a Pomegranate tree. He hated kids and would rather have the fruits fall off the tree and rot than give them to us. He was one of those guys who reminded me of the guy from "American Beauty," the stern, hardened, republican neighbor, who was a closeted faggot, putting his American flag out every day and saluting it.

I remember going to their house to sell candy bars for some charity, and the mom answered. She was a frail woman and I got the impression that she was scared of her husband. Once, she called my mom and asked for a recipe for the candy bar for her husband because he gave her an allowance and he wanted to know where she spent two dollars. Controlling behavior alert! Chris got in trouble but not many people were surprised it happened to him. He used to turn his lights out during Halloween and put a note up that said, "Get out! This is private property! No trespassing!" We lived on a street full of kids, what did he think would happen to him?

Mom had her "tools of destruction" above the refrigerator, so I couldn't get to it before she did. Jesus! Another weird memory: I was playing with make-up and got out of hand. I don't think I was supposed to touch the make-up or be playing with mom's clothes or jewelry either. The rules were, "Get out of the house until dinner!" I wasn't supposed to be in the house, but if mom gets that god damned metal fly swatter, I'm fucked! She could whip that sucker so fast and it stung like hell! I didn't care if she went for a wooden spoon or a spatula, but that metal fly swatter, OUCH! I went over to the kitchen table and looked in through the kitchen window at the den where mom was watching her soaps. "She didn't hear me," I thought happily. Fool. I tried to pull the seat but it was too loud. "She'll hear me," I panicked. Fuck. So what I did was I kept moving the chair five inches forward, and after every step, I would look out the window to check if I was busted or not, and repeated the cycle and ensured she didn't catch me. I think it took me about half an hour to get the chair next to the fridge.

I climbed the chair and started to reach for the fly swatter; I looked over and there she was. Mom was standing right behind me with that look. I started to play with the magnets on the fridge to distract her. She asked, "Jan, why are you in the house and what do you think you are doing?" My throat was dry but I still managed to say, "I forgot something." She asked again, "Why are you on that chair? Why do you have make-up on? I'm so fucked. I didn't know what to do. Flustered, I started to play with the magnets on the fridge and it was clearly not working, I started to push the chair back like that's going to help, but it started screeching across the floor. Now, this was more than bad and I flipped. "I didn't mean to do it, mom. I am sorry." I had no other choice but to accept what I did wrong and pray for some mercy. Without looking over her shoulder, she grabbed the metal fly swatter. "What did you do? Come on, tell me! What did you do?" She made sure I think a hundred times before pulling off a stunt like that.

Here is a thought. I think creative and artistic people get beat down more than other people because we can't hold back. We process things differently, not in a dyslexia way, but we think on a different level. Most artists try to see beauty in everything. The way they envision things is diverse. We take our blinders off better but get persecuted for it. I shouldn't have gotten into her stuff, but it was so much fun. That's my artistic bullshit excuse for getting into her stuff – any of you buy it?

I think it would be a great idea to gather people from very different backgrounds and see what they can do, artistically. It will be a No-Tech Art Day; all technology is banned for the day. Call ministers, priests, housewives, gang members, tax attorneys, chefs, every teacher you can think of, homesteaders, lifeguards, plumbers, gardeners, veterinarians, painters, truck drivers, politicians, bartenders, ballerinas, musicians, dog-walkers, bus drivers, construction workers, must have midgets, carpenters, mechanics, designers of everything; a plethora of people who just want to express themselves artistically for just one day. See the magic that happens. No egos, no grand prize for the winner. We would all enjoy the art; share in each other's company. That's it. I think it's a good idea; maybe the millennials can work on it. They're good for something, right? I think it would be life-changing for them to take a break from their tech stuff. I have witnessed that many of them can't be away from their phones for more than five minutes. This would be a "time out" for them. They would behave like the kids I taught swimming to once. They would whine for about five minutes when they didn't want to get in the cold pool, but after they got used to it, they were fine and enjoyed the water. We just need millennials to get their feet wet without their devices. Take baby steps. Leave your phone at home for an hour and see if you don't explode. We'll go from there.

When I was in the sixth grade, they made me play "Mary" in the Christmas play at school. My mom put them to it, I am sure of it! They made Pat, this blond-haired kid play Joseph. We hated each other and I made sure they knew it but my teachers obviously didn't care. All I heard was, "You're Mary and you're Joseph. That is final!" I didn't want to but my mom was playing piano for our play, and I couldn't get out of it. I sat there with my hands crossed over my chest, praying for a miracle and trying to behave. I would occasionally flip off Joseph when mom wasn't looking but what I really want to know is, why do white people think Jesus was white? I read that book more than once. No fucking way was he white. My mother has an allergic reaction to the sun. If she gets too much of it, she gets sick. Mom went skiing and went "snow-blind" for a day because her eyes are so sensitive. Do you think with the blazing sun in the desert, she would be okay for forty days and forty nights? No fucking way! If Jesus was white on that cross, he'd be freckled and burned. Maybe he looked white because he was scared, like a ghost? Maybe he was anemic, but no way was he white. The only people who think Jesus was white are the Mormons and we know how bright they are. JESUS WAS NOT WHITE!

I'm going to catch a lot of shit for the comment I just made, but at least I didn't say, "God doesn't exist," like my sister would say right to your face. She is a woman of science and her sense of humor is a little twisted, but I love it. I can just see her in discussion with Jim Baker. My sister would tell him, "I am an atheist, you sleazy crooked scumbag. God doesn't exist, you Bible banging dipshit!" I don't know how Jim would respond to my sister, but I know she would take him intellectually. Other than that, something tells me Jim doesn't go out to the gym much, and my sister wouldn't have a problem with beating the crap out of him either. If there was a fight between my sister and Jim Baker, and God had to bet, He'd put it all on my sister. God is all eyes and old Jimbo hasn't been a very good boy. My sister has no skeletons in her closet. Even if God knows she's an atheist, He will make an exception for her because she's a good person. She has no idea how much I pray for her. At least she's not fucking underage prostitutes, doing coke in hotel rooms, and stealing money from their congregation.

Just don't be a dishonest person in general. If you're a man of science or a man of the cloth, it doesn't matter whether you see God as black, male, female, white, or Latino. Just have faith. And if you don't believe in God or want to obey another "higher power," all I can say is, "I will pray for you." A higher power is only as good as you make it. Just because I like God, doesn't mean I'm going to heaven and you aren't. It just means I don't have to stand in line at the pearly gates! Have a look in the back of the Bible, you will find "The Pearly Gates Rule." If you are a good person, pray a lot for others, and you do selfless acts, you don't have to stand in line. You don't have to worry because everyone gets in eventually, at least whoever is supposed to be there, but I'd like to think the ones who think of others first before themselves get an advantage to meet God first. It's only fair. I would like to think the more selfless acts you do, it looks better with "The Big Guy" or "Girl," depending on your taste.

When we were kids, we went on a cruise to the Caribbean. I was eleven. On our flight to Florida, I saw Willie Ames from "Eight is Enough." I think he was in a band called "Paradise." I love Willie Ames! He was sitting on the plane with these girls about his age who were sitting behind him. I wanted them to say, "Come sit with us!" but obviously, that wasn't going to happen. Mom told me clearly, "You get his autograph and come right back. Don't be a pest." I went and just got his autograph. I didn't give a shit about Steve McQueen, but this was Willie Ames! WOW! I think it's a bit ironic that we were going on a cruise and he became a cruise ship director later on, which is the perfect second career for him. He's so personable and sweet. Willie was a really nice guy with beautiful hair. I had the biggest crush on him as a kid after watching "Eight is enough." I also ran into George Burns too at the airport, what a sweetie, typical L.A.X. airport.

When we got to Florida, it was so humid! There were big bugs that flew around, clearly not my cup of tea. We get to the ship and do the drill with the life vests on our way. Mom said, "Go have fun!" and we obliged like always. We went to Haiti, Nassau, Jamaica, and some of the private islands. We went swimming in the ocean, picked up a live sand dollar, and put it back in the water. Another exciting marine fish that we encountered was the baby shark. We also went to Dunn's River Falls. If you go there, take your shoes. The rocks are really sharp!

Mom struck up a conversation with a man who owned hotels in Bermuda; he was going to check out a rum plantation and invited us to go. Mom was always thinking outside the box, so she said yes. We piled into this bus and went up the hill. Wow, this was a third-world country. We were told that it was a road bullshit; it was a trail it was very lush and slick. In reality, there were no guard rails or anything. The driver would honk his horn, going around the corners but he never slowed down. It was thrilling, but a little scary too, as most fun things are. We should make buttons that say, "Everything that is thrilling is a little scary." We went to the top, and there were kids begging for money, and I'd never seen that before. Can you imagine? I lived in L.A., after all. I threw them some money and asked mom for more about three times. She said, "Jan, are you giving those kids all your money?" I said, "Yes. Why not? We have a lot." That's when mom realized I had no concept of money. Yes, I knew the word 'NO', but I thought everything was free. My parents never told us, "We can't afford it." So, my mom had a long talk with us about being white and being privileged. I think that's why mom wanted us to travel to experience how others live and open our eyes.

We got back to the ship, and mom gave both of us a roll of quarters to play with in the casino. She made us a permission slip and gave it to the guy in the cage. She didn't have to, but she explained to him, "I am these girl's mother this is our room and they are allowed to play on the slots only until dinner. Do you understand?" The guy in the cage said, "Ma'am, you don't have to do that. It is okay for them to be in here. Mom replied, "I understand. Just keep an eye out for them." She turned to us and said, "You have one hour, then come to dinner." We both started to play the quarter slots, but dimes looked like more, so I switched. [no concept of money]

I ran by this drunken woman playing the dollar slots. She was from Texas, and I showed her my Dixie cup of dimes. She exclaimed, "Oh, you're lucky. Come here. Give me your hand. I need some luck. You're my lucky charm. I'm going to pull this Handel down and I am going to win with your luck. Just wait watch, kid!" She pulled, and she won. She didn't let go of my hand for twenty minutes. I was begging her, "Please, I have to go to dinner. My mom is waiting for me." She kept saying, "No, you are my lucky charm. I need you." My sister came looking for me, and I told her this woman wouldn't let me go because I was her lucky charm. She asked the woman, who was clearly wasted beyond her limits, to let me go. But she wouldn't budge. "She is my lucky charm!" she screamed. My sister went across the way to a jewelry store and got this big black security guard. I know he was big because his head went to the top of the doorway. I couldn't tell what she was saying, but it looked bad. He comes over and takes her hands off me. The woman from Texas was yelling at him, but his face was ironically calm. He just told us, "You girls go have dinner. I got it." We thanked him and ran.

When we were rushing for dinner, my sister said, "I will tell mom what happened. Don't worry about it." My sister had my back! We went to the buffet and straight to the dinner table. We sat down and Mom was talking to this nice, well-dressed black man chatting. My sister starts to explain why I'm late. I look at this nice black man after Mom introduced us and say, "Oh, sir? Do you want some of my watermelon and chicken? That is what my daddy said you eat, and I have plenty if you'd like some?" I told you the "purple lips" thing was just the beginning and it was going to get worse, so there you go. This was right in front of my Mother. Now she had to tell this nice man that she was married to racist and that's where I got it. I thought I was being polite. Dad didn't say not to repeat that. When we got home, dad was in so much trouble. We didn't go to the kitchen table and opened up our luggage to show dad all that we did. That wasn't happening. Mom slammed down the luggage and said, "Richard, I want to see you in the bedroom right now!" I didn't hear any creaking in their room for a long time.

Dad pulled me aside and said, "From now on, don't repeat anything I say to Mom." From then on, I knew I had to play the "Pretty Princess" game with dad. If I wanted to know something Mom doesn't know, it may come to my advantage. The older I got, the smarter I got. When dad did anything sneaky, I knew about it. Not all of it but, enough to get me in trouble if I didn't have my eyes on it. I never told a soul about the K.K.K. stuff until right now. When my sister called me and told me that dad was dead, I had to make myself cry. I don't feel guilty for not missing him. He was a rotten guy and did more harm than good in his life.

I think my dad was a White stuck-up, rude, sociopath, schizophrenic, racist, insecure, and a white-collar criminal jackass! I know there's more, I mean, who knows? But he didn't die happy. The last time I talked to him, it wasn't good. I didn't go to his funeral and feel no guilt for it at all. After what he put my Mom through, fuck him! I hope he has a miserable time in hell with Hitler. It's true that if you are around someone who is a jackass and who uses slander that is really offending to anyone with common sense, but you're just a kid and don't know any better, it's confusing as hell and really destructive to the young mind. They just don't know it or they don't care if they are considered a racist person because most of their friends are the same, so why clean up their language for a kid? I was exposed to so much negative slander growing up in my dad's family. Even though mom didn't know about all of it, if you're a kid, it rubs off.

I am going to tell you a story I wish never happened but I'm going to admit to it. I was seventeen and went to the drug store by our house in Pasadena – an all-white neighborhood. I was waiting in line. A well-dressed black man was waiting with me and we said hello to each other. He had a U.S.C. pendent on his lapel. I asked him, "Did you go to U.S.C? My dad also went there." He said, "No, my son goes there." I, of course, thought like a stupid white person with her head up her ass. I said, "Oh, does he play football?" This well-dressed black man looked at me with utter disgust and said, "No, he plays books." I could only say, "Oh." From the look on his face, I realized what an incredibly stupid and offending thing it was to say. I wanted to apologize to him, but he took his drugs from the pharmacist and gave me a dirty look I well deserved and left. I can thank my dad for that one. I was a girl who was told by my sister, "Don't ever believe a word dad says ever!" She knew what she was talking about. I was young when that happened but it still is no excuse for doing that. If that man remembers that, I am sorry I offended you. I owe him at least that. I know we have all done some things we are embarrassed about or thought, "I can't believe I said that." This incident is one of them for me, and I will never do that again.

CHAPTER FOUR: CHILD STARS, PEDOPHILES, PRINCIPALS

I went to Jefferson Junior High. During that time, we somehow inherited a motor home. I think my grandfather won it in a bet, not surprising to the least. One day, I looked at dad and said, "We have new cars every year and now we have this. Why?" The look threw me off. It was a piece of shit, but we took it to Solvang for Danish days. Yeah, we are Danish too, white and whiter. It was fun. We would go to the "Anderson's Split," the pea soup place. Yummy! We would have apple doughnuts and fudge. Good memories as a kid.

I had this bright idea to take the motor home to the drive-in with my new friends from school, put the sleeping bags on top and watch the movie. Dad also agreed. Yay, so seven of my friends from the choir at school came over for the plan. Dad came in and said, "Okay girls, don't tell your parents, but we are going to see a rated 'R' movie called Halloween." Oh no! I hate scary movies, even to this day. Dad told some of the girls to get in the bathroom, so he didn't have to pay for them. So now he was teaching me how to steal, what a wonderful example. We got in and took the sleeping bags out; we climbed on the car roof and the movie started. I didn't make it ten minutes in. I got so scared. I went back to the motor home and sat on my dad's lap with my eyes closed. I wanted to ask him, "Why did you pick this movie, dad?" But I knew the answer already. "Oh yea, because you only want to see a movie you want to see?" That's why we were there. He never would have taken us to see Disney.

I went to see "Benji" with my mom and sister. There is a part where the dog, Benji, gets hit and I started crying like a baby. My Mom had to put me in her lap to calm me down, yeah no shit. I was balling inside that motor home, asking dad if we could go. All my dad was probably thinking about was, "Jan better not tell Mom about this." After that, I had nightmares and I could not tell Mom, we saw a movie with dad that scared me and was told, "Don't you dare tell your mom that we saw this movie or we won't ever go back to another drive in again." It was fine with me. I said, "Okay dad, I won't tell."

The girls were screaming, and people were turning around in the drive-in like, "What kind of an animal would let little girls see this kind of a movie?" My friends got so scared that they came inside the motor home too. Dad thought it was funny as hell.

I had a sleepover with those girls once. We snuck out to "T. P." Peter Altenburger's house he always stood out to me because he never missed one day of school, not one. Peter was a sweetie to boot. We wanted to T.P. his house because one of the girls had a crush on him. We did a great job but got caught. I can't imagine what we looked like, seven little girls in our jammies, running down the street holding rolls of toilet paper in the middle of the night in L.A. My Mom was so mad, she threatened to call the girl's parents and tell them they broke her rules. I begged her not to. "Mom, it was all my idea, ground me, don't punish them," I pleaded. She let them slide and I got grounded. The next day was one of the girl's birthday party and they all went. I got grounded for a month. Another girl I went to the choir with was Bonnie. She got a hold of a joint and convinced me to go to my old elementary school to smoke it. She was saying stuff like, "Oh, that's a good drag" or "Nice hit." She tried really hard to look cool. She got caught and told her mother it was mine and I was the only girl who smoked with her. The truth was

I only did it once with her. There were other girls who were doing it but she asked me to keep my mouth shut and cover for them. I took the fall and got in serious trouble. It was hard for Mom to trust me after that. I should have been in a gang; I know when to keep my mouth shut! I had their backs but not sure they would have mine, these white girls with no loyalty. Not all of them, just 75-80% of them.

One day, I wasn't feeling good and my Mom noticed I was not eating. I was a bottomless pit, and she made me a big breakfast, bacon eggs hash browns, usually it's a bowl of cereal and off to school. I looked at her and said, "I am not hungry," and went to school. I was in the second period and I felt like I was going to throw up. I walked to the teacher, and I must have looked awful, because she was writing and, and when she looked up at me, she yelped and said, "Oh my God! Honey, are you okay?" I could only mutter a few words and said, "I feel sick." She looked at Carrie, the sweetest girl in class who I have known since kindergarten and said, "Carrie take Jan to the nurse's office." Worried, she took my hand and said, "Okay Jan, let's go." We ran down the hall and I didn't make it. I threw up. We rushed to the nurses and I fainted. Turns out, I needed to get my appendix out.

My Mom came to get me and had to put me in a wheelchair because I couldn't walk. Mom and I went to my doctor who was nearby where we live, an all-white neighborhood. We were in the waiting room and a black girl who looked like she was in more pain than me, had the same problem I did, but they wouldn't see her. I just had a long talk with mom about blacks and whites and how we get privileged so I asked Mom, "They won't see her because she's black?" Mom replied, "No, it is because she doesn't have insurance." "What is insurance?" I inquired. We had another long talk.

I did notice security escorted her out of the office, never seen that before. We went to a private hospital and she was told to go to L.A. County hospital, the worst place she could go. I had a friend who was an actor from Canada and was working at a construction site. He got a blood blister that busted and got blood poisoning. He was rushed to L.A. County, where he was in a room with four beds, one small window, and one of the guys was handcuffed to the bed. They didn't even know what he had, and this was in 1988 during the aids crisis. Whereas I got treated like a princess, I went to a private hospital, and my dad called one of his buddies from college to do my surgery. He was one of the top children's doctors in California. I have a hairline scar but something in the medication that they gave made me break out in hives, and I had to stay in the hospital for ten days instead of three. The doctors said, "Well, your daughter has a low tolerance to the medication. Keep an eye out for bad reactions to medication from now on. It may get worse," and it did. I am allergic to everything but for some reason, I am not allergic to cocaine. YIPPEE. I don't know what to say to that. Maybe, Thank you God?

I loved choir. Our teacher was Mr. Doolittle. He was a tall white man who everybody liked; he was so talented and nice. You had to audition to get into the choir. My sister and I got easily selected. It was a privilege to work with Mr. Doolittle. My mom knew him because she was a pianist too. Mr. Doolittle did, however, have one problem. He was a Pedophile. I wasn't quite sure if something was going on but never said anything until my Mom told us, "Girls, Mr. Doolittle was accused of acting inappropriately with one of his students." Mom told us this about 12 years after I graduated high school because she was in the teacher's loop. When we heard what he had done from mom, my sister and

I said, "Yea, we kind of figured something was going on, but don't worry, we weren't his type." Can you imagine your daughter telling you something like that? She was floored. She said, "Why didn't you say anything?" We told her very frankly, "Mom, he would have kicked us out of the choir. We loved choir and he would have gone after you." He would have too. That's what guilty people do; they put their attention on someone other than themselves. He would say, "That's the mother of those girls who lied about me."

I can remember Mr. Doolittle stopping in the middle of our performance to tell everyone that a girl, Stephanie, was an alto and that she was leaving our school and going to another one. I didn't realize she was leaving. He went to her, gave her a hug, and continued our performance. I think she was a target. He always paid a little extra attention or gave a more appealing smile to some of the girls, but when you are only eleven, you don't think of that look as sexual because you don't know what sexy is. He sure was infatuated with Stephanie, like he was with a lot of girls. My sister saw it too but we didn't talk about it.

I couldn't help but ask Mom, "Did he go to jail? What happened?" She said, "No, now I understand why he did what he did." We said, "What did he do?" Mom told us, "When the accusation was made, he packed his bags, and moved in the middle of the night. No forwarding address, no nothing. Nobody knows where he went." I knew he was a pervert and he was caught! I can't imagine how many other moms asked their daughters, "Mr. Doolittle was your teacher. Did he ever touch you?" I always wondered after Mom told us that he was caught about how many of the girls I was friends with did he try any of that shit, nobody talked about stuff like that when we were growing up. It was the 70s.

When I was a kid, I went to church camp. Wow, a white kid at church camp? This is going to get exciting! I'll try not to bore you to death, onward Christian soldiers. Actually, I loved it as I was a geek. Anyway, it was fun. Church camp was where I learned the "Little bunny fru-fru" song and got a nickname because of it that stupid name has lasted my entire life. Oh, Yay, dork for life! My Mom calls me "FRU-FRU" to this day. We went to Wrightwood church camp. It was a Methodist church camp in L.A. and the last time I went, I was fourteen. There was a kid about eighteen years old, who was an assistant youth advisor, and he was escorted off the camp grounds because he was fooling around with a kid about my age and got caught. He wasn't arrested, just 'misplaced'. After church camp was over, we went down the hill to see our folks and he was there with a different set of kids going to camp. The church covered it up and no parents were told a thing. I wonder what happened to the girl he was fooling around with? She left camp too and nobody said a word.

I had a youth advisor from my church who once saw me and my friend, Sandy, out for a run and he was in his van. Of course, he was in a van. Pervert. He pulled his car in front of us and said, "Oh hi Jan, I saw you running. I had to stop because I thought to myself, that's a sexy woman and it's you!" I was a little shocked as I never had a man say, "You are sexy," to me. I said, "No, it's just me. See you later." Even my friend was uneasy with that remark. I was only fifteen years old, and he was around forty years old. Inappropriate! My sister had a run-in with a youth advisor as well, but I'm not going to get into it. There are predatory people everywhere!

We were a family in a nice neighborhood. My sister and I crossed paths with a guy who tried to flash us while walking home from skating; she saw it and I didn't. All the people who did that sick stuff were white men and lived in a very nice neighborhood but who gets blamed first for any problems? Black people, white people are really fucked up for doing that, but we get away with shit like that all the time. Just blame a black man for it. I know it was a popular belief before we freed slaves, "Yea, that black man is to blame," but now what's our excuse? I think white people are running out of excuses.

I'll never forget Vacation Bible School as a kid. We were really involved. That was the year I told everyone, "My mom will make her chicken and dumplings for everyone." I made this promise before they told her it was for eighty people. She explained why she can't just whip up chicken and dumplings for that many people at one day's notice, so she came up with something else, but her chicken and dumplings would have been better. Funny how you remember Mom's food you ate as a kid. Anyway, I was about ten and my perfect sister was twelve, I think. We were sponsoring a girl in South America and putting money in a big jar for her. This was the 70s, and people trusted one another a lot more back then. There was a thing where the most involved with church activities would participate in different games and whoever claimed victory, received a new twenty-dollar bill! Holy shit! I had no concept of money but it sounded like a lot.

When it was the big day, they announced the winner and it was us! We won! The twenty-dollar bill was mine! They gave my sister and I each a twenty. She looked up at me, went over and gave away her money to the little girl in South America in the donation jar. I'm going to fucking kill my sister, God damn it! I've never had any money of my own much less a new twenty-dollar bill. Now everyone was looking at me, expecting me to do the same thing. I wanted to scream a big fuck you at my sister and run, but mom was right there, no way is that going to happen. Fuck!! I go over, put my money in the jar, and everyone clapped for me. I wanted to flip them all off!

In my head, I was planning on how to get that twenty out of that jar without being noticed. I didn't always feel good to give. The older I got, the more I realized how good it feels to give. I was at church, and one of the girls I was in bible school with forgot her lunch. My mom made me split my Hats pastrami sandwich with her, I wanted to cry, but I gave it to her because that's what fucking Jesus would do. Damn it! "HATS" sandwiches feel like heaven, yummy goodness wrapped in between two beautiful warm buns, covered in mustard and pickles. You open the wrapper and your mouth starts to water. You pick it up and grease drips down your hand all the way to your elbow. It was like pulling teeth to give it up, but mom knew it was the right thing to do. I hope that girl knows how lucky she was to get that half sandwich.

I started eighth grade and met Vidal Peterson, a child star. If you don't recognize the name, here's what he was in. In Mork and Mindy, he was the little Morken Elder with the round glasses. He was the young Stewey in The Thorn Birds, and he also did 'Something Wicked This Way Comes,' a Disney blockbuster. They dyed his hair for that movie. He got most of his work between fourth and sixth grade. Vidal had these little round glasses that got him a lot of work! I don't care what anyone says, but Harry potter ripped him off! Vidal Pederson had those glasses first! Child stars don't have much time usually in the industry to be cute. Vidal is one of a kind! He was always going to land on his feet. He was really smart, funny, and never got into anything fishy. I think I bragged to him once that I saw a scary movie. Of course, I didn't tell him I saw it with my eyes closed. He said, "You want to see a movie that's funnier than scary? Come over and watch with some of your friends if you want. The movie is called 'Creep show'. You'll like it, it's funny!"

Remember that movie with Ted Danson? He was a middle-class kid like most of us. The famous misconception is that all kids in the business are rich, but we were middle class for L.A. People in the Midwest may think we were all rich, some of us did better than others but we could give a shit whose dad made more money. We never discussed it; we just had fun together. I went to his house with a couple of friends to watch the movie on the V. C. R. That's how old I am.

Vidal showed us his headshot; it said 'Peterson' on it. I assumed he was white until his Mom walked in. She was Hispanic. I never told him this, but when his Mom walked in the room, I thought, oh he has a maid. I asked him, "Is that your dad's family name?" Vidal said, "No, are you kidding? That's my stage name. I can't use my real name. I would never get work." Confused, I inquired, "What do you mean?" He explained, "It's a business thing. My real name is Pelasious, and I can't use that. It's not white enough. I have to be white to get parts, and I'm white enough to play a white kid, so I changed my name." I asked, "How can they do that to you? It's your family name." The blame goes to my dad with the family name bullshit that he kept going on about all his life. The Williams family name is sacred! Vidal said, "I don't care if they take my name or put me in different clothes. They can dye my hair, I don't care. I'm a trained actor and I can play anything." He was eleven at that time.

Vidal was so funny and talented, he reminded me of Leonardo Decaprio when he was young. I want to be a serious actor. He was just like that! I went back to school after I graduated and saw him get on stage, as he was back to the theater. He played this goofy kid who kept running into stuff. Vidal ran into the set so hard it fell down. They immediately dropped the curtain, and fixed it; Vidal never missed a beat! The last thing I saw him in was Beverly Hills 90210. He wasn't just talented, but he was a funny and good all-around person. We didn't hang out much. He didn't go to my church and he wasn't on the swim team or in my dance class either but he did turn me on to sushi. I thought he was crazy, I mean, raw fish? He was right though. Surprisingly, it was great! He had good taste even as a kid. Miss you, Vidal!

I know a lot of child actors who tried to stay in the industry after their child-star status is over. I know the kid from The Courtship of Eddie's Father. He was in a punk band for a while and then he got into production. I think I saw him at one of the studios when I was a kid. He wasn't acting anymore but still in the business. I sometimes wonder about what happened to the child stars that I remember, like Roxana Zal from Something About Amelia, Quinn Cummings from Goodbye Girl, the woman who played Leather Teskadaro on Happy Days, or the baby girl everyone was so infatuated with from Baby-Boom.

I think Willie Ames had it good. We have all had our little bumps in the road, but he managed to pull it together. I will never forget an episode of Eight Is Enough, where Willie's character found a present from his mother who passed away and I balled like crazy. He was such a good actor! I know Billy Mummy from Twilight Zone; "Monster" was one of my favorite episodes. He was in Lost in Space and Babylon 5. He turned out great, and he was from home; San Gabriel, but there were so many kid actors that just disappeared. I wish they would write a book to explain how to make that transition for child stars but it doesn't exist, as of yet. I think that would be a great idea. A book with a title "How to be well rounded and Happy When It All Ends as a Child Star" Maybe we can write a book for the stage parents too called, "How to Get Your Kids into the Business, Without Screwing them Up!" I can think of a few people who could benefit from that information. I know they could have when I was a kid.

When you're a kid trying to get into the business, it's not unusual to get new headshots and show them to each other or talk about auditions. "Hey, you get that part? No? Yea 12 sucks. I can't play 9 anymore either." I modeled for kids' clothing. Mom got me into it because I thought I was ugly. If a kid has low self-esteem, usually it's not a good idea to get them into modeling but for me, it was a boost of confidence I needed. I never took the business too seriously. For me, it was just fun for a while. I chalk it up to experience. Whenever people asked me if I was ever a model I'd say, "A little, nothing professional."

I would lie because I didn't want to get interrogated with questions like who have you worked with and where did you model last? Who's your agent? A lot of gigs I did were a little "expressive," if you know what I mean, and if you don't, use your imagination! I wasn't model material; I just was enough of something to get noticed. I had a good body, I was an athlete, I took directions well and I think that's the problem with some models. They're hired for their looks and not their opinion. Shut up and do your fucking job! I really think that's why I got a lot of work. I just did what the director told me to and kept my mouth shut. Usually, a difficult thing for me to do but when I have to, I keep it shut! Does anyone look at the cover of Vogue and ask, "I wonder what's on her mind?" No right? Except when Katelynn

Jenner was on the cover, then I just wondered, "What the fuck was she thinking?"

There were kids in the industry weren't as lucky as Vidal Todd Bridges, and Corey Feldman, both molested by white men in the industry. They were both talented, funny kids who were good at their craft and those perverts got to them. The only mistake Todd's Mom made, she trusted the man who molested her son, and it's not her fault. Now they stand up for kids in Hollywood against pedophilia. Thank you, Todd and Corey. I commend them both.

I met Todd once. I was really high; who wasn't in the 80s? He was at Sushi on Sunset. I was there with my friend, Lori, and Cindy, from Caddyshack. Cindy was a blast, she did Tron, and everyone is entitled to their bombs. I was only eighteen when I met her, but it was the 80s. Nobody was too young or too old for parties. I swear I did a line with a guy who could have been my grandpa. Jesus! Cindy had a house on Queens Road, and the view was gorgeous! I don't know if she will even remember me as some dorky kid from Pasadena, but Cindy was a very nice woman. Now I can say that I had a little crush on her. We went hot tubing at her place and she was so beautiful. I was so confused about my sexuality. I never told her or anyone if I had a little something for them. I knew she wasn't into women, but Cindy was wonderful and really nice to me. Lori was drop-dead gorgeous! When she walked in a room, heads turned. She met a N.J.B., nice Jewish boy, got married and settled down in L.A. Last time I spoke to her. He's a lucky guy! She was a true survivor. Lori was in a student film and a guy became obsessed with her. He followed her around and was taking pictures of her without her knowing it. She came home one night and he was waiting for her in her underground parking lot with a knife. He tied her up with her seatbelt, blindfolded her and repeatedly raped her in the front seat of her car. A security guard saw them and did nothing about it because he thought she was just having sex with her boyfriend. Lori got stabbed in the armpit but managed to survive. Her parents got her a trained attack dog to protect her. Theresa Sladano, Rebecca Shafer, all these actresses got attacked in Hollywood and a lot of those attacks went unreported. Lori was a good actress, she is very lucky to be alive. I hope she reads this. I miss you, Lori. She was the first person I told I had lost my virginity. What a dear girl.

Todd was going through a rough time when I met him, and I'm so glad he's okay now. What a good actor. He was really not treated well by the business at all. I don't think people took notice of Todd's accusation of molestation as well as they should have at first. It was when Corey Feldman, a white kid came out is where they went, "Oh, maybe it is true." They wrote off Todd as some black kid who fell off the rails and his career took a dive because he was on drugs. He turned to drugs to cope. I think if he was a shining good Christian white kid like Kirk Cameron, they would have arrested the man who molested him, given him financial compensation, and put him up on a pedestal as the poor white Christian victim, but that's just my take on it. Welcome to white Hollywood.

Woody Allen, and Roman Polanski, both white directors, and pedophiles', we let them slide because they're so talented. We love their work and stay in denial, believing they would never do anything like that. Well, all I can say is that's a crock of shit. We let them slide because they're white! A white director who's famous and people like his work is protected in the business. Where do the funds come from? Whitey! Even if the funds were available to a black director, he would never get away with molesting a boy in

Hollywood. I'd like to give a warning, don't ever let your kids alone in a Hollywood setting, not at the beach, pool parties, or in a photoshoot. To put it simply, don't let them out of your sight! Hollywood pedophiles are out there! Don't leave them with an agent, manager, publicist, photographer, or any white male adult in the business.

I can remember working at a place in Hollywood. Some parents would drop their kids off and let them alone in a dark restaurant with an agent or publicist and we were told to give them privacy. Ask around, and you will hear that it is like that. Sometimes, their Mom can't always watch them and that's where the sick bastards go in for the kill when mothers are not around. It doesn't matter how famous they are. Those kids are just that, kids. They're your responsibility, not your meal ticket. The business will fuck them up enough; don't lend it a hand by leaving them in a dangerous situation. Natalie Wood was raped by a studio executive when she was fifteen. Her mother told her, "Don't tell anyone about this or it will ruin your career." Not kidding, don't let your kid become another statistic, don't let him/her become one more kid getting fucked in Hollywood for fame. That's one of the problems with Hollywood, people are so desperate to get in the business, and they sell out their kids to do it. They want to be in the spotlight where their kids have the Hollywood Kid Star title that they are so proud of, and once they get a taste of it, the more work he gets, you don't see your kid as much. But his manager, director, publicist, and photographer get to spend time with your child, and they tell you it's because he's talented and one of their favorite kids to work with when the real reason why is because they want to fuck him.

Fuck Kevin Spacey and Brian Singer too! I don't care how talented they are, they're sick fucks! These vile men can't keep their hands off little boys in Hollywood. Both of them passed boys around in Hollywood like their tick-tacks. "Oh, here, try this one, no? I already did. He tastes great. I'll have that one later." Parents of boys they molested and people who love their work think they are not guilty because they don't want to accept the reality, because it will lead to acceptance of their horrible crimes. Oh, he's so talented he wouldn't do that, right? You have to be fucking kidding me! How would you feel if your sixteen-year-old son invited Kevin Spacey over for dinner and he goes up to your son's room and you walk in on them and Kevin Spacey has his cock in your son's mouth? Would you still think he's talented and would you still love his work? Then after Kevin comes all over your son's face, maybe he can take him to Brian Singer's house for a little pool party? He comes home a little dizzy and his jaw is sore but he got the part in Brian Singers' movie. Aren't you proud of him? Everyone knows what's going on. They both deserve to be seriously punished! How is it that I'm the only one to say it out loud: Brian Singer and Kevin Spacey should have their dicks cut off! I'll do it.

I can disassociate between a human and an animal, I'll cut it off! Isn't 'Q' going after pedophiles? Go for it Q, knock yourself out, have fun. I have a sharp cleaver if you need it. You can cut off Warren Jeff's cock too while you're at it and any other child molester as far as I'm concerned. If they need someone to be The Hatchet Man, I'll do it. I'm a professional chef. As I said, those fuckers aren't human beings, they are animals. I can kill, skin, gut, filet, and cook almost any animal. I would treat an animal I hunted with more respect than I would treat them.

Call up Joe Rogan. He's a good marksman and the father of a little girl. Joe could make a head or chest shot with no problem, but I'd bet Joe would shoot him in the dick if I asked him to! I will bet Joe's daughter is a good shot too, give her a gun too. Joe could tell her, "Take your time, okay sweetie? Focus, line up your shot, breath, be patient, and now take your best shot right in the crotch!" I think Joe would agree with me when I say that they don't deserve a quick death. Let them suffer like the kids they molested did but worse. Give those kids they molested a "weapon of their choice," tie the bastard, go into a room with the offender, and let them go to town as long as they want to. That's justice!

I feel for so many people who have gone through any kind of assault, but when it's a child, I have no empathy for the abusers at all. I would love to be on a jury for a child molester case. If I even remotely think he's guilty, I would tie him up, get a full gallon of gas, pour it over to him, give a lighter to the kid who was molested, and say, "Don't burn yourself, have fun, and run away." If someone is caught for pedophilia on their first offense, cut their dicks off. But if you think that's too much, if they have to be in prison, tell everybody that he is a child molester, and give them a little "alone time" with the prisoners who have kids. If the sick fuck gets out of prison and does it again, give them the electric chair, but pull a Percy from The Green Mile, "He is on fire! He is not dead yet! Hit it again, hit it again! Don't get the fire extinguisher! He is not dead yet! Hit it again!" Problem solved.

Yeah, I am not a maternal person at all. Hate to say it, but I don't think any mother or father anywhere with an ounce of maternal instinct would mind setting a pedophile on fire if it was their kid who was abused. I think like a lioness, if you hurt my cubs, I may tear you apart. I'm not a violent or angry person, I don't like scary movies or rollercoaster rides, but if someone came at one of the kids I took care of, I would rip them to shreds if they hurt those cubs. I wouldn't care if I'd lose, get all beat up, or wound up in the emergency ward, I'd recover knowing I did whatever it took to protect those kids. Children go to adults for advice, kindness, support, love, safety, honesty, and trust. Any adult who mistreats a kid like that should be burned at the stake. Hey, maybe the Klan will come on handy after all. They like burning steaks! Perfect! We'll have a Klansmen Pedophile Burning Party. I think I would go to that Klan meeting. I'll bring the marshmallows!

Have you seen the documentary "Bully" on Netflix? It is about a kid who gets bullied at school. The poor kid is a bit odd-looking so he gets extremely picked on. The parents tell the principal and she does nothing about it. Until they get a film crew involved, then she has to do something about it. That's some bullshit. They had to hire a film crew to get her attention. I had a similar situation with a principal not too long ago.

I used to babysit some of my neighbors' kids occasionally and the mom had a drinking problem. In simple words, she was a drunk. She got fired from her job for drinking. I would always catch her playing all kinds of games. I know all the games drunks play, so I was not too thrilled to see her playing this game with me. The drunk Mom needed a ride to her doctor's office and she told me her car wasn't working. We got in my car and her son said, "Mommy, what's wrong with your car?" There was nothing wrong with her car. She was drunk and didn't want her doctor to find out, so she asked me to talk to her doctor on her behalf. She needed more medication so she won't drink anymore. That was her excuse to go back to drinking, "I ran out of my medication so I started to drink, but I can't help it." We reached the doctor's office and the minute we entered the appointment room, her doctor said to me, "She's drunk right now, isn't she?" I said, "Yes, I think so. She asked me to come here and talk to you, because she ran out of her medication, and she didn't want to talk to you, because she's drunk."

I told her the truth. I think she was expecting me to lie to her. She was giving us "the act," that she was playing with some papers pretending not to be able to hear us talk when she's five feet away. Her doctor sees her playing this game, and I'm sure she's seen this kind of thing before from drunks trying to get away with acting like the victim! The doctor said to her, "If you come here drunk like this again, I'm going to call social services. Do you understand me?" She looked up and nodded. She got her drugs and I took her home. I told her husband, "I can't watch the kids anymore, I don't trust her." He understood about it. Social services got involved, and as expected, she lied to them and told them that when she wasn't around, I was there their primary caregiver because she knew I didn't drink and was sober. She asked me to talk to her like I did for her at her doctor's office, takes a lot of balls. Drunks think they can take advantage of people with the whole, "I am not feeling well. Can you do it?" It's a fucking game. I told the social services lady, "I'm the neighbor who occasionally watches the kids, but she is out of hand with her drinking, so I'm out. Her husband knows." I told the truth. She understood and gave me her card.

The last time I watched the kids, I was walking up her driveway to the house and she was leaving waving goodbye to me. I thought her husband was home but he wasn't. She just left her kids with nobody to watch them. She knew I was on my way over but she didn't know I was going to be right there when she left. I gave her money to get the kids signed up for swimming lessons she never got them signed up and she took the money I gave her and spent it on booze. They had a pool and she lost her keys to the gate, so she thought it would be a good idea to try to climb over the gate and she fell and fractured her ankle in front of her kids, drunk. Those were some of the games she was playing and I got sick of it. I asked the eldest who was eight years old back then with my best friend in the car next to me, "What happens when mommy drinks? You can trust me. I won't tell anyone." Do you know how you can get a kid to trust you? Don't break your promises and don't lie to them ever. That's it. It's not complicated. He said, "Mommy passes out all over the house all the time. She takes us to the liquor store when she's not supposed to, and hides it in the house, but we're not supposed to tell dad." My best friend looked like he wanted to throw up. He was sick to his stomach. The kid's eight, and she's driving drunk with the kids in the car. Now, the water was way above my head and I had to say something to the school. I wasn't not going to watch them anymore, but they were in danger.

First, I went to the liquor store right around the corner from her house with a photo of her and told them not to sell to her. The drunken mom went to rehab for ten days and did an experimental treatment. Her parents took ten thousand dollars out of their retirement to help her. What does she do to repay them? The first day she's out of recovery, she goes to the liquor store, gets booze, and gets drunk. Thank you, mom and dad! They don't deserve that but they enabled her. When her husband couldn't take her drinking, he didn't want his kids exposed to her like that, she would go to mom and dad's house where they helped. "Oh, she just needs one more. She gets the shakes if she doesn't have a little bit."

Yeah, the tremors she's having will lead to seizures soon and just one more won't do it. She's going to die if she doesn't stop completely! I know from personal experience.

I gave a heads up to his teacher because he wasn't listening in class and his mom wouldn't talk to her She would pick up her kid from school, or she would just wave to him and didn't get too close, so they couldn't tell that she was drunk. She even missed teacher-parent meetings. So I pulled the principal aside, and asked her, "Do you know who I am?" She did, "Okay, that mom is a drunk, and I'm worried about the kids. She's drinking and driving with the kids, and I'm not able to watch them anymore. I don't trust her at all. Social services got involved, but she's not in jail she's driving drunk, so don't let them go with her if she's been drinking, okay?" The following was her reaction. "Well, if you think it's gotten that far, you should call the police or social services yourself." She was looking around and at her watch like I was wasting her time. I looked at her and said, "I'm telling you, social services got involved, I can't watch her all the time, so heads up please, if she's drunk, don't let the kid go with her! Please!" I'm a concerned woman, who is warning her about one of her students in trouble and she was not paying attention at all. The principal looked at me and went, "Well, I don't know why we are having this conversation? If you think it is that bad, you need to call the police. This sounds like something you need to deal with, not me." She smiled at me with a smug grin on her face like, this is your problem, honey. She started to get up to leave and I realized she was not going to do anything.

I have had people in the past tell me, "Do not be a pushover. Sometimes, you need to get mad, don't hold it all in. Get angry if you have to. It's okay to get mad! It doesn't make you a bad person. Stand up for yourself." My friends are right; I needed to stand up for the safety of those kids. Who cares what she thinks of me? So now I had to treat the irresponsible principal like I would if it was a man who wouldn't listen to me. I had to become a bitch, so that's what I did. I stood up, raised my voice, and got in her face. "Okay, princess! This is how this is going to fucking fly! You are going to keep an eye out for her, because if those kids get hurt, it's going to be your fault, and I am going to tell everyone we had this little chit-chat, so you can't ignore this conversation. You fucking got it?!" That really got her attention.

I'm not a screaming-blow-up kind of person, but when I get mad, I tend to act like that, and it takes everybody back! All the girls in the office were looking at the principal, and she wasn't going to ignore me now. I don't even like to yell at my dog, but she wasn't going to listen to me if I didn't scream at her. So I marched out and told all the parents and teachers the following; "Heads up, everyone. The kid I'm friends with has a mom who's drunk, and if she comes here to pick up her kid, I told the principal to watch out for her, so don't let the kid go with her if she's been drinking but listen to this, the principal doesn't think, she needs to worry about it!" I smiled with disgust and walked away. I'm sure she was very surprised to get that kind of reaction from me, and I hate the fact that I had to yell and use profanity to get her attention, but I'm glad I did.

Two days later, the mom showed up at the school drunk! The principal took them home, and then went back to school. Not her problem anymore! Really, that's it! I will protect those kids even if it is from their own mother if I have to. If this doesn't get her attention, it was at Eastridge Elementary School in Aurora, Colorado, in 2020. I wonder if she's going to listen to this or if she is going to ignore it like she did when

I spoke with her. I told my mother, who was a first-grade teacher for 25 years. I asked her if I had gone too far with her. Although, I didn't tell Mom that I cursed, she was still on my side. She said, "No! She needed someone to tell her what was going on. It's too bad you had to snap at her to get her attention. I'm so proud of you for standing up for those kids." I said, "Thanks, Mom!"

I liked the other teachers at that school. Mrs. Heinz was a wonderful teacher, she just got married, and I hope her husband knows how lucky he is. I was picking up the drunken mom's kid from school. I got out of the car, went to him, and asked, "How did he do today?" I think that's what you're supposed to do when you pick up a kid from school, right? You say hello to the teacher and make sure that everything is okay with the kid in school.

I went to Mrs. Heinz and asked, "Is everything alright? The kid got his head down and he's really crying." You have ever seen a kid so hard on themselves; that they hold their breath and choke up? He was doing that and it was breaking my heart. Mrs. Heinz looked at me and motioned for me to come close to talk to her. This isn't good. I asked, "What's the problem?"

Mrs. Heinz says, "Does he know what the f-word means, or what the middle finger means?" Oh, God! He was in first grade. I said, "No, he doesn't. Did he learn that today at school?"

She replied, "Yes, he did, and does he knows what it means?" I said, "No, but now we need to have a long talk about it, don't worry, I'm on it." She thanked me but what I had in my mind was, "What my mom would do?" I wanted to find the kid who started it and have a little talk with his mom instead, we went to the car.

I asked him to sit down. We were sitting outside the car and now he was bawling. He must have thought that he was in real trouble, and being his best friend, that's what he told me, "Janny, you're my best friend." We were in the car when I said, "I'm not mad at you. Look at me, you don't need to cry. I'm going to explain to you what that means, and why we don't do that. It's not your fault, and I'm not going to tell your mom and dad, okay?" He looked up and said, "You will not tell my parents?" I said, "No, but you're never going to do that again, and I'll explain what that sign and that word means when we get home. You're not in trouble, and I love you, okay?" He nodded and said, "Okay." He told me who started it.

I took him to McDonald's. I told him I was proud of him for telling me the truth. Later, I took him home, explained the word and the sign, and let him know that it was bad and sometimes it's funny too, but I'll tell him about it when he is older. I could only give him the PG Disney version of the word. I did tell his dad, I needed to. He thought I handled it well. I told him he understands the basic meaning of the word, but if he does it again, feel free to spank him. He knew better! I can't spank him; I can only get in his head! He laughed and thanked me, and that was it. The kid didn't do it again.

I talked to Mrs. Heinz after we had that talk, and told her that she was very helpful and kind. I shared that I talked to his dad. Obviously, the kid didn't know that, but he was aware that he's not supposed to do that anymore. I let her know that if she catches him repeating his behavior, she is free to call his dad. Mrs. Heinz said, thank you. I couldn't ask her to talk to his mom, as it wouldn't have done any good, but the dad was on his game with his kids. I feel so sorry for him; he works so hard and he's dealing with his drunk wife. The kids are lucky to have him. This incident made me glad that the kid has Mrs. Heinz as a teacher and others like her to count on whenever they need any sort of help. I was also proud of doing what I did, even though I'm not a parent.

It took me a while to understand but oh my God! That's what it was! I was not a parent! That is what the principal must be thinking. "She's not a parent. Who does this woman think she is? I have more important things to do. She's wasting my time, and I don't want to get involved with the police or social services if I don't have to. They are a pain in my ass. Sure, she said she's talked to them already, let her deal with it. It's not like this will ever get to the administration! If she complains, she's just a babysitter. I have the authority here. I don't technically have to listen to her at all. She is not a parent, after all."

That's what I thought she was thinking when we first sat down, and the following were my thoughts, "What if she's right? I am not a parent she doesn't have to listen to me. What if the administration finds out about this? She's going to be so mad at me. She has more important things to do than to deal with me." But then I started wondering, "What if I am right?" I felt like I was a kid in high school being pushed around by the mean girls. Then I stopped and realized, I was my mother's daughter! Don't let her push you around; you're doing the right thing. Then I let her have it!

I know for a fact that mom being a teacher for 25 years in the Los Angeles Public School System wouldn't have done that, not at all! She would have gotten up and dealt with it immediately all by herself. My mom was a teacher from age 50 to 75, when she taught tough old broad! Mom's been all over the world, literally, and is well versed in everything.

So everybody knows not to mess with her, she never would have passed the buck! My mom would have gotten in touch with social services, called the police, talked to a therapist, and sat down with both parents with the kid and made sure the kid was alright that day! She wouldn't have waited two days until she showed up drunk to do anything about it.

My mom doesn't care about what anyone thinks of her. She was going to do the right thing anyhow. Mom knows how to deal with all kinds of people. If the police wouldn't be on her side, she knows the law and would explain it to them if they don't get it. A badge means nothing to her if a kid's in danger. Mom's in charge, and the police would do whatever she said, not the other way around. If she thinks they are wrong, she will let them know. Mom will explain it to them until they get it! Mom will get her way as long as it's in the best interest of the child, not the badge. She would make sure the kid, no matter whose kid it was, is safe. Mom wouldn't have ignored it or passed the buck like the principal did.

I think what bothered me the most was the principal's attitude. I was a concerned woman, and she being a woman herself, didn't help or provide any kind of support, which is what I was looking for desperately. If I received such a response from a man, it wouldn't have bothered me as much. So much for Girl Power! It was a slap in the face from her as a woman. I know I'm not a parent, but I still have a pretty good understanding of how to be a positive example to a kid. I'm not perfect, not at all, but when I see a kid in danger, I can't turn the other cheek. I mean, doesn't she get paid to not turn the other cheek? I went to her for help, and I got shot down because I wasn't a parent? If the parents and administration found out about this, a concerned babysitter warning their principal about some student in their district had a “drunk mom” showed up and all the principal did was take her off the school grounds and didn’t act immediately when I warned her, what excuse do you think the principal will use to get her out of anything that might make her look bad?

Other people there ask around, the principal wasn’t the only one to see the drunken mom at school that day, and she wasn’t the only one aware of the situation. The principal didn’t even have a sit down with the kid and the parents both. I talked to the dad and he said she asked him if they wanted therapy, but she said she had to offer it because that was what she was supposed to do and dropped it. I know how hard it is to teach and work with kids, and I am talking about firsthand experience here, and so did my mom. I’m sorry to say this about someone who works with kids, but the principal dropped the ball here. Regardless of my opinion, any sane person would agree with me here, but what do I know? I’m not a parent, right?

CHAPTER FIVE: HIGH SCHOOL, CARS, COMEDY

I went to San Gabriel High School, which catered to 5000 students. Thirty-seven languages were spoken at my school, making it extremely diverse! They split the school into two separate schools after I graduated as it was so overcrowded, they started to put trailers in front of the school. That's where I saw the big difference between where I live and the other kids. People used to rent houses in some of those areas but not ours. My ignorance led me to think that everyone owned their homes.

Our school was literally on the other side of the tracks, very John Hughes. The vibe there was very 80s. The first day of school requires a good first impression, right? I wore a periwinkle blue Polo shirt, tan Ralph Lauren shorts, penny loafers, and my hair looked like "Diane" from Cheers. Yep, I've been a weenie fan my whole life. I have desperately tried to be cool forever and to no avail. The cool kids got away with a lot of shit while I got caught for everything, and my mother didn't trust me after I was accused of smoking pot with Bonnie. I didn't want to be labeled 'The bad girl', so I thought, if you dress a certain way plus you were a virgin, you wouldn't be labeled as a slut. And if you had sex outside of marriage, you were a whore. I had this notion until I was about sixteen, but I made sure everyone knew I was a virgin. I thought the worst thing anyone could call you was a whore. My mom was a twenty-six-year-old virgin when she was married. Now you understand?

A senior boy asked me to senior prom; it was my freshman year. Upon asking my Mom, she said, "It is entirely inappropriate, as you are not a senior or a junior. You are not old enough, so you tell him, no thank you."

Yeah, mom was strict. I had to tell him, "Sorry, my mom won't let me go. I'm not old enough." I was so embarrassed. I was asked as a sophomore too, but mom wouldn't let me go to that either. The rules were, if a boy asks you out, you give mom his mother's number, she talks to her, and you wait until she gives her thumbs up and approves for them to come over. They meet dad, and you either double with your sister or tag along with another couple until you're sixteen.

I wasn't allowed to date on my own until I was sixteen. My parents didn't have anything to worry about. Every boy I liked in high school was gay. James, Johnny, and Eric Evavold, oh God, he was the cutest! They were all such sweeties, so polite. They dressed well and loved their mothers. My senior prom date became the first male cheerleader at our school. RA-RA-RA! GO TEAM JAN!

I think I was a virgin until I was eighteen because I didn't have a cock. Although, if Eric Evavold, one of the gay boys I liked, hears this, he'd say, "Honey, even with a cock, I don't think so, but you're fun to shop with." What a sweetie! Also a wonderful swimmer! He was such a fun faggot! He's going to laugh when he hears this!

Our school was right next to The San Gabriel Mission, which is an all-girls Catholic school. Girls, there were so beautiful. Naturally, I felt very jealous. Those girls got to wear make-up and they looked so mature I looked like I was in the third grade. I was such a late bloomer I didn't get my period until I was sixteen.

If you are an athlete and have very low body fat, a very active long-distance runner, a swimmer, a gymnast, or a ballerina, it stunts your second growth to spurt. I didn't stop growing until I was twenty. I went back to the 10-year reunion and the response was, "How did you get so tall? And are those real? I don't remember those!"

I wasn't allowed to get my ears pierced until I was thirteen, mom's rules. She went with me to get her ears pierced too. Before that, she wore clip-ons. Mom wouldn't let me wear big earrings either or lots of makeup, it was very obvious that mom was conservative. I did like the Latino girls, but they kind of scared me. They were intimidating, like "I'm going to beat the shit out of you," intimidating, not the way white girls do it. Those girls were more stuck-up and annoying. I always thought Latinos were really pretty. One setback to going to school was crossing the Nuns. They are the worst drivers in the world. If you see them coming, watch out, and say a big prayer. They don't use their brakes very often and the Nuns station wagon is all fucked up. They're not worried if they sideswipe you. God has the right of way and peace be with you. Now move it! I would always say hello to them. Most of them liked me and said hello back with a smile, but some of the nuns weren't very happy, and not many of them had a good sense of humor. Not going to tell you what I said. OOPS!

I was a very active kid, and so was my sister. I was on two swim teams, two theater groups, choir dance ballet, plus I did extreme hiking with my church fellows in the Southern Sierras. We did practice hiking in the San Gabriel foothills, and I went to my youth group three days a week and did volunteer work too.

I was constantly going! I'm A. D. D. and Dyslexic to boot. I wish they had C. B. D. for me when I was a kid. It would have made my life a hell of a lot easier. I don't believe in drugging kids, but C. B. D. is all-natural and it would have helped "slow things down." I have a very high IQ but I still spell my name backward on occasions, it's annoying. I also hate the fact that I have to defend myself for being dyslexic and A. D. D by telling everyone that I have a high IQ. It's like a defense mechanism.

People used to label me, "Stupid" I was just misunderstood. We process things a little differently, no biggie. They gave me an IQ test, they said something like this to my mom, "We don't get it, she's very bright with a very high IQ, but she spells her name backward, and why is she hanging from the rafters? Tell her to slow it down or keep her really active all the time." So, that's what mom did, she kept me active. I'm glad, at least now I know what it is.

I heard about this guy who was being teased for being dyslexic by his teacher. He was in a typing class and the teacher was ripping into him. He was a football player, a very quiet student. He was just having a hard time typing, so what? Many people with Dyslexia do the same goes for me. She went overboard and said to him, standing over him yelling, "How can somebody be so stupid? You can play football, but you can't type? What's wrong with you, huh?" The guy looked at her, picked up his typewriter and threw it out of a two-story building, and shut her up. He wasn't stupid, just dyslexic. Yeah, he went a little too far, but the teacher should have done her homework, he's dyslexic, not stupid at all.

It is so frustrating to explain Dyslexia. They didn't know about this stuff when I was a kid. Oh well, "Live and learn." I'm not going to blame being dyslexic for everything that goes wrong in my life, it's just the way it is and I will figure it out.

I know people who think, if you don't go to college or get a diploma, you're not that smart, bullshit! My dad was a doctor and he had no common sense at all. A lot of people think if they are in a position of power with a diploma, a family name, or connections and that a piece of paper is proof of their smartness. They live with an idiotic false image of themselves, "I know everybody, you better listen to me."

You know who some of them are, the famous ones Nixon, Trump, Oliver North, Hitler, Saddam Hussein, Osama Bin Laden, my dad, and those sex offender pricks such as Harvey Weinstein, Kevin Spacey, and Brian Singer. Just to mention a few. My point is, I don't need a piece of paper to tell me I'm smart, I know I am. Regardless of what people think about me.

When I was sixteen, I hit a guy's car while I was leaving someone's house in the Arcadia Foothills. I hit it and took off for home. I admitted doing it. I was drunk and my dad paid the guy for the damages. The same guy asked me to a school dance before this happened, so he was stuck to going with me. His dad was a dick. He was a teacher and full of himself. He sat me down and said, "You know, I could have called the police." My spoiled cocky ass was thinking, "Go ahead, see where it gets you, asshole." But instead, I being half-assed, apologized. I still had to go to that dance with him. We were doubling with Karen, so I had to go. The guy sits me down and says, "You know I could go by myself if I wanted to." Like I'm supposed to squirm because I hit his car, fuck him! The only reason I was there was that my friend Karen was going, we were doubling to the dance, you schmuck! I looked at him and said, "Fine, I'll call my dad to come to pick me up." He didn't expect that. He goes, "Well, I am the school president, they would be disappointed if I didn't go." Like he's Mr. Important, so we went and I avoided him.

I went to church in Arcadia, California. They had a little drug problem at their High School, pot and coke to be precise. They sent an undercover cop, an Asian female officer, to go to the school and make a drug bust. It was a joke. All those white kids had dads like mine their fathers paid the fine that got them out of jail. Just for kicks, they made up T-Shirts that said, "I survived the arcadia drug bust," and wore them to school to mock the police. All those kids had dads with little influence and money. They didn't learn a thing, white privilege! That would never happen to blacks or Latinos. If you are white and have money, you get a "get out of jail free card!" That's how it was when I was a kid. White cops are going to hate my guts for telling you all this truth, I'll bet some guys my dad knew from the police departments in L.A. will get a little nervous when they get a load of this, and they should. Some of them, not all, but a few of those white guys my dad knew were crooked as fuck.

When I turned sixteen, I got a new car. I kind of expected it; we always had new cars. Dad once said, "Don't give rides to anyone!" He meant people who weren't white. So when I got to school, I asked, "Anybody need a ride?" and I gave rides to anyone who needed it. I offered a ride to a couple of Mexican girls I really didn't know well. They needed a lift, and so we got into the car, and one of them said, "Is your family rich?" I replied, "No. Why?" They said, "You and your sister always have new cars." My answer was, "Yeah, doesn't everybody get new cars every year?"

I didn't know any better. That's how "sheltered" I was. My dad used to put gas in my car, and check the odometer reading every night. He was really controlling. I still snuck out a lot! We would go to the beach, the Beverly Centre in Beverly Hills, and drive to the Rialto Theater in Pasadena, to watch foreign films we weren't supposed to see. Like

Another Country Testament, Maria's Lovers, and Sophie's Choice. We weren't bad kids. I went to church three days a week. Sneaking out like this for such innocent adventures was being bad to us. We didn't tell our parents about it, obviously.

I stole my dad's brand new Camaro and put a scratch on it, and as expected, he got really mad about it. I didn't care though. Now you know why I was a spoiled brat! Dad let me get away with it. Meanwhile, mom would have beaten the shit out of me and I would have deserved it.

Dad let me get away with everything because he was a shitty father. He never punished us, and he left that up to mom. Dad thought, "Spare the rod and spoil the child." Don't do that to your kids; punish them when they do something wrong. Don't let them get away with it or they will think they can get away with anything. It's sad when an adult does that, especially if it's a guy. I know it's old-fashioned to think he's a grown man, and he can fix his own problems.

Then he calls daddy to fix it. Pathetic! I think that's how a lot of white kids are. They don't have to take responsibility for anything. A white kid whose parents have a little pull, says things like, "I don't have to worry, dad will fix it." Or, "Do you know who my father is?" I was like that too when I was a little kid, then I grew up.

I was sixteen when I tried to give my first blowjob. YUCK! Not that blowjobs are bad, but you have to be into it and I wasn't. The kid was in my youth group, Todd. He was a cute but typical, immature white kid with rich parents who probably spoiled him too. We were going to go to the drive-in movies was his idea. He picked me up and I warned him beforehand. I instructed, "Tell my dad your parents are

Republicans and shake his hand firmly." He came to the door, dad saw him, looked at his car, and said, "No way is my daughter going anywhere in that car, you can take her car. Where are you going?" Todd replied, "The drive-in movies." So dad made him leave his car in front of our house and we took my car. Just for your information, Todd had a Honda. Dad was just against foreign cars, no joke.

We got to the drive-in and the first thing he asked was, "Have you ever given a guy blowjob before?" I replied, "No, I like you but I have never done it." He said, "Well, if you want to go home, we can." I didn't want to go home. My best friend Karen had done it, and she told me how it was supposed to be done, so what the hell? I'll give it a shot. It's not sex, it's just a dick in your mouth. You can take it out or if he's a real asshole, bite it!

I agreed, "Well, I can try but don't force me or shove it in my mouth or anything, okay?" He shrugged and said, "Alright, I will talk you through it." He pulled it out, and we were in the front seat. I leaned down and started doing what my friend had taught me. He pressed his hands against my head and pushed me down, which made me sit up instantly. I told him, "Not so rough. Let me know when you are about to cum." I only continued when I knew he understood what I meant. He nodded his head and I got back to the deed. I was not enjoying this at all, but he was having the time of his life as he started to cum in no time. I pulled back and he came in his hand. Breathless, he muttered, "Oh, that was great, thanks. We finished the movie and we started our journey back to my home. I couldn't believe it, he was still horny. He was trying to finger fuck me in the car, I told him to stop. He then looked at his hand, all wet. He examined it and said, "Man! Look at all of that, what a waste! Ha-ha kidding." We got to my street, so I buckled my pants and glanced at his car that was parked in front of my house. It looked like it got hit. I got out, the back end of his car was smashed and it was a brand new Honda.

He flipped, "Jesus, what happened?" I got in the house and dad was not home. I asked mom, "Did you hear or see anything?" Mom came out to look, she was floored. "What happened?" I told her, "Dad didn't want us to take Todd's car, you know why, so we took mine instead, and someone did this to his Honda." I yelped while pointing my fingers towards the thrashed vehicle. I asked our neighbors, but nobody saw a thing. Todd went home pissed off and I don't blame him.

Two days later, Todd came over to my house and asked me, "Did your dad hit my car?" I looked at him so pissed. "Are you kidding me, he wasn't even home and mom asked him about it too. We asked everyone we know, I'm sorry about your car but it's not my or dad's fault." He left and dropped it.

It got me thinking, though. Dad may have followed us to the drive-in or had someone else do it. He must have seen what we did. My dad did say to me later that night, "I don't want that boy with the Honda around you, I don't like him." That was strange. Dad always liked most of the white boys I went out with, as long as they were Republican. It can't just be his car that he didn't like. I had a feeling that dad asked some of his buddies to warn Todd – if that is the case Todd's lucky to be alive.

I bet that's what happened because about a month later, I was going to a dance with a different boy, who was gay! My dad called me into the bedroom and asked me, "I need to ask you something, you don't do that, do you?" My dad was motioning in a rather poor way giving a blowjob. Jesus,

I am so lucky that the boys who followed us didn't tell dad everything. Dad doesn't know what really happened. I said to dad, "God! No, dad. I have to tell you the truth, I can't lie to you but don't tell mom. Well, that guy you don't like, the one with the Honda, tried to get me to do that but I didn't do it. I'll never do that ever, it's gross." To reassure him more, I repeated my words as dramatically as I could, "No dad, I won't do that. No way."

I figured this little white lie is either going to save my ass or I'm fucked. Was dad stupid enough to believe his pretty princess will never do that dirty thing again and he will be glad that I told him the truth, which I never do? But he never knew that or do you think dad will go have Todd killed? I didn't care as long as I didn't have to try to blow him again.

I managed to turn on the waterworks a little and I said, "Dad, I know you are disappointed. I'm sorry, really. Don't tell mom, please." Dad looked at me and said, "I'm glad you are honest with me about it, bunny." Bunny was my nickname for dad. "Don't let a boy try that with you again, I know boys get aggressive, that's why I gave you a gun. Just don't do anything until you are married like your mother, okay?"

That was it. That was our sex talk. "Don't do it until you are married and oral sex is dirty." I'm shocked, I'm not screwed up, I mean, I'm a little twisted sometimes, but at least I'm not Karen! Speaking of Karen, my ex-best friend, she was sexually active when we were sixteen. She was always talking about it and once she started having it, she would go into details about it with me. I found it fascinating she would tell me about her experiences. It was like she was my teacher but the older I got, I realized I shouldn't listen to her advice on sex or relationships but she was a cool friend, she got away with everything.

I can't tell you how many girls got pregnant in my high school. There were 5000 students but I personally knew ten girls who, either got pregnant or had an abortion by the time we got out of high school and no, the girls were not all middle class I'm talking about opulent white girls whose daddy wanted to keep it quiet. I'm going to admit this and I am not ashamed of it that I have taken four girls to get abortions.

I won't tell you their names. That's why they asked me to help them, because I can keep my Goddamned mouth shut! I didn't judge them or put them down for the situation, I was there just to listen to them if they need it or just be there. I would do it again if any similar circumstances would arise, but who am I or anyone else to tell someone what to do with their bodies?

Shame on anyone who does that, especially men. Yes, I am pro-choice and a Catholic. I didn't say I was a perfect Catholic, but I do my best. I go to confessions and do a lot of penance and praying. Not going to lie here, but I have never walked away from a confession empty handed then I always feel better.

So for all of those people who think I'm going to burn in hell because I helped a friend, God will forgive me, and that's between us, so if you don't like it, tough shit and peace be with you. I do have a friend who thinks abortion is a sin that's killing a baby, I understand and I have heard both sides of pro-choice and pro-life and so has my mom. Mom, the most level-headed, smart and kind person you will ever meet. Her response to all of it is, "I believe in pro-choice. I don't speak for God or the government, but it's every woman's right to choose, that's it." I love my mom.

When I was sixteen, we did a performance of 'Grease', and guess who Sandy was? That's right, it was me. While casting, I was double cast with Bonnie, the girl who rated me out for smoking pot. We got cast together as arch-rivals, she was the bad Sandy and I was the good Sandy. Everyone thought it was funny because she was a slut and I was a virgin prude, so it was perfect.

We went out for lunch and some kids wanted a ride, so they piled in my car and we got pulled over. I talked my way out of a ticket because the cops were white. We were in our Grease outfits and I offered the police tickets to our performance and one of the cops said to me, "That would be illegal, bribing a police officer with tickets." I told him, "It's not a bribe. If you see our performance, you would arrest me, ha-ha."

The cop didn't laugh but his partner did, and I said, "Look how about this? They have to get back to school and I'm the only one with a car, I'll take some to school and come back for the rest. I can't just leave them there, please." The cop who laughed said, "Okay, go ahead. We will let you go this time. Just don't do it again." I thanked him and made two trips to school to get everyone back to class.

I was lucky because I was white. This is bad but when I was twenty, I crashed my car drunk in front of my parents' house and I uprooted a small tree from my neighbor's house and dragged it across the street to my parent's driveway. I was so drunk, I thought nobody heard it, so I got out of the car. My mother came out in her bathrobe, "You are drunk, aren't you?" I said, "Nope! I just lost control of the car, sorry." I immediately ran into the house.

My dad was on his way home, my sister protected me from him in my bedroom. Dad goes to the door because someone called the police. Dad said, “It’s okay, she lost control of the car and the breaks went out, she’s fine.” The cops knew my dad and said, “Okay Doc, see you at the range,” and they left, white privilege! I was so drunk that I couldn’t get my panty hose off and tried to get them off with a pair of scissors. Safe to say, I’m really glad my sister was there. The next day, dad taped a note to my door about what a fuck up I am. That was fun to read.

In 10th grade, three boys came to school for Halloween, dressed in ‘K. K. K. Cloaks 1983’. They were very authentic because I had seen them before. One guy was dressed like Hitler. Nobody liked him, he kept getting pushed down and some of the big guys would launch him, it was great. I don’t think he stood up straight all day. The guys in the cloaks offended some of the teachers as well they should. The principal was white, he went to U.S.C., like my dad, he told them to take off the cloaks and put them in their cars and go back to class.

That’s it, I stood right there and witnessed them taking off their cloaks. As I turned around, one of the teachers, who was so nice – she was an English teacher and Hispanic – looked at the kid I knew and asked him, “Boy, what were you thinking? Where did you get these outfits?” The kid I knew looked at her and said, “I got it from my dad, what are you going to do about it?” He laughed at her and went to his car.

The principal was standing right behind him when he said that. The teacher looked at him in disbelief, expecting him to do something worthwhile, he shrugged his shoulders and went back to his office. He didn’t have her back at all.

You know why? The kid's dad was a cop and a Klansman, the principal knew him. White privilege! I knew that kid. He was a piece of shit, and so was his dad.

I was in Keywanettes – a female version of the Kiwanis Club. It's for geeky white girls, I fit in perfectly there. My Grandpa, my dad's father was in it, so they were happy I was in it too. It was the only club my dad said he was proud of me being in besides Junior Republican League. Yep get 'em while they're young!

I was in a club called "Kahanakai," an all-girls club. They said it was a Christian girls club, what bullshit? I went to church three days a week, they never opened up a bible once. It was all the popular girls in school. I had to audition to get in and I was going to get in that club no matter what. I was teased a lot when I was in elementary school and I knew for a fact that it wasn't going to happen again!

I knew if anything bad was going to happen to me, those girls were going to know about it. As they say, "Make your enemy your friend." I didn't like most of those girls but at least I wasn't left out. Those mean girls were not very nice to a lot of girls in our school. I found out at my ten years reunion, how bad they were. Two Mexican girls I didn't know very well at the reunion told me, "You were nice to us, not like those other white girls you hung out with." I told them, "I didn't really hang out with them. I was just in Kahanakai, I went to church three days a week, and was really involved in a lot more than just stuff at our high school. I just didn't want to be left out, I'm sorry that they were so mean to you, I hope I didn't come off that way." They didn't know I went to church three days a week and was on other swim teams and theater departments. I didn't know them very well but I didn't realize how bad the white girls in our school treated them. I apologized for their bad manners and they told me, "You and your sister weren't like those other white girls." My sister and I got along with almost everyone because our Mom raised us well.

I have to tell you all about plastic surgery. It's not an uncommon thing in L.A., but I knew four girls who had surgery before they got out of high school. Though I won't tell you all their names but two of the girls I knew wouldn't care if I told you about their experience. Sandy was a girl I was in dance class with. She was Asian and had her eyes done to give her an upper lid. She and her parents went to a credible doctor and she was happy with the results. I thought why not? Her parents permitted her.

I was happy for her, for a fact I knew a lot of Asian people do it. Jackie Chan did, another friend of mine Carrie, the girl who took me to the doctors when I got my appendix out in junior high, she got a breast reduction. I knew her from elementary school and she developed before every girl in school. She was really shy and used to cover it up a lot and couldn't play tennis without being in pain, so she got a reduction.

That is no walk in the park. Punky Brewster did it. She was in the same boat as Carrie. What a good example she is setting for young girls; anything related to the female body and sexuality is not an easy subject to talk about, especially for teens. YOU GO PUNKY! I also had two friends who were Jewish, who wanted to get their noses done. Again, I won't tell you their names, but I loved their little Jewish noses. I thought they were perfect just the way they were, but they wanted their nose to look like every other white girl in L.A.

It is very normal for a girl here about to turn sixteen to ask daddy for a nose job if they want it. He will ask his daughter, "Do you want to go to Cabo for your sixteenth birthday or do you want a nose job?" As I said, it's pretty common in L.A. I just wish we had more women like Justine Batemen who wouldn't falling into the plastic surgery trap like most of the women in business. Justine is aging gracefully and naturally, and I truly commend her for being her!

I do have a kind of funny story. I knew a girl who was a stripper, whose tits exploded on stage and she kept working until her shift was done because she really needed the money. The minute she started to dance, her tit was leaking on the side next to a tube she had to fill up her tits; it was so gross. She told the men she was dancing for, "Oh! I just got out of the shower and didn't dry off enough." She kept wiping her tits with a scarf like nobody is going to notice it.

She was telling me this story right after I had my third martini. I was dying laughing, picturing her asking men for dance while her tits spring a leak all over them. It was too hilarious of her to say, "I just got out of the shower." They'd go, "Does this seem sticky to you? I don't think this is just water." She was like, "No! That's my body wash, that's all. Do you want a dance? Here, let me get that for you. Hey, busboy, I need another towel."

I didn't ask her how much money she made that night but hope it's enough to get a new tit. I don't know if they sell them in pairs like tires or what, she just needed a little fill-up and a patch or two and she was good to go. She was not going to the hospital right away for an exploded implant for a few table dances. I can bet she was probably not saving her money for grad school and didn't have a lot of career opportunities lined up other than stripping, so maybe working that extra few hours at the club with a busted tit was something she could comfortably work around if she was in a pinch.

When you think about it, it's kind of impressive on a white trash level. You rarely see that anymore, except in Louisiana, according to Tom Segura. I saw a one-armed stripper in Texas. There was something about the symmetry, I couldn't stop laughing. I had to leave because I didn't want to hurt her feelings. I just couldn't help it. I'm sure she has a very nice personality. I guess that the girl I saw might be saving for grad school. There is no doubt that if she ever gets a leaky tit at work, she'd be smart enough to go to the hospital right away, because I can't see her boss saying, "Yeah, we hired you with one arm because you are really pretty and the rest of you makes up for the stump, but get to the hospital and fix that leaking tit. How are we going to explain that shit to the customers?" That girl was really pretty, even though she just had one arm. I give her credit for doing a job most people could never attempt to do.

My friend Ted Jon Dominico, decided to chauffer Kay and Robert to a dance we had in Old Money Pasadena. I think it was at a historical building, really pretty. The area we were in was not too far from us. If you have seen "Pretty In Pink" the house where Ducky and Andy look at where the rich white kid lived? That's the area we were in.

Where the Ritz Carlton is, it used to be the Huntington Hotel back then. It is a really pretty neighborhood. It looks like Beverly Hills, that's why they do so much filming there and tell everyone it's Beverly Hills. It doesn't cost as much to film there. Anyway, Ted was really funny and smart, but he was a stoner. He once drove off with the gas pump still in the car. Yep, stoner.

He had this old 50s Cadillac that was fully restored and he took them in that. We left the dance and while driving home, Ted got pulled over with Kay and Robert in the back. Ted was stoned and he was out on the sidewalk talking to the cops. I pulled over because I was a cocky white kid who thought she could talk to the police to get them out of there.

I was with another couple and they said, "What are you going to do?" I cockily replied, "Don't worry, I'll be right back." Now mind that I was in a purple satin prom dress and heels, I got out of the car to converse with the officer. "Excuse me, officer, I don't mean to interrupt, but we are doubling with them, and if they get late for curfew, we're going to be late, and I'm going to get in trouble, so are they. So, is it ok if they come with us, so we don't get in trouble?" I said, batting my lashes like a puppy.

He turned back to his partner, and it didn't look like he was going to let them go. So I said, "My dad's a cop." He said something to his partner and returned, "Okay, you can go with her." They came with me and I dropped them off. Can you believe that shit? My dad's a cop, that's all it took, white privilege!

I don't think Ted got in trouble. Looking back on that scenario, if I was black and tried that stunt, the cops would have shot me and covered it up in that neighborhood, and I am not kidding. The Klan has a lot of money in that neighborhood to pull off all kinds of stunts. When I was a kid, they used to have small parades down Orange Grove with Klan. Back in the day, grandma told me about it. They were proud white men back then, that's all.

I got pulled over right in front of my dad's office, once. I knew the cops were well acquainted with my dad. To my advantage, his office was in front of the police department. I said to the cop, "I was going a little fast, I know. I have a curfew, I'm coming home from my youth group, give me a ticket if you have to, just don't tell my dad." He looked up, there's dad's sign, Dr. William's D. D. S. He said, "You are Doc William's kid, aren't you? Oh shit, I knew it." I said, "Yes, I'm his daughter." The cop said, "I saw your picture in his office, didn't you go to the range with your dad?" Yup, he was a clan. "Just slow it down honey, I won't tell him," and he let me go. White privilege!

I was in Aurora Colorado not too long ago and this black man was parked on the side of the road, his car broken down. I pulled over to see if he needed help. I asked, "Are you okay? Do you want me to call someone for you?" It looked like he didn't have a phone so I offered. He said, "I just called someone. They're on the way, thanks." After hearing that, I got back in my car. I stayed just out of concern. I saw some white guy pulled up next to me in a truck and signaled me to roll my window down and I did. "Yes?" I asked. He said, "Did that guy hit you? I'm a cop, and if he hit you, I can call someone if you want right now." I said, "No. He broke down, I'm fine." He smiled and said, "Just checking," and drove away.

Now, I don't know if that white cop was just playing the "My hero" act to get laid or if he was a racist motherfucker. If that guy was white, broken down on the side of the road, he never would have done that but he was black, so he must be guilty of something, right? You see that's the kind of shit black men put up with every day and I saw it firsthand. Nobody can tell me that stereotyping isn't around in the police department, the fuck it doesn't! I experienced it several times and I'm white; it was 2020 Aurora Colorado, I should have asked him for his card, goddamn it!

Even though I'm going to get in so much trouble for all this, but I am still going to put it out there. The truth is, I don't think any white cop will like me much after this gets out. My adopted little brother is a cop and he's not too thrilled with me either but he is not in the same standing as the cops, who are the 75-80% of them, the troubled bullies who are fucking with black people. I don't think all white male cops do that. They just need to prove it, that's all.

My brother doesn't have a racist bone in his body. He would never partake in any kind of cruelty to anyone. He is just as disgusted with the cop who killed George Floyd as I am. Unfortunately, all white cops are being persecuted for it. It's fucked up on both sides. Blacks will say, "They are getting what they deserve now they know how it feels." They may be right to an extent but we need to figure out how to work together better, or we are all fucked!

I witnessed a lot of levels of white privilege, from the middle class, upper class, higher class to multi-millionaires, and billionaires, I've seen it all. It still doesn't make them any better than anyone else. Some white people will always think they should come first because they're white and for no other reason, some of them will never learn. I think it would be a good idea if privileged white people should have to go to a third-world country and see how good they have it.

Make them do a hard day's work in Haiti, India, or fuck it, Mexico. It's not like a hard day's work in the States, 12 hours shift with no breaks plus, lunch is not included and all you get paid is, well, nothing. What you get goes to feeding your kid, if you're lucky. I don't think most white privileged people could handle it, not even for a day. People who live there struggle every day and I think it would be a good idea if we did that to give a new perspective on life. To have them taste their own medicine for once.

I'm sure you can think of many white people you would like to see do that or here's an idea, take the kids who are in cages at the border and switch places with a white privileged person's kid to see how they like it. We expect people from South America and Haiti to do it for months and years, some of them even die there like caged animals. It's less than fair. Those kids need our help. It's not like we can't do it. Let's help, pull up our sleeves, and use our white privilege for something good, at least for once. Get in the horn, and make some calls. Those kids need help, so do their families. Fuck the Rose Parade and big-budget pictures in white Hollywood where our priorities don't make a movie about helping others. Start from within, help others!

My dad took me to one of many stupid formal Christmas dinners at his undergrad in Whittier College. He was in his uniform, the military one. Dad was a General, two stars, and a Klansman, not the highest-ranking either. He wore his uniform to feed his massive ego. So, they sat him at the head of the table. Dad sat next to this dude in a suit, and I was next to a woman wearing a linen outfit dressed in white. She told me she was one of the head nuns in Mother Theresa's Orphanage in India, not kidding, jackpot!

You never get to meet interesting people at these things. Dad was talking to the suit, and he interrupted us. Of course, dad didn't interrupt politely as mom taught us to, "Excuse me, please may I borrow my daughter for one moment?" Oh no. It went something like this. "Jan, do you know who this is?" I turned to dad, "No, I don't know who he is, but I'm sure you're going to tell me."

I gave dad a look, which clearly showed that I don't care who this suit is and he knows I'm going to embarrass him if he does something stupid. I was at an age where I didn't give a fuck about what anyone wanted, especially the people acquainted with my father because they are full of shit. Dad just hadn't caught on to it yet. I still played pretty princess with him, and he liked that. So dad said, "This man worked for Nixon, remember him?" I confusingly asked dad, "The crook?" Dad shook his head, trying to conceal his embarrassment, and said, "No, she gets that from her mother," to that man. Then, he looked at me and said, "This man was the secretary of transportation under Nixon, shake his hand."

I shook his hand and he started to say something about my dad, but I turned around and continued my conversation with the nun. He can go blow hot air up my dad's ass if he wants to. I was clearly not interested. You meet a lot of people like that at those things, and they are all boring. However, the nun wasn't boring at all. I really enjoyed her company.

She made my night. Dad wouldn't even shake her hand nor the suit. They both were busy just listening to their own voices too busy patting each other on the back. It's a Klan thing, to shake anyone's hand. Especially a nun's hand, God forbid. Touch a Non-Republican? God forbid!

That guy was lucky that the nun had my attention. I mean, if they started with open-racist stuff with me there to hear it, I would have embarrassed dad so badly. I would have to walk home from Whittier, where I'm not familiar at all. But I would have ripped that Nixon fuck apart. If I didn't get a rise out of him with, "Do you think Nixon was a crook? Did you go to jail? Have you ever spent the night at the Watergate hotel? What do you think of Oliver North, a liar, or not?" I would have mentioned a girl or two who are underage that he might know, and no their not his nieces. Hey word gets around, that would ruin his appetite for sure. Come bring us some figgy pudding, this motherfucker!

Once, I went to Hawaii for a choir tour, and it was fun. We got to see Berlin – Pleasure Victim album tour in Waikiki. If my mom knew I went to that, she'd kill me. I went to a lot of cool concerts in the 80s. I saw Amy Grant at a church concert, and she was great. Baby, baby, I love her. I saw one of the best concerts I have ever gone to in my life. O.M.D. opened up for the Thompson Twins at Universal Studios in Hollywood. How 80s is that? I saw Bob Dylan and the Grateful Dead. Wow, you really experience the dead. Elvis Costello, Motley Crew, U.2. The Red Hot Chili Peppers Oingo Boingo, and Duran-Duran. It was fun, and I don't regret that I had to sneak into some of it.

In L.A., there's a lot to get into. I started to go to comedy shows. I used to get a ride with some older kids when I was really young. Mom never knew, it was one of the only things I didn't get caught for. I started writing then but never kept what I wrote because I didn't want my mom to find it. I saw Rosie O'Donnell, Jim Carrey, Kathy Griffin, Drew Carrey, and Bob Saget, who had a really dirty mouth. I can honestly say everyone that knew Bob Saget would say he was a wonderful performer and a good guy. I hope he's having a good laugh with David (Deacon Grey) in heaven. You are both dearly missed! Oh, I saw David Spade as well and so many more.

I had a drink with Tim Allen, the Home Improvement guy. I had a skin-tight polka-dotted dress on. We were at the Icehouse in Pasadena. We left, I expected him to get into a Range Rover or a big jeep but to my shock, Tim Allen was driving a canary yellow Geo Metro. He said it was a rental, and I laughed my ass off. If he hears about this, he'll never live it down, but it's the truth. He didn't mention that on Jay Leno's Garage.

When comedians are starting out, they take what they can get. It was probably the least expensive car they had. Tim did a really great set and was very nice. The first time I did stand up in L.A., I knew I wanted to be a writer. Stand-up is not for me, full-time working up to getting past newbie sets. Everything I wrote then was way longer than two minutes, but you only get two and three minutes. You have to build up to get five minutes on stage.

I don't mind being on stage, but I couldn't handle the constant traveling. It's a pretty lonely lifestyle. I can do stand-up; I just didn't want to do it for a living. I have worked in some sketchy rooms! Performing is fun, but there is a lot of drug use that goes along with that world, and now that I don't drink, I couldn't do it. I write every day, I'm good with that. I can't see myself acting again, not unless there is a part for me where the character just spouts off whatever she feels like and doesn't give a shit about what she just says just to be funny. If it is a job to just make you laugh, I'm pretty sure I could pull that off, I wouldn't even have to do any research for the character or anything.

When I moved to Denver, I met my friend Deacon Grey David, that's his real name. Deacon ran comedy works in Denver. I would tease him and say, "Deacon is a vampire name, I'm calling you David." He encouraged me to keep writing. He told me, "You're a good writer, don't stop." David was the only person I told anything about the Klan stuff, which he took to his grave. What a good friend! I knew I could trust him. He was a dear man. Deacon was one of those friends I wouldn't see for a year, and the next time you see them, it's like you saw each other yesterday.

I came into the club once with my ex-girlfriend Brianna. Deacon just laughed and gave me a big hug saying, "Call me later." When I finished writing this, I tried to get in touch with him and found out that he passed away. It caught me really off-guard I wasn't expecting that news at all. Last time I talked to him was about seven years ago. I wish I hadn't turned off my computer. He used to say some day we will work together on this and he was going to help me put this together. I hope he's looking down on me and smiling, saying, "Jan, don't lead up to a joke, get them right off the bat." Our little joke.

We became friends because he knew I did a little stand-up and was a writer. I told him how I snuck into comedy shows in L.A. and saw so many people when they just started, I worked at The Icehouse Comedy Showroom as a ticket taker. I wanted to see that world, and boy oh boy did I.

I had to go into the green room, turn off the alarm and spray down the leftover cocaine from the night before off their glass coffee table. It was the 80s. That's how I met a lot of comedians and got the inside skinny in the business. It was fun, but the more I saw, I knew I didn't want to be a full-time comedian. When I was around people in the business, I didn't talk much. I watched, tried to learn, and had fun. I was invisible. I went to so many places to see comedy; it was fun.

I think Jerry Seinfeld is a dirty old man. He went out with a girl twenty years younger than him. What's she going to talk about with him? Nothing, for him it's a sex thing, that's it. Pervert!

I know people like him, but whenever I think of him, my mind gets a picture of a dirty old man. I hope she's visually impaired because in ten years or so, he isn't going to be so charming, and funny. Maybe, when she's old enough, she can hire another teenager to fuck him so she can have friends of her age to hang out with. Who's going to go with her to Disneyland? They don't let geriatrics on the rides who complain about everything. I don't think they'd let him on the log ride with his cane. She needs to look at the big picture. What's best for you in the long run? Do your friends think this is a wise move for you? I know they can't relate at all.

It seems like you have to be so careful about your comedy these days to not be labeled as the racist comedian or the comedian who's the bad guy for telling it like it is or being too honest. Well, for those people who are like that, all I can say is, don't read or listen to anything I have to say. I am not going to clean up my act to appease you Karen; and Joe Rogan is not a racist, neither are a lot of comedians! Stop with all of the politically correct bullshit already. If it makes you laugh, shut up and laugh, you idiots! Yes, most of the people who think Joe and other comedians are racists are white bitchy Karens with too much time on their hands and the dudes who are like that are big faggots.

CHAPTER SIX: BOYS CLUB, STREET RACE

As far as I can remember, I was always a curious child, and if there was one person who fueled it to no avail, it was my father. Dad used to wake up in the middle of the night to check up on the office. I had a guy who said to me, "That's weird, your dad goes to his office in the middle of the night and you don't know where he goes?" I shrugged my shoulder and told him that it isn't any of my business. But how could that be? It seemed weird because he was a dentist, after all. I didn't tell the guy the truth. I followed him more than once to quench the thirst for my curiosity.

Dad went Monday and Wednesday at 9:00. There was always a meeting at a church that really bothered me. I followed him and I watched a number of men go in, and guess what? They were all white men. I also noticed two guys who were in The Kiwanis Club who went in. Dad wasn't in the Kiwanis Club, but his father was. Even I was a Kiwanette. I got the courage to go in after dad left. I remembered one of the buildings from when I was little and I still had long hair. I remembered the handicapped ramp going up; I didn't want to go up the stairs. Dad had taken me to this building before when I was little without mom. It was just us.

I remember men patting me on the head and telling dad how proud he must be. I waited for dad to leave and I went in and there was a long table set up and two bins on it. I looked in and it was full of Klan stuff. I knew it. I left and never told a soul. Mom had no idea. None of us did for a long time. It was all a front, a façade. They were using government buildings to have their meetings. No big surprise though, because they were backed by the government. My dad was a Brigadier General, inactive but he still held rank. He was sneaky, and so are a lot of those guys. They used to brag about being in the Klan. I do know if you check the Klan roster from 1935 to 1975 and compare it to the white cops in the Los Angeles police department and all the counties surrounding it, it is pretty astounding. I know some of the higher-end Klansmen try to keep it quiet now.

Anyway, I know that stuff is all over the internet. I think if you are a police officer, you have freedom of speech like all of us, that's fine. But there should be limitations to what you're searching for on the internet. If you're a white male cop, looking up 'hate groups' on the internet and downloading it to your home computer, how do we know if you are just looking or you are doing your homework?

They don't have the advantage of going to the meetings like dad did, with a secret handshake, a pat on the shoulders, and the old merit, "Okay guys, just between us." I think all white male cops who are affiliated with any hate group, even on the internet, should be segregated to work in all-white areas. They shouldn't be allowed to work in predominantly Black and Latino neighborhoods because it's too big of a risk for the people who live there. I think it would have saved a lot of Black and Latino lives if we implemented it.

I'm not saying all white male cops are in hate groups, but we should be a little more vigilant with what they are viewing. If it's about hate groups, it raises a big red flag. If they are investigating hate groups for work, that's one thing, but I don't think recreational viewing of those sights is something I'm comfortable with by a white cop. I don't buy sentences like, "I'm just browsing at it. I'm not doing anything wrong. Just because I look at it doesn't mean I'm into it. I'm only looking for fun."

I mean, what? I'm not buying that horseshit, are you? You have ever seen a cocky white cop at his desk sitting back, putting up his feet, shooting the shit with other white male cops, laughing together. Don't you wonder what's so funny? I'm sure it doesn't have anything to do with putting another black man in jail, beating another black man to the ground, or getting away with anything because no one's around. Come on, it's just for fun!

I'm sure that smile has nothing to do with anything like that, just like looking at hate groups is not a big deal. It's only for fun. I'm just looking, so what's the problem? Does anyone buy that, not me!

I think the only thing you can do with the Klan is to ignore them. Unfortunately, some of those cloak-wearing jack-offs do have some pull and a few badges. Ignoring them is fine, but I think we should treat them like spoiled children when they rant and rave. You ever seen a kid that wants attention and isn't getting it? They go nuts like a kid throwing a tantrum, holding his breath, kicking and screaming until he runs out of steam and quits.

Those guys would be funny if they threw a tantrum with those cloaks on until they collapsed. We could treat them like we did in church camp. When they fall asleep, put their hands in a bucket of water and watch them wet themselves. We can also draw all over their faces when they are asleep. When they will wake up and see, "I'M HERE, I'M QUEER! GET USED TO IT, AND I LIKE CHOCOLATE LOVE!" written all over their forehead, it will be a pretty amusing sight.

It would be funny. Here's an idea, my mom hates it when I start a sentence like that because you never know what's coming, but who can come up with the silliest way to offend the Klan and not get in any real trouble or get arrested for it? Good Lord, I would love to see that!

I am speaking to white people, no way is a black guy going to be able to do this. So come on, I dare you Whiteys, go to your closet and get out your cloak and get back to me after figuring it out. I know not all of you white people have cloaks in your closet, no it's just a costume! Sure it is yeah, so was my Grandpa's! But alright, not all of them, just 75-80% of you.

I hosted the talent show at school with Tony Albers, my first kiss, at the top of the baseball field when I was fifteen. He was so sweet. We were announcing a Chinese girl to sing and all the white kids, not all but a lot, started to boo her. Tony wasn't having it. He reprimanded the audience and I backed him up. He re-announced her and she was beautiful. Tony was not like the majority of the white boys at my school, he had ethics and I wish more boys in school were like him. Tony, tweet me!

Asians took a lot of flak back then, especially in Arcadia. We had someone who spray-painted "Gook, go home" on the house across the street to someone who just moved in. Pretty sure it was the clan. Welcome to the neighborhood! My mom went over there with a basket of goodies to welcome them. Once, I had to try to get this Asian kid's bike back from some popular, racist white kid I went to school with. He stole the bike just to fuck with him. The kid didn't speak English; he did that just for fun, what a prick!

Some white kids, mostly male kids would ask for trouble because they knew they wouldn't be answerable for anything because our principal was white. So was the majority of the police department, and they knew it. Since they are only judged by looking at the color of their skin, Blacks, Latinos, and Asians don't ever get a fair shot at justice. You ask any guy I went to high school with that was Hispanic, or Asian if I'm telling the truth. It was like that for them at my school, where the white kids always got favored.

I have Trumper neighbors. All my neighbors are armed, with the pandemic on their guard. Let's imagine for a minute, what if a black man gets shot trying to rob one of my neighbors and gets killed by a white man? Even if the police, white cops, show up, I doubt they would get in any trouble at all. They would just call it self-defense. They wouldn't give a shit about the black guy who gets killed and ripped off by a white guy. Whose side do you think the judge will take? Since most of the judges are white, they will take the side of their own 'species." That's just my opinion. Having said that, I also think we need more black judges.

I'm going to tell you something that I never wanted to tell anyone. This is one of those triggered memories that popped up and I couldn't ignore it. My dad had his dental office about ten minutes from our house in Temple City. His office was across the street from the police department. Dad had his buddies from the department. They used to go out of their way to keep a close eye on his office so he didn't get robbed. White privilege!

I also know for a fact that some of them were in the Klan, it was in the 70s. Dad told me this story when I was a kid and I think it's true but I hope it's not. Dad's office got robbed; I did know he got robbed. He got a call at home. Most of the time, he got calls for dental emergencies. It wasn't unusual for the phone to go off at all hours. It didn't happen often, but it happened that day. Dad went down to the office and told me later about what happened.

Dad had a trick gun. I asked him, "What's a trick gun?" Dad replied, "A trick gun is a gun that will fire back at you if you pull the trigger, and it kills you instantly." I asked outrageously, "Why do you have one of that, dad?" I wish I hadn't asked him and I wish he hadn't told me. Dad said, "This is what happened. Two Mexicans broke into my office, where I planted the trick gun in the top drawer of my office desk. One of the guys who were robbing found it and tried to use it. He killed himself." I asked him, "You said two guys? What happened to the other guy, did he get away?" Dad replied with a freakish calmness, "I shot him and killed him, but it's okay." I inquired, "Were the police there?" He said, "Oh yeah, they know all about it. Who's going to care about two spicks? Good riddance." I, with numbness creeping into my bones, asked, "You're not in trouble or anything? Does mom know?" Dad shrugged, "She knows I got robbed but she doesn't need to know about everything. It's over, everything's fine."

He was all smiles about it. My dad killed two Mexican men who tried to rob him and the police, white cops, covered it up. I wish I didn't remember that. That's kind of shit that goes down in, not all, but some white neighborhoods. We aren't supposed to talk about it and I know this is going to be really upsetting for most of you, I don't like it either, but the truth hurts. I wonder if any other white people, after reading this, will come out and tell some stories about their experiences growing up with a dad like mine. It's really hard to admit you have a family like that.

I'm going to throw everyone off with this comment, but just hear me out. I think that we should legalize street racing, they're going to do it anyway. We should shut down the street where they can do it safely and set everything up. People can get professional paramedics to work there, just in case someone gets hurt. They can have sponsors and we can place bets on the racers.

There will be commentary as well. They can put it on a cable station. I know that they have some street racing stuff on T. V., but I'm talking about the kids who are doing it at three o'clock in the morning. They don't all have the accessibility to those events. Why do you think they do it where they do it? It's more convenient and a lot less expensive there. It will be revenue for the city to repair the streets if they get damaged. The people who live in the areas where they do the racing will have a heads up about street racing between these hours. We will also shut down the highways and get food trucks and have cooking competitions to see which one is the best food for the day. Aaron Sanchez can be the top judge. Another idea is to call the food network. To have food critics in the areas where they do the racing will add an interesting element to the overall scenario. They will do a full write-up in the city's paper. It will be great publicity for the food trucks.

They can have women street racers displayed on the calendar. We will ask Estevan from L.A. to be the photographer. He can take all the pictures because he captures women like nobody else. In simple words, he's brilliant. By the end of the year, they will have a street parade with marching bands, floats, and authentic Mexican dancing. We can add up puppet shows and big bubble shows as well as face painting. People can check out all the cool cars and the mechanics who work on these beautiful machines and can talk to people who are interested in racing.

Mr. Cartoon can make a guest appearance, painting cars and showing drawing techniques. Everybody can get their favorite racer's autographs and get photographed. There will be a Queen of the parade like the Rose Parade. The host will be George Lopez, of course. He can invite other comedians to do a live show at night after the parade. Any proceeds from the races or show will go towards a scholarship to a trade school for mechanics and artists, who want to learn the trade and to the kids, who do street art and murals. They can further compete for a spread in a street racing magazine.

I think it would be a blast. It's a win-win situation if you ask me, but what do I know? I'm just some white woman with some pretty good ideas. If you have any doubt about the creativity of my idea, call up Mr. Cartoon, Estevan, George Lopez, and Aaron Sanchez and see what they think about it. Maybe if we stop fighting about street racing and learn to enjoy it like the racers do and also learn to live with it together, it wouldn't be so bad, right? White people need to lighten up. I think whiteys are the ones whining about it, so here is a solution, and this idea is coming from a Republican herself. See, we aren't all bad, just 75-80% of us are.

There were two really bad car accidents in high school that I'll never forget. One was about this girl Dana and her boyfriend. They were so cute together. They would walk arm and arm down the hallway, eating popsicles always happy, kind of Romeo and Juliet. Dana's boyfriend and his buddies went out to lunch for someone's birthday and got drunk. They drove and got into an accident. The car rolled on her boyfriend and killed him. They told her at school and everyone found out about it the next day.

They sat in a different area than I did for lunch but I saw them. They looked so sad, their skin pale and eyes filled with sorrow. I said to some of the girls I was in that Kahanakai group with, "Don't you guys think we should get some flowers or say something to them?" Upon that, a girl Jennifer

Vemp, I think that was her name, looked at me and said, "You can if you want to." She turned her back on me because they weren't white or rich enough for her. I went over to them and said, "I'm sorry for your loss. If Dana needs anything let me know, okay?" I didn't know Dana's boyfriend very well but Scott, one of her friends, said, "Thanks." He had tears in his eyes. I had to run away. I didn't want them to see me cry and make it worse. Dana was such a sweet girl. I still pray for her.

The second accident was of a girl in Mr. Doty's class. Mr. Doty was a great teacher he really cared about his students. One day, he made an announcement about a girl. She got into a bad accident with her family and he wanted to know if anyone knew her well enough to find out how to get in touch with her and her family. Since I had a car, I was willing to drive to her if anyone knew where she was.

So after class, I went up to the podium and so did a Mexican girl who I didn't know, to find out how we could help. I went to school with five thousand students; it's not unusual to not know everybody you have a class with. I wish I could remember her name; she was so nice. Tweet me if you remember me! Her friend knew her aunt. She said, "Her aunt is in East L.A." I said, "I've been there. Let's go, I have a car."

I've been to Olivera Street for Mexican food, and never the residential part of East L.A., but I didn't care. We wanted to know if she was okay. It was like a war zone. We got a little lost, but we found it. We went up to the gate. A pit bull came up and barked. It scared the shit out of me. I stayed next to the car. The girl I knew and her aunt spoke fluent Spanish. She came out of the house, her head was shaved from the accident, and she had a house dress on. She was moving very slowly down the steps to talk to us.

I almost cried. I couldn't understand what she was saying, but somehow we got the info we needed and went back to school. I told everything to Mr. Doty. When I was walking down the hall, Jennifer, that cheerleader bitch I was in Kahanakai with, who never gave me the time of day said, "Who was that?" I would speed talk when I got nervous, so I replied, "Well, there is a girl in Mr. Doty's class, she got in a wreck. So, she's going to be back in two months. We went to east L.A. to talk to her aunt."

She said, "You went there?" Snubbed her nose and walked away. I mean, all she got out of that was that we went to East L.A.? Some of the girls in that Kahanakai group were so stuck up. I'm glad that I didn't have much to do with most of them. Not all of them were stuck-up bitches, just 75-80% of them. I'm sure some of those girls are going to read this and say, "I wasn't like that she's not talking about me." Yea sure; I'm not, honey. I'll bet all the Mexican girls I went to school with will agree with me.

I started going to the range with my dad when I was five. My dad gave me a loaded forty-five for my first shot. I could barely hold it up. He had to hold the goggles in the back because they were too big and so were the earmuffs. Dad said to me, "Okay honey, do you see the target? I know you can hit it, but if you miss, you can't come back to the range with dad." All I wanted to do was spend time with dad, so I lined up the shot and pulled the trigger.

BOOM! Dad didn't tell me about the kickback. It blew me on my ass. Dad picked up the gun and let me fall. "Get up," he said and pulled the target towards us. I hit it dead center. All of dad's friends started giving him a pat on the back and applauded me, "Good job kiddo, do it again."

You have got to be kidding. No way, so I wet my pants. Dad thought me wetting my pants meant that I was happy because once, I wet my pants when I saw snow white at Disneyland. So dad goes, "When she gets very happy, she wets her pants." I was jumping up and down, smiling, as it was my only defense. I knew I couldn't do it again, no way!

I liked shooting at the targets, never the figures of people. I could never kill anyone. I couldn't kill scorpions when I was little. Do you think I could kill a human being? Get out of here, no way. I'm a chef. An animal is different. I can kill a cow or a pig because that's food; you don't get emotionally attached to them. I could never kill another human being, and no, it's not a Catholic thing. I just could never do it. There was a white cop who said to me, "Well, what if someone had a knife to your mom's throat and you had a gun. Would you kill him to save your mom?" Yeah, like that is really going to happen, not even in a million years. My response was, "What moron gave you a badge and a gun?" He didn't like that but fuck him. That was such a stupid thing to say. Is he in the fourth grade? What kind of "I'm rubber, you are glue," kind of bullshit that was? God! I hope he doesn't figure out that I'm talking about him. Just Kidding! Oh, fuck it! I'm not too worried. I don't live in his district.

I think there should be an owner's manual for racist Republican gun owners. On the cover, there will be a picture of Meghan McCain, who will tell all her Hitler youth to just pretend we're not racist. While we all know, Meghan's a total bigot when the cameras are off. Also, Rush Limbaugh for all the young gay male Republicans that will get their attention.

Indeed, they are not into books, so tell them that they'll get a blowjob from Meghan and a free tie from Rush if they read it. A lot of those guys aren't into academics so we'll keep it simple. It will be written by Dr. Seuss, that's about their speed. "One fish, two fish, Nazi fish, blue fish," illustrated by the guys from South Park. We'll use a lot of visual characters for them. We will have Uncle Jimbo, who can teach them about weapons. Mr. Mackey will show a film that says, "Guns are bad, mm-kay."

We can have Kyle's mom, she will teach them about the holocaust. Mr. Garrison and Mr. Slave will teach them about homosexuals by using visual aids because they all say they know what gay men do even though they say they don't know any faggots, so Mr. Slave will show them what faggots do. Then Craig will just flip everyone off and Chef will teach them a new dish called Cracker Stew and show them his new technique on hunting, killing, and gutting Klansman. And of course, there's Eric Cartman. He will do an awful impersonation of Hitler, and Wendy Chesterburger will be offended and beat the shit out of him.

Afterward, Stan will tell everyone what we've all learned today, and finally, in the end, Kenny dies, you bastards. We will make it fun to teach them about racism, homosexuality, and gun safety. Maybe they'll learn something. Hey! We could make copies of it and pass them out as constructive literature to kids at Klan meetings. Let's make a popup book for the little ones. We will pull a "Dad, don't tell your mom." If we keep the words small and the premise is simple, maybe it will work. I'm a writer, I'll figure it out.

Anyway, I didn't like the attention I got at the range from dad's friends either the way they talked, "She's a good shot, isn't she?" It made me feel uncomfortable. When I would shoot at figures, they would say, "Get 'em in the chest, and the head like I showed you, good girl!" They also used a lot of racist slander without keeping it under their breath when they all got together and thought nobody was listening. They didn't hide a thing, it became Hitler's heaven. My sister and I both are good shots, but I don't want some Klansmen over my shoulder telling me how good I am.

This handshake with your fingers out while shaking someone's hand wasn't the gunman's handshake. It was the Klan handshake. That's what dad told us it was. Every guy my dad introduced me to at the range did that, they were all Klan. The range in L.A. was one of their meeting places it was when I was a kid. The guys in the Klan don't want you to know this but there is no such thing as a Klan-free gun range in L.A.

Personally, I can tell who is in the Klan and who isn't just by the way they talk and move. They're not very subtle. I love target practice; I just don't want to be around the Klan. I can assemble, disassemble, fire, load, and re-load. Basically, I can do all that crap with a number of weapons, but I have no interest in it. Honestly, I only went to the range a few times with dad, but that's some of the stuff I can remember. Dad tried to clean his guns on the formal dining room table once. Mom just had to give the look, and he never did it again. He then did it in the den, and I watched. I didn't like the smell of the gun cleaning oil. It's not like wood oil or scented oil, it's gross, but you have to use it. I can't use anything else.

CHAPTER SEVEN: MEXICANS, REDNECKS, MOVIE LOTS

When I was in Kahanakai, there were a lot of girls I didn't like much. One was Jennifer; she was a stuck-up bitch. I mean, get off your high horse, girl. There was a part of me that desperately wanted to say to her, "You know my dad makes more money than yours and he went to USC too." But that would be such a stupid rich white girl response. Jennifer usually didn't give the time of day to me unless she was trying to be mean or when she was trying to deliberately insult someone or put them down.

She returned to school after graduating just to tell us about her little sisters in Kahanakai and how fabulous her life was at USC. Of course, she went there. I'll bet her daddy did too. I don't understand the big deal with the college admissions scandal. My dad told me, "If you want to go to USC as I did, I'll just have to make a call, and you are in." That's been going on forever. I am not saying that everyone who goes there has rich daddies to get them in, but it happens more often than you think. It will still go on. They just have to be more careful.

Jennifer gave a presentation to all of us and told us about how they wanted to do a show for everyone with her sorority sisters. They love the musical cats, so one of her sisters went to New York and got a really good makeup artist to do their makeup so they would look authentic. Jennifer also told us how they have the best sorority on campus and if you want to be as special as she is, do what she does and maybe you might get lucky and all of a sudden, beep, beep, beep. The boys in school knew where the popular girls were.

Half of the girls got up to go see what was up, so did I. I saw her wicked blue eyes. "How dare you get up?" I shrank back down into my chair, she was that intimidating. When the girls came back, she waited until it was completely quiet and all eyes were on her. She said, "None of my real sisters would have left me. Do I have your attention now?" Then she continued on and on about herself. I can't imagine what she's doing now, probably Botox parties. How many husbands do you think she's going to go through? Or maybe she's a nun and I'm a cunt. Sadly, every school has a Jennifer in it.

There was one girl who stood out to me, Danice Dilts. She could touch the tip of her tongue to the bridge of her nose. We danced together and choir in Junior High. She was a good dancer, but she stood out because I only met one other person who could do it. Try it. It's hard to do it. I can't, but she could. She was really cute as well. And Kara Miller, she was a Methodist, a P.K. and a darling kid. I think she had A.D.D. too. Either she was a little spaz like me or she was really full of energy but really sweet overall.

In my senior year, I became friends with another girl named Jennifer. She got me into pot and coke. She was a real winner from a broken home, she didn't go to church and she was having sex at the age of twelve. She was everything that I wasn't. I wanted to see the other side of life. I was privileged. She did stuff I could never get away with. I only hung out with her for a year or so, that's all. It took a long time for me to realize how much good I have. Jennifer convinced me to take my car to the Mexico border and buy smoking stones for pot joints. Yeah, she was trouble.

I can't imagine what she's up to now. I guess she's either a congressman or in prison. She was one sneaky white girl.

All I know is that I'm glad we didn't spend more time together. She was trouble. She did get to go out with this really cute guy, Gullermo. He sat in one of my classes, kitty-corner to me, and he had the most beautiful cocoa-butter skin. I think he was Dominican. He always wore cut-off t-shirts and his arms were so defined. WOW!

Once he accidentally lifted his shirt and he was ripped. That's when I found out what the word horny means, like, Hello! He was so sweet and nice. I wanted to tell him about the girl he was going out with, "Wrap it up! She's dirty!" I don't think they went out long. He was too good for her. I can't imagine him taking her home to meet his mom. He was such a good guy. He had to have a good mother. I hope he's doing well. Such a sweetie! He probably wouldn't remember me. I was just a dorky white girl theater geek. I don't think he would remember my performance of Grease, Blyth Spirit – you're a good man, Charlie Brown, The Fantastics, Shakespeare, or any of my dance recitals. Not a lot of cool kids watched that stupid stuff, just us weenies.

When I got out of high school, I knew I would go to a performing arts school, and I did. I went to The American Academy of Dramatic Arts in Pasadena. My dad was signing the tuition check when he looked at me and said, "They don't let any of those homos in there, do they?" I said, "No dad, that's the Pasadena Republican discount because the school is owned by Republicans, didn't you know that?"

Dad replied, "Well, that's more like it, Republicans are getting recognized again." I don't know what the hell that meant, but I had to go to an audition in order to get in and I did. Going there was fun. David Roundtree, who also worked at Strasburg, was my main director. He was wonderful, as were a lot of my teachers and choreographers.

Here's a heads up, don't watch the Academy Awards with a bunch of actors because they can't keep their mouths shut. "Oh my god, look at her dress and did you see that movie? I can't believe she got the nomination." They have to critique everything as you watch the show.

If you are in L. A and you get the chance of going to Hollywood, see it live. Jump in your car and go. You can then brag to your friends back home, "I saw the Academy Awards in Hollywood live." I went to school with a lot of kids who think I've been performing for years because I know everything about the arts. No, I don't, jackass! You may have been hot shit in Colorado, Georgia, Ohio, or Kansas, but you don't know shit about the business in L.A., so pull it back.

I knew a girl Beth, a white girl who had a lovely voice but she had a big ego that matched her fat ass. We went to see a performance in Hollywood and she said, "I hear that girl sing, and she's off. I can hear it. I have better training than her. I should be in this, my voice is so much better." I never acted like I was a better actor or performer than anyone else, but Beth was in competition with every young girl who could sing because she couldn't act her way out of a wet paper bag.

There were a lot of kids with talent at school. They don't need Beth's bullshit on top of an already challenging school that will make you work really hard to get your craft fine-tuned. I had more experience with training than most kids I went to school with. My mom was in the arts, music, dance, acting, but I didn't compare myself to anyone else. Beth had some experience with singing and was a little more trained, maybe, but look at the statistics, less than two percent of all actors get work, not full time just one small gig, if they're lucky.

Actors that say things like, "Oh, I'm a trained actor, I'm going to get an academy award." Break a leg but don't think that just one part will make you a star. I saw a lot of students who had the upper hand when it came to specific training, but you are not any better than anyone else and the people in the business will tell you, "Who let her in here, lose some weight, fix your hair, I don't know what you're doing here, you're never going to make it, get me a woman who looks better." That's why nobody needs negative criticism from actors like Beth.

I went to school with a guy with a really big ego, who booked a part in a T.V. series, 21 Jump Street. He came back to school like he was a rock star. A year later, the show got canceled and that was his last gig as an actor. His acting career was over, so one part was not to get him that Academy Award he wanted. He came to school to gloat, and now he's an unemployed actor just like Beth, so welcome into and out of business. When Will Smith slapped Chris Rock across the face at the Academy Awards in '22, he's lucky he didn't hit him and really fucked him up. I understand he snapped, but what was he thinking? Will is so lucky he didn't get arrested. Being banned for ten years is nothing. I like him as an actor, but he went way too far!

I'm going to talk about the 80s in L.A. My nose was running a little, and it was going to get weird. When I turned eighteen, I went a little nuts. I did more eye-opening thrilling stuff in the 80s and 90s than most people will do in their lifetime. As they say, "You are only young once." The first restaurant I worked in, I had my very first crush at a restaurant called The Hungry Tiger in Pasadena. It was with one of the Mexican chefs. He was so cute. He was only about five-four, but he had eyelashes for days. I always went out of my way to say hello to him.

When I was seventeen, I still had my braces on. I sent him a belly dancer for his birthday so all the chefs could see it. I wasn't there, I would have been too embarrassed. The next shift I worked with, he had someone help him with writing me a thank you letter as he didn't speak English well. I didn't care. I still think about him to this day. I hugged him and told him, "I just wanted to do something fun for your birthday." In fact, nobody knew I liked him, but if he hears about this, I'm sure he won't remember me; some dorky white girl with braces.

He looked like a young Emiliano Zapata. Do your Latin history, ask John Leguizamo. He knows everything about Latino history. Oh, if you have a chance, watch John Leguizamos, Critical Thinking. One of the best films I've ever seen. Goddamn, he's talented. Critical Thinking, Critical Thinking, Critical Thinking. Don't forget it, go watch it.

I'm going to say this once and stand by it. Mexicans are the backbone of this country, tear down that fucked up wall at the border and let them all in. They are the most hardworking, faithful, honest, kind people around. They were here first. We invaded like we do everything else. We're classically well known for it. We go in, we invade, and we fuck it up. We go in, we invade, we fuck it up, leave, and we do it all over again.

This gentrification is bullshit to give the people in those areas a break. They have been there a long time now. We white people are shoving them out of their communities for what? It is just because we can. It's fucked up, to say the least. Mexicans deserve a hell of a lot more respect than the Scotts do. Fuck the Scotts! What did they do for us? Oh yea, they gave us the worst president we ever had. Thanks a lot, you dicks. I knew a Scottish guy in college, I couldn't understand a word he said. That's all I could hear, and well I know it's English, right?

"Lay off the scotch."

It's hard to understand Australians too. Do you know what did Christian Finnegan say about Australians? "An Australian is just an Englishman who's been left out in the sun too long." When an Australian speaks that twaddle good day mate, not fucking English either.

I studied dialects; open your mouth when you speak. For example, I can't watch Rob Shutter talk. He looks like "Chicken Run" chickens when he speaks. Just watch him; it's hard not to laugh when he speaks because all I think when he talks is Chicken Run. I can't watch The Osbornes, it makes me upset even with the closed captioning.

I met my first boyfriend, David Lagel, when I was nineteen. David was an actor. He was a white boy from South Carolina. When he first got to L.A., he had a wicked twang. The directors at school told him, "Lose the twang hill-billy or you will never get work." They were kind of cut to the chase at school. He did lose his twang, which was not easy to do, and he learned standard American dialect. I never told him this it would have gone to his head. David Lagel was a great actor, not just good, great.

He had it all, looks, wit and talent. He was a very versatile actor and an amazing character actor! It kills me to see someone so talented not make it. David did however make one mistake. He trusted the wrong photographer, I would have warned him but he wouldn't have listened. Some very young cute eighteen years old boy with a twang and a nice body, let's see what we can get away with. I can just see it. "Oh hi, son! You're a good-looking kid, do you mind taking off your shirt? You have such a nice body. Has anyone ever told you that before? If it's okay with you, can I take some shots with you in your underwear? It can't hurt, but only if it's okay with you? A lot of kids take more seductive pictures to get work. It might help your career. Why be ashamed, you look great."

I'm pretty sure that's how it went. The headshots he got were mediocre at best, but the provocative pictures looked great. I asked him, "David, did you sign a model release form?" He answered, "That's standard. Everyone signs one." I said, "So, the photographer told you that. Did you look in the dressing room for any cameras?" He understood, "It wasn't like that, he was a professional."

Two months after he took those seductive pictures, they wound up in a gay porn ad. Welcome to Hollywood. He didn't read the fine print. The photographer who took those pictures can use them for anything, anytime. You don't get a dime or have any say in the matter. Stuff like this happens a lot. People will take advantage of you in every aspect of the business.

That photographer wouldn't have cared if David was only thirteen. Don't trust anybody in the business, especially if you are a young man. That may seem odd to say, but the casting couch is not just for girls. The people doing the most harm in the business are white males. They aren't straight, only in public.

I'm not trying to put down people from Tennessee, not like Tom Segura rips on Louisiana but, have you been to

New Orleans? It is underwater, and kind of smells like they could use a little Febreeze. I think most people from L.A. and New York think everyone from the Midwest is a little slow. Do you know why? Because we're stuck-up dicks and we think everyone's beneath us. Not all of us but 75- 80% of us. The white people at least.

This kid I went to school with was from Tennessee, yee haw! This kid got into the American Academy of Dramatic Arts like I did. You have to audition to get in. The hick kid was from Tennessee and invited his two redneck buddies to come out to Las Angeles to see some movie stars. Very nice guys but they were very naive, to say the least. I think this is how their talk went when they planned their stay in L.A.

"Hey Bubba! Get the map, we got to look for a house in L.A. and we have to have a garage because they steal trucks out there a lot. Give it here. Oh, Las-Angeles is big. Look here, Pasadena. That's where the school is, that's too expensive. Look here, Oh boy, that's expensive over here. That looks good, and right off the highway too, what's it called bubba? Boyle Heights, East L.A. Perfect!"

Those dumb hill-billies had no idea that's the heart of east L.A. where the gangs live, mostly Hispanic. Their house was right next to Boyle Heights East, L.A. Talk about a fish out of the water, these guys weren't racists. They just didn't know any better than to write up to a Mexican and say, "Are ya'll a cholo? Can I take your picture?" YUK YUK YUK, shit like that.

They called me in the middle of the night, it was 2:30 in the morning. "Jan, you have to come out here. They are filming down the streets, Whoopi Goldberg's down there." I think my initial response to them was, "Jesus Christ, it's 2:30 in the morning. Why would I get out of bed to go down to that shithole in the middle of the night?" They replied, "Please Jan come out here!"

"I have the script to go over in the morning, Jesus." They begged dramatically until I had no choice but to give in. I dragged my ass out of bed and got down to Boyle Heights at three in the morning unarmed. Yea, that's safe. Just as I arrived, I saw five gang members sitting on their porch. The hillbillies were on the sidewalk observing the set.

I looked at one of them and he smiled at me. Did I say, "Well, you don't see that very often in this neighborhood? Do you?" He laughed, so I went over there. They didn't have their guns out or anything, they were just sitting there. I introduced myself, "Hi. I am Jan. I know those guys. One of them goes to school with me. They are harmless, don't be surprised if they ask to take a picture with them to send back home to give an impression, look I met a bunch of cholos." Yuk Yuk Yuk. One of them said, "Jan, like Jan Brady from the Brady Bunch?" I answered, "Yea, like Jan from the Brady Bunch." So one of the guys goes, "Marsha, Marsha, Marsha." Great.

They started to laugh. Thank God, to be perfectly honest. They were all really nice, all of them. Those gang members who are supposed to be so dangerous and awful were pleasant. The gang members were enjoying the hillbilly show better than cable and a lot more fun. One of the gang members offered me a beer and I accepted. We chatted a bit about school and art. Turns out the gang member I was talking to was into art. As I always say, "Don't judge a book by its cover." I told them, "I'm going to see what those hillbillies are up to, I'll be back."

I went over to them, "You guys shouldn't be out here. You are going to get shot." They said, "No, we are not. We got our guns right here." They had their shotguns right next to the door. I looked back at the gang members and shrugged my shoulders. They started to laugh. They were watching this whole thing and enjoying themselves, laughing. I went back to my car, passed the gang guys and I said, "I might need another beer after this." They laughed and said, "We got one right here Marsha, Marsha, Marsha, Ha-Ha." Jesus Christ.

I went to my car, took my makeup case and my parking pass, put it around my neck, shoved it inside my shirt, and walked down to the set. I asked about the makeup room, "Makeup?" They pointed the path, "Right this way." I walked right onto the set. Do you know why they let me in? I'm invisible in California, there are skinny blonds everywhere. I'm invisible and unassuming. I was a wallflower, I blended in. That's how I got into a lot of parties by just following the pack and the blow and blending in.

Anyway, I went over to Whoopi. She was standing outside where they were filming. I bum a cigarette either from her or the woman next to her. I don't smoke but I just wanted to look cool. I looked at the Tennessee kids, "Hey, guys!" They looked at me, "How did she do that?" She was going over the script. Don't know the film, but Whoopi had short dreads. I love Whoopi; she looks so huggable with those poufy shirts she wears. I just want to hug her. Whoopi, Whoopi, Whoopi.

My mom was so mad at her when Ted Danson did the black-face. My mother was looking at the TV going, "Oh Whoopi! That's so inappropriate. How could you let Ted do that?" I said, "Mom, they can't hear you." My poor Mom, she gets so attached to her favorite people in the business like Tom Selick, Ted Danson, Steve Gutenberg, and all the guys in Three Men and A Baby. Come on, all sweeties! Mom has good taste.

So when mom saw Ted Danson, one of her favorite people and Whoopi, another one of her favorite people do something that stupid, it really let her down. Being ashamed of yourself is worse than being in a movie. She just didn't like much. She took it very personally. It is a bad example of doing something stupid just to draw a crowd. I still have no idea why they pulled that stunt, but it really hurt mom's feelings.

Anyway, I checked out the set and went back to the hillbillies to let them know what was up. They were spraying down the streets, and the hillbillies were like, "What's that? Why are they doing that?" I had to explain, "They wet the streets at night for effect, and it looks cool on film at night." I grew up watching stuff like that and that's why they called me. They thought I would have more information about filming and I did, but it was past four o'clock in the morning. If I stayed any longer, I'd get stuck in the rush hour traffic and I had school in the morning.

They asked me, "What's Whoopi like?" Jesus. I said, "She was going over her script, I didn't interrupt her." They were filming outside a little A. and P. it had a pinkish or maybe purplish car in the movie. I didn't know which one it was. I told them, "If you want to see more or a movie set, I'll try to arrange it. It's not safe out here, go back inside." I went over to the gang guys and had a beer, talked about art and old movies. It was fun, then I went home. I didn't get very much sleep that night.

What they didn't know and I couldn't believe but I'm going to admit I never told anyone ever. I used to sneak into the lots. From 1984 to 1989, I snuck into the lots in Studio

City Burbank in L.A. Hollywood. I did it for years. I couldn't tell anyone, especially actors. They would try to do it, get caught, and fuck it up for me. I got the idea from my mom. I hope to God my mom doesn't hear about this. If she does, mom, I was just kidding. I'm making all of this up and I never curse. Think she'd buy it?

Mom was a part-time security guard for the '84 Olympics. Mom just wanted to add that to the résumé of weird stuff she's done. She also sang in the opening ceremonies. Moms are operatically trained. She hates it when I say that she's so humble. When mom was seventeen, she was the lead in Madam Butterfly. I think she's got it. Mom used to sing so loudly when she wasn't playing the piano and we sat together at church.

It embarrassed me to stand next to her in church. People would turn around and look at her, "Wow, someone loves to sing for God." Mom was the first soprano and very well trained. I took mom's pass and mocked it. I mocked all the passes for all the studios. I usually didn't get in through the front; I found the side entrances worked better.

I saw Willie Aimes, I almost wet my pants. Who cares about Scott Baoi but Willie Aimes. Oh my Gosh, I love him. I wanted to go up to him and say, "I met you when we went to Florida when you were in a band." I don't think he would have remembered me. I was only eleven when I met him. I think he was doing Charles in Charge in Gower Studios around that time.

I met so many people but he stands out to me, Willie Aimes come on. It was fun. People ask me, "Have you ever seen any movie stars?" I couldn't tell anyone, well most of them between 1984 and 1989. I didn't meet all of them. I really just walked around checking everything out. If you see any old footage of the lots back then, you would just see me walking around saying Hi to everyone. I did do something I probably shouldn't have. I helped myself to a lunch buffet they had for the cast and crew. I was hungry, so I made a plate nobody gave me a second glance. I sat down next to a guy that ran the boom.

He was nice. We shot the shit and then I went home. It kind of feels good to get that off my chest. It was like I had this really fun secret nobody knew about. I'm glad to share it with you. I hope I don't get arrested. I don't know what the charge would be being a sneaky little white girl. If that's the case, arrest every skinny blond bitch in Southern California. Okay, not all of them, just 75-80% of them. Warning, don't try this, especially if you're black. The only reason I got away with that was because I was white once again, white privilege!

I must admit; the more I got into the business, the more I got turned off by it. I think if you want to make it big in Hollywood, you have to sell a little piece of your soul. I was not willing to do that. A lot of people in the business won't agree with me but that's how I really felt. I loved doing theater and dance, but films and modeling weren't really my thing, I just did it.

Writing was something I always did, but I didn't really share any of my work much until now. I never thought I'd see my name in lights as I was very realistic about it.

So many young actors who went to L.A. didn't really know what they were getting themselves into. I'm not talking about the hillbillies from Tennessee finding a house with a garage. I'm talking about kids who have never lived in Los Angeles. It's not like Denver, Little Rock, or Seattle. L.A. is a completely different cup of tea altogether.

Like any big city, you have to be extra cautious. Trying to get in the business is rough. Even just trying to just get an agent is a little sketchy. Some actors have a little advantage from a family name or connections in the business to get their foot in the door easily or they have an advantage of being from L.A.

I didn't even have a full-time job to support myself. I did have more opportunities than them in terms of auditions, parties, and networking with people. I was lucky I guess, but I wasn't really trying to win an academy award. I was just having fun. They say it's a dirty business for a reason.

Be as careful as you can, watch your back, know who you're going to that party with, don't leave your drink unattended, take pepper spray, look for cameras in dressing rooms, don't sign anything unless you have completely read it and understand it, don't think a business card is legit. In the end, you'll regret it and no, you don't have to get naked or show some more than you're comfortable with. Just be careful.

If anyone in the business tells you that you have to show some skin to make it, no you don't! And I'm not just talking about the women.

Be brave and take chances; there's nothing wrong with nudity but it must be your choice. Just always keep your guard up. I can't tell you the countless stories of Hollywood where kids and actors have been exploited. Even the thought of it is too depressing. Notwithstanding, I have some funny stories too but once again, for that, we will have to write thick sequels to cover that information.

At the academy, I had some friends who played a prank on a kid we went to school with. A guy from Tennessee told everyone, "I ain't no homo!" What a dumb fuck. Sixty percent of our school and administration was gay.

He got messed up with all year long. He was going back to Tennessee and they took him to L.A.X. and decided to play a little prank on him to bid farewell. This was way before the security was tightened. They took a ten-inch black dildo and placed it on his carry-on. That's not all! It was a vibrating dildo covered in Vaseline and aluminum foil.

Therefore, when he went through the x-ray machine, it started to vibrate. The guards yelled, "What's in the bag?"? They pulled it out before him and he went on, "That's not mine, they did that. I am not gay!"

After that incident, he didn't come back to school. He wasn't invited, and he was pissed off at the administration. "I ain't no homo" didn't sit well with them. Even though I can't remember the guy who told me that story, I'll bet he's a comedian for sure. That kind of stunt is something only a comedian would be able to pull.

I'm not ripping on Tennessee. I think Tennessee is a nice place. I have never been there, but I'm sure I'd like it. Brad Paisley lives there with his lovely wife, Kim. Every time I think of her, I think of the movie, "Father of The Bride" and it reminds me of home.

Nate Bargatze lives there too. I think with his daughter, Harper. I only mentioned her because apparently, Nate doesn't read much and I wonder why he named her that. To be honest, I liked it, very original. "You go, Harper! Knock em dead, kiddo! That's a name to be proud of. I don't know why it just sounds strong, cool, and confident! If I ever hear another Katelyn, I'm going to puke.

I'd like to say Jeff Foxworthy's not a racist! He's a redneck through and through, but Jeff Foxworthy didn't have a racist bone in that bow-legged body of his not one! He treats everyone with great respect and kindness. It wouldn't be a bad idea if Jeff Foxworthy ran for president. But that's a great idea, don't you think? Larry the cable guy could be the V.P. GET HER DONE! Ron White can be the press secretary.

I can just imagine it, Ron standing in front of the press shouting, "You guys are fuuuuccccked!" Standing there, with a glass of scotch in one hand and a cigar in the other, Bill Engvall can be the speaker of the house. I can just visualize him saying: "You call to calm down, settle down, now let's get it together, I had a contractor that moved this slowly, I don't have the runs, but I'm losing my patience, if you don't settle down, I'm going to get the hose!"

I think there would have been a lot of changes in the White House if Jeff Foxworthy was President. How about this, our new Olympic sport would be Inner Tubing, without a life-vest, while holding a case of beer. The winner wouldn't get any metal. He and his lovely family would go for four at the sizzle and a case of Aqua Net for his wife. His kids would get a free beer, and they would be cozy with a missing child on the back. That is how they kill two birds with one stone. "Hey daddy, it's pretty!" They'll have a pie-eating contest in the Piggly Wiggly's parking lot and they will have a contest to see who has the best farmer's tan, presented by the runner-up to Miss Georgia. They will have corn hole and B.B.Q. It will be great.

By the end of his term, the national drink would be Pabst Blue Ribbon. The wine country would produce the country's best Moonshine! Nascar and Monster truck races will replace the rose parade and the Macy's day parade by the end of his term. He can make up a new law to protect good strong rednecks.

Rednecks are not racists. There is a difference; it may be hard to see at first but look closely. Do they have a confederate flag anywhere? No, you might be a Redneck. Do they use racist slander? No, you might be a Redneck. Do you dismiss anyone who isn't white from your circle of friends? No, you might be a Redneck. Do you think God loves you more because you are white? No, you might be a Redneck.

Do you worship Hitler, or are you part of any hate group? No, you might be a Redneck. Do you treat others with compassion and kindness? Yes, you are a Redneck, not a racist. They don't hate or like the clan. They are just Rednecks; good people who love country life and good old-fashioned fun like the Inner Tubing, without a life vest while holding a case of beer. God, love them.

CHAPTER EIGHT: POKER, JUST A GAME

Let me tell you something about me, I had a lot of interest in poker. I loved playing it. There are things I have never told anyone before, not even my best friends. After hearing this, countless people are going to say, "Goddamn it, I knew it." Yes, it's true. I am a very good poker player. It kind of feels good to finally admit that I have no tells. I play very comfortably, casually and I never think about the money. I just play.

If someone asked me, do I play poker? I'd say, "A little." I never bragged or showboated. I would put my ear to the ground and sit in as many games as I could. I never told a soul that I played all over California, Colorado, Wyoming, Nebraska, Texas, and once in New York. It was fun for the most part. I never lost everything. When it got old or felt uncomfortable, I left.

I was underestimated from the get-go because I'm a woman. It came to my advantage. They never saw me coming. I always pretended I didn't know anything about the game. Right now, as I am writing this book, I am thinking to myself, should I open this can of worms? But I'm not worried because I am never playing poker again. I am not going to tell you everything, we will be here all night and into tomorrow, but I'll tell you a little.

I have played for a long time. I started to play in the fourth grade, and I guess it's just something I was natural at. I don't know but it comes to me easily. I'm not a big fan of blackjack, bridge, or any other card games but just poker. I learned from my grandfather, he was a good player. I only took money from assholes with big chips on their shoulders. I'd walk up to them and go, oops. Knock it off.

They used to be so baffled and say, "Did she just take all my money? What happened?" It was fun. I never told any of my friends or family members because if I'd tell them, they'd probably think I had found a new addiction other than alcohol. I admit it, I was a drunk, but poker was not an addiction. If it was, how did it affect me exactly? I know it didn't.

I also dated more than my share of people with gambling problems. Two of them were Wayne and Darren. I would watch Darren lose. He never won and he used to say, "I couldn't understand what happened to my rent money? Oh yea, I played poker with the guys again." If they knew about my moral skills in the game, they would think to themselves, "I will get Jan to play. If I lose, it won't matter because she is good. Jan will win, so she won't get mad if I lose."

I went to a tournament with Wayne and figured out his gambling problem. They were both addicts, takes one to know one. People knew about my addiction to alcohol, I didn't hide it well but I never lied to anyone or stole money to feed my addiction. I may have been a drunk, but I am not a liar or a thief. People will tell you, anything too excessive is bad for you. Folks with a gambling addiction are no different from any other addict.

There are so many lies you can tell before you get caught. I never lied about me playing poker. I just didn't tell anyone, until now. I was good at it and that was nobody's business but mine. Wayne and Darren would both say, "I'm not addicted to gambling." Sure, you weren't and you weren't drunks either.

I tried to quit drinking with both of them, but no way. My alcohol addiction was on and off for years, but neither of them could quit, much less slow down. Once, Darren came home drunk around three o'clock in the morning, and he locked himself out. He lost his keys but remembered the two bottles of wine he won for selling the most specials at work that night. "Hey, honey. Look what I got us?" and I'd dodge him away, saying, "Maybe later, okay?" he did that when I was trying to not drink, yeah real supportive.

Wayne would drink day and night. They both had addiction problems. I couldn't risk telling them that I was good at playing poker, no way. Wayne would have figured out a way for me to play, so he didn't have to work for the rest of his life because he was spoiled, lazy, drunk. On the other hand, Darren would have given it a shot to play poker, but I have seen him play cards poorly, he would fail at the game and I would be stuck with his debt for the rest of my life.

Poker was fun, now it's not. Because of the guys like that, I'm never going to play again. My life didn't revolve around poker, so I can leave it without going berserk. I'm also a really good swimmer. I have expertise in ballet, cooking, working with kids, and writing. There are lots of things I'm good at, but that doesn't mean I want to do them all the time. I want to play poker casually with someone who plays well, keeps it low-key and doesn't smoke any cigars. Most importantly, someone who can keep their ego at the door and can hold a conversation that doesn't involve poker or money, someone who just enjoys the game, even if they lose. I'm not holding my breath, who I am kidding? I am never playing again.

I wanted to play at Bill's Chicken in Altadena, California. It's an all-black area by Pasadena. It was a front for poker, craps and God knows what else. You should have seen the comings and goings from the back of that place, wow. I was a sheltered white girl; I never saw anything like it. It was a little scary but at the same time, thrilling. I just thought it was really neat. I would get mad if they would get busted and shut down, I couldn't get my chicken. Bill's Chicken was so good, I dream about it to this day.

I got the courage to ask Bill once while he was putting together my chicken with the bread and brown paper, real old school. I said to him, "Bill, you got any games going on?" He winked at me and replied, "Not now, honey." I knew it. I was dying to ask if I could play with the guys, but I didn't think it would go well. How I would have been introduced? "Hey, guys. This is Jan, she'd like to play with you. By the way, her dad's in the Klan. Go ahead, honey." They would take one look at me, "Your dad's in the Klan, huh?" I think they would just shoot me or I would give them everything, my money, earrings, wallet, watch, rings, or my car keys you just name it to know when to lose! But honestly, Bill was a very nice man, I miss him. I really want the recipe for his chicken. If anyone knows it, please let me know. It's Bill's Chicken in Altadena, California.

I played in Wyoming as well. One of the most fun games I played to this day. All the guys were pretty good players, no egos, and they were very polite smokers. I was sitting next to the window, it was nice for me. With the wind blowing, I was next to the freshly cut wood, it smelled great. They were all smoking cigars. I tried to get into cigars, but they made me gag. Once, my mom was a little girl, and she got onto a boat with a jerk and he wouldn't put out his cigar though it was making her sick. So, she threw up on him. Go, Mom!

They knew I had asthma and didn't like the cigar smoke, so they were polite about it, appreciate that! I was really enjoying myself until this big faggot cowboy came in, "Hey, look at me, I am here." He made it sound like I know him. That was weird. He looked like, just picture Gomer Pyle in female drag trying to impersonate John Wayne. I thought to myself, "Well, there goes the game." He got his chips from the dealer and his friend introduced me to him. I leaned across the table, but he didn't shake my hand. He was too busy talking about himself to the guys, strike one. He has no idea what he's in for.

We started to play. He leaned back and put his gun on the table. I'm so desensitized to guns. I glanced at it but didn't give a shit about it. Though it was only a 38, a pop gun but it was a gun, no less. I could see him looking at his gun from time to time. I didn't respond to him the way he wanted me to, so he started spinning it on the table with his finger to get my attention. I think that's what he wanted desperately. I said, "Excuse me. Is that loaded? Could you stop that?"

He started to look at the guys for approval. "Oh, I'm sorry, Kitten. I'll just put that right over here for you. Is that ok, Kitten?" Then he leaned onto the table and said, "Kitten, do you know how to play this game? It's called poker." I looked at him like I'm a twelve-year-old learning the game and said, "Well, a little. Do you play a lot? I don't and I'm not very good, but I'll try, okay?"

The guys I was playing with knew I could play. I winked at two of the guys and thought, "Let the games begin!" I started to play like I didn't know what I was doing. I was playing with my chips poorly, looking at my cards a lot, and asking stupid questions. I was being his silly little kitten, just like that guy wanted.

Two of the guys I was playing with caught on pretty quickly about what I was up to. I was playing with this big faggot cowboy, and he had no idea that I was going to take everything he got. I was deliberately losing, building up his ego so much that I got into "stripper mode". I started saying stuff like, "Are you a real cowboy? Do you have a horse and everything? Do you hunt? I think that's really neat, I would love to do that sometime. Wait, do you have a truck, real cowboys have trucks. Let me see your belt buckle. Oh, it's so big." I was feeding his ego so much and the guys I was playing with were trying not to laugh out loud.

I knew exactly what I had to do to take him as it was so easy with his inflated ego. I also think he was farting under the table and was trying to pretend it was okay to do so. What a pig! I played the game well, and from the time he walked through the door and didn't shake my hand, he pissed me off. I was playing him from the first hand. They were waiting for it, so here it comes. I thought it couldn't be this easy, so I did it, I dared him to go all in, and he did.

I said to him, "I really think you have it, but I'm not sure. I'm not going all in unless you do. You play this game better than I do." Of course, I had it. That stupid motherfucker with that "Kitten, do you know this game?" went all in. We flipped our cards and I saw the look on his face. He was really hurt. The guys were, of course, making fun of him, really letting him have it, this poor big faggot cowboy. It was too much for me.

I don't mind taking anyone's money, but he was really hurt; I couldn't take it. So, I said, "I thought you had it, you let me win, didn't you? You're so sweet. Are you going to be here tomorrow night too? I'll try to be here if you're coming, I'll give you your money back. You are such a sweetie."

The guys were looking at me like why are you being so nice to this dick? They didn't know what to say, but they stopped teasing him. The cowboy said, "I'll try to be here, kitten." I wish he didn't say kitten. I kind of cringed and said, "Goodbye." I usually don't play in the same game more than once. I couldn't handle that crushed look on the guy's face.

One of the guys I was playing with before the faggot cowboy showed up, said to me as I was leaving, "Why did you do that? You had him way before that. Why did you take so long to take him down?" This guy knew how to play well and was very nice too, so I just told him the truth. "I know you play well, so do I, but I don't believe in kicking someone when they're down, that is why I threw him a bone. I don't like mean people and I'm not a mean person myself. Please don't tease him anymore. I let him play as long as I could ignore him being obnoxious. Now, I'm done. I had fun with you guys, thanks."

He was nice, but I also think he was looking to get laid. Nope! I just wanted to play poker, that's it. I only took three thousand dollars from him, not much. But I didn't want him to feel bad. It wasn't about the money. I don't care if I win or lose, I just loved the game. I usually won.

I need to tell you about my ex, Wayne Crawford. He was a drunk, belligerent, and an abusive asshole. If I had the balls, I would have had him arrested. Wayne was a perfect example of a spoiled white kid who drinks too much. Alcohol is like any other drug addiction except, it's readily available at your disposal and welcomes you at every dinner party "Oh, he's just drinking wine with dinner, he's not a drunk." Bullshit!

Same with the guys who just do a little drinking when they watch games, no they don't have drinking problems either, I hated when they said, "I only drink with my buddies at the game." It's the same thing with the women who just go out with the girls at lunch or brunch and have a couple of bottles of wine or the businessmen who have their three martinis at the luncheons. I am not talking about all of them, just 75-80% of them. I'm stating the well-off white people and the middle class both that's my experience.

Anyway, poker was a thing Wayne wanted to try to get into another addiction. Wayne put on a good game when I first met him. He was a chef and very charming, but he did drink a lot. Drinking is not a big issue but within no time, Wayne used to go from having a good time to "Fuck you, get me a drink" and ruin your night. Wayne managed to pull it together when we first went out. We tried to slow down our drinking together but couldn't do it.

Wayne drank more than anyone I ever met!!! I've met a lot of people who drank, but Wayne was the epitome of a fall-down drunk. I met his parents and friends. Wayne was getting his act together Wayne was trying to re-connect with his friends and family after his divorce and seemed to be headed in the right direction and I was happy to lend a hand, but it seemed like the more his parents, and I would help him get on his feet, the less he worked to help himself.

The typical addict and their thinking, "I will tell them that I'm not drinking but it's just for show. They won't know that I'm still drinking, I can hide it." I asked Wayne if he had ever been arrested and this was his reply, "Once my ex-wife got bent out of shape, filed charges against me for the destruction of private property, and called the police. Nothing happened. I just put my fist through a door, that's it."

I cannot imagine what Wayne put his ex-wife through. Wayne was a good chef and pretty good-looking, but the police showed up at his door more than once. Wayne told me, "If you have me arrested, you'll regret it. I will break your neck. Take a look around, I will break everything you own." I remember the first time when the police came to the house. I told him, "I'm calling the police if you don't stop screaming at me and calm down." So, he stole my car and left before they got there.

Wayne knew if the police came there, he's going to jail. After that incident, he came back hours later, he was drunk and said, "I'm so sorry. It will never happen again. Don't be mad, please forgive me." A typical answer for an abuser is, "I'm sorry it won't happen again."

Here's a heads up, if the person you are dating or married to is someone who hits, slaps, or chokes you, they are an abusive asshole. Get out and get help. Wayne scared me into silence. It was interesting watching him try to pull it together and look like a good guy in front of the police, but I knew as soon as they left I was in trouble, so I kept quiet. We were together less than a year and Wayne started to show his true colors within four months. I gave him more than one chance to turn himself around.

We played Poker in a tournament about 20 years ago, when poker was the big new thing. All those poker movies came out. Everyone thought they knew how to play. He said to me, "I'll see you at the final table". He got kicked out in the second round. There were twenty tables. I was at a table with ten people. My first-hand surprise royal flush never happens. It was between this kid and me.

He stood up an amateur move at the game like this and He said, "Do you have it?" I said, "Yes, if you want to keep playing, don't go all in." He didn't listen. I cannot tell you how many times that happened. He went all in. I didn't even look at my cards, I threw them down. Everyone went like, "She had it right off the bat." The kid dropped his head. I shook his hand and said, "Good game. Look, if you want to take my place, you can. I don't want to be here, you can play if you want." He nudged his head and said, "No, you won, fair and square."

I felt so bad for him, so I kept playing and winning. I went over to Wayne, who was now getting drunk with some of the guys that kicked off my table, and he was telling them, "She plays like a pro, right?" What a prick. I told them, "No, I'm not a pro. Can we go now? You're not playing anymore, so let's go, okay?"

He said, "I know, you can make it to the final table, right?" I looked at the guy he's getting drunk with and said, "I guess I could try, why?" Wayne replied, "Make it to the final table, then we can go." I did what he said and I kept winning. When I got to the final table, I said to him, "Wayne, can we go now?" Then the press showed up. My dickhead ex announced, "Interview her, she made it to the final table."

I got interviewed with channel 7 or 4, I don't remember but I was so mad. The last thing I wanted to do was draw attention to myself, so I told Wayne, "Don't tell anyone know that I'm a pro. Please, can we go home now?" I said this more than once but he was drunk like always, he was pushing me because he thought this was cute and I think he was placing bets to see if I would win with the guys he was getting drunk with.

When the press left, we sat down to play and I threw the game on purpose. He got mad at me. Wayne yelled at me, drunk behind the wheels of my car all the way home. Wayne was such a prick. We went to Vegas with his parents. They paid for everything, and Wayne got to be in a poker tournament and his dad watched it while he got drunk and eventually lost.

Wayne was a perfect example of a guy who thinks he knows the game but doesn't. Just because he gets drunk and played, "Hey, get me another one," that attitude is what I always looked for in a player who plays when their wasted or when they let their guard down that's when I take all their money, and that's what happened to him in Vegas. He got taken by a guy who knew he was drunk, and Wayne wasn't paying attention. Fucking moron! Wayne's parents were really nice but Wayne's dad did dental work on him and told him not to smoke at all, so what does Wayne do, he smoked right in front of his dad. His father did nothing about it because Wayne is a spoiled brat who does whatever he wants to and his daddy lets him.

When I broke up with him and he moved out, Wayne opened a fraudulent account with my ID because his credit was so bad that he couldn't get cable. He used my ID to get it, so he ordered his porn on it and I got a bill from the cable company for eight hundred dollars. He got one hundred and eighty dollars in parking tickets on my car. I couldn't understand why Wayne collected the mail every day. He didn't get any bills and wasn't receiving any letters from friends. Later, I realized that he was collecting the mails because I was getting warnings from the city, "We are going to boot your car. We will issue a warrant for your arrest if you don't pay these parking tickets."

He didn't want me to know about the tickets so I asked him about it, "Wayne, did you get all these tickets on my car?" Wayne replied fiercely, "Just shut up. I will take care of it. You're overreacting again."

If he was in a mood to stay away or stay quiet so I had to call his dad to straighten out this mess of opening this fraudulent account but his dad made it very clear to me, "Don't call me about the problems you had with my son again." For some reason, Wayne had the wool pulled over his dad's eyes.

Wayne told his parents, "I'm the executive chef at a restaurant and have worked there steadily for months." What a total crock of shit. He had one job for a month and that's it. We were together for almost a year and he never paid a bill, not a single one. I paid all of our rent! Whatever money he had, he spent on booze. Wayne got money from his parents or took it from me. He had been trying to get a job for so long. Once, I finally asked him, "When are you going to work?" He said, "I am looking." Sure he was looking, nope!

I found his resume in my car and he had never tried to get a job. That's when I found all these parking tickets shoved under my car seat with his resume and I figured out where he was going in my car in the middle of the night. He was going to poker games.

Wayne was going to poker games, losing money he didn't even have. He was playing with my money or his parent's money. Let me tell you this, Wayne lost every job he ever had because of his excessive drinking Wayne tells everyone he was fired because the restaurant wasn't running well and the management was bad that's bullshit. Excuses, excuses.

Even Wayne's close friends said to me, "He's a drunk. He is never going to change. You're a nice girl, get rid of him. You are never going to get him to stop drinking." They were right. Wayne borrowed a truck from his mom to move his stuff out. He was shitfaced behind the wheel of his mom's truck and he didn't care. Wayne left a bunch of his stuff because he was drunk and didn't look around that well. I called his friends to inform them that Wayne has left his stuff behind. Their reply was, "Throw his shit out. Fuck Wayne."

His friends have seen this kind of behavior from Wayne before. Wayne gets sober for ten minutes and expects everyone to trust him, then he falls off the wagon and goes back to being a drunken loser all over again. His friends were sick of it, and I don't blame them. I know all the tricks drunks have, and Wayne had played them all. Yet, he still opened a fraudulent account in my name and I had to get it closed.

I told his dad, "Give me his number to close this account or I will call the police and have him arrested, then you can bail him out of jail. It's your choice." Looking back at that time, I should have had him arrested right then and there. He wasn't living with me and I think the cops would be on my side, but you never know. The police were there before for me and I didn't press charges; why would they help me now?

When we lived together, we had a roommate named Steve, a nice guy. His dad died out of the blue. He was a waiter and didn't have enough money at the time to go to his dad's funeral. I went into a drawer that Wayne didn't know about and pulled out five hundred dollars in cash. I gave it to our roommate and said, "You don't owe me a thing. You bought us a washing machine so we will call it even. Go bury your dad." He said, "Thank you."

Wayne was livid! He asked me, "How much money did you give him? You are never going to get paid back." I told him, "His father died, who cares about the money?" Wayne went through the entire house looking for money, "Where's the rest of it? I know you're hiding more." That's when I realized he was stealing my emergency money. I used to hide it just in case of an emergency.

I used to drink back then. I wasn't on top of my game but I knew he was taking my money. I have gone out with some great people. Not all the men and women I dated have been drunks or bad, not at all. Some of the people I have gone out with have been really great.

However, I'm still pissed at Wayne and I want everybody to know about him, so it doesn't happen to them. Beware of Wayne Crawford, a fall-down drunken liar and a thief. If he wants to come forward and try to sue me for defamation of character, that would be a joke, but okay. If you want to do that, then go ahead. I'll have your ass thrown in jail for stealing my ID to get your cable and assaulting me. You dick.

Fuck it, I will call my brother and tell him what you did to me, then you are fucked. Not because he's a cop but because he doesn't like anyone beating up his sister. Not to mention my boyfriend and your friends who know what you did to me and all of the other people who would love to take a shot at you.

Mean drunks can't keep friends for long. They burn bridges everywhere they go so they can get drunk. Wayne did the same. We went to a restaurant where he used to work before he got fired. I had a black eye, the bartender looked at me and said, "You okay? What happened?" I didn't know what to say. Wayne said, "Yeah. She won't get out of line again. ha-ha."

The bartender looked like he was going to jump across the bar and beat the shit out of him. I said, "He's just kidding, it's from boxing." I didn't know what else to say. The bartender backed off, but Wayne thought it was funny. I had to throw a baby shower with a black eye.

Once I was on a plane coming back from L.A. I was waiting for the bathroom to become available while I struck up a conversation with one of the flight attendants. Her name was Leslie or Lindsey, something like that. I told her I was a chef.

She told me that she just got out of a relationship with a guy who was a chef as well and a total drunk. Turns out, it was Wayne who she dated after I did "It's A Small World". We shared war stories about him, and she told me he fell down the stairs on their first date. Have you ever heard of the terrible twos? Wayne was the terrible thirty twos.

She thought, at first, it was funny until every time they were together, he was drunk. I said, "He also comes from a good family, right? His brother is alright, what happened to Wayne?" She agreed, but she couldn't take his drunken bullshit anymore, so she broke it off with him. I told her that it was a smart move.

I asked her if he ever got violent with her. She said that he almost did once and that was enough for her. I told her how he got violent with me and her reply was, "I am not surprised." I think some people who drink just have a violent reaction to alcohol or maybe that's his real personality, alcohol just brings it out.

Wayne is going to wind up in jail if he hasn't already. He will go to jail and his daddy will post bail. When he gets out, they'll get a case of wine to celebrate and get drunk. Wayne had stacks of wine boxes for the decoration of our house. When we moved in, he said, "My dad gave me most of those wine boxes. He loves wine."

He did drink with his family too, but they thought it's acceptable to have wine with dinner. I believe that's fine, but the problem is your son is a drunk and he can't have just one glass. It has to be at least a bottle. Every time we went to his parents for dinner, they had wine and Wayne would get drunk. His dad let him get drunk in front of him.

Wayne was a good chef. Unfortunately, he liked to drink more than he liked to cook or do anything else. Everything is a learning experience. What I learned from my relationship with Wayne is that you cannot change someone for the better if they are an addict. Even if they are from a good family, it's a waste of time and patience.

Nobody gets better unless they're really trying to get sober. All you do is get disappointed and hurt trying. From now on, I'm leaving it up to professional therapists to work on people like that. Wayne is not the first person I've gone out with whom I asked to stop drinking or smoking.

I dated a wonderful guy, Shane. The only guy I dated that drank. I asked him to slow down and he couldn't, so we stopped seeing each other. But I really liked him. I had a drinking problem too; if a drunk can recognize someone's drinking too much, that says a lot.

Shane was a good man. He just drank too much and if I wanted to be sober at all, I couldn't afford to be around him. I tried to get over the addiction for years, but you cannot get sober when you are around people who drink all the time.

That's why I am so blessed to have a partner who doesn't drink, smoke, or do any drugs at all.

I have been sober for over a decade now, but I don't think Wayne will ever get sober with his dad helping him. Wayne's dad was very nice, but his dad failed as a parent by helping his son, trusting him and financially supporting him. I mean, stop it. Wayne will keep taking advantage of that. If you really love your son, cut him off. It's called tough love. You are hindering him, not helping him. The saddest part about Wayne was, he was a guy with tremendous potential. He just chose to drink over anything else like most drunks.

The last poker game I played is the reason why I don't play anymore. My girlfriend just re-modeled her basement and invited me over to see it. Don't ever live in your house when you re-model, it is a total nightmare. On and off with the water and electricity. They told her that it was just for two months, bullshit.

Have you ever watched The Money Pit for two weeks? Right, it took six months for her basement, two bedrooms, and one bathroom. When it was finally finished, she asked us to come over. As I went down the stairs to look at the basement, I realized why it took so long. She had set up a poker area for her boyfriend.

I knew he played but I never talked about poker with him. He invited me to play, but there was money on the table. I told him, "I don't play for money, there's money on the table. No thanks, I am just here to see the rooms." I went back, the rooms were okay but the bathroom was very nice. It better should have been after six months of waiting, Jesus.

I went back upstairs, they took off all the money and her boyfriend said, "It's just chips now. Jan. Play with us, do you play?" I said, "A little." So I sat in. Her boyfriend introduced me and there was this one spazzy kid. He just got back from Vegas. "Hey! Do you know this game? I'm pretty good at it. Have you ever been to Vegas, do have any tells? I know all about tells." I have to sit next to this fucking guy. Great!

I was trying to ignore him. Every time he won, he used to shout, "Fuck yeah, I'm the man." And every time he lost, "Why are you giving me these fucked up cards. Goddamn!" He never played casually. I threw my hand to him twice because I didn't want him to throw a fit. I was playing like I usually do and winning, but I didn't have my eye on anyone to take down; I was just trying to have fun.

It was our last hand. It was between me and the spazzy kid. He said, "Do you have it?" I said, "Yes, this time I do." I took my hands off my cards to adjust my seat. He reached over and flipped my cards, a big poker no-no. I said, "What the hell?"

He threw back his chair and said, "She's cheating, I just got back from Vegas. I know a cheater when I see one. Nobody can come into a game like she did, and win like that. She is cheating, I know it." His friends start to defend me, "What's your problem, dude?" I pushed all my chips in front of him and said a few choice words and said, "I'm done with this game."

They insisted, "Come on, Jan. He is a dick. You can stay, he can leave." I said, "No thanks, I'm out." That's the last time I played poker.

When you play poker often enough, you either get the feel for it or you don't. For me, it's pretty easy to tell when someone is going to slip and let their guard down. You can tell who can play the game well fucked up and who can't. It was kind of my little game. See who's doing the most coke or drinking too much.

That's when I figured out who was going to go all in. That's one of the reasons you don't draw attention to just some girl at any game. When you add booze and coke to the game, it is bound to get a little tense. When you take money from someone you don't know, you don't know how they will react until you see the look on their faces.

That's when you decide what will be your excuse. "Good game, I'll have another drink or time to go, thanks guys. It's late, I'm going home." I was good at the game but never bragged about it. I don't like people who brag about stuff like how good they are at something. I say never brag about it. Prove it, and when someone compliments, you say, "Thank you." Don't be rude.

I never wanted to play professionally. I don't like a lot of the players. I never sat in a game that was more than a few thousand. I once played for ten thousand. The guy gave me the money to play because he knew I wouldn't lose and I didn't. Pro players like Bill Hellman, who is a stuck-up dick, I wouldn't mind taking all of his money, but I don't want to be around his inflated ego.

Some of them are okay, but I don't play to be praised or to be famous. I liked playing with guys who weren't all about themselves. It's kind of like the guys who only play chess. That's all they do and talk about. Just putting it out, Chess is so boring. Their social skills suck, and they can't talk about anything else. I loved the game, just not the people who take it too far but that makes a lot of them.

Most of the guys who play are serious addicts. I wasn't looking to get laid or get rich. I just wanted to play the game, that's it. I have to admit, it drove a couple of them a little nuts. I was like this wallflower that just showed up. I kept it really low-key. Nobody gave a shit about me.

I would play and disappear. I was invisible. Just in case someone I played with hears about this, I will never tell any personal information about anyone I played poker with, ever. It's a private game for a reason, it is for their protection. It is nobody's business but theirs. Yes, I played with some names in the industry, and all I can say to anyone who wants to know who they were, "It's none of your business, so fuck off." There will be folks out there who will be happy to hear that.

CHAPTER NINE: GAYS RIGHTWINGERS, MODELING

I'm going to use my new favorite word, Faggot! Faggot! Faggot! And guess what? I'm allowed to use that word because I am bi-sexual. Yep, now there it is! Who cares, right? My next confession will be fun. Don't worry, my priest is gay. I don't think he'll give me a hard time. I used to go to The Denver Detour after mass and get lunch, it was a gay bar. Unfortunately, it's not there anymore, but that's where I used to go to be around women and sit by myself in my "Bi-sexual" corner. There, I got a lot of looks from lesbian women, which said, "What's she doing here? She is not one of us?" Not all of them, just 75-80% of them.

Let me tell you, it's not easy for bi-people out in the world. We don't really fit in, and it also doesn't help when you don't carry the typical "lesbian" look. Anyway, I don't really like to talk about my sex life with anyone but for some reason if you tell a straight man you are bi-sexual, they suddenly want details. They think it's an open offer to have a three-way. I hear stupid comments like, "You're bi-sexual, well, would you like to meet my girlfriend? She's thinking about becoming bi-sexual. Can you give her some pointers?" Stupid guys who do that deserve a good kick in the groin. I usually don't have a very pleasant response to men who want to do a three-way with me.

My sweet next-door neighbor and I were talking one time the subject of sex came up and I stated that I am bi-sexual. He said, "I didn't know that some people I am friends with want to do a three-way with me. Do you have any advice?" I understood the curiosity, but I'm not a sex therapist. I told him, "I did a three-way but it was with three women." He was a little taken back by that and inquired. "What was that like?" he asked with his pupils dilated out of excitement. I just laughed and advised, "If you want to do a three-way with anyone, know who they are and don't let them film you without your permission." He thought about it for a moment, and then told me, "I didn't think about that." You have to be really careful now about that kind of stuff. Whatever two consenting adults want to do is fine, but I still think the age of eighteen is too young to get involved in the adult entertainment business. If you ask me, even the age twenty-one is pretty young, but eighteen is way too young. That's just my opinion.

I worked in the adult entertainment business, and it doesn't mean I want to do a three-way with anyone. I dated a guy who said to me, "You know a lot of pretty girls who work with you I'll bet you could hook that up for me." I made it clear with not such gentle words, "I am not a pimp!" What I really wanted to say was, "You can't handle me alone in bed, and you think I would bring another girl into bed with us? I am not worried but you should be. I've been holding back buddy, you don't want to embarrass yourself." I think he thought it was okay for him to talk that way because I showed him some of my bondage gear just to see what his response would be for a good laugh. He was in way over his head. He was one of those guys who would say, "Tie me up! I can handle it, I promise." Sure, the fuck you can. I have seen it done by the best. Don't make promises you cannot fulfill. Also, have you ever seen Gerald's Game? Ouch! Always keep your key at arm's distance. I know if I pulled out my big black strap-on and made a few calls to a place where women and men I know would love to get a hold of him, it wouldn't have been that exciting for him. Especially the gay guys I knew, if they showed up, geared up and ready to go, that big tough white guy would run like a motherfucker.

Anyway, I'm not fully accepted in the L.G.B.T. community, though. I'm not gay enough. Or maybe I'm not woman enough, I don't know. My gay male friends are okay with me, my trans. Friends like me but T.E.R.F.s. 100% gay from birth, no cock ever, and hardcore lesbians snub me, just like my Mormon relatives. Yeah, we're the real gay women over here, can you stay over there? We know you're here, but you're not gay enough to be around us "real women," so you stay over there. They're just like that to me because I like a cock sometimes. Sorry, I'm not more like you. I know I make you feel uncomfortable, so I'll stay over here in my "bi-sexual cave" so I don't disturb you, real women.

Don't believe me? Okay, I lived in Durango, Colorado, the mountain biking capital of the world. We would go watch the races and cheer them on. I knew Ned Overland, the World Mountain Biking Champion. I didn't mountain bike but it's a small town and everyone knows everyone. I knew Missy Giovi, Women's Mountain Bike Champion. She did the Nike commercial where she was painted gold, then she got busted with marijuana and the Nike attorneys had to get her out of a mess. NIKE didn't want to look bad.

Missy wasn't a drug addict; she needed the marijuana for her pain from all her mountain biking accidents. She was on painkillers, traded it for pot. What's the big deal? It's legal now, thank God. When you think about it, she's pretty smart to do that. I ran into her in the market before I moved to Denver. Her dad was a chef and we struck up a conversation. She was gay, but I remember when she came out, it was kind of "in your face" like Missy. She didn't know I was bi; yes, this is me formally coming out.

I said to her, "Missy, we have known each other a long time. Yes, we don't really hang out, but, we know each other, right?" She nodded, "Yes." I continued, "You always say hello to me, even though we don't really hang out or anything, but, when I say hello to you, you always return a friendly hello back. But none of your lesbian friends ever say hello to me back, is that a prerequisite for a friendly hello? Do I have to be a lesbian?" Missy kind of laughed, and said, "They are like that to you? I will say something to them." I muttered thanks, was feeling too vulnerable to say something else.

Missy, with a sweet smile planted on her face, wished me luck and gave me a hug. She was always nice to me even though I wasn't in her little click of lesbians. I have always admired people who went outside the box and became friends with someone who isn't just like them. You never know, see what happens; you might surprise yourself. I became friends with people I never thought I would hang out with just because they're different. I took a chance and made some really good friends with individuals I didn't think I would normally hang out with. About a week later, one of her lesbian friends who never gave me the time of day from across a bar goes, "Hey, Jan! What's up?" And she's all smiles. Oh, I guess it was permissible to say hello to me now that the Queen of the Dykes said it's okay. Wow, how disingenuous. It was fake and I don't need that fake shit. If you like me, great if you don't pretend to like me just to save face, it's cheap.

If this gets out, I don't want Ellen DeGeneres exclaims to the troops, "She is okay, she s newly out, gives her a break.” I know she would, Ellen is very sweet. Thanks, but I don’t need some lesbian who wouldn’t be nice to me before coming up to me and saying, “We’re not like that. We like you.” I’d definitely say, “You are not like that, and I’m not a racist. We’re even.” I don’t understand it; the concept of women fighting against each other, aren’t we not supposed to do that? They say there’s no racism in the L.G.B.T. community, I beg to differ.

This reminds me of a personal experience I had with a lesbian woman I worked with. I thought she was nice but it turned out she was nothing close to it. Kim was a chef, and we worked together. She was going to a school, and her then-girlfriend broke up with her. Since I had a three-bedroom apartment, I offered her to stay with me for a couple of weeks or months, however long it takes to find another place to live while she’s in school. She took me up on it and stayed with me for seven months. She was the invisible roommate. I didn’t tell her I was bi. She was one of those lesbians who usually wouldn’t give me the time of day and I wasn’t comfortable talking about it anyway. She dated my friend Ann, a sweetheart! When she moved out, I found out she dumped Ann on her ass.

Once, I asked her for a favor as a friend but more so as a woman. Her response was, “I’m sorry you are having a problem, but I don’t want any part of it. I can’t help you, click!” Thanks for nothing, Kim. If I was one of her lesbian friends, she might have helped, but I got the feeling she was really out for herself! She wasn’t the strong woman I thought she was. If there is such a thing as a lesbian Karen, guess who would be number one Kim, obviously. Maybe her ex-girlfriend knew what she was doing when she kicked her out. I hope Ann hears about this, I love and adore you. You deserve so much more than Kim. So Ann, this one's for you. GO FUCK YOURSELF, KIM! She deserves that.

I helped an older woman recently who side-swiped a car in front of me. It was in Aurora, CO. 2021. She was very old and she got hurt. The poor lady fell down pretty hard and was on the way to the hospital when it happened. We pulled over and a sweetheart of a guy on a motorcycle helped. We both said it was her fault, but she had more damage than the other guy who was in a Toyota, whereas she was in a high-end Mercedes with new plates. She had a hard time telling us, "I've had a hell of a day already." That's when she told us she was on the way to the hospital. The guy she hit was okay with leaving, but she didn't have any identification, and her dog was with her.

The lady needed to drop the dog off at the doggie daycare before she went to the hospital, so I told her, "I'll drive your car and someone can come to the hospital to pick it up later." She, panicking, stated, "I don't want you to drive my car. Who will take you back home?" I told the guy she hit, "I'm going to follow her to the doggie daycare, and then the hospital." Sweet guy said, "We should call the police if she needs to go to the hospital." He was right, but I thought it was a good idea to follow her because she was going, no matter what!

I followed her, took the doggie to daycare, and followed her to Rose Medical. As I parked my car, I ran over to her in front of the hospital emergency room entrance and got a wheelchair to put her in it. Roll her in, talked to the sweet security guard, who deserves a big thank you. She was so helpful; thank you so much! I got her checked in with no I.D., and told the nurses, "This woman, here in this wheelchair, is alone, and you need to take care of her until her family gets here." I made sure they all listened and looked me in the eye and all of them answered me. I was inspired by mom, of course. I was peering right to them, "Okay, ma'am. We understand, we'll take care of her." And I gave her a hug. She said, "I need to take you out to lunch or something, you sweet girl." I replied, "Don't worry about it, anytime. Here's my number." She kept asking for my number to thank me, "Let me know you are alright." I gave her a hug and went home.

I reached home and told my boyfriend. He said, "You were her guardian angel today." I replied, "Nope. That was my guardian angel sitting on my shoulder who didn't want me to leave this elderly woman all by herself. She's hurt, if you don't help her and do the right thing, you're going to burn in hell, and you don't want to see your dad again, do you? So help her!" Sometimes, it sucks to have a good guardian angel, but I can't live without her! Just because I've been dumped on in the past by people like Kim, and others of the same nature, doesn't mean I won't help those who need me. I'm just a little leerier when it comes to helping others. That woman genuinely needed help. She talked to me and told me that she fractured her pelvis, broke her nose, and had a concussion too. I went to the hospital to see her and took some flowers and to my surprise, she sent me flowers too. Anyways, I'm just glad that she is okay.

Of course, use good judgment. Some people are dangerous and need mental help. I'm all for giving out a bottle of water or a sandwich, and I have done that, but it's difficult to trust the homeless. A lot of them are on drugs, that's why I usually don't give them any money. They use it on drugs, not all of them, just 75-80% of them. I commend anyone who works with the homeless at all on any level. I'm not going to start to talk about the homeless because I'll end up crying, but I still think if you can ever lend a hand just because you can, do it! That was just one example of helping others, your guardian angel is watching, karma, what goes around comes around, W.W.J.D., you shall love your neighbor as yourself, the heart of the person before you is a mirror see others as you see yourself, or just stop being a selfish dick, and help out a little. Yeah, that last one is pretty direct; it works in any tax bracket.

Speaking of faggots, do you know who the Boogaloo Boys are? They are the guys with the Hawaiian shirts and the machine guns. What a bunch of faggots! No girls anywhere. I don't think they are just faggots, I think they are sexually, socially, intellectually retarded faggots! No, not retarded, I don't want to piss off a bunch of retards, but you get it, right? I think the Boogaloos should be punished. Put them in a dry cabin in Juno, Alaska, where there is no running water, no electricity. Nothing sharp, no knives, tweezers, nail clippers, or bobby pins. Just give them the necessary supplies. They can have their guns but no bullets. They have to have their guns; it's like their little security blanket. They will have crayons and coloring books, but the crayons have to be non-toxic in case they try to eat them. They can have that really cheap toilet paper, the one-ply with the wood chips in it, and that's mean. They can have a copy of Highlights from the doctor's office, which is for little kids. It has puzzles and mazes in it that will take them forever. And a copy of Vogue for fashion tips, which they desperately need. We'll leave them there until they stop being dicks.

I'll bet most of The Boogaloo Boys live in their Mom's basement, and they probably had no idea what they're up to. I think their daily conversation would go something like this:

Boy: "Mom, bring me some meatloaf."

Mom: "What's going on down there? You are not playing with your paintball gun in the house again, are you?"

Boy: "No, no more paintball in the house, I know. Will you get me more batteries for my remote can? Put it on the list for me?"

Mom: "Okay sweetie, have you looked for another job? Maybe if you apologize to your boss, and tell him that you won't bring your machine gun to work again, you can get your old job back, at the A and P?"

Boy: "He doesn't like me, he's big and black, and he's jealous because I'm white, and he's not. He also doesn't know why I'm doing this, so I'm standing my ground, Mom. I won't compromise!"

Mom: "Honey, I know you don't compromise, but why are all of your friends' young Boogaloo men? Honey, have you thought about finding a girlfriend? If there is something you want to talk about, it's okay. I'm your mother, I'll understand."

Boy: "I'm not gay, Mom!"

Mom: "Well, we could try some new shirts? Maybe something a little more manly?"

Boy: "No! Mom, I like my shirts. Will you get some more color-safe stuff for me? It keeps my shirts bright."

Mom: "See honey, that's what I mean. Do you want to talk?"

Boy: "Mom, I'm not gay. My guy friends like my shirts. They have the same ones too, but my machine gun is bigger than theirs. But, I'm not gay, Mom."

Mom: "You know sweetie, it's not about who has the bigger gun, you know that! Are you being teased again by those Boogaloo boys? They're just jealous of you because you are special. We've always told you that it's okay to be different. I love you no matter what. We'll get you help if you need it, no matter what it costs. I'm just checking."

Boy: "I'm not gay, and I know I'm special. That's why, I got to ride in the short bus, but now I have a big truck of my own. I'm all grown up now, I'll get a girlfriend later. So mom, is it okay that I won't compromise? Okay, mom?"

Mom: "Okay honey, but do you mind compromising the trash out today?"

Boy: "Sure, mom. If I do it, will you still think I'm gay? Just kidding! I'm fine. I'll keep taking my meds, don't worry. I won't shoot up the garage again. I was blowing off steam with the boys when that happened."

Mom: "Thanks sweetie, you're my big man. I love you so much. Now, go take out the trash."

You know, mom is probably thinking he's an adult. I could have him committed, it's cheaper than rehab. Hopefully, then his ridiculous faggot friends won't come around anymore. God, that's a great idea! "Hey Fred, Google lonely, sexually frustrated white men with radical behavior and past presidents, see what comes up!" I know they wouldn't get any help if they googled 'safety lessons for gun owners'. I doubt the Boogaloos would read about any of that. Or how to handle a gun with respect and not like a toy. Experienced hunters, get it!

Hunters are disgusted with them; they take care of their weapons. My dad had some beautiful guns, and he took care of them. The Boogaloos treat their guns like their fancy umbrellas. Oh, look at my new fancy machine guns it matches my boots, faggots. I bet they can't fire a weapon with any accuracy at all. Give any one of those dipshits a real weapon like an actual hunting gun. They wouldn't know what the hell to do with it. That's one of the reasons an experienced hunter would agree. The Boogaloo boys are ridiculous, dumb-fuck faggots! They're just missing their tinker bell wings and fairy dust. Why don't you ask mom to put that on her list too, faggots! We need guns! You can't go camping or fishing, especially in Alaska, without a gun; only if you're stupid.

My best friend is from Alaska. If you are fishing and you see a grizzly bear a hundred yards from you, and it starts to charge, you better be a good shot and kill him. If not, the bear will maul you and eventually, kill you. It happens every year in Alaska, usually to hippies with no common sense. I'm actually okay with that, no big loss; at least it's not an experienced hunter or fisherman. Those guys are okay by me. When we went camping, we always had a weapon. You never know when you could run into a bear or mountain lion, so we needed it for protection. I firmly believe in the right to bear arms! Just do it wisely. No assault weapons, dickheads! Let me say it again, no assault weapons! Colombine School and all of the mass shootings. When are we going to learn? You need to master time, skill, and patience to make your shot. If you can't do that with any precision, you shouldn't be allowed to own a gun, much less a machine gun.

White hippies with dreadlocks, who think we should ban all weapons with their, "Hey man, will you sign my petition?" can go fuck themselves. Take a shower, you smelly fuck. I think a black man with dreadlocks needs to teach white men with dreadlocks how to bathe because they don't stink. How about you impress me and go join the Peace Corps. That's hard work. I had two friends who did that. Or help with habitat for humanity. Don't go around and tell everyone how to be organic when you can't shower properly. I think all useless hippies should be punished as well. We should trick them. You can tell them there's free hemp shit out at the burning man in the middle of the desert, they'll go! We will rip out that fucked up wall at the border because hippies love recycling! Then, we will lock them in and leave them there. I don't have a punch line for that. I don't think anyone will mind. At least you won't have to sit next to one on a plane ever again. YUCK!

I have lived in Durango, Colorado. It's a condensed version of Boulder. Lots of hippies spent daddy's trust fund on weed and sage. They wind up in Durango because daddy won't pay out-of-state tuition. So what's the furthest school from Denver? Durango Fort Lewis College, they call it Fort Leisure College – the number one dropout school in Colorado. That is the same as Humboldt State where the men are men, and the women are too and the sheep run scared. It's in California, the longest distance from L.A. The furthest school from daddy! My sister did that, and she's not stupid! That hippie weirdo that wants you to sign their petition is driving daddy's old range rover. Oh, how sad for the environment, it's not a high-breed. I'm sure it will make it to the Fish concert. When Jerry Garcia died, oh Lord, those hippies went nuts. Now, who are we going to follow? I don't care who you follow, just do it downwind!

Do you want to know about another big faggot? Tucker Carlson. That big fat Baby Huey looking soft, obnoxious, weebly-wobble, who I know has a rubber corset on under his shirt. That racist faggot on Fox News, you know him? I think Tucker Carlson sucks cocks all the way down to the taint, rubs his chin on it, sticks his fist up their ass, and pumps. I think we should make buttons that say that; little buttons the size of a quarter, so people come up close to look at it and go, "Everyone knows that." The buttons will read, "Tucker Carlson is a cock sucking, fist fucking, racist faggot." I'd wear one, just not to Church. Do you think his wife knows he's a faggot? I think the more conservative the man, the kinkier the sex. I'm sure his wife has a big black strap on for old Tucky, probably in the prenup that she gets to be on the top. He's definitely a bottom! That's a lot of wobbling flesh. Bad visual again! Dead puppies, dead puppies, dead puppies, that's better.

Do you know who Megan McCain is? She's that overfed right-wing, white conservative, racist bitch on the View. I'm sure that she's friends with Tucker Carlson. That fat cow is going to ride her daddy's coattails until the day she dies. She always has to have the last word in. I hope Whoopi gets sick of her and punches her in the face. Forget Tyson/Holyfield, I'd pay big bucks to see a Goldberg/McCain fight! All my money on Whoopi! I know deep down, Whoopi just wants to slap the living shit out of Megan. I don't think Megan could take a hit from Whoopi, but a good old-fashioned bitch slapping would be so much fun to watch, don't you think? Can you imagine the turnout for that gig? Jesus Christ, on Megan's corner, would be all the people who are far right-wing, uptight, rigid, racist assholes that only look good on paper as long as it's been doctored and thinks Richard Nixon was our greatest president. Oliver that North would never lie and Donald Trump was robbed of the election put them on Megan's side. On Whoopi's corner would be anyone who isn't a racist and has a good sense of humor.

Megan McCain is such a typical white girl with a name, throwing it around to get noticed. I will bet if her dad wasn't a big wig. I'll also bet she would be happy, no, overjoyed to be the head of the Daughters of the American Revolutionary Party. I wouldn't be surprised if she was already a member. She's the kind of white girl who would say, "Well, our family-owned slaves. Didn't everyone? It's not like we are proud of it or anything. I'm not going to be ashamed to admit that we did because everyone else did." She would say that with a smile on her face. She's so holier than thou, maybe she is a Mormon and we don't know it. She's white enough. I wouldn't want to throw her in the same standing as Mormons though. At least they seem a little nicer to your face. What they say behind your back is a different story.

I think it would be interesting to meet Megan face to face. I wouldn't have a problem with her if someone gave me a needle and thread to sew her mouth shut! There is something very Handmaid's Tale about her, and it bothers me. I'll bet she's never done any volunteer work. She might have the strength to write a check, but only if it's for a white charity. I think Megan McCain does the same thing my dad's family did. They would piss on the poor as anyone who isn't white and below their tax bracket is a waste of their time.

Modeling! I modeled when I was a kid. It was for a children's clothing brand - Robinsons and May Company. But I never thought I was pretty enough to model, not professionally or so I thought. I wound up doing some professional work but didn't think much of it. I got pulled into a few jobs; I just got my foot in the door. "You need another girl," they'd check me out. "Get her in hair and makeup," happened more than once.

I did two hair shows, one for Vidal Sassoon in Santa Monica and one for a private salon. The stylist saw me in the market and asked me if I ever modeled. I said, "Not really." I lied. He asked me to model for him, which happened all the time. Maybe, I was in the right place at the right time a lot, I guess. I was a Bud Girl. Do you know how I got that job? The guys thought I was funny and I fit the dress, that's it. I did model nude as well, and I would get compliments on my body a lot. It's just I wasn't used to it.

When I was in high school, a boy I was on the swim team with called me "two-by-four" and "flat as a board." I tried to ignore it, but it hurt. The next year tenth grade, I still didn't have boobs. The boy came up to me on the first day of practice and called me the same name again, fucking 'Two-by-four'. I just started to cry because I couldn't take it. All the girls were developed but me. One of my coaches saw me cry and I told him why. That was the end of that! I don't know what the coach said to him, but he never did it again. Thanks, coach!

I've always been skinny until I had to go on steroids for my asthma. Then I put on an extra fifteen to twenty pounds, but guess what? I was still fairly slender. I'm really small framed like a ballerina, but when I sprouted, I had tits; natural D cups. Tits on a stick; be careful what you wish for. I never got bigger than a size ten at my top weight. I gained weight all over, not in one place, but I felt so fat! Unfortunately, there was nothing I could do about it. I think I was pretty uncomfortable with it, but it wasn't the end of the world. I do have a problem with the severely obese; someone's feeding those people way too much! Stop it! When you get to be over five hundred pounds, how do your friends not say, "You are way too fat. You are going to die if you don't lose some weight."

I understand about trauma and eating disorders, but someone has to say something to you about your health, right? Shut your mouth and open your ears. Your friends who care about you are telling you to stop killing yourself over food! Listen to your friends, stop eating yourself to death. I was an athlete, that's why I had a good body and some are genetic, but I do know some people who are just big-framed. It's hereditary, not everyone is going to be a size two or four, and people just don't get that. I was in that category, the skinny chicks.

When I finally got tits and got tall then, I started to get compliments. I modeled for the students at two art schools. It was all very professional. I would go in, undress, and get in for makeup and hair that was usually done by students. Other team members would set up the lighting, the students would come in, set up with their easels, and they would chalk you, paint you or pastel you. It was fun, but the only setback was that sometimes it would get a little chilly or too hot from the lighting. You sit for an hour or so, get up, get dressed, and leave. That's it. There was nothing dirty about it.

One of the best parts about modeling for the students was waiting until the class was over and looking at the students' work. It was inspiring to me. I think the human form is beautiful. I hate people who shame anyone for showing their bodies. There is nothing wrong with wearing your birthday suit. However, if you're wearing something really inappropriate like to a funeral, wedding, or to Church, that really fucking bothers me!

There was this woman who came to Church with rollers in her hair, sweats, slippers, and she was smoking outside the church steps too. She was a complete slob! I guess she wanted to look good at the disco that night, so she had to leave her curlers in, so when she meets Mr. Right at the club, she'd look good enough to get laid later. Are you fucking kidding me with that shit? How do you get communion and not be ashamed of yourself? Don't you see the look on the priest's face when he gives you that piece of Jesus? He's disgusted with you. I know if you're a homeless person, it doesn't matter, but we always dressed for Church. Pull your act together, for Christ's sake. This was also the same woman who kept showing up pregnant with curlers in her hair, pregnant but with no husband. Go figure. Heads up, honey! You are pissing off God, you are never going to find Mr. Right if you show up to mass like that! I'd clean up my act if I were you. God may go all Old Testament on your ass. Your kid will be born with three heads, and all your hair will fall out. You'll get Leprosy and Locusts will eat your home and oopsy-daisey, you're a young mother during the killing of the firstborn of Egypt, and your son is all boy and will never pass as a girl, so goodbye! And just for kicks, God knows that you hate feet, so He will make you give a foot massage to the Elephant Man, and clean toilets for Mother Theresa because she doesn't like you either. The priest you offended when you took that piece of Jesus "guilt-free" at mass will give a heads up to God, "Hey, that piece of garbage from Colorado is on her way, put a note up at the pearly gates that said, 'Sorry, full up with people who dress appropriately for mass. Have fun at the disco," and see what she does. My Mother had us dressed for Church, no matter what. If my mom saw that woman, she would kill her with a look.

Anyway, I don't think girls now get what modeling really is. Taking selfies is not modeling! I never bragged about the modeling I did. It was professional but not worth keeping or talking about. I've been in a few magazines, been on television a couple of times too, did voice-over stuff here and there and done some runway work. Occasionally, I would do extras work too, but who cares if you were the girl in the tenth row on the right? If you're on the cover or doing an expose, that's one thing, but I was more into my theater work and dancing. I liked stand-up too, just not full-time. I prefer a live audience. I wasn't worried about callbacks; I didn't take it too seriously. I just went with it and it really pissed a lot of people off who were trying to make it. Actors would talk about the auditions they went on, and I thought it was a bad idea to do that; you could jinx it. Don't set yourself up for failure. Wait until you have it in a contract before you blabber to your friends that you got a gig. I never talked about any of my auditions.

I had a girlfriend who modeled nude. She came to me once and said, "They need nude models, and I think you should do it. You have a great body." So I did for two different art schools. I usually had one area for me to get ready in but these days, there are two.

On the shoot, there was a man, and this guy was beautiful! Every inch of him was perfect. He was sitting in a director's chair with his legs crossed, wearing a bathrobe, reading a paper. I looked at him, he glanced up, and I felt like dad with Faye Dunaway with that stupid look on his face. I asked the director, "Is he modeling today too?" He said, "He's with you today, go get ready." I, not being able to digest what he just said, inquired, "We're both going to be naked, together?" He just stated as a matter of fact, "Of course, go get ready." I couldn't keep it in and had to say, "What if he gets an erection?" The director said, "He won't. He is gay. Just ask him. Now, go get ready!"

The director clearly didn't have time for my insecure bullshit but I didn't want to offend him. This is the 80s, also the height of the AIDS epidemic too. I went up to him and bombarded him with my questions to confuse him, "So are you from here? Do you have friends here? Are you gay? What's your favorite color?" He stopped reading and went, "Is that an issue?" I innocently replied, "No, I just don't want to see your penis." He was very sweet, one of the most beautiful men I have ever seen, and queer as a three-dollar bill! Thank you, Jesus!

In all honesty, the last thing I wanted to see was another boner. This modeling was just after I had sex for the first time, and it was awful. Thanks for nothing, Jeff! I told him, "I'm a student, not a professional model. You're beautiful you must be a professional, right?" He even smelled wonderful. I was a little embarrassed to ask. He was so nice. "Yes, I'm a professional model, don't worry. It will be okay. I'll keep a handkerchief over my privates, don't worry, alright?" His words made me feel instant relief and I was grateful. "Thank you so much, I appreciate it," I mumbled and went straight into hair and make-up. We went to sit together where the student had set up and the director said, "Lose the handkerchief." I looked at him with complete terror in my eyes, but this sweet gay boy declared to the director, "No, the handkerchief stays. She is more comfortable with it on. If you don't like it, too bad, but it stays!" He stood up for me and the director tried to say something like, "Hey, I am in charge." No, he's not. He starts to say something, but this gay boy stops him.

This beautiful gay man turns, covers me up, sits me down, and says with calmness laced in his sweet voice, "I'm just going to talk to him." I have heard my dad say that when I was a kid and he talked to the neighbor's dad who grabbed me. But he is naked and honestly, faggot or not, this guy could handle himself if he had to. He tells the director, "I'd like to have a word with you in the other room." Fuck. I've heard that too from Mom. I was wondering if someone dosed me or something. It was so surreal. Now, I couldn't start thinking about my parents. I was nervous enough already. If my parents knew about this or a quarter of the shit I did, I would be in sooooo much trouble!

Both the men left the area we were in for a few minutes. I was sitting by myself in front of all the students with a robe over me. The students were like, "Why is this fucking model holding us up?" They came back, the director apologized to me and said, "If anything makes you feel uncomfortable, let me know and we won't put you in that pose, okay?" I looked at the sweetest fag on the planet and he asked me, "Okay with you?" I said, "Yes, thanks. I'm sorry, I'm just a little nervous." They reassured me at the same time, "That's okay. We all get that way sometimes." They were trying to make me feel better. I don't think I have ever been treated so respectfully by anyone in the business before that or since. Not that all modeling gigs are a bad environment, but I could tell you a few stories. I don't know if they are all true but funny as hell and other kinds of disturbing. The hardest part about modeling with him was giggling. It was like sitting with my sister, but he was prettier. A few years later, I was driving down Sunset Boulevard. I looked up, and he was in a Tommy Hilfiger ad, half-naked. You go, girl.

I also did a shoot in California, nude. During that time, one other girlfriend of mine modeled for an adult magazine. After I called off my wedding, I took pictures of myself naked and sent them to Playboy, thinking well I did it when I was in L.A., why not. I got them back with a rejection letter. Ouch! I thought I still had it, maybe not. Now I'm glad I didn't pose for playboy after seeing 'Secrets of Playboy'. I'm lucky I wasn't one of those girls! When I moved to Denver, my girlfriend told me, "My photographer is always looking for models with experience so call him. He's really good." I was working out a lot and knew I looked good, so I called him and he sounded so gay, like really gay. We chatted then we met in L.A. just like I pictured, his gay energy was loud and clear!

He started with his, "How are you, sweetie? Oh God, look at you, perfect!" You should have seen what he was wearing. I was a little taken back but he was supposed to be good, he was an artist. We went to the San Gabriel Mountains to do the shoot. I knew those mountains as we used to hike there. So I knew exactly where we were going, and he didn't. He was such a little bitch about the hike. He even asked me, "Do I have to wear hiking boots?" I said, "It's probably a good idea."

The hike wasn't bad at all, but he was so uncomfortable. He was annoying me with his idiotic questions such as, "Is it much further? Where is it?" I get to the place where he wanted to shoot, but I told him, "We don't have the license to be here and it's too close to the trail. We have to go further up." He wasn't happy, but we got there and set up. We took the pictures and left. About three weeks later, he called me. "I got you in the magazine you have to go to the magazine signing, okay?" I didn't want to, but I said I would. He did not prepare me at all. I got there and I am wildly underdressed. The women who modeled for the magazine had on glitter, big hair, long nails, lots of big boobs; they looked like hookers. I looked like I had just got out of church.

I sat at the end of a long table and none of the women would talk to me. The men got all of their autographs but didn't want mine. The men would go up to the really pretty women and say, "Wow, love your tits. You have such a nice ass! Great legs! I love it!" Then they came to me, checked me out, turned around, and left. This was not the ego booster I was looking for. I sat there for about an hour and a guy said to me, "Are you the photographer?" I replied, "No, I was the model." The business cards from the photographer were in front of me with the magazine. He looked at the picture. It was only a three-by-four picture of me, naked up against a tree profile shot. When I got there, I looked through the magazine and went, "That faggot is a liar! Where the fuck am I?" I couldn't see it at first because it was so small. When I saw the picture, I should have left then and there, but the guy continued, "Well, you can sign it if you want to." So I signed it. "Bite me!" with a little smiley face.

That's why I don't brag about any of my modeling stuff. I'm not even that impressed by it. Some models brag about their work because they are not professional models and they are trying to impress you. "Hey! Look at my portfolio! I was in the penthouse." Really, my response would be, "Me too in '99. Eat me." She would be like, "Huh?" And that would be the end of the conversation because most models who think they are the shit when they are not, what can I say? I like to fuck with them, but most of them don't have a good sense of humor. I had a portfolio too, but I didn't whip it out to impress anyone and go, "look at me!" I look at that shit now and think, "God, I hope nobody sees this." The 80s sucked, what was I thinking? I think a lot of models who survived the 80s would look back at what they did and go, "Yep, she is right. The 80s sucked for me too."

I went to see my girlfriend's final runway for school at Otis Parsons Fashion Design in L.A. Janine Oats, a wonderful girl, so talented. It's amazing what she can do! I was floored. One thing I did notice in the whole show, there were only two black models. It was in the 80s, but is it still like that? I'm not sure what to think of that. It was a fun show. The models for her show were all top dog models! I could never hold a candle to them no way. It's such a cut-throat business. If you don't have a lot of confidence, you're fucked! There's a lot of drug abuse and a lot of eating disorders too. Sorry, I couldn't starve myself for a modeling gig, no way! I met Al Bane. What a wonderful tailor. He did a pair of custom-made chaps for me and did all the leather works for metal bands in the eighties. His shop was in the whisky and his house where he did his work was amazing. He was the best of the best at what he did. Nobody could hold a candle to him when it comes to leather work and he was a sweetie to boot! Going to the Whisky, and The Rainbow Room was fun, but now it's all clean and polite. Nobody hands out fliers anymore. That's where you get to know people on the street and find out where the parties are. It's way too clean and politically correct now.

CHAPTER TEN: TRUMP, HOOKERS, A.A. [VOMIT BAG REQUIRED]

I danced at four different dance studios in my life. It was always fun to witness how others implemented their techniques. I was little when I took classes, and my mom also joined me. I was chorus line good, not prima, but I loved it. My girlfriend tried to model, act, dance, and sing, all of it. She couldn't make up her mind. The thing was, she was new in L.A. and wanted to do everything. She was always breaking the rules. When you get into school, they tell you very clearly, "You cannot get an agent or do any professional work. Or you will be kicked out." But she wasn't the kind who'd listen. She, even after the warnings, broke all the rules.

She called me, "Jan, when you finish your ballet class, stop by, okay?" I met her in Studio City, where she instructed me, "Okay, Jan, play along." I couldn't stop thinking, "What are you getting me into?" She was at a modeling gig and introduced me to the photographer. She said something to him, I don't know what, due to which he looked me up and down and remarked, "Twirl." I did. All he said after was, "Okay, get her into hair and makeup." It was as easy as that. I got thrown into a chorus line once. They were short of a girl, good timing, I guess. Shit like that happened a lot. Anyways, back to the story. So, I got into hair and makeup and we did the shoot. It was only about three hours, but it was fun. I struck up a conversation with a girl whose birthday was three days after mine. She was just turning eighteen, and I, nineteen. She invited me to go to a party with her and some other girls who were from New

York. I told her I just got back from there, and she replied, "These girls are fun, you party right?" I gave her a big, "Hell yes!" She said, "We were there six months ago, you'll like them."

After she gave me some clothes to wear, I was all dolled up. Why not?! We got into the limo with the women who were from New York. They were beautiful. One of the women was a really famous model. I had to act like I didn't know who she was. I was definitely intimidated. The champagne was pouring, and the little plate of coke was going around. These girls had some good coke. They started to talk to me, "So you were in New York?" I took a toot and said, "Yes, I was there a couple of months ago. I stayed at Omni Park Central. We did all the touristy stuff for fun. The places I enjoyed the most were Stages Deli and Windows on the World." Windows on the World is a restaurant on the top of the old World Trade Center. I remember getting into the elevator to go to dinner, and some Arab prince had four men at the elevator telling us to wait. So, out of courtesy, we did.

A came out in a full Nights of Arabia outfit and four other men. I smiled at him. I don't know if you are supposed to do that but when I did, one of the men gave me a dirty look. I looked at the guy I smiled at and he smiled back, so fuck that guy, but when I got in the elevator, we went to the very top. I almost shat myself. VROOM! The elevator makes you feel like you're rocketing comfortably to the moon.

I further blabbered with the women in the limbo, "We hit the Russian Tea Room, Radio City Music Hall, and Trump Towers." They asked, with smiles stretched on their faces, "Oh, do you know Donald Trump? We saw him about six months ago, show her the pictures." Now, at that point, I have seen some pretty fucked up shit. I mean, what do you expect from a person who worked at a dominatrix place? But I kept going. "What is that?" I would keep asking, to add the element of shock, just for their sake. It was really sick stuff and a little out of focus, but then the girl who I was talking to said, "Look at this one." She was laughing. It was a picture of her snorting a line of cocaine off someone's cock. It looked like it was gasping for air, and it looked bent really weird. The girls said it belonged to Donald Trump. I was really taken aback. All I can say was, "Donald Trump's dick looks like a shriveled-up hot dog that has been left in the microwave for too long."

They started to talk about the stuff "The Don" did and what he liked to do. It made me want to throw up. I've done some pretty weird stuff, but "The Don" is a filthy pig and a disgusting womanizer! So are some of his so-called friends. Those women could really fuck them all up if they wanted to. I heard a lot of conversations I wasn't supposed to, but I kept it quiet, and they didn't. I thought Trump paid off his hookers. Apparently, not well enough.

I was only in the limo for ten minutes until I realized I'm not in a limo with a bunch of models. I'm in a limo with a bunch of Hookers. I'm in the wrong place! The door to the limo opened, and that was my cue to escape. I said, "I remember, I have a class in the morning. I have to go, have fun!" I heard them say as the door closed, "Oh, we scared her away." I was embarrassed, but I'm glad I got out of there. I went home.

I wasn't surprised to hear Donald Trump likes hookers. I think almost everyone knows he has to pay for it. I can't imagine anyone having sex with him without a lot of laughter or money involved, maybe both. His dick was weird. I wish I could get that image out of my head. Dead puppies, dead puppies, dead puppies, that's much better. The thing that really bothered me wasn't just his cock the girl who was snorting coke off it was only seventeen in those pictures. They were taken six months prior. We were talking about our birthdays being three days apart, and I just turned nineteen, and she was eighteen, so she was underage in that picture. Isn't that illegal? I mean, she got paid, and is it pedophilia if she's paid? I hope those girls come forward and show everyone those fucked up pictures, but I never want to see them again! God, no dead puppies, dead puppies, dead puppies; that's better.

If Donald Trump got drafted, there is no way in hell the Don's going to get his suit dirty for anyone, much less fight for his country. If Donald Trump had to go to war, if he couldn't find someone to go fight for him, I have a feeling that he would get killed by his own troops on the first day. I don't think anyone outside his group of "Yes men" would have his back for very long. The first day at war, if the Don doesn't pull his own weight, I don't think he could buy or talk his way out of it. That lazy fuck couldn't even walk a full golf course, much less walk in the gear the guys in the military wear! I think they would get sick of him pretty quick. "Hey Donald, get up! Let's go." The Don would say, "Go ahead, I'm taking a break call. My attorney, he'll fix it all. I need a nap and I don't cheat at golf either. Call my lawyer." They wouldn't take it for long. They would be like, "M.A.G.A. This motherfucker!" BOOM!!! Who is useless in the military now dickhead? I don't think the marines would put up with The Don for more than one day. I even think my Pops would have killed him, for the love of his country.

I should have done rallies for Trump. In my dominatrix gear with a big banner saying, "SUCK MY DICK TRUMP!"

But, I can't do that; I stopped drinking. I can just see it; get drunk, go to the rally, wake up covered in Maga hats. How did that happen? I am a Republican, but I voted for Biden because I'm not an idiot. It was the first time I didn't vote Republican. I just couldn't do it. When you stop drinking, they give you Valium, then Benzos. I got hooked, I'm a white woman, after all; another white privilege. It wasn't hard to get a prescription. Paxil, Prozac, Zoloft, Xanax, Clonazepam, Lyrica, Wellbutrin, you name it. With THC and CBD, I got off eight medications in two years. I slowly weaned myself. Getting off benzos isn't easy either. You have to do it slowly, so you don't try to kill yourself because the thoughts of suicide increase with benzo use. I never felt suicidal before except once, when I was coming off benzos. I told off my sister and thought everyone wanted me to go away. I had conversations with people I don't remember. Fucking benzos, I can't do those drugs; I have a bad reaction to them. I know they are supposed to make you happy, not make you want to shake and die. Doctors said I would be on those medications for the rest of my life. I don't take my seizure medication or my high blood pressure meds either. They were wrong. I'm still here. I wish we had more people like Klee Irwin, who help people get C.B.D. and T.H.C. at an affordable cost for people like me with A.D.D., or people with any number of reasons they need to take C.B.D. and T.H.C.

I went to A.A. meetings by myself for years. Every meeting I went to, at least one guy would cross the room to meet me. They would say, "Would you like to go to another meeting with me or maybe coffee?" I never stopped to ask, "Are you a convicted felon or a sex offender?" They need to change their rules! A.A. says, they're not affiliated with the government, but people are being court-ordered to go to those meetings. Here's an idea, if you are court-ordered to be there, you don't get to stay anonymous at all. You have to give your first and last name, why you were arrested, and your parole officer's number. Keep people safe! Because they're not safe! I struggled with alcoholism my whole adult life! People who go to those meetings are looking for a hand to hold. Someone who cares and will be nice enough to help them people are being preyed upon in those meetings. Predators know where to get their prey. Criminals shouldn't be allowed to stay anonymous. That's just my opinion.

I dated a guy Darren. Nice guy, but he was a drunk and had a gambling problem. He fell off the wagon big-time and was on the streets of Denver as a meth head for seven years. He was once an educated and smart guy but got wrapped up in it. I saw him years later at Sam's club. He told me that he was living in a sober house and he wanted to take me to an A.A. meeting to apologize to me. It's part of the A.A. thing. So I went. Everyone was happy to see him. All I heard about him was, "Oh there's Darren he's so helpful and nice." He didn't take me there to apologize at all. He took me there to gloat. "Look Jan, I'm doing great!" He didn't apologize to me, so I did it for him. I told everyone some of what he put me through and said, "Okay, Darren, I forgive you." One of his A.A. friends came up to me and said, "We are really not supposed to be negative, we are supposed to be more supportive and tell about the positive things he's done. We don't bring up negative subjects." I said, "Not my rules honey, he brought me here to apologize and he didn't, so I did it for him too bad."

I hate it when someone who's done A.A. and is in recovery tells me, "You can't get sober without A.A. Nobody can. You have to do all of the steps or it doesn't work." Excuse me, but I don't think so. I'm glad you are sober and A.A. worked for you, but don't tell me how to stay sober. It's none of your business. I also don't like people who are in and out of rehab and brag about it. "Hey, took me four rehabs to get sober." I want to say to them, "Are you planning on paying back the people who put your sick ass in rehab four times?" Some of the people who go to those meetings treat sobriety like it's a game, and I think the meetings are great for some people, just not for me.

Darren and I went out for coffee. He wanted to pay, but I wasn't going to let him. He was living in a sober house, going to school in the church choir, trying to learn the violin, and helping others. I have seen people who try too hard at their recovery, always going to meetings, taking people's numbers for a hookup. They get all pumped up with, "You're doing great! See you at the next meeting!" That attention they start getting as a newly sober person never lasts long. The smart would take it easy.

That's the problem with addicts. They overdue everything whatever they do, it's all too excess. When the bubble bursts, watch out! They fall, and they fall hard. Darren and I sat down for coffee, and he told me how well he was doing but he was talking in the language of bumper stickers.

"This is my path today."

"I'm glad I can have this coffee with you as a sober person."

"Today is a healing day for me."

All I could think of was, "Do you fucking hear yourself right now?" But I let him go off, I listened. He used to live with me. He was also gambling all his money away for rent and it was getting worse and he was drinking way too much, so I threw him out. He moved downtown to a studio apartment. That's where he got into meth. I told him, "I'm sorry you were downtown at all. It's a bad environment for drug users. If you weren't down there, this wouldn't have happened." I was expecting him to say some cheesy bumper sticker response. Instead, he said, "Well, it's kind of your fault I was down there in the first place…" And, there it is. It's not all his fault. It's someone else's fault he became a drug addict. He wasn't taking full responsibility for his actions. Hence, proves: never trust an addict. He looks good now, but he was living on the streets of Denver for seven years before. He's been sober for four years. He's got some catching up to do if you ask me. I don't trust him, sorry, not completely. He's still not sober enough for me to trust. He has a cute little smile that makes you think he's a sweetheart. I also saw that cute smile when he was wasted too. Darren also lived in a sober house full time. I know he's been sober a long time now but he's lucky because he's white. Did you know less than ten percent of sober living people are black? It might be less than that. White privilege.

I don't trust anyone who is newly sober. It also depends on how long did they use it and what? I don't trust them, my apologies, but I don't. I don't follow the rules of A.A. either. I wouldn't feel very uncomfortable with someone in my house that was newly sober. Okay, hide the silver, put away your purse, hide the car keys, lock the liquor cabinet, tell Rover to stay in the doghouse, saran wrap your daughter. Maybe they won't steal from us, only if we are lucky. Is that too much?

Look, if you did A.A. and it works great, addicts who get the privilege to go to treatment, don't care about how much it costs. Or think about how it affects the people that love them, and who want them to get sober. They have put up the money to save their life and after they get out after a month or two, they go right back to using. "Oh well, Mom and dad, I tried. Can I have my old room back?" No! Kick their ass out. I don't have any sympathy for any of them.

The moms and dads who lose their kids but keep using don't deserve to get their kids back. I know a lot of therapists will say, "That's not fair, they should get a chance to get sober." Um, nope! They didn't learn their lessons the first time they were in rehab. Too bad, you lose! There should be stiffer penalties for moms and dads who are drug addicts and drunks, who go to rehab and it doesn't work, so they go back to using. You lose your kids forever! Some of these parents who have supervised visits take one pretty picture and expect a judge to believe they are sober. A picture doesn't say a thousand words! I'm glad kids in a position where they have to have supervised visits don't get to be alone with their drug-induced parents. Don't trust them as far as you can throw them. Being a kid is tough enough. I'm so lucky my parents never exposed us to coming home from school to find your parent passed out unresponsive or to a drunk and abusive parent who beats them. We were lucky, and it's not a white privilege thing. There are plenty of rich white drug addicts too. White people try to keep that stuff quiet if they can. We are experts at keeping things quiet, especially if we are in a pinch and don't want to be embarrassed in front of our friends.

Did you see what Trump did to Kathy Griffin? She's the red-headed comedian who held a fake likeness of Trump's head with ketchup on it, and he got all offended by it. If you heard about the stuff he's into sexually, you'd vomit! That offended him? He went after her and her family. What a schmuck! He went after her sister who was dying of cancer. I don't even think the devil would do that. If the devil saw him do that, I think this is how that would go down:

The Devil: "Dad, come over here! Look at what Trump's up to now. Look at that! That's Kathy Griffin's sister. She has cancer, good job dad! That's low. Even I couldn't do that. Uh, what? It wasn't you? That prick came up with that all on his own? Do we have to take him, dad? Can't we put him in purgatory? Why not? dad, I told you to stop gambling. Leave Poker up to Jan, she's good at it. And no, we don't get her, but, we got her dad! He is over there, with Hitler, they are old friends. Dad, did you get a look at Trump's cock? What happened? Were you playing a joke or something? That's a good one, dad. You did it to all of the men in their family, nice one! They are all coming down here, right? I know we have to take them, but tell Trump, his money's no good down here. Leona Helmsley knows all about that. Now, she's mopping floors and Trump can join her, oh how much he'll hate that… Welcome to hell, Trump!"

How could our President go after a woman who did her American duty and more by entertaining our troops? She went overseas during the war and made them laugh. Kathy Griffin strengthened our country doing that and he shot her down for being funny. That's un-American! Go back to Scotland! Isn't that where his ancestors are from? The Scotts must be so embarrassed.

I like Kathy. She's hilarious, but Anderson Cooper didn't have her back at all. He didn't want to lose ratings. I liked his mom, Gloria Vanderbilt. She was lovely. I don't know where she went wrong with him. I think Anderson Cooper is a spineless faggot. I think he sucks Tucker Carlson's cock and fists, Andy Cohen. I think we should make buttons that say, "ANDERSON COOPER SUCKS TUCKER CARLSON'S COCK AND FISTS ANDY COHEM!" Little ones about the size of a quarter, so people have to come up close to see it and go, “Oh yea, I agree.” I can’t see anyone looking at it and going, “I don’t believe it.”

Even if you don’t like Kathy Griffin’s work, you have to give her credit for how she stood up to the worst President we have ever had, and she did it with humor and as much grace as she could muster. She made him look more foolish than he already was. She’s got a big heart. I hope her cancer is treatable and she gets through it okay. Kathy is in my prayers. She’s a fag hag, and I’m a fag-hag too, but maybe we can both work on the lesbians who don’t have a sense of humor. Lesbians are a tough crowd. I know lesbians hate cock. Why can’t you just act as my Scientology friends did? We’ll just keep cock out of the conversation like we don’t talk about religion with my Scientologist friends. Then maybe we can enjoy each other’s company. Is that too much to ask? Don’t we get enough negativity from men? I’m not less of a woman than you or anybody else just because I like cock. I guess I should call Patton Oswald for ideas on how to make lesbians laugh. He used to get mistaken for a little lesbian.

Speaking of cock reminds me of Harvey Levin, that cock from T.M.Z.! Fuck that faggot too! All he does is bitch like a little girl, and tries to get people fired up about nothing but lies and innuendos. Harvey sucks a lot of cock. I’m not even going to get into it. When he’s not giving Trump a rim job, he’s probably sucking off that annoying jack-off, Perez Hilton. There is a match made in heaven. Something about Harvey makes my ass itch like I need to wipe again. He’s just icky. Oh, what a disgusting visual those two assholes sucking each other off Trump’s weird cock. Dead puppies, dead puppies, dead puppies, that’s better. They are two of the most annoying assholes on the planet. Whenever I see either of them, I think that Hollywood has really taken a nosedive. Why are they wasting film on those cum dumpsters? Where is all the money for black and Latino performers? What about Tanya Saracho the woman who gave us Vida. She's brilliant! Where are the funds for her work? Oh yeah, it doesn't exist. Welcome to White Hollywood folks, yet again!

I wonder if we should go back to the Hattie Mcdaniel days. Put all the blacks in the back. Why not? White people do it anyway when it comes to putting up the funds for black and brown artists. Not all of them, just 75-80% of them! I know some people in the business will think she's never going to work in Hollywood again when this comes out! All I can say is big fucking deal! I don't care if Don's dickheads come a-running either or any of the people I will offend with this piece of shit. That's what all the critics will say about it, so bring it on fuckers. I got nothing to lose. Harvey can suck my left tit! I always wanted to use that phrase, "Suck my left tit!" That's for Shelly and Jeff who introduced me to The Rocky Horror Picture Show. Those crazy fuckers would perform that shit every Saturday night at the Rialto Theater in Pasadena. They let me perform once when I was a kid, I was Janet. It was fun. If you two are out there, don't quit doing what you are doing. They were both terrific entertainers, thanks for letting me perform with you.

I think Donald Trump should be punished. I think he should go live with the F.L.D.S. in Colorado City, Arizona. It's perfect for him. He can teach them how to cheat on their taxes and file for bankruptcy. Besides that, they are all white. That's what he really wants. He's halfway there. He's already fucking his daughter, it will be perfect. You don't think he's fucking her? Have you heard the way he talks about her? "Oh isn't she beautiful? I'd fuck her if she wasn't my daughter." He said that on national television. Do you know what her reaction was? "Oh daddy, you are so charming and clever, isn't he?" Oh, yea. She's shining his knob.

You have seen the wife? That can't be fun to fuck! She doesn't move. It's like she was dipped in wax. Do you know what she is? She's the ugly ornament left in the bottom of the box when you're decorating the Christmas tree. Where do we put this one? Oh I know, maybe in the bald spot. See, that's perfect! Well, not any better but it is there, just taking up space. Yep, the same job she had when she was in the White House. Just hanging around taking up space did she do anything productive except take some pictures with people she normally wouldn't give the time of day to and acted like she gave a shit? The only reason Melanie went to other countries without the Donster is so he can go fuck his daughter. Don't you wonder what their prenup says? Yuck! Let me get this straight I can fuck my daughter, but Melanie has to be out of the country to do it. Sounds good? Where do I sign?

Did you see that piece of shit she was wearing when she got off air force one the last time? Jesus, she's lost it. It looked like the Joker and a Hare-Krishna vomited all over her with those diamonds and that sack. Disgusting! If she's trying to get her husband to keep his hands off her, that dress will do it. I met Dan Quail at an event. What a dumb shit! I think he should get together with Melanie Trump. Nobody wants to hear anything about either of them. They can tell each other, "You know I'm gay, right?" I would love it if Melanie shaved her head and told her husband, "Fuck off, Trump! I'm in love with Rosie O'Donnell." I don't think Dan's wife would be shocked at all. I think she has known for a long time that he's a faggot. That's what the enema bag in the shower is for. My ex-girlfriend had one too. She was transgender, and she really needed therapy. Nothing to hide or be ashamed of, Dan, we understand! I hope your wife understands too!

I know when this comes out, people are going to ask me, "Did your dad know trump, were they friends?" The answer is no. My dad was such an all-American white bread stuck-up prick he wouldn't have anything to do with Trump because he didn't know how to fire a weapon and he had foreign cars. My father was well educated, Trump is a fucking idiot, no way would my dad, as crazy as he was, ever be stupid enough to be associated with a low I.Q. embarrassment like Trump. The guys my dad knew ran the show. Trump never had control over this country or his finger on any make-believe button that he bragged about. That narcissistic ass wipe had people he had to answer to, and he knows it. The guys my dad knew were military; we don't talk about police and some politicians say, "Oh, 75-80%!" They know who they are.

This is for Bill Maher and W. Kamau Bell. Trump was never a politician. He was a joke. The man had someone take his S.A.T.s for him. I seriously doubt he could pass his G.E.D. on his own. The only reason he wanted to be President is because he wanted to brag about it to all of his rich, stuck-up friends who laugh at him behind his back. "Look at me, Na-na-na. I am President." When all they think is, "You are still a social retard with a weird cock." All Trump has are his Yes Men to make him feel superior and get his hands on hookers. He has to pay to fuck him, but he doesn't have real friends or self-respect because you can't buy that.

There is a small part of me that feels sorry for him. Then I realize, I must be having a "bad trip" or something, because no sane part of me would feel sorry for that piece of shit. Donald Trump deserves every bad thing that happens to him and more. How did that twisted, pathologically lying, and racist, homophobic, arrogant, womanizing, tactless, classless, and motherfucking stupid jackass become our President? I hope he finds out about this, “Hey Trump, get your daughter off your cock and listen up, I am a Republican, but I think you were the worst President our country has ever had. I didn’t vote for you twice! You never had the kind of power the big wigs you used to answer to have. They are laughing at you, you just can’t hear them. Ha-ha Trump, you loser! I know you can’t hear them, but everyone with more money, power, and pull than you have is laughing at you saying, Jan’s right! You’re a joke, Trump!” Do you think Trump will pull a Hitler? I’d like to say I hope so, but I’m pretty sure he doesn’t have a clue how to fire a weapon. Maybe he can call the boogaloo boys for some advice. The blind leading the blind.

CHAPTER ELEVEN: '80s PARTY, '80s TRAGEDY

I met David Lee Roth from Van Halen. He used to come into the place I was a hostess at. David was very nice. He would go into the back of the restaurant and read a paper. David came into the restaurant once with his little Jewish mother, she was so cute. He was fine when he was alone, but it's when he gets around a group of people is where he gets a little nutty. The restaurant North Woods Inn, it looked like a big log cabin. We wore barmaid outfits and peanut shells on the floor; it was fun. Those girls partied hard! I worked with this sweet girl Georgie who drank and did a lot of blow. She let it get way out of hand. It ruined her marriage, she lost almost everything she worked for, and surprisingly, I saw her at an A. A. meeting. She was still a lovely woman but broken. You could tell that she was very sorry for putting her family and husband through that, but at least she was trying. That's one of many reasons I don't like to go to those meetings. You run into people you knew, who you partied with, and who didn't do well in the '80s. Or you go to a meeting, and find out they are dead. That happened too often and more than once.

I met Robert Hayes, one of the nicest guys! I had the same allergist as his son. I think it was in Santa Monica. His wife paid me a compliment when I knew I looked like shit. I told her that her son had beautiful hair. He was a strawberry blond, like my pops. Robert turned around and told me, "You do look beautiful." What a liar, but it was so appreciated. He had no idea how sick I was and I looked so bad. I really didn't say more than two words to him. His comment was very touching, so thank you, Robert. I have met and partied with people in the business I actually had a real conversation with, but his simple, “You look beautiful,” really made my day. Thank you to your wife and you, Robert.

I also met Kevin Costner, once again, a nice guy. I met him not too far from us, at Sports Chalet. I think he lived in that neighborhood. I really liked his work except for Waterworld. What a disappointment. I did a little girl-on-girl amateur porn for fun, and I can guarantee it was more fun than Waterworld. It had a beginning, a middle and an end, and it didn’t drag on and on. The women who saw our show had a good time. Some of the people who saw our work wanted us to do a sequel. The people who had to sit all the way through Waterworld only got disappointed, seasick, thought what a waste of time it was. They wanted their money back.

Again, I like Kevin Costner’s work; I was just really disappointed in this film choice. If he makes a Waterworld 2, I’m going to have to have a serious talk with him. Everybody’s entitled to their Clunkers. Look at Halle Berry, another actor I really like but Cat Woman was a total bomb. But nobody looked better in that outfit! I just want to say, “Halle, please do some comedy, or Disney, for all the wimps like me, and Mom, who can’t take all the scary, “shoot ‘em up”, violent, terrifying films you make! Jesus, Swordfish, The Call, John Wick 3?” I hate really scary, violent or suspenseful movies since I have a very vivid imagination. I have nightmares from scary movies to this day.

The only reason I watched John Wick 3 was because Halle Berry was in it. The first scene she’s in, her character shoots someone. I can’t take it. We know you’re a badass, and you can make any part work, except Cat Woman nobody could help that disaster, but please do something, maybe

P.G. of a romantic comedy, where everybody lives in the end. Could you do that? Is that too much to ask? I love Halle Berry and will see anything she has any part of because she's brave, funny, talented, kind, compassionate, and a good Mom. It's too bad that she's so ugly. Well, looks aren't everything. There is always plastic surgery. Look what they did for Caitlyn Jenner, oh fuck, bad example. Follow what Justin Bateman is doing, ageing naturally like we are supposed to. Don't worry Halle, you have a great personality. Looks aren't everything. Hehe. If Halle reads this, I'm kidding. You're beautiful and I do really love your work!

You want to know a perfect example of how a little fame can turn you into a complete asshole and egomaniac? Byron Allen asked me out. He said, "Your birthday is coming up and you have no plans, so why don't I get a limo, pick you up, we'll go out to dinner, or wherever you want? And maybe we'll go see a show too, how about that?" I said, "Really? I barely know you, are you sure?" He stated with a smirk on his face, "Yeah, it will be fun." He took my number and I took his. Then he called me up the night we were supposed to go out, and said, "Well, the limo fell through, and let's just take it easy. Why don't you come up here, and we will watch a movie?" I replied, "You didn't get a limo, and we aren't going out to dinner. You just want me to come out where you are and take it from there?" Without an ounce of shame, he said in the phone, "Well, it's better for me if you come out here." I said, no, thanks for nothing, Byron." Click. That's so classic Hollywood. I've had a little time in front of the camera, but she'll come to me. I'm famous enough. If he hears about this, I'm sure he will deny it, but if you ask around, I'll bet there are other women out there that will agree. Byron Allen is a cheapskate schmuck!

I went to this club, Vertigos. I think for a long time, people wanted it to be another Studio 54, but there will never be another studio 54. This club had a red carpet around it. A guy on a podium decided who got in and who didn't. I always got in, even when I didn't try. You just have to be confident and act like you belong, but it didn't hurt to be 6 ft. 1, and I dressed to kill. They just picked you to go in according to a certain "criteria." This one very sweet guy was trying to get in. He told me his friends were all in there and they wouldn't let him in. That is a game they play, just to fuck with people. I told him, "I'll get you in, don't worry." The guy pointed to me, signaling a "You" gesture. I looked at him, "He is with me, he is with my agent." He replied, "I don't see him with you." He was fucking with him, so I kissed him. After the kiss, I looked at him with a face that said, "Now do you see me with him?" And guess what? He let him in. The guy thanked me as we walked inside with a genuine smile plastered on his face.

I don't know if that guy would remember that night or me, but I'm glad he got in. He was really sweet. I went to say hello to the owner. He first introduced me to John Voight. Next to him was Sylvester Stallone, and behind him was the woman who played Ginger from Gilligan's Island. I swear to god! I had to get out of there before I said something stupid. I was high and my mouth sometimes got me in trouble. A big part of me wanted to go, "Well, Sly, did you shrink in your last film? I didn't know you were a midget." I could only hope he had a good sense of humor. Or I would turn to John, and say, "I love your work, will you go with me to school for show and tell them that I'm a student at American Academy of Dramatic Arts? I know all your work, they'll love it and I will be a hit at school." I don't know what I would say to Ginger, but she would probably have someone ask me to leave her alone.

I needed to get out of here as the press was there, and I never wanted to get my picture taken. I was half-naked, my mother would kill me! I ran home, wrote down all the shit I saw and who I met. You can't keep a pen and paper on hand when partying, it's a small setback for a writer. Let's see, do I bring my pen and paper in case I come across something I need to write down for a book or a set later? Or do I bring the coke and say fuck the pen and paper? What do you think I did? I had my priorities.

You are only young once! Safety pin it, dye it, mohawk it, tattoo it, pierce it, paint it on, turn up the stereo, go to that country, see that concert, go skinny dipping, live it up! Don't look back and go, "I wish I did that." Do it all. I did. Some of it was scary but isn't everything a little? I'd like to say don't do drugs, but it would make me a hypocrite. Enjoy all of the attention! Take lots of pictures! You have the advantage with that, pictures. Most of our pictures turned out like shit. It's kind of hard to fuck up a picture now. You can take ten pictures every two seconds. We didn't have that privilege. Ours would be out of focus or blurry, or the pupils in your eyes would glow. Now you can doctor that shit up and make it look okay and good. Unless it's a picture of Madonna's pussy, not with all the doctoring in the world, but if you see a picture like that on your phone, delete it immediately! It will haunt you for the rest of your life.

The worst first impression I've ever had in my life from a famous person is of Madonna. You think she's filthy now? Jesus Christ! She looked like she needed a flea dip! This was before the blond ambition tour where she had a pixie cut. It was at this little hidden gem in the heart of Hollywood foothills. Coyote, I think that was the name of it. She was with a security guy that was massive, the kind of guy that could walk up to you and kill you with his pinky. She was wearing a T-shirt with no bra. She's famous for that. Her legs were crossed Indian style. My mother told me never to sit like that in a restaurant. Her elbows were on the table and she was hunched over her food like in a prison movie. Her napkin wasn't even in her lap and she was holding her fork like a shovel. Madonna was chewing with her mouth wide open with food in it. Yuck. You know how you can tell a lot about someone's table manners? She didn't have any at all. I liked her music, even though it's not hers until I saw "Truth or Dare." She laughed when one of her make-up artists got sodomized. I'll bet she wouldn't be laughing if it happened to her daughter. Madonna's a piece of shit for doing that. She's a piece of shit for many reasons.

Someone introduced her to me. Madonna dropped her fork and wiped her hand on her mouth and armpit to shake my hand. I was so grossed out; I ran to the bathroom and washed my hands immediately. She should be doing herpes commercials. I can only imagine what her yucky twat looks like. You ever seen imitation of corned beef? I'll bet it looks like that but kind of flowered out, like someone sneezed on it, blew some dust on it and left it there to die! I've had a case of raging Hershey squirts that I was embarrassed about. I thought if anyone saw this, oh my God! But now, if someone saw what I did in that toilet and compared it to Madonna's yucky twat, I don't think they would give me a hard time about it. The worst diarrhea in the world wouldn't be as bad as Madonna's yucky twat! I think her twat should come with a warning sign. Caution! Enter upon your own risk, vaginal leprosy, beware! Oh God, what an image! Dead puppies, dead puppies, dead puppies, Oh, that's better.

Someone needs to tell her to hang it up! Madonna's not getting better with age; she's not like Ralph Macchio or Dick Clark. She's looking more and more like the witch in Hansel and Gretel. Does Hustler have a dirty pussy page? Madonna would win first prize for that for sure! I don't think my mechanic would put it up in his work. He'd lose business. Her sex book didn't win any marks with me. All it just made me want a shot of penicillin.

I'd love to hear what Amy Schumer would say about her. I'd like to get together with Amy and shoot the shit about Madonna's filthy twat. I love the way she describes things in such detail. That would be a great afternoon, sitting down with Amy. She could have her bottle of wine, we'd share some T.H.C. and chat a bit and tear Madonna a new asshole. I am sure her old one could use a break. I bet Amy could give her some good advice. She has always been such a sexually responsible woman! Very conservative, yeah. Amy's not a risk-taker at all; I rarely wet my pants when she does stand up. Bullshit! I have to put on a "Depends" when she does stand up. I can't help it. I am so glad there are more female comedians pushing the envelope like Kathleen Griffin, Kathleen Madigan, Rachel Feinstein, Monique, Fortune Feimster, and Tiffany Haddish. I would love to meet Tiffany Haddish. I think she is going to be the next black Meryl Streep. Tiffany is so talented and funny. I think there is a lot we have not seen from her yet. Just watch as long as her agent doesn't fuck up and make her do films that suck, just for money. I don't think she will sell out, she's too good for that. I will bet Tiffany Haddish gets nominated for an Academy Award in the next five years, if not sooner, and Monique? She did stand up at an all-women prison. Give it up for her because that takes some balls. Kudos to Monique. I know a few comics who entertained in prisons. That's crazy, but I would do it if another female comic was with me. I'd do it just to say I did it.

This next story was told to me by a guy I dated in L.A. when I was going to school. The guy I dated was a house painter. I can't remember his name, maybe it was Joey? Something really Italian, he was tall, skinny, adorable and really cute and funny. He painted the house of Mark Harmon and Pam Dauber. I think I may have mentioned I went to school with someone who worked with Pam on Mork and Mindy, Six Degrees in Hollywood. So, he got me an autographed picture of Mark Harmon, which I thought was nice then he told me this story. I have wondered if it's true or not for years. I mean, if this story was told to you by someone from Ohio, you would say, "Get the hell out of here," but it's L.A., so here it goes:

Mark Harmon and Pam Dauber have a son, Sean. He was about three, he had a favorite toy. It was this little jelly-like thing. Mark Harmon gave it to my friend and said, "That's Sean's favorite toy, what do you think of it?" My friend replied, "That's neat Sean, I like it. Almost feels familiar for some reason." Mark Harmon died with laughter and said, "I hope you like it. It's a breast implant." My friend threw it up, and screamed, "What?"

Mark told him with a sinister smile on his face, "Yeah, he likes the feel of it. Can't hurt him." He told me this story in the '80s. I don't know if it is true or not but I think that's brilliant! If it is true, does Sean have a boob fetish? I wouldn't have believed it, but he told me the story with such sincerity it had to be true. Mark please, I have wondered if it was true for years. Could you help out? I really don't think he made it up. Also, could you tell Pam to have Vidal get in touch with me? I don't live in L.A. anymore, and I miss him.

Typical L.A. story like two women having tea at lunch. One would ask, “Hey, what’s your son got in his mouth?” The other one would reply, “Well, nuts! He got in our ‘GOODIE’ drawer again. That’s our anal dildo; he likes the feel of it, it can’t hurt him. You should have seen him last week; he put my husband’s cock ring on the neighbor’s cat. Meow! It was so funny, at least for us because the cat didn’t think so, but how’s your tea?”

Yep, typical L.A. story. I can’t start to tell you all the weird and fucked up things I experienced and saw when I was in L.A. in the 80s. We would be here all night and into tomorrow. I also don’t think you would buy half of it. It would be a tough pill to swallow but very funny, and some not so much.

It is true, though. Once you’re around kids, nothing really shocks you anymore. I will tell you about my friend, the devout Catholic, but I’m not going to tell you her name in case she hears about this and doesn’t like it. I’ll burn in hell! Kidding! I love her and her eldest kid, not telling her name either or her stage name. Hehe. Don’t worry; I worked the pole once too! She’s going to get a kick out of that. I have a feeling the devout Catholic Mom and my mother have a lot in common. The Mom took a picture of her eldest with her best friend Andy, when they were four years old, naked from the waist down in a waiting pool with their underwear on their heads. Now that’s a classic shot! She should put that picture out during the holidays! So when she brings her friends over when she is all grown up, everybody can look at what she did when she was four! Kids love to be naked! Jesus, we don’t really get embarrassed until… Okay, I never really outgrew it, but maybe someone else can tell you.

Kids don't get uncomfortable with their bodies until they're ashamed in some way, which is really fucked up if you ask me. My mom never told us, you need to lose weight, that's making you look dumpy or anything negative like that to us. It pains me to see mothers do this to their daughters. I don't know if it's a white girl thing or a black girl thing, or is it a fucking crappy mother thing! Don't tell your kid anything except you love them, no matter what they look like. Period!

Anyway, when I was a teen, I was babysitting the little girl; the eldest from the devout Catholic. We were at her house and we went swimming. When the kid got out, she said, "Let's take a shower Janny, Mom always does after we swim." Oh fuck is this crossing the line or something? I thought, but I mean, she trusts me. I'm a girl, but I have never been naked in front of her or any kid. I didn't know what to do. I said, "I'm going to call someone real quick, okay? Stay here." She looked at me like I was acting weird; I was! I went into the other room and called her Mom, no answer. I wanted to call her dad, but if I tell him I'm embarrassed to be naked in front of his daughter, I think he'd just say, "Lighten up Janny, we have seen you in a thong bikini, what's the big deal?" I think he would laugh his ass off. I couldn't get in touch with either of them. Okay, pull it together; it's only a body; don't make her feel ashamed of her body. This is the same kid who would run around butt-naked in the front, and not backyard when she was three, no biggie, don't body-shame this kid! I got undressed. I acted like a confident girl, and she checked me out. I could see she was smiling ear to ear. Okay, here it comes. She looked up at me and said, "Janny, your breasts look just like my mommy's did when she was pregnant, just like them!" I said, "Well, thank you, honey." I really didn't want to get in that shower; I still didn't know if that was an appropriate thing to do with their daughter. I was also thinking, what if her dad sees me naked? Oh my God, I'll just die! I wouldn't give a shit if her mother walked in, but her dad, no way. Just because you work with kids doesn't mean you know how to parent! I don't know all of their rules, but I was trying to be responsible. We turned off the shower, she pulled out a squeegee to clean the doors, which was a good idea, but she wanted to do it with me naked. I was so uncomfortable at that point, she had no idea. When we got out, I don't think I've ever gotten dressed so fast.

When her parents came home, I told them the truth. They said, "No problem Janny, she trusts you." I guess I handled myself okay, but I can laugh about it now. It was uncomfortable when I was younger. Mind you that I was a virgin teenager when I did this but just watching the news with all the pedophile crap, it could be taken out of context. Remember the McMartin School? Think about it, a teenage girl in a shower with a five-year-old naked and she's not her Mom. It might look bad to someone who doesn't know her. You have to be so careful nowadays, and I think I would be a very worried, Mom. Like all the time!

Just watch the news; it's in the paper and on the internet everywhere. I just know about the dangers of the world, not just in your backyard. You hear about abductions in other countries or just missing kids, it breaks my heart. My hats off to John Walsh for doing what he's doing and with what happened to his son, no less. God bless them both! I'm very maternal, and I always was. It was disappointing, not being able to have kids but I feel lucky. I had some great times teaching, swimming, and working with handicapped kids. The times I have spent being an activities instructor at a daycare belong to the fondest chapters of my life. I babysat the neatest kids as well, so I have great memories forever with kids. Why do I need one of my own? I tried to keep positive about it but it wasn't in the cards for me. Truthfully, it sucks. I'm not saying anything more or I'll cry. I'm in my 50s, and it still makes me sad.

The worst job in modeling I ever had was at the Governor's Ball. Jerry Brown was the Governor back then. I've met a lot of politicians; don't really trust any of them. I got hired to do this gig because the guy who asked me to do it owned a jewelry business and needed a model for the event and knew I could handle myself in front of famous people. So, I was in the lobby putting on the jewelry, and I said, "This kind of looks like my grandma's jewelry." The jeweler replied casually, "Look around at my target audience." I looked around, and there were all these people with blue hair. So here is the deal, you don't talk. Never. You hold out your left hand, show the bracelet and ring, you present the necklace and earrings, you keep the left hand visible at all times to the security you don't talk! It's pretty easy, right? I was wearing two hundred and fifty thousand dollars' worth of jewelry. I acted like it was nothing.

The music started, we were there for about an hour, and all of a sudden, I felt this hand around my waist, which went inside my dress. I was in a very low-cut black dress.

I looked over and he was this very famous old guy, Rich Little. But I'm not supposed to talk. He smelled like a mixture of scotch and old spice, yuck. He looked at the jeweler and slurred. Unsurprisingly, he was drunk. "Can I steal her away for a dance?" I looked at the jeweler, and I am sure that my face read, "Oh God, please do not make me dance with this dunk old fuck." The jeweler slyly replied, "Why? Certainly, she'd love to." As if the existence of that disgusting prick around me wasn't enough, now I was getting pimped out. Rich Little's hands were all over me, but not just grabbing my ass. He was trying to shimmy his finger down the back of my dress and trying to fingerfuck me on the dance floor. Nobody was helping me. The security was like just there for the jewelry. I was not supposed to talk, and he was not letting go of my hand to get him to stop. He was all over me. I couldn't take it. I took the hand I'm not supposed to move off his shoulder; out of the security's eye shot, I took his hand, pulled it up and whispered harshly, "Stop it." The rest of the song, his hand was up and down my back. The music ended; I pushed him off me as he tried to kiss me, yuck! I clapped and turned; everyone was going, "Did you see what he did to that girl?" I rushed towards the nearest exit security followed. I needed a little air. I was at the exit and really wanted to run. The jeweler came up to me and asked, "You okay? I said, "Yep." He checked out the jewelry, spanked me on the ass and said, "Thirty more minutes, let's go. Giddy up." So since I had a job to do, I went back. I did say hello to Jimmy Stewart, but I made an exception. What are they going to do? Fire me after that disgusting display on the dance floor? Bullshit! I didn't care if they did! I was so mad at myself for taking that gig! I wasn't very happy, but I went out there again.

I got to see Bob Hope perform. Jesus Christ! Bob should have hung it up a long time ago. People were like clapping nervously. Is he still funny? Keep clapping, he's an icon! It was sad. It was like watching Sinatra when he used to forget the words he was singing. Then I met Jerry Brown, I hate to say Jerry Brown reminded me of Ted Bundy; he gave me that creepy white guy serial killer vibe. I know why he used to wear turtle necks with sports jackets, just like him. I was in no mood to meet him; He asked me a direct question. I didn't care what he was asking, he was a politician, so whatever it was, it was going to be bullshit anyway. I didn't talk to him. He asked me again, and the jeweler had to answer for me. Jerry Brown was smiling at me, and I just walked around him. I was counting the minutes. I can't stand most males in politics like Mayor Hancock, what a piece of garbage. Hancock was involved in a sex-swinging in Denver. There was a building off Alameda where he would go for his orgies. I know a girl who blew him. I hope he didn't give his wife anything. Hey, I'm all for adult sex, even if it's with more than one person. If you are an adult, it's okay, but Mayor Hancock was doing that shit on the tax payer's dollars. Mayor Hancock took off during the pandemic to go see his family for the holidays when he told the rest of us to stay home. What a jackass! He said, "Let's all set a good example." That's so typical, do as I say, not as I do. Fuck him!

Anyway, I was standing there and another very drunk, very well-known man started to bee-line towards me. I'm not telling you who he was, he has passed away and he didn't hurt me. All I can say is that he was an icon like Bob Hope. Fuck! I thought I could not go through that again, but I couldn't leave at the same time. I was working. So I thought, okay Jan, you're a trained actor, you can do this. He came up to me, the jeweler wasn't around, and he was busy sucking up to Jerry Brown. I shook his hand and said in a singing voice, "I know who you are." He replied, "You do?" I confidently stated, "Yep, and do you want to know a secret?" He was amused. He replied seductively, "Oh yes! Tell me your secret." This fucking guy reeked of booze and cigarettes. I said, "It's my birthday, I just turned seventeen. I had to lie about my age to get this job, don't tell!" He, with an uncomfortable look, just quickly murmured, "I won't.

Happy birthday!" He left quickly. It was funny. The bell tolled, and I put the jewelry back in the case. With that, I sternly told the jewelry guy, "Don't ever call me for a job again." That was my stint at the Governor's Ball. Some people say, "You are so lucky to have gone to those formal events. You meet so many famous people." Surprise, it is not as fun as you think. It's more fun to be a guest, but still, it's still pretty boring. I met Ross Perot once, he's a little guy, but very nice. He's the only politician I liked who didn't give me the creeps.

I danced at four different studios on and off for years. I liked to see other techniques from different choreographers. I was young, so why not! I danced at one place called Rudnunsky's Art Center Studio in Studio City. Dana Landers was one of my choreographers from school, and he was wonderful. I say "was" because he died from AIDS. The tragedy of the '80s, we lost a lot of talent. I don't know if Serge Rudnunskys is still with us anymore, Serge was one of the original L.A. cats. He could do fouettes for hours. He was brilliant!

For a while there, every time I went home to L.A. to visit, someone else was dead. I went to a restaurant, and found out my friend of ten years Allen had passed away. I was stunned. I knew him from a restaurant where we worked at when I was 18, and I didn't even know he was sick. He was in such great shape. He was going to come out to ski in Colorado. "Sometime soon," he said, and now he's gone. One of his friends called me when I got back to Colorado, and told me all about it. I asked, "What about Paul?" His boyfriend. Turned out, he died too. It was like they fell like dominos, one after another.

I personally lost a dozen fends, all gay men between 1985 and 1995. Back then, if you got a positive AIDS test, you were supposed to say your goodbyes and make out a will. A lot of gay men were doing a lot of drugs to mask the pain of all the death around them. The rest of us were just irresponsible dicks.

That was during the time Freddy Mercury came out. The good Christians in L.A. banned *We Are the Champions* from being played at high school graduations. Back then, if you were a gay man, you had to keep it quiet around anyone who was not gay. That's also when little Ryan White and his mother took a stand for AIDS patients. She is such a strong woman. She was and is a ground breaker. She lost her son but still stands up for AIDS research. What a brave woman. My friend Eric Evavold, a gay boy I liked in high school, made a patch for the quilt for a friend and his family. He went on a houseboat trip to say a final farewell to a friend of his who was sick. I thought that was very nice of him, what a good guy.

The 80s wasn't all a barrel of laughs. I went to an A.A. meeting, and one of the people there told everyone she was H.I.V. positive at the end of the meeting. Nobody wanted to talk to her except me. I talked to her for about an hour. She got it from using heroine-shared needles. She was shunned even though she wasn't a gay man and she wasn't getting help because AIDS meant death back then. The next meeting I went to, I wanted to talk to her, but I found out she had killed herself. I didn't go to any meetings for a long time after that. She was the only person I knew who killed themselves when they found out they had AIDS. Thank God we have come a long way with AIDS medications. Now, this disease is not a death sentence. I think Billy Porter and Andrew Sullivan are perfect examples of a man living with

AIDS instead of dying with AIDS. I wish the men I knew had the benefit of the medical care with AIDS that patients have now.

I went to see the last performance with Joel Grey in Cabaret at the Dorothy Chandler Pavilion. One of the guys in the show was in my school. It was great! I got to see so many wonderful performances in L.A. and I'm lucky. I sang with my choir at Disneyland with my Mom and her choir during Christmas. Michael Landers from Little House was the speaker for the show, and he was really sweet. I went to so many performances and got to work with a ton of talented people. I do miss some of the business, but the bad outweighs the good. I don't trust anyone enough to get back in the business, but I chalk it up to experience. My first experience trying to get an agent wasn't too bad, but I had a friend who told me a story that I will never forget.

I won't tell you her name, she knows who she is, but her first attempt to get an agent was pretty bad. She went alone, her first mistake, and sat down in his office. Keep in mind that this is 1986. She had her portfolio and résumé for him to look at. He told her, "Sit down. Do you want something to drink?" She should've started to watch out right away. Poor honey. She wisely refused, "No thank you. Here is my work and I am looking for an agent. I am from blah, blah, blah," the information didn't matter. He looked at her, and with a menacing tone, he said, "Who referred you? Do you have any talent or are you just pretty because I have plenty of pretty girls who would love me to be their agent, but I can't help everyone, can I?" She didn't know what to think, "Well, I would really work hard. I have a lot of experience in theater, and I can change my look if you want or lose weight. Whatever I need to do to get work, I will do it." This dirtbag agent looked at her, leaned back in his chair, spread his legs and said, "What do you think it takes to get anywhere in this business? I don't want to be rude but you are nothing special." Now keep in mind that he was saying that about the prettiest girl at her school in not butt-fucking North Dakota but in L.A.; she was nothing special.

He continued, "But I could make you a big star. You know, I think you might have that something, like an ugly duckling under there, I can bet." He got up and went over to her and said, "I can help you out, but I need some attention. You don't have a boyfriend or anything, do you? I didn't think so. You will meet so many people in the industry, we can network together. Get you new headshots because these suck! We will get you some new clothes, you will like them. Okay?"

The douchebag kept going on and on about how he could help her fit in with being new in town with his "I'll take you here and there." She let him feel her up but she didn't want to and he kissed her but she stopped him. He was getting way too aggressive. She had enough and said, "Is this what you do to all girls you work with? They just say alright, ill fuck you?" The guy was a cocky jerk who should have kept his mouth shut. He replied, "Yeah, the ones who want to go on auditions do." She without hesitating, but scared as fuck said, "You mean, they don't get the part from you being their agent, they just go to the audition like all the other actors in Hollywood do?"

This girl thought, if you have a really good agent, you will get better parts. Since she had no agent and beggars couldn't be choosers, she was desperate. Hollywood can smell fear, but she was smart enough to stop before it got too out of hand. She got the message and decided to leave. "Okay, look. I am going to go." She started to pick up her stuff and he shrank into his seat and leaned back like he's the most let down jack-off that ever lived. She looked at him and stated, "Sorry, I am going to make it in this business without fucking anybody for a part or an audition."

He still didn't want to give up his manipulation. He told her, "No, you won't, honey. Trust me you won't," and she went home and cried. After she told me this, I confided in her with some things I experienced and others' stories I won't get into. That stuff happened more often than you think, which is why I think the business is crooked, vicious, heartbreaking, and there is so much hidden stuff going on in Hollywood. It's too scary for me to think about much less want to be a part of. Yeah, I'm not going to lie, I had a lot of fun in the '80s but for a lot of kids who I knew in the business, it wasn't fun. So, I don't understand kids and especially parents who think it's a healthy environment for children. I think it's okay to let kids work, but they should change the rules to favor kids in Hollywood. If a child is going to work a full-time gig in Hollywood, they have to sign a contract that says that the child will be involved in other activities with other kids like baseball, swimming and fishing, regular stuff kids do. Other than that, the child and their parent have to take once a week for an hour individually with a therapist to discuss how the child is for their safety. Finally, no child will be alone with any white male adult in the business unless they are their father. Something along those lines to start in a contract signed by all-white male studio executives, producers, directors, agents and photographers. Yeah, I will never work in that town again, fine by me.

CHAPTER TWELVE: DOMINATRIX, MIDGETS, NO ME-TOO

I was eighteen when I lost my virginity. Most of my friends were having sex at fifteen and sixteen, but I waited until I was an adult. The first guy I slept with was awful. He didn't even pay for a room. It was in the back of his van, and he knew it was my first time too. Jeff, that was his name. He was a waiter in a restaurant, where I worked as a hostess. Jeff said he was in training for the U.S. cycling team, and he liked my nice firm body because I was an athlete too. After we had sex, he asked me to marry him, no joke. He had to marry a virgin like I wasn't fucked up enough from my parents with the whole "You have to be a virgin when you get married" bullshit. All I could say to him was, "No way." That was the last time we went out, but he told everyone we worked with that he popped my cherry. I told everyone he was terrible sexually. I said I didn't have any experience but told everyone what a loser he was and a pervert too. I was barely eighteen and he was almost thirty. I guess he couldn't find a virgin his own age. After I said "no" to him, he found another virgin and asked her to marry him because he had to marry a virgin. He was like my dad with his rules about women "Do what I say, woman!" I pity the woman who marries him!

Soon after, I got a feeling something was wrong. I thought I had a bladder infection or something, so I went to my children's doctor so he could have a look at me. The first question he asked me was, "Are you sexually active?" I answered honestly, "Well, yes. Why?" He said, "You have Gonorrhea. I need to give you a shot of Penicillin but I know your dad is allergic, so I need to know if you are too." He called my dad, they went to college together, so they knew each other. He asked him, "Hey doc! Is your daughter allergic to Penicillin? She needs a shot, she got the clap! Haha! I will see you at the reunion." Doctor-patient confidentiality, my ass.

I drove home and found a letter taped to the door of my bedroom from dad. That's how I knew I was in trouble. Dad would type out a formal letter to tell me how disappointed he was in me and sign it. My father had no communication skills, even with his own kids. My father thought anyone who got any type of V.D. were dirty, filthy people and beneath him. From that point on, my dad thought I was wasted for anyone. I asked my dad, "Dad, were you a virgin when you married mom?" He replied, "Of course not, but I am a man. It is different." My curious tongue continues, "Does mom know about it?" He changed the subject and diverted the question.

I could never tell him I liked girls too, or tell my mom about it. It was not like my mom wouldn't understand my bisexual status, hell, I didn't even understand it, but I think it would be very confusing to her, to say the least. I was dating women in secret because I didn't want to be rejected by everyone, not just straight people but gays too. I was afraid of notions like, "She can't make up her mind what you are anyway." Yeah, that's fucked up no matter who it comes from. I started to go out by myself because I didn't want to talk about it with anyone and offend them or say something wrong. Nobody had an "owner's manual" for newly bisexual people. I was on my own to figure this out for myself, and when you don't know how to approach this comfortably, it's a little scary. Not because I was in L.A., but I was new with everything, and I was so sheltered. That's why I went to my children's doctor to look at me. I didn't know any better! I couldn't talk to my mom about sex; I was expected to be a virgin until I was married.

Most of my friends went away to college but I stayed home, where I went to school, so I didn't have my friends' support for spreading my wings with nobody to catch me if I fell. I will tell you about one woman I dated, she was fun, but she was really just using me like a sugar-mama situation. I didn't let her buy me things. She just paid for us to go out. All of her friends had younger girlfriends, and she had to have one too. Just like the guys who are married, who have their cake and eat it too, she only had me around for looks. We would go out to places I couldn't afford but she could, so it was fun for a while, but she got to a point where she was calling me all the time. She would be anxiously asking me, "Just checking to see if you still love me." I didn't know how to tell her that it got old. I tried to communicate to her that I needed some space, and she accused me of being with men behind her back. I had enough of it and called it off. She wasn't happy, but we were really using each other. I wanted to go out, and she wanted a young girlfriend to make her look good. It was clear that neither of us was in it for the long haul.

I also went out with a woman who I never slept with, but what a joy it was! She was fun. I have to admit that I miss her. She was a dyke and a blast! We were polar opposites, but what a fun woman she was, the only woman I really ever loved other than my sister. She let me be myself and didn't try to make me feel like I didn't fit in. She was the easiest-going woman I had ever met, but I was too young and wanted to just party and have fun. I wasn't looking for commitment. We parted as friends but I miss her to this day.

There was a time I took a job as an assistant. Well, I mostly was just a gopher. I worked with a dominatrix. Very interesting I think she hired me because she knew I was new with sex in general. She hired me to see how I'd react, just for laughs, but some of it was shocking. My mistress only had high-end clients. I am talking big money, guys. I still have some of my old gear; my whips, a leather corset, a big black strap-on. I even got to model some of it! AAHHH, the good old days! I can just put that on my resume of weird jobs I've had. YEP!

I do have a bit of advice: don't loan out your padded cuffs! It takes all four to make a lasting impression. You need all four, even if the guy is blindfolded. He'll know and might think, "Is this a bungee cord?" It ruins the mood. It was just one of those jobs that made a lasting impression. I would love to see my mistress work on that guy from Shark Tank, Mr. Wonderful. He could use a good thrashing if you ask me. It wouldn't surprise me if Kevin hadn't already seen her. What an ego that guy has. I'm sure he's friends with Trump. What do you bet? I know he comes from a humble upbringing but is not very polite to some of the people trying to present their ideas. Barbra, Lori, the rest of them don't lose their manners when they do a deal. Why can't he? You would think with all his money, he could afford some manners. He should change his name to Mr. Asshole! If Mr. Wonderful hears about this, he will probably say, "She is some nobody comedian she's dead to me." I wouldn't know what to do if he did that except to laugh in his face and say, "No thanks, I'm out."

In my list of the weirdest experiences I have had in my life, one of them is when I started a midget fight. Yes, you heard me. I started a midget fight, but it wasn't my fault. That little shit started it! I was in Hollywood, of course, in

1988. I was meeting some friends. It was way before the "little people" shows. Now keep in mind that I didn't know about the whole "little people" thing. I found out that night. I walked into the restaurant, and there was no place to sit because all the seats were taken up by men with no manners. There was one seat available. It was next to this woman who was a midget. I looked over, and guess what? There was a whole booth full of midgets! I started smiling, who wouldn't? I love midgets! It always reminded me of The Wizard of Oz, the first film my Mom saw in color. I also loved Snow White with those cute little dwarfs! So I asked her, "May I sit here?" She said in her little midget voice, "Yes, be my guest." So I sat down. I had to kind of squish down because I felt like a giant.

I said, "Hi, I'm Jan, and you are?" She replied, "Jan? Like from the Brady Bunch Jan? I continued, "Yes. Like Jan from the Brady Bunch. Marsha, Marsha, Marsha!" Jesus! She laughed hard. I had to ask, as it was Hollywood, "Are you all in the business? Is there a movie you're in that has a lot of midgets in it?" She told me, "No, some of the girls are, but I don't live here. We all know each other."

She was really pretty. You couldn't tell she was a midget from just looking at her face; she looked like an average woman but from the neck down, definitely a midget! We chatted about her family and she was nice, and I said, "You live in Vegas?" She said, "Yes, so do some of the other girls too." I wanted to desperately ask her if they worked at Circus-Circus, but that would have been too much.

Further in the conversation, she told me, "We don't go by midget anymore, we prefer little people." I said, "Don't you find that offending, like you are beneath us?" I didn't know this was 1988. She explained, "Well, we don't and some of the girls get a little offended by that term." I asked, "You mean midget?" By this time, I had spewed out the word midget like three or four times and this tree-stump midget – I know all their kinds, I just don't know what they are called – looking like a tree-stump disco ball, was eyeing me. Her dress was silver and had tiny beads on that shimmered when she moved. She was glaring at me. I asked the girl I was talking to, "You mean her?" She looked over her shoulder and shifted her gaze towards me again, "Yep, her, alright?"

I smiled at her, midgets usually make me smile, I can't help it. She had started to get really mad at that point. She thought I was making fun of her. She asked, "What did she say?" The women she was with were watching her get riled up. Her friends were trying to tell her, "She doesn't know any better. Let it go."

She placed her drink down and grunted, "Did you say midget? You can't say that!" I quickly responded, "I am sorry, I didn't know." I realized I was laughing while I was apologizing because this was so funny to me. The midget I was talking to said to her drunken little friend, "Leave her alone. She knows now, let it go." I looked at her and I couldn't stop staring at her panties. Her mother didn't teach her how to sit properly in a dress, her little legs were sticking straight out. I could see her flowered panties. Maybe the tree-stump disco ball midget should have dinner with Madonna. Neither of them knew how to sit properly in a restaurant. Tree-stump midget was so mad, she jumped off her chair, and I lost it. I laughed my ass off! She was shorter than she was on the chair. She looked at me and stated, "I'm a black belt. I'll kick your ass." I thought, okay. Let me tee you up. KICK. See ya, midget! Kidding couldn't do that. I stood up, I must have looked like Jolly the Green Giant. I was in a green dress. I told her friend, "Thanks, I'd better go." She said, "Sorry, she gets like this when she gets drunk." I replied, "Yeah, I get it." I didn't want it to look like David and Goliath. I thanked her for letting me sit with her. I looked back at her drunken friend and said, "See ya, midget," and I ran. That was all I needed to get a bunch of ankle-biters after me. Can you just picture it, me running down the street being chased by a bunch of drunken pissed-off midgets? Only in Hollywood!

I was watching Naked and Afraid. I'd do it if I was in my twenties. They would let me have shoes and sunglasses, underwear, my toothbrush, a pillow, a blanket, a tent, a fishing gear, and a thirty-out for hunting, along with a lighter and all my cooking gear. I would also get a mosquito netting and a bag of gummies with T.H.C. Then, I'd do Naked and Afraid. There was this half-midget on it, Frodo. He wasn't really super short, but he was considered a midget. He had the worst case of short men complex. I'd never seen that! Look, I can do it, and I'm a midget! Yeah, we know you can do it, but you are still four feet tall. Unless your cock is twelve inches long, I'm not that impressed. I have dated guys who were shorter than me. They would say, "Oh, it is okay. You're taller than me." Really bullshit! I went out with this guy, who took me to a Christmas party. I was dolled up! I was wearing an outfit that looked smoking hot! I took off my jacket to reveal my dress. He looked at me, up and down, and said, "Thanks for wearing your flats for me tonight." Boy, you are so not getting laid tonight. I felt like saying, "Look at you, when you are naked, you look like an albino Gorilla, you hairy little Scottsman!" I let it go. I wish I could say, "Yeah, you're not uncomfortable with your height. That's why you wear those cowboy boots all the time with the lifts in them because you're okay with your height." I should have worn stilettos and called him "Shorty" in front of his family to see what they said, but I held back. It was Christmas.

I guess I shouldn't make fun of short people; I was the shortest kid in my class growing up. I grew up tough shit, get over it. So if I offended that little guy from the Naked and Afraid, if he comes after me, I'm not worried. I will just use humor to defend myself. If he doesn't like it, I'll run. I may be old, but I still have a good foot and a half on him. He'll never catch me. I know I'm probably going to get a lot of shit for this. Live and learn! I'd love to go to the "little people" convention! I wouldn't even need to talk to anyone to have fun. I would just smile, and hum to myself 'The Yellow Brick Road' and think of Willy Wonka, Leprachauns, Snow White, Willow, Court Jesters, Star Wars With The Little Ewoks, Santas Elves, Midget Tossing, Michael J. Fox. Danny Devito, Napoleon, The Old Midget Medium From Poltergieste, Billy Barty, Lil-Kim, and anyone under five feet tall, and enjoy myself. Without anyone telling me, I'm inappropriate for being happy in my own way!

I would never run up to someone and say something that would hurt their feelings unless I was defending someone and backing them up! I'm not going to be polite to someone who is an asshole and tell him, "Oh excuse me, you slightly big-boned person, would you not do that? It hurts him, that's not nice." No, I'm going after anything I can if anyone is going after someone's weight, height, sexuality, dick size, his mother, his voice, mannerism, the way they dress, and all of it. I won't worry about his *wittle-fweelings*. I will treat any midget or little person equally like the same way I treat regular-sized people so if you're a dick and you are being mean to someone, midget or not, you're a dick! You're nothing special.

I'm a comedian and a writer, and I don't care if you don't like it all. All I can say is, lighten up, you little people/midgets. If you are all worked up and having a little midget fit, go ahead. You can yell and scream all you want. I still think it's kind of amusing as long as you're not a drunk pissed-off midget. Then stay away from me. I do carry pepper spray, but if those little guys were in a crowd, I... no... I was going to say, "I might be scared," but really, I still think I could take them unless those little fuckers whipped out a sword, a dagger or some medieval crap to defend themselves with. I know it's not the fifteenth century Scotland or New Zealand, but that's how I vision them defending themselves like Snow White and The Huntsman. I don't know, I guess some of them hunt; they would be great for gopher hunting. Sadly, I have never seen one at the range before.

In 1989, I was 21 and I took a job at a restaurant in Pasadena. This very nice Jewish man who owned it and quite a few restaurants in Pasadena he was a successful restaurateur. I liked him but his son Robert ran the restaurant I worked in and he was a scumbag, a womanizer. He made a rather aggressive pass at me. It made me sick to think about it. I rejected him and he fired me, in front of my co-workers. They were right behind me. He looked at me with a smile on his face and said, "Well, I think I can do better than you for an employee. So, I'm going on vacation with my new fiancé and you can look for another job." I was crying. My friend, who was an assistant manager was next to him. He couldn't even look at me. He started to leave, I stood up and said, "You're firing me because I wouldn't fuck you." In front of everyone, he stood up and said, "I don't know what she is talking about." Right after, he left. I was so upset. My assistant manager told me that he'll call you later. I looked at some of the faces of the women I worked with, thought how many times this guy had done this before.

I got home, and my friend called me. I asked him, "He's done this to another girl before, hasn't he?" He replied, exhaling a heavy breath, "Yes, it's not just you." I told him, "Give me her number, I want to know what he did to her." He gave me her number and I talked to her. After we spoke, I talked to other women. Eight women in two years were victims of his disgusting advances. Eight women in two years! I told those women what he did to me, and I found out that they got it worse than I did. I told them that I was going to talk to an attorney. All of those women wanted justice, so did I.

It was way before the Me Too movement. It was just me. I couldn't tell my mom I was fired for not sleeping with my boss, and telling my father I worked for a Jew was not an option. My dad hated Jews more than blacks. He used to say, "Jews are sneaky, you can't tell who they are." What a prick. I really liked his dad. I wouldn't let anything bad happen to him and after what happened to Todd's car, if I told my dad a Jew made a pass at me, it wouldn't have been good for his father. I just wanted justice but didn't know how to go about it and I didn't want to tell anyone, but I had no choice and this was not his dad's fault.

I went to a friend's dad who was a lawyer. I didn't know who else to talk to and it was so embarrassing. He was a contractual attorney, but he listened. I couldn't tell him the details of him making a pass at me, but he told me, "You can file a wrongful termination case against him. Go to the fair housing and employment agency of California, and get a wrongful termination form. We will fill it out together. Okay?" For that, I had put a suit on. I had never been to a building like that. I went to get my license at the D.M.V. but, that's it. I didn't know what to expect. I was wildly overdressed. I took a number and waited for about an hour. I did notice, I was the only white person there. My number was called. I went up to the woman, and she was not very excited to see me. The woman was black, and probably didn't like most white people. I looked at her and said, "I hope I'm in the right place. May I please have a wrongful termination form?" She went to get it and came back. "Here," she handed it over to me. I said to her, "I hope you don't mind. I can't talk to my Mom about this, and I'm not quite sure that I'm handling this properly. I need a woman's opinion, do you mind?" I think she recognized from the tone of my voice or the look on my face that I was scared to death, and embarrassed.

She dropped the whole "fuck Whitey" attitude and said, "Sure honey, you can talk to me." I looked up at her, and started balling. I hadn't talked to anybody about this. I was so upset and embarrassed. "My boss fired me in front of everyone at work because I wouldn't sleep with him. He tried to get me in his bed, and he was all hairy. He said we were electric, so sleezy. I rejected him, and he did this to eight other women. I talked to them, and it was worse for them! Some of those women slept with him, but I didn't, so it is not sexual harassment for me, but it was for them. But they didn't go to an attorney. I am not sure how to help them, my Mom doesn't even know I lost my job, and I like his dad. I don't want him to get hurt, I don't think anyone will believe me because nobody saw it. Now he's engaged to some girl who has no idea he's a schmuck. Someone should warn that girl. I don't think she has a clue. God, I don't know if I'm doing the right thing. She stopped me, "Okay honey, you don't have to cry. It's okay." She handed me a Kleenex and told me, "Here is what you are going to do, fill this out with your friend's dad, and you are going to list all of those women, and their addresses, so when he does this again, and he will, this will be on the record. He can't run from this." I said, "I can do that?" She explained, "Yes, you can and have him served at his work. He fired you at work. It is only fair he gets the same treatment, so everyone knows about it." I was shocked. I really thought nothing would happen at all, but she said, "This guy is caught. He just doesn't know it yet. You're doing the right thing." I thought she was trying to get me to stop crying. I cannot forget how she was so nice to me. I think she did everything for me she could, and more. Wonderful woman! I hope she hears about this. I didn't get her name but thank you!

So I did it. I had him served at work in front of everyone, and he was fuming mad! My friend, who was the assistant manager, called me and told me in the most amusing tone, "He is pissed!" I settled for one month's lost wages and dropped it. I know he got engaged, but I hoped she was a smart woman and called it off! It wasn't about the money; it was the principle of the thing. I do know that about a year later, his dad fired him for embezzlement from his own father's restaurants. What a schmuck! He was stealing from his dad. I think even some of the chefs knew what Robert was up to, but they didn't want to lose their jobs.

I went to a taste of Pasadena or some fair we cooked for with the restaurant. I was talking to the chefs, and one of the guys told me Robert would come to the event and steal all of the cash they made. I think a lot of people knew what was really going on. I don't think my wrongful termination case was anything Robert needed to worry about. That jerk was a thief after all. I can't believe he would do that to his dad. His dad gave him everything and it wasn't enough for the bastard. His dad was so nice too, what a shame for him. I hope his dad hears about this. I hope for your sake he has grown up and gotten himself together. I know you didn't know about anything your son was up to, but you're a good man and I respect you. I wish you all the best.

I met my ex-fiancé Eric shortly after that, and his mother wanted to go to one of the restaurants the guy's dad owned while the case was pending. I told her in the car on the way over there, "I shouldn't go in there, I have a pending case against the owner's son." But she acted like it was nothing and when we got out of the car and started to get out, I said again, "I am sorry. I can't go in there." She gave me a dirty look and rolled her eyes, and said, "Well, I guess we can change our plans for you." Then we went someplace else. I should have known then, this is not a bitch to trust on what she says, and her son is never going to back me up. When I said I can't go in there, my ex said to me, "It is not that big of a deal. My mom wants to go here, come on." I didn't tell her the details of what happened, but I don't think she would care. I was embarrassed about what happened, but I didn't want everyone to know about it. That's the thing about being in that position; you don't know if anyone will believe you and it's so humiliating.

I have been friends with drug dealers, not ashamed to admit it. There were two in L.A. and one in Denver. I'll tell you about them a little, but I won't tell you their names. I'll tell you this: I didn't sleep with either of them, we would just hang out. The one guy who lived in L.A., his apartment was right next to the Hollywood police department. I thought that was funny. He wasn't a flashy guy. He showed me some of his Rolexes. I knew what he did but we really didn't discuss it. He wasn't my dealer. He introduced me to his Mom, who was a cancer survivor. She was so funny. She threw her breast implant at a co-worker as a joke. She had breast cancer and was such a good sport about it. I thought she was great.

He also got a little chow puppy. I mean, this guy had a heart of gold. We only saw each other a couple of times but he was a sweetie. He gave me a heads-up once at a club. He told me and a girlfriend I was with, "Heads up. Something's going to go down here, you should go." I said, "Thanks." My girlfriend was like, "I want to stay." I said, "Go ahead, I'm out!" He was looking out for me. One of the other guys was in Denver. We didn't really date so much. It was all about hanging out. He took me to a few clubs, he was sweet. I was kind of over the party life. They had no idea how much I partied in the '80s in Los Angeles. The parties I went to in Denver, they were all doing coke but not me. I think some of them thought I was a cop. It wasn't like I didn't do coke, I just didn't do shwagg coke! I was an L.A. coke snob. I don't know if either of them will even remember me at all. They were both good-looking and surrounded by girls everywhere. I was just some chick they hung out with a few times, but not all drug dealers are bad guys.

In the year 1987, I was in Los Angeles and at a drug dealer's house, and I knew it. I walked in and I'm in a 'barely there dress'. It was the '80s, bad make-up, big hair era after all. I worked part-time as a dominatrix and I thought, "What the hell? I will wear this and see what happens!" I'm not going to describe what I had on. Use your imagination. I think I would need paint remover to get that outfit off. The drug dealer didn't know who I was. He was checking my outfit out and I couldn't decide whether I should laugh or shoot my ass, but he was smiling. The guy I was with left, and I was there alone with him.

I have to say that his house was beautiful, really stunning. He had good taste in art. I was dying to ask, "Where did you find this beautiful piece? What gallery? Was it here or New York?" I know art fairly well, but I didn't want to push it because there was a gun on the table, only a nine mil. Chick gun, but if I started with what I know about weapons, he could've thought that I was a cop, and POW! Maybe I'll keep that information to myself.

I smiled, he smiled back. Thank God! I said, "Hi, I'm Jan." He joked, "Like the Brady Bunch Jan?" Yeah, I acted like I never heard that in my life. Showing my big smile, I replied, "Yes, Marsha, Marsha, Marsha." and we both laughed. He told me, "Have a seat, please." I was thinking, "Okay, he is polite." I don't think he wanted to kill me yet. We start to chat, and I'm not going into any specifics, private conversations. We did talk about food, I told him, "I'm a chef." he snorted in a cute way, "Ah, a skinny chef? They say never trust a skinny chef." That's true. It's a saying, after all. So, I told him, "I used to weigh three hundred pounds." He was shocked and said, "Really?" I was joking. I thought to come clean to him as his face was making me lose my composure. "No, I'm fucking with you, but I am a very good chef. Ask me anything," I challenged him. Cooking is something I do well, so I was not worried about him asking me anything.

He asked me a few questions, and he didn't think I could answer, but of course I knew what I was talking about, but he didn't know me so it was a little test to see if I was full of shit. I think I passed, so we got along. It turned out that this guy liked to cook. You never know where the really good recipes come from! My Mom has the best recipe for New York Cheesecake. She got it from a guy who looked like Motley Crew, and she met him where she was taking a class at P.C.C., just for fun. His name was Philip, and he gave mom his recipe, and it's wonderful!! My mom would strike up a conversation with anyone, you know why. My mom doesn't judge a book by its cover, and neither do I!! Just because he was a drug dealer doesn't mean he didn't have any other interests.

I gave him one of my favorite recipes. He showed me his beautiful kitchen that night. I told him, "I am so jealous." My friend came back, and told me, "Let's go." I said to him, "It was lovely meeting you, thank you. You're a darling man. Let's do lunch sometime." He looked at my friend, giggled a little, he continued, "Maybe sometime." He was mirroring the big smile on my face, gave me a hug, we left. I hope he hears about this. I'd ask him, "Did you try my recipe? Hope you liked it!" I'm pretty sure he was just being nice to a silly white girl from Pasadena. I told him the truth when he asked me something, I answered him honestly. I don't think he was expecting me to tell him the truth. I think he got lied to a lot! He was very pleasant, kind and he had good manners too. He was a drug dealer, so what? His mama raised him right!

I was stuck in Chicago when I met a guy who, I'm pretty sure was in the mafia. He knew I was stuck there and invited me to go hear Big Band Music. I was thrilled to go, he was so charming and polite. The people who owned the place knew him, so we didn't have to wait in line. They welcomed us right in. It was Jilly's in Chicago. They made some women move for us, so we had a nice table. He got us a bottle of champagne. All these big Italian men came over, gave him the big Italian bear hug. Boy, those guys liked to eat and introduced themselves to me. He even took me dancing, and he even danced well! That will always be one of the best dates of my life! I wish to God all my dates were a tenth that good. But I know these experiences are always once in a lifetime! I'll never forget it! He and the guys who dealt with drugs, we never talked about their business and I liked it that way. It was none of my business. Just because you're a drug dealer or in the mafia doesn't mean you are a horrible person. Some of them go to church and have kids, the same stuff we do. They just do this or that thing on the side. My experience, the drug dealers and mafia I have met, were polite, funny, kind, and delightful. I have only good memories of all of them. They will always be in my thoughts and prayers. It's funny you would think they were dangerous, but they were so fun to be around. They were just lovely men, all of them.

I was in the Hollywood foothills in 1986 and saw the biggest cock I've ever seen. Of course he was black! I walked into the wrong room, I guess. He wasn't a very big guy, but I swear to God it went down to his knees. This guy turned around and went, "What do you think?" I said, "Why is your dick holding its breath?" I laughed and ran away. At least I didn't tell him he had neat purple lips! Never got his name but I'm sure he does porn. There is such a thing as too big! Jesus! I'm smiling while I'm writing this. The visual image of his huge cock reminds me of Boogie Nights, but bigger and more purple-ish. I hope that was him with a hard-on. If it wasn't, somebody out there is in real trouble!

I went to so many parties with no invitation and didn't know a soul. I would put my ear to the ground when I walked onto all those lots, I would just follow a crowd. If anyone asked, I offered them a little bump and skated my way around. The question isn't that terrible, but if you had a good blow, it opens doors. I would ask people who worked on the lots, that what was going on, where were people going, and what parties to go to? Why not? I was young and I wanted to see everything! Nobody gave me a second glance or said, "Hey, who are you?" It was like I was invisible. It was fun, mostly.

I don't look back and say, God, I wish I didn't do that. I never got arrested or in serious trouble. I look back and go, God that was so much fun, scary but fun. Glad we didn't get caught! I consider myself very lucky that I didn't get into any serious trouble. I had a very Hollywood moment when I drove right next to Billy Idol on Laurel Canyon drive. I had just left Yamachiros in Hollywood. It was above the Magic Castle, one of the best views in Hollywood Billy had a maroon white wall-sided Porsche, with the top off. I looked at him, smiled and waved. He wove back with that crooked smile on his face. It was great!

I have a recommendation to make to everyone. Don't go see The Little Mermaid with a friend who is with you after he's done a window pane hit of acid. That was embarrassing. We almost got kicked out when she got her legs and walked out of the ocean to her Prince. He went nuts with, "Oh yes, she loves him forever!" Shut it down buddy, it's only a movie. There are times and places to do drugs, not in a crowded movie theater. Do that shit at a Grateful Dead concert. I did have fun dropping "one hit" of acid and going to Griffith Park Lazer Show. Wow, was that a trip! No, we didn't drive! I have babysat so many people when they've done a little too much. It got old after a while. The older I got, the less I had to be the responsible one at the party.

I've left many parties with puke on my shoes. Most of them had no idea what kind of trouble they could have gotten into. I had to remove a couple of girls from clubs and parties so they wouldn't get arrested or make a bigger fool out of themselves than they already did. I had to take a girl out of a wedding reception in front of my boss because she was making a fool out of herself and he was the best man. He called me the next day to thank me, I felt for his best friend and his family. They were really nice people. I wanted to stay for the reception, but she needed to go. Same thing happened to me in L.A. We were at Vertigos and the girl I was with was getting out of hand. I had to remove her before she got arrested. The owner was nice to me. I told him, "Sorry about her. I will get her out of here." The owner, he said, "Thank you. You can come back if you like."

Sometimes, it sucks doing the right thing. I saved a girl from getting arrested, and she didn't even thank me the next day. It was in Denver, Colorado, when we were leaving a bar about sixteen years ago. She got into it with her drunk-ass boyfriend. I broke it up and landed on the ground. The police helped me to my feet, he backhanded me really hard. I've never been hit like that before. He had a ring on, and I was a little stunned. The cop that helped me to my feet asked, "Are you alright?" I said, "Yes, I'm a little shaken up, but I'm alright." I looked up and they were putting her and the boyfriend in cuffs. I said to the cop that helped me up, "This was his fault she didn't do anything except try to leave him. Please let her go, my dad is a cop." Sad, but this usually got them on my side. They related to me and let her go and arrested the boyfriend. I don't know what happened to the drunk-ass boyfriend, but I never saw her again, no thanks, nothing. Well, not nothing, I got a black cheek.

I think if I was black in that scenario, it would have gone very differently. White privilege; I was white and the cops were white. I'm really trying to see things from a different perspective. It's hard to do when you're white and that's all you know. I'm glad we are seeing more information about racism on T.V., the internet, in magazines, on billboards, and on our phones. Keep cramming that information down our throats!! Until then, I'm not going to give false hope but until we kind of get what you mean. Wise up and try to get a clue about what's really happening in this world. Let's try the truth for a change. If we can't see the injustice in this country, we are either very stupid or blind. I'd like to say something poignant, but nothing comes to mind except, wisen up Whiteys. How's that?

I went out with some girls who really partied. They dressed like preppy whores; I guess that's the best way to describe us to you. God, some of the stuff I wore out. Sometimes, I'd have to change at a friend's, and you couldn't tell from here to there. I was wearing anything until I moved. Oh, I guess she does have clothes on, that kind of stuff. It was fun! I had a great body, I showed it off and got a lot of attention. Fuck it. I was not looking to find a husband, I wanted to party! I knew I was never going to be able to wear any of that stuff when I got older. But some of the older actresses and performers who think, "I still got it." Like let's say, Madonna. In my opinion, either donate their old sexy stuff to the Smithsonian or burn it, but please don't think, "Hey, I can still pull this look off!" No, you can't and your friends are dicks to tell you, "Oh, you look great in that!" No, you don't. Leave that stuff for the twenty and thirty-year-olds. Hang it up, grandma!

We went to dinner and were going to a party in the Hollywood foothills on a Saturday night. The girls were going with their guys, and I knew who I was going with. The guy who had the best blow I've ever had in my entire life!!!! Yep, I'm going with him for sure. This blow was a champagne blow that glistens down your throat and makes you tingle all over, that kind of blow. It makes my nipples hard just to think about it. Don't judge, it was the '80s. In

L.A., sorry Nancy, I couldn't say no. We were at the valet's and this guy was so 80s. He was only about 5'4. I towered over him; I'm 6'1 in heels. He didn't care, thank God. He was dressed like Don Johnson from Miami-Vice. His hair was slicked back on the sides, and he was wearing a white suit with the sleeves rolled up. He had on a T-shirt and loafers with no socks, gold chains. He almost looked gay. He was also Jewish and didn't look like Don Johnson at all, but he sure wanted to. He looked at me and said, "I hope you like Lamborghinis!" I think that's a line from a cheesy '80s movie and here came a Lamborghini. I was not happy in that dress. I looked at the valet with concern in my face and he went, "Don't worry, I'll get you in safely." He took off his jacket, and helped me in. "Here you go, I have you." What an angel. I got in, gave him a twenty, and said, "Thank you so much!" He replied, "You're welcome." and shut the door. The doors went up on this car. He shut me in. It was like being in a sardine can covered in soft leather.

The guy I was with didn't tip the valet. I looked at the guy who helped me in, showed him the twenty I gave him, and he shrugged. That was a cheap move but the blow was so good. I'll let it go for now. He got in and I told him, "I know exactly where we're going, it's just up King's Road, not far. Just go slow, I don't want to get car sick." I warned him more than once. He didn't listen, but my stomach heard it. We started up King's Road, it was really windy and I didn't make it. I projectile vomited from the corner of the dash, over the top of the steering wheel, up his sleeve, across his neck, down his chest, and into his lap. He was covered in it. Not one drop on me! Do you know why? Because I tipped the valet, he didn't. That was his bad karma! He should have tipped the valet. For every guy that's ever valet-parked for him or anyone like him, fuck him, that's for you. I didn't know how to get the door open, the valet shut it, and the doors went up. Oh no!

He was screaming, "FUCK, FUCK, FUCK!" I was yelling, "Get the door open. I can't get it open!" He leaned over with the arm that was not covered in puke and opened the door. What he didn't know was that I had a sinking feeling that would happen so when we started up King's Road, I took my shoes off. I opened the door all the way and he said, "Go get help!" I could just say, "Okay, and ran." I was running, top speed, coked out of my mind, half-naked with my shoes in one hand and purse in the other.

Yeah, nothing could go wrong in this scenario. I flagged down a car. This sweetheart of a guy picked me up. He asked me if I needed the police or wanted to go to a hospital. I must have looked awful. My eyes where all dilated and I was a sweaty mess from running. I said, "No, bad date." He was so sweet; he offered me his driver's license, in case I thought he was a psychopath or something. He told me, "Here is my ID, if it makes you feel safer." I just said, "Let's get out of here, okay?" We got stuck in traffic; it was a Saturday night in Hollywood, so I told him what happened. He laughed his ass off! I got home safely, good guardian angel, thank you again! I got cleaned up and I suddenly realized. Oh God! I was such an idiot, oh fuck! I forgot, I wasn't thinking. Jan, you moron! You left the blow! How could you do that? That was the best blow I ever had. Only if I was really thinking clearly, I would have stopped, dug through that vomit and then ran.

Oh well, live and learn. I'll bet if this gets to the ears of, I don't know, say Johnny Depp, Christian Slater or anyone of those guys during that time, they'd go, "The 80's gold Lamborghini? Yeah, he had some good blow alright." I hope the guy that helped me that night hears this; thank you so much! And I'm sorry I couldn't share any of that great blow with you. Oops, my bad.

CHAPTER THIRTEEN: DURANDO, CANCER, AND RIOTS

I fell in love and moved to Colorado, like all the other California dicks. I did it a long time ago, so I've paid my dues. So I tell dad I need a jeep! Yeah, I know, spoiled. We were packing the jeep and dad said, "You can take the gun!" I told him, "Dad, I think they have guns in Colorado. I don't need one, thanks." He answered, "You can take the one in your car." I was driving around with a loaded 9 mm in my car and didn't even know about it. Dad just randomly continued, "If some spick tries to steal your car, put one in his head like I showed you." I was so glad to get out of there!

I didn't move to Denver, nope. It was Durango in the S.W. corner, about two hours from Telluride. I lived in a little log cabin ten miles outside of town for the first year. No cable or T.V. Love makes you crazy! I was with my ex, Eric for five years and when I describe him to you, you are going to go, "Why did she put up with that stoner loser?"

Well in my defense, I didn't have a lot of experience. He was my second boyfriend, and I prayed day and night, "Lord, please let him grow up." It was never going to happen. I put up with Eric for a long time. I tried, I really did. I have a lot of patience with children and that's what Eric was, a big stoned child. We did go to Mesa Verde, saw the Luminarias during Christmas. It was really beautiful! They also did the hot air balloons in Durango, and that was really beautiful too. They did cowboy poetry and drove the cows down from the mountains every year. The duck races were carried out in the Animus River. We would vacation in Telluride, and see festivals there. We would go see the colors change during the fall. It was stunning! There's a place in Telluride called The Peeks, it's a hotel with the most gorgeous view from the bar. They have the best sunset, the most splendid I have ever seen! All the colors of the mountains come out. If you get to Telluride, go see it in the fall but be careful in La Plata County. They have the highest D.U.I.s in any county in Colorado. Small ski town, a lot of people drink, and cops don't have much to do.

I found out pretty quickly that the largest K. K. K. membership in Colorado was in Bayfield outside of Durango. I'd get information in the mail without an address in it for meetings. I never told anyone about getting information in the mail. This happened when we moved into town and I started to go to church. I knew some of the guys I went to church with were in the Klan, but I didn't get involved with church, like I did in L.A. I just went for me but, someone knew I was there and I've had more than one run in with them. I guess when you're white, the Klan, no matter where you are, will invite you to their club and welcome you. They don't want to miss out on a new recruit. A lot of them stand behind the cloth to look more presentable, and sometimes it works.

The Klan did want to go up to Fort Lewis College to give a lecture about "White superior supreme howdy ho bullshit race power show" or something stupid, and they couldn't do it because they couldn't get enough security for it and I think it is funny. What are a bunch of hippies going to do to the K.K.K? Blow pot, smoke in their face, burn them some sage, play on their bongos, or make an eye-opening deeply spiritual banner made from hemp? The worst thing they could do to them is just stand next to them downwind. None of those fuckers were armed except with B.O. I'm pretty sure the Klan have some experienced hunters in their group, so if those hippies want help fighting them, it's not going to happen, not in that town. Do they know how many guys in the police department are in the Klan? No, they don't. If anything happened, the police would probably back up the Klan. It's a good thing they didn't do their little hate speech. The hippies should consider themselves lucky. When I moved to Durango, some stupid dumb fuck hippie had a banner that said "Free Mandella." This was after he got out of prison. Go smoke another bowl, you stupid hippie.

I worked at the Teddy Bear camp at Purgatory Ski Resort. It's where I saw how fucked up rich white people were. These rich white parents treat their kids like luggage. "Oh, here is my kid. I can't remember his name, but I know who designed his outfit, go make him ski!" Those rich white fucks didn't care about their kids. They weren't all like that, just 75-80 % of them. I would always rescue a kid who didn't want to ski and take him under my wing. I felt bad for some of them. They come on vacation with their family and they are put in a room with hundred kids they don't know in an unfamiliar environment at an altitude they are not used to. Some of the kids would get altitude sickness, which is not uncommon. The kids haven't had anything but a high-top tennis shoe on their foot. Some of them had never been in the snow; they just wanted us to put them in ski boots and expect them to be comfortable?

These parents would get mad at the kids and us as we didn't make them ski because they were sick or just overwhelmed? Why couldn't they play with their own kids? I guess it was too much of a stretch for them to give a shit; just pass them off to someone else and let them do it. It's no wonder these kids wind up with separation anxiety and turn to drugs. Not all white parents were bad. I met Dan Marino there, as he was there for a charity skiing for the blind. He was a good daddy. I watched his daughter Markie? I think that was her name. She had the most beautiful hair. I knew he was a football player. I asked him if he played for the broncos, and he told me who he played for but I forgot. No offense, but I don't pay much attention to the game. He was nice. Dan Marino is a loving father.

I worked at a couple of restaurants. One was owned by this total dick with the name Jerry. The place was called Old Timers. That prick made his employees come in once a year and made them clean, fix up, and paint the place without pay! He told all of us that we were required to be there or we would get fired. He was one of the cheapest bastards on the planet; he didn't want to waste a dime on anything. I don't know how that asshole got away with that. Hey Jerry, remember me? That shit that you do is illegal! I hope he gets sued for not paying his employees because he did that shit for years. Heads up, if you worked for Jerry at Old Timers in Durango, he owes you past wages. Find out others he did that to and get an attorney! It was a small town, and jobs were scarce, so this white prick could do whatever he felt. Also, Jerry hated kids. I remember that he used to wear his polo shirts with the collar up, and walk around like he was God's gift to everyone. His wife, she was a piece of work too. They were both assholes. I guess there are arrogant assholes in every town, but this couple sure gave every one of them some competition. They were rude and full of themselves I hope they enjoy each other's company because nobody else does.

I worked with a sweetheart of a girl, Michelle in Durango. I catered her wedding reception at our church. It was a sit-down dinner with individual stuffed Cornish game hens for sixty people. Whew. It went beautifully. I think her dad was a cop. I threw her a bachelorette party too, but I kept it low-key. I surely miss her.

I also went to a hippie wedding, and it was just like you think it would be. We climbed up a hill outside the wedding with bongo players, and there was a black guy playing guitar; Bob Marley stuff. Once again, I was wildly overdressed! It was a lovely wedding though. I just stood downwind from all the Patchouli. Halloween was fun too. Once, we went as Mama and Papa Bears. A friend of ours put pasta in his hair with a big red, gold and green hat on. He said, "I'm a Pastafarian."

Other kids put on dress suits and looked like they were in a wind tunnel. They would all walk by and go, whoosh! It was very clever. I dressed up for a white trash party like Peg Bundy; wore a one-piece dark red velvet body suit, a gold belt, big hair and stilettos. The guy I was with dressed like the cousin Eddy from vacation. They served Twinkies and Pabst Blue Ribbon. It was fun. I wish my cousin Walt could have seen it. I think he would fit in, but I don't know how everyone would take his Bible banging. They did this thing in Durango in the off-season. It's a small seasonal town, so the restaurants would do a buy-one-get-one-free dinner. A lot of the higher-end restaurants do that, so we would take advantage of it. It's the only time my ex took me out to dinner. Eric would only offer something as long as it didn't cost him anything, cheapskate! The only thing Eric had going for him was looks. Eric was really good-looking, but the longer I was with him, the uglier he got.

There was a Reggae Festival with Ziggy Marley. We went to Telluride where it took place. It was fun, of course I paid for everything but I got us a hotel room because it was our anniversary. Eric and I were at the festival, and he told his hippie friends they could use our hotel room. When we got back from the festival, they were in my bed and getting up to go. Now our room smelled like Patchouli. I was fuming and questioned him, "Eric, why did you let them use our hotel room?" He said, "So what? They just wanted to take a nap." I reminded him again, "This is our anniversary weekend." Eric didn't care and he didn't get me anything for our anniversary either. He didn't have to pay for the room, he was a leach and so were some of his friends. Once, Eric and I were going to drive to Boulder and see a concert with friends, and his bronco broke down. We were stranded for a day because Eric couldn't get the part he needed and he had no money for his truck. We missed the concert. Eric called a friend to get us and we were two hours from the house. He was the kind of person who was always going to have to rely on someone else to bail him out but hey, he never ran out of weed!

There were also a lot of strange deaths in Durango while I was there. When I worked at the Teddy Bear camp, I worked with a girl whose boyfriend was killed in a plane accident. We were skiing and his name came up for some reason. One of the guys we were skiing with knew him and I spilled the beans about his death. I had no idea they knew each other. A kid going to Fort Lewis College went out with his friends, got drunk, was walking home and he passed out ten feet from his house while it was snowing like crazy! They couldn't find his body for a week. He was buried in snow, only ten feet away from his house. He was nineteen years old; what a life wasted. Another kid was a new rider with his mountain bike and he was stopped at a light. He couldn't get his foot to release from his bike pedal, and he wasn't wearing his helmet. The boy fell – over, smacked the side of his head on the sidewalk that killed him instantly. He was eighteen years old, another life wasted. A chef in town, Dave, went on a hike with another couple of chefs. He was sitting on a snow-overhang. He realized that pretty late and fell about a hundred yards down while his friends tried to help. One of the guys fell too, badly but lived. Dave was not so lucky. He was killed on impact. He was good friends with my girlfriend, Brenda, who was a pastry chef. Yeah, a lot of strange deaths and those were just a couple and weird accidents too. One poor kid was snowboarding and got out of control and slid into a tree with a stick poking out of it and it went right up his ass! They had to cut the tree away and remove it surgically. What a fun vacation! There were more weird stories, but I don't want to get into it all.

I modeled for Durango magazine as well. I saw the advertisement in the paper, "Model wanted for the Durango magazine." I went to the audition thinking I won't get it. This town wanted a tough mountain bike chick or a lumberjack girl. I was too L.A. I gave my portfolio to the woman and she said, "Wow, what size? Okay, when can we do this?" I was the only fucking model in the whole hick town. I did it, didn't even keep a copy of the magazine. It was fun but funnier than anything. We took pictures by a train on mountain bikes. I can't even ride a mountain bike but it looked good for the magazine. I did a shoot with the sweetest guy. I can't remember his name but he married a beautiful red-headed girl. I worked with two of the nicest people. I remember that we had to change in the woods for the mountain bike shoot and he was so sweet. He kept saying, "Don't worry, I won't look."

I did meet a lot of really good people in Durango. There was this kid who was always protesting everything, but he was so nice. Adam, what a character I adored him. He didn't have a single mean bone in his body. Yes, he was a hippie, but he treated everyone well. Unlike most hippies who couldn't stand me because I was a Republican and I go to church. I also worked with a girl who went Rhubarbs picking on a bike ride. We went on, and when we came back home, we made rhubarbs pies. It was fun. I miss that stuff in a small town. I would go get my roasted green chillies for the year with my good friend JAMES. He loved to cook too. I would have loved to have more time to do fun stuff while I lived there, but I worked two, sometimes three jobs just to get by. There was this wonderful guy, Biker Mike. He was a Harley rider, and he had a chopper. Such a sweetie! He was 6'6 or so, and they would put bells on his toes. He would sneak up on you without warning and he came into a place I worked. I went on a ride with him during a parade in town. I wore an American flag bikini on his chopper, it was a blast! I weighed more than when I was on steroids, so my tits were huge! We were in the parade with Ben Nighthorse Campbell, who led the parade. He's an American-Indian politician; a typical politician making promises he can't keep. He uses whatever means possible to get votes, like his American Indian status. When he would come to town, people would bow down to him. He loved it, but I never liked him and I think he knew it. Like most politicians, Ben Nighthorse Campbell is a lying piece of garbage. He doesn't really care about people who live on The Reservation unless he could get their vote. Almost all of his friends and associates were white. He only took pretty pictures with Indians to look like he gives a shit, and after he got what he wanted, he dumped them like most politicians.

Anyway, there was kind of a rally of sorts where a bunch of hippies went marching down the street to March for pot legalization, Save the Gray Whales, Stop De-Forestation, the Right to Stop Bathing, or some hippie shit. Eric loaned the Mama and Papa Bear costumes I had made for us for Halloween. I never got them back. Eric didn't ask for permission to take the costumes, he just did it. Those costumes cost three hundred dollars to get them tailor-made for us. Eric didn't have to pay for them so who cares? I probably wouldn't want them back anyway; they would smell like sage and B.O. Eric did stuff like that; took my things and never replaced it. He was living on that cheap mindset, "What is yours is mine, and what's mine is mine." I knew he had the ability to be supportive but Eric was only interested in doing stuff he liked, just like my dad! When I first moved to Durango, Eric told me, "Jobs are scarce, take what you can get, and don't complain." I was not taking money from my family. Except during the holidays, I would get Christmas money which I used for presents. I worked a lot! Even though he made more money than I did when I was first in Durango but we split things 50-50. And I didn't complain.

We went to Navaho Lake and did mushrooms. Prior to this, I had never done this before. Not the best drug to do. If you have a weak bladder you laugh a lot. My girlfriend Theresa grew mushrooms in her bathtub. It was a way for her to make extra money. I gotta say that now, Theresa was a blast. She was one of the few hippies that I got along with, just like Adam. She didn't judge me because I went to church or because I was a Republican or conservative. She was just a nice person all the way around.

I don't like any kind of smoke. I'm asthmatic, and so the reason for me never smoking pot wasn't just because it was illegal, so I didn't exactly fit. We went to this guy's house, and the party was in the backyard. Eric went through the gate first because he's a pig with no manners. He only used his manners in front of his Mommy. Anyway, I went in after him, and I passed through the gate. This hippie girl, who had a basket in her hand and her armpit was full of stinky hair, brushed right by me and I went, "Oh Jesus Christ!" I think I overreacted a little. I mean, her armpit hair was stuck to her arm. Oh God, no, so filthy! She looked at me and asked me with a disdainful expression on her face, "What?" I couldn't help it. I just said, "I'm sorry, I thought you were a guy." I didn't know how to get out of my bad reaction, but I couldn't shut up. "Thought you were a dude for a minute, sorry about that." She asked, "Do I look like a dude?" I said, "Your armpit does!" I was trying to be funny. She, very proudly, stated, "That's how God made me. What's wrong with it?" I couldn't help it. I thought let's really throw her off. I told her. "Great! You go to church? I'm new in town and I am looking for someone to go to Church with, so would you like to go with me sometime?" She looked around, utterly confused. She took a minute to come up with a comeback. She said, "Well, the Earth is my Church." I couldn't help it anymore. I just said it. "Well, you wear it well." As I said that, I had a big smile on my face.

She snubbed her nose at me and walked away to the compost pile. "Who invited the girl in the polo shirt?" She screamed. I should have asked her, "Do you know the book of Mormon Latter Day Saints?" I don't know what the hippie chick would have done, but it would have been funny to me. I didn't make a lot of friends who were hippies in Durango. They were hygienically challenged and they refused to accept most people who weren't just like them. They would say, "Oh let's all be one, and let's accept one another." That was a load of crap! They only wanted to be around other people who conform to non-conformity; become vegetarians and wear that hemp crap. Sorry but that wasn't me. Not all of them, just 75-80% of them. My girlfriend Brenda, Theresa and Adam were not like that at all. They were big fucking hippies, but we still got along great. They didn't have the hippie attitude. If you don't know what the hippie attitude is, just go to Boulder, Colorado, and if you still don't get it, move there and stay there, you clueless dickhead.

I did have a nice run-in while I lived in Durango. They filmed City Slickers while I was there. I have to say, I don't know what Billy Crystal's WIFE is doing, but she should write a book on how to raise two beautiful, smart, funny, sweet, and adorable young ladies. She's a wonderful mother. Whatever she's doing, follow her lead! I met Billy too! If I ever got to hang out with Billy, I'd like to go to a baseball game with him. Billy seems like the kind of guy you could go to a game with and just enjoy the beauty of baseball. I don't think people respect the game as much as they used to, but baseball, I have always loved it. I know Billy likes it too.

I would host theme dinners at my house, and my friends would sit on the ground or anywhere they could, and we would have the times of our lives. My friend David and his girlfriend Lisa would make up music tapes to match the food I was preparing. David was a professional pianist, they are really nice people. The first year I was there, I got Pleurisy; it's a lung infection. I broke my ribs. I used to cough so hard that my ex made me sleep on the couch because my coughing was keeping him awake. He was going skiing in the morning and needed his sleep.

Since I worked at the ski area, Eric said, "We are going to get married anyway. Let's get a common law marriage so I can get a free ski pass. We are going to get married someday, you know? I love you. Let's do it." So we did anything for free for Eric. He would take parts off my bike if he needed to fix something on his bike and didn't want to pay for it. I asked him, "It's my bike. Are you going to replace the parts?" Eric told me without shame, "Well, you don't ride as much as me." He didn't care about my stuff ever.

Eric was on a mountain bike ride and got stung by a bee. Due to that, he had an allergic reaction to it. I told him, "You are having a systemic reaction. Get in the car, let's go to the hospital!" We went to the hospital, and they told him exactly what I did. Eric was supposed to keep an epi-pen with him at all times because they said, "The next time you get stung, it will probably be worse, so keep it with you at all times." Stupid dick never kept it with him, and never got it re-filled. They expire, dumbass!

It's because of guys like Eric who smoke a lot of pot and make it look bad, half-assing shit, stoned all the time. This is why it was illegal for so long. The hippie dickheads with the signs and marching for the legalization of it is all white Middle America sees. They don't see the kids with seizures, the woman with post-partum depression, the guy dealing with P.T.S.D. from coming back from war protecting his country or the woman with Chorne's disease who needs it for her chronic pain. No, they just see stupid dicks like my ex. Getting high and wasting space, that's why it was illegal for so long!

None of those hippie fucks could ever do anything successfully. I bought a ceiling fan that I wanted to put in our house, and I asked Eric if he could install it. He had to call an electrician to do it and made me pay for it because the ceiling fan was my idea. He benefited by having it, but it was my idea so I should pay for it! Eric took until he was twenty-eight to get his undergrad work done. He got it by the skin of his teeth. Without informing me, he told two girls that I didn't smoke pot, and it was okay for them to ask me to pee in a cup for them so they could get a job that required a drug test. Since I was the only person they knew who didn't smoke pot, they offered to pay me to pee for them, and I didn't know them, but my ex did. I clearly refused their offer. He got pissed because I wouldn't do it. That jackass didn't care if I got in trouble.

Eric was just a spoiled white boy who didn't have to care about anything. I got the feeling from the start that his family was very inclusive. Our family always did work with the needy. We didn't put ourselves first just because we could. I know we were privileged, but Eric and his family were living on the impression that they were above charity work. They were very stuck-up. They were the kind of people who would say, "We don't look down on people who were Democrats, as long as they have the same tax bracket as us." I know if they get wind of this, they will go, "She is making all of these accusations about us up. You know we never really liked her." They were very fake people. They never liked me but pretended to like me. It felt insulting but I was determined to make it work.

There came a time when I wasn't feeling good at all. I didn't know what it was. I went to my gynecologist, who performed a biopsy. I still remember when I heard the words, "You have cancer." It was stage one endometrial cancer. She gave me my options. I didn't want to have a hysterectomy, I wanted kids. So they did an experimental treatment not covered by my insurance. I couldn't afford it. I had to go back to L.A. for my treatment. My treatment was about four hundred dollars a month. My treatment was drug-induced forced menopause. I actually went through menopause twice! I'm just that lucky. It was worse the first time; hot flashes, no sex drive at all, weight gain, and hair loss. I was up and down because of the chemo. It attacked my lungs, and I was already asthmatic. I had to go on anabolic steroids because I couldn't breathe. I also lactated and took pills to dry up. I hope I never have to go through that again. I didn't tell my parents that I was sick. It was stage one and I didn't lose all my hair. I cut my hair because I'm a natural blond. You could tell I was losing my hair, so I dyed it red. So it wasn't so obvious. I think they knew something was up, but I didn't want them to worry. I would go to my doctors and have blood drawn every three months along with frequent biopsies too. I went through all this alone. My ex was no help at all. He told me I was getting fat and hated my hair. I should have left him, but I still had hope and I was sick. Eric treated my cancer like I had a cold. He would say, "It is only stage one. It's no big deal."

I couldn't have picked a worse time to go home. It was Los Angeles in '92 during the riots. Let me just say, Rodney King was a good person, and nothing that happened to him was his fault. He was traumatized and was molested as a child. As a kid, he was horribly abused and didn't stand a chance. He turned to drugs to cope with the emotional trauma he endured his whole life. If you saw him off-drugs, he was very pleasant and warm, a very nice guy. He didn't deserve anything that happened to him. All white people did was see a man who wasn't listening to the police. He was bombarded with questions like, "Why won't he stay down? Why won't he just listen to them?" Nobody realized he was having a psychotic episode. He couldn't hear anyone. I can't wait to get to heaven to see him and tell him, "I'm sorry for misjudging you." I hope he's happy up there and I pray God forgives us, the white people, for treating him so poorly. God bless Rodney King! For the record, Daryl Gates can go fuck himself! The day of the riots, he took off and went to a big black-tie charity dinner. Let them eat cake. He blamed all of L.A.'s problems on the Mayor and left. Someone needs to look into Daryl Gates's involvement with the K.K.K. My dad knew him, guilt by association.

Before the riots, there was a lot of tension in L.A. for sure. Mom and I were home, but where was my sister? She's a biologist, and we call her the bug police. She doesn't like it much. My sister used to work with the Med-Fly project. This is the fly that could wipe out crops and really demolish California if it didn't get stopped. California's main export is fruit and vegetables. If that fly got to the wine country, they were royally fucked. My sister knows everything about plants and any vegetation, bugs, insects; she's an encyclopedia of all of that. Going on a hike with her is a total nightmare. She can't go two steps before she sees something and tells you all about it. "That's a plant from South America! You can tell if it's female, from the veining at the bottom of the leaf, and this is a rock from the Pacific Ocean, it only gathers moss on the North side, and it is only found in this region. This dirt, the topsoil, is very good for those plants but they don't do well in the summer. If it gets too hot, these plants, their flowers bloom in the fall." I would have to stop her, it was all Greek to me and I would say, "Jesus, sis! Look at the pretty blue sky" What am I talking about? It's L.A. look at the grey! It's only a simple hike. My sister is brilliant, and very funny.

They did overhead spraying to get rid of the bugs but had to stop. The overhead spraying was taking paint off cars and killing, not just the med-fly but Sparrows, Hummingbirds and Ladybugs, to mention a few. My take on the reason they stopped the overhead spraying, "Don't ruin our precious Roses, the Rose parade, and stop killing the Ladybugs!" What do Ladybugs kill? They kill the AFIDS that kill roses. It's all about saving face for whiteys. It would affect the revenue for the city of Pasadena, so they went to give an end to hand spraying. That's a great idea! Put some unknown biologist at risk and exclaim, "Just don't kill our Roses." Pasadena is going to be really pissed off. I told you this shit, no biggie. If you look into Pasadena's past, they had a lot of Klan back in the day. Everyone knows that they did. They just wish we wouldn't talk about it, oopsie. I'm not one of them, I don't give a fuck. My sister had to set traps for bugs in some pretty unsafe places. The second I thought that the phone rang. I ran to the kitchen. I heard her on the other side of the phone, thank God. She said, "It's okay, I'll be home by five." Guess all of the biologists who were out in the field were told to get back to the main office two hours before the verdict was read, just in case. It's a good thing they did. My blonde-haired blue-eyed sister was in Compton, just two hours before. Yeah, it would have been bad.

Mom and I watched the T.V. and just tried not to cry. We were watching it live on every channel, over and over. Los Angeles was on fire. We saw the guy get pulled out of his big rig and get beaten down. Our area didn't get affected at all. There was a little smoke in the air, a siren in the far distance every once and a while. We lived in a very nice neighborhood. Dad came home all smiles like it was the fourth of July. "Don't worry, don't go anywhere. We got this covered," he stated. He runs down the hall to gear up. I look at mom, "What's he up to?" I'll never forget the way she looked at me and said, "I don't know, and I don't care anymore." Mom was on her last leg with dad. They got divorced shortly thereafter. I go down the hall and play pretty princess with dad. "Hey daddy, what's up? What are you going to do? I won't tell Mom." He said, "I'll tell you about it later." He smiled, grabbed his guns and left.

My sister came home and said, "Well, I guess that I won't be wearing my uniform for a while." I asked, "Why?" I guess the gangs were targeting anyone in uniform to shoot. They tagged the buildings with words, "You are in uniform, we'll kill you," or something like that. I restricted her, "Don't go anywhere near there. It's not safe for you." My sister said, "Look, this is not those people's fault who I know. They're nice people. I go to their houses, they know me. I'll set my traps, and I'm not worried. When it's safe, I'll go back." My sister has balls of steel! She's also very level-headed. She's perfect for her job. They were lucky to have her. Dad came home hours later. He told me what he did. I followed him again and really found out what was going on. Dad, the Klan, and the cops (white cops) set up roadblocks to all the white neighborhoods. Martial Law for whites only! They stood with their shotguns at roadblocks they set up they would stop anyone that was black or Hispanic; they would shine their lights in their faces check their I.D. and say, "I don't know you boy, turn it around or we'll kill you," and laugh. When I say the white cops, I mean all of them. I was there the police came up and checked in on them. "You guys ok? Did you get any tonight?" They replied, "No, we're good." They kept that shit on a different signal on the police radio. This went on for days. Nobody said anything, white news. They said there are still missing kids from the riots, not just from the day it happened. Even after days, nobody bothered to look for them. My best guess is that they killed them. Darrell Gates is a motherfucker, Martial Law was his idea and all the white male cops knew about it. They may not have been hands-on, but they all knew. I said it before, I will say it again, I got nothing to lose and nothing to hide. All we need is one really guilty cop to come forward, or one clan member to just come and tell the truth about what happened. No priest or minister in the world will ever forgive you. You are going to burn in hell, and take your family with you. God's not going to forgive you or your family. You're going to burn in hell with my dad. Take a look at your kids and tell them, "Daddy's a racist murdering heathen," and that would be the truth. Live with that!

I worked at a restaurant called The Ritz Grill in Pasadena. That was the year of the Super Bowl, Cowboys/Giants. I remember all these guys coming into the restaurant looking like Joey Buddafucco. Another fashion disaster! My dad did this thing. It's a white, rich thing, I think. He never donated anything. We did, though. Mom always said, "Someone else may need it, don't throw away. Donate it." But my father and his family didn't ever do that. Dad said, "I don't want some spick wearing my clothes." Those were his exact words. He was throwing away all this good stuff, Stetson hats, three pairs of cowboy boots, all they needed was to be re-soled, shirts, a suit, bola ties, you name it. He was putting all of it in big trash bags. I played the Pretty Princess game and said, "Daddy, why don't you let me take this junk to work? There are big trash bins by where I park my car. I'll get rid of it for you, daddy." He gave it to me, and I gave all his clothes to the Mexican cooks I worked with. They loved it! They thought it was great. I think I liked it more than they did. I can just imagine those guys wearing my dads hat to their daughter's Quinceanera or his boots to church. It makes me feel all warm and fuzzy inside.

I've always gotten along with most of the chefs I worked with, even when I was waiting tables. Some of the front staff, usually all white, treat the Mexicans we work with like dirt. They won't even say hello to some of them. They're kind of stuck up. The people in the kitchen work much harder than the front of the house does. I don't think most of the white people I worked with would make it one day in the kitchen. I'm a Chef, and I know how hard they work! The chefs and the guys in the kitchen, in general, deserve more credit than they get. They are the hub of any restaurant. I wanted to learn how to make tamales, and a friend of mine was from a big Mexican family. She asked her grandma if I could watch her make them and she let me. It's an honor to be invited into someone's kitchen to make a family dish; I was excited to say the least. Her grandma sat me down and showed me. I was the only white person in the kitchen, and I'm sure they were all laughing at me trying my hand at making tamales. They were all speaking Spanish, and I had no idea what they were saying, but it was so much fun! A quick question, what does *Puta* mean? Just a little joke, I know what it means. Her little hands worked so fast, I looked like one of Jerry's kids, trying to cook, but they were very nice to me. That's how I learned how to make tamales. Theirs were much better than mine, for sure. I was blessed to have had that experience with them. I also learned how to make wontons from scratch from a friend's mom who was Asian. That was so much fun! You want to open your minds to culture, get in the kitchen!

CHAPTER FOURTEEN: PROPOSAL, COP DATE, TEKASHI 69

When I went back to Durango to spend some time there, my ex proposed out of sheer desperation! I have had five marriage proposals, and they all sucked. Eric's was the worst one!! We went to Ouray, Colorado. He already knew he was on thin ice with me. Eric taking and never giving back was getting old. So he pulled out this plastic ring he got in a quarter candy machine and said, "Well, here! This is for you. Now you can plan your wedding." That was it. I guess I shouldn't have expected much. I called my sister, and she asked with great concern, "Do you really want to marry this guy? What has he ever done for you?" I started to think about our lop-sided relationship, and realization hit me like a big fucking truck. I was in it for the long haul from day one. I supported him through the last year of college. I realized I was actually the only one invested in this relationship. Heck, I sold my truck because we needed the money. I remember putting an advertisement in the paper to sell my truck, and some hippie stoner wanted to trade it for some hippie art. I asked him, "How much do you think that art is worth?" The answer I got was, "It is priceless to me." I said, "Well maybe, you can trade your art for my credit card bills. Do you believe people think your art is worth eight thousand dollars?" The hippie didn't buy my truck, obviously. Someone with brains did. I got a scooter and had a basket put on the front so I could go to the market. Eric never paid for any groceries, never! Naïve me used to think that he would pay me back when we got married just because he said he would. I worked two jobs, I wasn't taking money from my family, and Eric didn't have a job, or so I thought.

He took me to Telluride for my birthday, and I paid of course. There was a concert in the hotel we were staying, and it was Crosby, Nash and Young. He didn't get us tickets, and I shouldn't have been surprised. I asked one of the stage hands if I could sit in the hallway and listen because we didn't get tickets and it's my birthday. My ex kept suggesting, "No, let's just go to bed." I was adamant. "No, I want to hear this." The stagehand said, "It's your birthday?" I nodded a pleading yes. He instantly said, "Here! I have a seat for you. It is your birthday." Eric interrupted, "What about me?" The guy looked at him with such pity and said, "You're the guy who didn't get tickets for her birthday? No shame. Whatever, I guess. Come on." He must've thought, what a leech he is. But Eric didn't care as long as it was anything free.

We sat down in the V.I.P. area. I looked down at the audience and one of our friends was in the audience, and he was fast asleep. I started to laugh and looked next to me. The guy on my right looked familiar. I couldn't help but ask, "Are you Keith Karadine?" He said, "Yes." I was too ecstatic to be careful with my words. "What a treat! It is my birthday." He replied, "Your birthday? I will go sing for you." I thought he was kidding. He didn't just sing for me but made my birthday such a nice day, with no help from my ex. Thanks, Keith.

I had my birthday party at our house and my oh-so-amazing boyfriend didn't even bother to get candles for me. Only after I asked him, he put a big candle in the middle of my cake. What a lazy fuck! I made an authentic Jamaican feast for his birthday. One of his hippie friends came for dinner and said, "I'm a vegetarian. I can't eat meat and neither should you. I'm just going to have whatever that isn't meat." This is after I told what was on the menu for dinner. Great! To be nice, I also let them smoke pot in the house because it was Eric's birthday.

The guy who was a vegetarian who told me that I shouldn't eat meat went outside and lit up a cigarette. I went outside and told him, as a matter of fact, "You stupid ass! You won't eat meat, but you smoke cigarettes? That's funny, real smart." And I went back inside. He looked at me through the screen door and said, "I didn't take a life for this cigarette." I threw him a glance, and said, "You're a fucking idiot." The same night some mentally Ill dude Eric got high with came over, I told Eric to get him out of here. Eric politely ushered him out and told him under his breath, "I will see you later." He had a lot of strange friends, but they helped me clean up. He never did anything helpful when it came to me or anyone else, but I think I got it worse than his friends did. I had to put up with his fucking family who put on an act with their fake smiles. All they used to think in their thick skulls was, "When is he going to break up with that girl?"

I had a feeling Eric was dealing, but I wasn't sure until my sister came out for a visit. This schizophrenic guy had the audacity to come by my house high when my sister was alone and I wasn't. He knocked on the door, and she answered it. "Hey, is Eric here? I need some weed." My stupid ex had gotten him high once, sold him some pot, and told him where we lived. It wouldn't have been hard to find Eric. He had red gold and green roll bars on his Bronco. We should have just put a sign on our porch saying, "I deal weed." My sister replied, "No Eric is not here; get off my porch." My sister told me and I confronted him. I asked him clearly. "Eric, are you dealing pot?" Of course, he denied. "No, I'm not. He made a mistake." I didn't buy it.

I told him to keep the pot crap out of the house from now on. So, Eric kept his pot at a house down the street. I don't have a problem with pot. But it was illegal and I didn't want to get in trouble. I also knew some police and people from my Church couldn't come over because it looked like Bob Marley threw up all over my house. There were pot seeds and bongs all over the place, and the house smelled like weed. That's why I had to install a ceiling fan. I would be watering the lawn, and the police would drive by and say hi to me. I knew if they came inside my house, they would find a lot of pot stuff. It was everywhere.

Eric didn't care. He probably thought, "Those guys know Jan. They wouldn't do anything to me." He would be right. I knew those guys, and they wouldn't let anything bad happen to me. But Eric knew I was friends with them and if he got in trouble, I would get him out of it because I knew some of the cops in that town. I did all the cooking, that was fine with me, but Eric never cleaned or helped me with anything in the house. He didn't even bother about the laundry. Eric did the laundry once and put a ballpoint pen through the wash, fucking idiot.

I would make Eric really beautiful lunches, and his friends would tease him, "What's on the menu today, Eric?" I would think he would be thankful, but no. He came home and told me, "Don't do these gourmet meals for me anymore. They are teasing me about it." I was so confused. "Eric, you are complaining about your lunches being too good. Are you kidding me? Okay, Eric. I'll keep it simple." So from then on, I gave him peanut butter and jelly. Fuck you Eric, you pussy. He should have been proud and said, "Yeah, my girlfriend loves me. She makes me really good lunches." Eric was going on field trips with school, and his friends told me they were jealous of his lunches.

We went to a Chinese food restaurant and he walked through the door, didn't even hold it open for me. The hostess pulled out the chair, and he sat in it. I still remember the hostess looking at me like, why are you with this pig? He looked at me, "What?" I looked at him and said, "You want to try this again?" I marched out and he followed. I couldn't take it anymore. "Where are your manners? Is this what it's going to be like when we get married?" He replied, "I wasn't thinking. Sorry." He did that right after we got engaged.

I came home from work early once. I asked Eric not to smoke in the house, but he didn't listen. The screen door was locked, the fan was on and the house smelled like pot. I banged on the door. Eric came out of the bedroom with two guys I don't know. He looked so guilty. "Oh, I didn't know the screen was locked." We had a screen that he had to physically lock. It didn't accidentally happen on its own. I asked, "What is going on?" He came up with the dumbest excuse. "Hi! They haven't seen the place. I was just showing them around." It's a one-bedroom house. They leave to go on a mountain bike ride. I looked through the entire house. Do you know where I found four individual baggies of pot? In the back of my underwear drawer, buried under my panties, perfect! He didn't think I would look there and if the police came over, the blame would be on me. I took it and hid it.

He came home. His friends were waiting for him outside. He went to the bedroom. I could hear him slowly open my drawer. In seconds, he came out, flustered. "Where is it?" I said with a smile on my face, "Where is what? Eric was furious. "That's not mine!" I was more than furious. "You're not dealing? Bullshit! I flushed it down the toilet!" It looked like he was going to have a heart attack. It was funny. I have never seen him get that upset or excited about anything. It was kind of amusing. I gave him back his pot and warned him, "No more pot in the house, I mean it."

I was at a bar with Eric, and this drunken guy groped me. I told him to stop. Eric had his back to me, so I turned to him and asked, "Are you going to help me?" He turned around and said, "Hey dude! Knock it off, man." Eric turned his back on me and the drunken guy did it again. I looked at my coward of a boyfriend and called him a pussy in front of his friends. He came outside and went, "What is the problem?" I said, "You couldn't hit him, or try to do something?" He started going off. "What do you want me to do? I'm not going to hit him! I'm not gonna start a fight." He couldn't fight, not for me.

I tried so hard for Eric, just to give a shit about anything except pot! I was starting to think what a waste of five years and that's not all of it. That's just a small part of some of the ridiculous stuff he did. I felt like I needed to talk to someone about my engagement with Eric because I wasn't happy and had serious doubts about marrying him, so I made an appointment to talk to a minister at a church I went to. It was a Baptist Church. I wasn't a Baptist, but I didn't care, I went to get closer with God; I would find wherever the minister or priest or pastor was, who gave good sermons and go to them.

The minister was wonderful, and we really talked. He told me, "It sounds like you know in your heart what is best, but you need to make the decision. God will be on your side with any decision you make." I think I knew what to do, but ending a five-year relationship is tough, especially when it's a small town and everyone knows you. I went home, Eric and I were supposed to go on a weekend break to plan the wedding, and he got a call from his friends. "Hey man! You want to get high and go fishing?" Eric told them without a second thought. "Yeah, I will pack." I looked at him and said, "Wait a minute! Aren't we going to do some planning? What is your priority? Our wedding or fishing with your buddies getting high?" He had the audacity to say, "Well, you knew what you were getting into when you met me. I am not going to change. This is it, and you can do the wedding planning with my mom." He left. His mom never liked me, but I had to call her.

I called his mom, who pretended to like me before we got engaged and pretended to like me even less after we got engaged. I told her, "We got formally engaged, let's plan a wedding!" This was her response, "Well, I thought he might do that. I always thought if my best friend was a little bit younger and he was a little bit older, they'd be perfect together, but if this is what he wants, okay I guess." That was her response after five years with her leeching son and putting him through a year of school. What a bitch.

She was married to Eric's dad, who was a pretty good-looking guy, but he didn't make enough money for her and she wasn't happy. She wanted more. She re-married this man who was well off and lived in a very nice place in L.A. Perfect! She stayed married to him until the kids were out of school and divorced him. She cleaned up pretty good too. She was a typical Karen. "Oh no! It's not about the money, I really loved him." No you didn't! He was four hundred pounds, and I don't think it was a sex thing for you. There are all different levels of gold-diggers and Karen. They are sneaky like that. I was watching The First Wives Club and I was cheering on the first wives. Eric came into the room and said, "That's terrible. They don't deserve all that money." I felt like telling him, "Really? Call your mom. She knows all about what they are doing." I told Eric that his mom insulted and said that he should marry her best friend. You need to talk to her. He called her and then came up with, "Yeah, Mom thinks you are overreacting. It is no big deal."

I couldn't take it. Eric never backed me up on anything. He was so selfish and didn't support me in any way, even when I had cancer. I couldn't make any excuses for him. If I married him, people would say, "Jan, why did you marry that stoner loser who treats you like shit?" I had dreams about getting married, I could see myself walking in my wedding dress and looking at Eric, but I couldn't see myself saying, "I do." So, I called off my wedding. I finally said this to Eric: "Call your mommy and tell her she can set you up with her best friend now." I packed his shit up and told him to get out. He acted surprised. So Eric moved in with some people he used to deal drugs to, so he didn't have to hide it anymore.

I tried to stay friends, but he was never going to pay me back; he didn't care. I took Eric out for his birthday, and I told him pretty clearly that all I could afford was a Mexican restaurant. I could have taken him to an expensive place, but I really didn't think it was worth it. He even commented on it. "Why didn't we go to someplace where we could get a nice bottle of wine or something?" I said, "I can't afford it, you know that." He just laughed. He never cared about me; I was just a chick who paid the bills.

Eric did something to me when I was sick in L.A., getting chemo and going through those god-damned anabolic steroids. In addition to supporting him, and putting him through a year of college, Eric said, "This rent is going to be too much while you're gone. I might have to move someplace cheaper." I had to convince him. "I'll get a job that makes more money, please. Don't move. I have all my stuff here, okay?" So I sent him my portion of the rent. Eric took money from me when I had cancer, and he almost got us evicted for not shoveling in the winter. He was so useless! Eric had no common sense at all!

Once, he was surfing in California. I told him to put silly putty around his ear so the water wouldn't get in. Eric took my advice but put the silly putty in too deep, and it wouldn't come out all the way. I did this when I was a kid for the swim team and never got it stuck. I had a problem with the handrail on the oven getting loose, and Eric just stuck some toothpicks around the oven handrail to jimmy rig it until it broke again. Eric was the laziest jackass on the planet. A picture fell off our wall when he was smoking pot, and I asked him to fix it. The picture sat on the floor, broken for six months. We didn't have a vacuum cleaner, so I would borrow it from my neighbors, but we really needed to deep clean, so this Kirby vacuum guy came over to give us a presentation for a free cleaning because Eric didn't want to pay for it. When we got a common-law divorce, five hundred dollars Eric made me pay for it. He said, "Why do we have to get a divorce? Just keep my name. I don't care." I said, "I don't want anything to do with your name!"

The worst thing Eric did wasn't to me; it was to my girlfriend, Theresa. She got arrested and needed bail money badly. I had no other choice but to call him. "I don't need money for me, it's for Theresa!" He said, "All I have got is ten bucks on me, sorry." Click. Eric could have called his drunken mother and asked, "Mom, I need some money. It's an emergency." She would have sent him anything he wanted. I needed him to help a dear friend, and he couldn't give a shit. It wasn't like she was in Denver or Durango. She was in jail in Mexico!

She flew to California and rented a car, drove to Mexico, got into an accident. The Federals saw her little white girl, cha-ching, 5000 dollars to get her out. Theresa was handcuffed to a seat in a Mexican jail. Can you imagine how scared she must have been? Her friend, who I had never met before, called me and broke the news. "Theresa's in jail in Mexico. Break into her house, get her money, and wire it to me as soon as possible she doesn't have enough. Send me everything you can. Okay?" I broke into her apartment, and there was money hidden all over. For your information, she sold mushroom. I sent this guy all her money, all my money; I borrowed money from my mom, who was a school teacher herself, not that rich. I borrowed money from my boss. My rent was due; I called my landlord and asked him if it was okay to be late on the rent, and he said that it was okay because my ex, the looser, wasn't involved. I was the only one living there, and he liked me.

I gave her everything I had except twenty dollars in my checking account. I got her out! She came back, thanked me, took her a year, paid me back every dime! I would have gotten her out of jail in Thailand if she needed it because she would be there for me too; she was that kind of woman. My ex, Eric is a piece of shit for doing that. Theresa, if you hear this, miss you sweetie! I ran into Eric's friend from Pasadena about three years after I called it off. He told me that the stoner Eric, my ex's nickname in Durango, married a hippie girl, moved to Oregon, and was selling used cars. I'm so glad I paid for his last year of school. That degree came in real handy, didn't it? Well, at least she smokes pot, and I hope she doesn't mind paying for everything unless she has a rich daddy to help them. Hopefully, she gets along with his Mom.

Watch out, girl. She's a phony, stuck-up witch, so don't trust her. Remember, her son comes first and he can do no wrong, so if she asks you something, agree. Eric's Mom was planning a trip to Europe with him after he graduated from college, and I wasn't invited. She was going to take Eric on vacation the same time we were going to get married. She was going to take my new husband on our honeymoon without me. I really think Eric should just fuck his mother and get it over with!

If Eric hears about this, he will probably take a long hit off from his huge bong and go, "What was her name? Don't I know her from someplace?" He's probably leaching off his wife and her family, re-loading his bong as we speak, listening to reggae music, and barely getting by. I'm sure he's not thinking about retirement. He will leave that up to his in-laws and his Mommy to take care of it for him or an inheritance he gets, but it won't be from him really working for it. I'm so glad I didn't marry into that family. I would have been very unhappy, but they wouldn't give a shit unless Eric was unhappy. It would be more like, "Oh poor Eric, look at him with that woman who doesn't deserve him!" Calling off my wedding was the best thing I ever did for myself. I started to write again, feeling like myself. I lost who I was with him. I hope his new wife hears about this. She may be his ex-wife by now. He told me once, "When I have kids, I am gonna let them get high with me." He never said, "I'm going to teach them how to ride a bike, swim, paint, fish, or go to church, but he's going to get them high." That was his game plan to get his kids high for the first time. Eric tried to explain his idiocy in the following manner. "It will be a bonding thing, just like when a kid has his first drink, it's the same thing."

I can't imagine what his life is like now. If he did have kids, I would pray for them. They are going to need it. I can't see his mom being a very warm grandma. Her house was like my grandmother's in Palm Springs, like a museum. I hope the in-laws are kind people with a lot of patience because if they are expecting much out of Eric and his Mom for support or comfort, they're going to be disappointed. No kid wants a stoned parent, or worse, a drunken grandparent! Who knows what he's doing now? As long as he's not leaching off me anymore, he can do whatever the fuck he wants. I always had Eric's back but he never had mine.

When you go through a break-up, it shows you who your friends are. My bridesmaids came to my rescue! Jodi, what a sweetie her family would take me in at Christmas; my ex's mother would pay for him to go home. I stayed and worked to support his lazy ass. Thank God for Jodi, what a sweet friend. She gave me a copy of The Frugal Gourmets book for Christmas because she knew I liked him as a chef. I liked him because he always had kids on his show and showed them about cooking. Then I found out The Frugal Gourmet was a pedophile. That's why he had kids on his show. My Mom told me this and she doesn't lie, but God! I wish that wasn't true. I loved his work, and now I can't even think about him without being totally disgusted. It is always the nice white guys you don't think could do that kind of thing, but it almost always is. Their family would do Monday Night Football together. When we saw the games, honestly, I didn't pay much attention to football. I liked their company and I loved to tailgate. I miss you, Jodi!

Brenda, a pastry chef, wonderful woman and fantastic chef! She let me stay with her for six months. I love Brenda, everybody does. She was a saint but sometimes her little hippie friends kind of get on my nerves. One time, she got a

D.U.I. The day she got her license back, she was out next to the restaurant I work at with her so-called hippie friends for drinks. She paid, they leeched off her. I went over to Brenda who was drunk, and I said, "Brenda, you are not driving." I had to go to the bathroom and thought, I will drive her when I am back. But when I returned, she was gone. I went to the useless fucking, jack-off hippies. "You fuckers got free drinks, and I told you not to let her drive!" I screamed.

All they could say was, "She is a big girl! She can handle it." I found out the next day from a friend in the department who pulled her over that night. "Jan, don't you have a friend called Brenda? I gave her a D.U.I. last night." He told me this the next day at work, small town. She gets her second D.U.I. that night, driving home from the bar. That's another reason I don't like hippies. All they do is leech on others, smoke pot, and tell everyone else to be organic, and to conform to non-conformity.

None of those hippie assholes would help you out in a real crunch, like if you needed bail money or if you needed to have someone watch your house. I had more than one friend in Durango have me take care of their house when they were on vacation or use help with moving out or put a dinner together, but if you ask a hippie for help, all they do is protest, get high, and pray to Gerry Garcia. They are worthless, like my ex. Not all of them, just 75-80% of them.

Nichole, she is a hairdresser. Sweet, kind, and darling woman, we had them over for dinner one night, and we were getting up. I said, "When we get married, and done with school, no more of this 70-30 relationship. It is fifty-fifty." Eric replied, "I kind of like it, 70-30. Fine with me." Nicole was a little taken back by that remark. After they left, we had a little talk that did no good. It didn't change a thing. I asked

Nicole after my break-up. "If I didn't call it off, would you have let me marry him?" She said, "Hell no! We wouldn't let you do that! You can do so much better." They were super supportive and good friends. I don't know what I would have done without them. I hope they aren't mad that I broke all ties with them; it's not like I died. I really am anti-tech. I don't do the internet. Long story, tell you later. Everyone I know has the internet! I love them all very much. I just wanted to move on and not have anything to do with my ex. That's all, nothing personal when this comes out and anyone wants to talk to me later, tweet that shit and I will try to get in touch.

It's a small town when you're single. Everyone knows about it! Everyone wants to set you up. So I got set up on a blind date with a cop! I just started writing again; I thought maybe someday I'll write about this, so here we are. I thought, what the hell? Maybe this will be amusing. He picked me up, and his usual car was an undercover cop car as his regular car. I remember thinking, "Try not to laugh. Be on your best behavior. He doesn't know you are a comedian and smartass." He had the cop mustache and haircut fresh on the force. He was a very nice guy, we got in his car, and he had the police radio going on. I asked, "Is it okay if we listened to the radio?" He told me, "I like to keep the police radio on, just in case."

Oh boy, this is going to be a long fucking night, I thought. He said, "We are going to a new place for one drink?" It was a small town, and the new place we were going to was called Horney's. It was a bar outside town, brand new. When I said to him jokingly, "Are we going to the bar and get horneys?" It was a little joke but he didn't get it. He said, "What? The name of the bar is Horney's bar. Yes, we are going to Horney's bar." Yep, he didn't get it. I wanted to reach over, grab his gun, and shoot myself in the mouth, but I got that image out of my head because I could never kill myself. So fuck it. I'm going to keep a smile on my face and get drunk if at all possible. Why not? He's driving.

We got to the Horney's bar. All he wanted to do was look around and check out stuff. See if anything was about to go down. He didn't talk to me. He just looked around and waited to arrest someone, anyone! We left, got in his car and I just said, "Shit." I forgot something back in the bar. He told me, "Don't say that. Don't cuss." I was irritated now. "Can you take me home now?" If he was going to be upset for me saying shit, I don't think he would be into anything kinky, much less be okay if I grabbed him by the back of his head, pulled his hair and screamed, "Fuck me!" or anything close to that. I kept thinking of my mistress and what she would do to him. Who knows? He might have liked it, but I don't have the patience for him. I think having sex with him would be too much like screwing Donny Osmond; too missionary and proper.

I'm not into Mormons, so this isn't going to work for me at all. I was hoping this date would be over soon. This fake "I am having a nice time smile" is painful. All of a sudden, I hear my ex over the police radio. Eric was getting pulled over. Ding, ding, ding, jackpot! I'm with a cop who is foaming at the mouth to arrest anyone, and Eric is a drug dealer! I never wanted to listen to the police radio as much as I did at the moment. I asked him to turn it up! The cop was really paying attention to this reaction. "Oh, I get to arrest someone!" ERIC always had pot on him and I knew where he lived, his roommate's names, where his phone book was for all his connections. I remember thinking that he is so fucked! I'm listening to the cops. He's got two squad cars there. I knew two of the cops who pulled him over in small town. All I had to do was say the word.

In my head, the fight between the angel and devil started. The devil was screaming. “Fuck Eric!” This cop thinks pot is the same as heroine. He’s going to put his ass in prison, not jail. That pretty boy who can’t throw a punch will never make it, not one day! They will take turns beating the shit out of him and fucking him! That motherfucker left you ten thousand dollars in the hole; you will never see that money again. Eric didn’t help when you had cancer. He took money from you when you were sick; let him have it. Tell him about all the kids he deals to. They will all go down. This cop will brag about this bust for years, and none of them will get out. They are not your dad! You wouldn’t be in jail for two minutes. He’d get you out, but Eric and all of his friends will all be fucked. Ah, sweet revenge!”

The Devil had a point, but I had to shake that off because then my angel spoke. “Don’t do it. Your heart will heal; you loved him once. And all those kids? Do you want that kind of guilt? What did those kids do to you? This cop won’t stop until they all go down, hard! You won’t have to help this cop to bring them down. They will tear his house apart, and what they don’t find, they’ll plant or make up just to get a big bust in a small town. This cop will brag about his drug bust to all of his friends, he will be a hero. You know how it really works. Don’t do this to them, you’ll regret it for the rest of your life. You’re going to leave this town, start over. Do you want to ruin those kids’ lives? That cop doesn’t care about them, do you? Could you look their mothers in the eye and tell them, sorry about your son getting in so much trouble, I was pissed off!” My angel said, “Let it go.” Karma! So I listened. I looked at the cop and said, “I am sorry, I thought it was something else.” He knew I was lying. “You know, if you heard something, you have to tell me, I am a police officer." I said, "It was something else, can I go home now?" I let it go. I let it go.

Eric has no idea how lucky he was, so were his friends; all the kids he dealt to are lucky too. I'm not a vengeful person, but I do believe in karma. All those kids would go down, and I didn't want that for them. Everybody deserves a little forgiveness, even if you don't know them. So, listen up, you hippie fucks, this Republican Christian girl you would never hang around with would have had your back and Eric, the cool stoner would turn you all in just to save his own skin. Eric was only loyal to himself. Don't judge a book by its cover. When my friend Theresa called for help, if Eric had answered the phone, she would still be in jail in Mexico. Eric was a selfish prick, kind of like TEKASHI69.

TEKASHI69, do you know that kid? The rainbow-haired, talentless little bastard who set up all those gang members to take a fall to boost his ego that piece of shit should be put in solitary confinement for the rest of his life, cut off his fingers, cut out his tongue, sit him in a corner and let him rot. That's the best torture for a needy, arrogant, self-absorbed asshole like him! Total seclusion forever! None of those kids, or we should call them gang members he set up, should be in jail. Those people, again gang members, are not disposable numbers. I know they get treated like that but they are people too with rights! If the K.K.K. has first amendment rights, shouldn't gang members too? Maybe we should start to listen to them instead of putting them down. At least gang members aren't all about hate. Open your eyes a little. Those people have sisters, and mothers, grandparents, friends, and children. TEKASHI69 didn't take any of that into consideration when he set those men up. The police thought, "Great! This little white kid will help us put twelve black men behind bars, and that looks good for us. They are gang members. People will like that." Are you kidding? No, we don't! Let them all go! They don't deserve to go to jail. The accusations made against them were all doctored to make them look as bad as possible. TEKASHI69 helped the white cops set them up. TEKASHI69 never understood the concept of a gang. You don't rat out your fellow gang members. They don't deserve to be put in prison, just for showing their colors. If that's the case, go arrest the next guy you see in a cloak.

There is one thing I'd like to know about TEKASHI69. I'd like to ask his security guards, who are black, "How do you sleep at night?" They helped a white kid, to the police he's white, put twelve black men behind bars who don't deserve to be there and not feel any regret or guilt of any kind? Do the Mothers of these security guards know who they are working for? Someone should tell their moms what's going on. I know they have had their pictures taken, blow them up. Put it on the internet or put it on the billboard at church or at the market they go to, and let's see what their mothers have to say. Well, put a warning out beforehand, "Moms, do you know who your son works for? TEKASHI69! He's a mini Hitler." They would be in so much trouble if their moms were like my mother.

Ask yourselves this is it worth working for someone who has no soul? I'm going to pray for those security guards; they are going to need it. Not to be all Catholic, the big guy is watching! Do you think he will forgive you for causing so much pain to those family members and friends of the men who went to prison for an ego boost for your boss? Explain that at the pearly gates. TEKASHI69's security guards should be ashamed of themselves. Now I understand why blacks say, "Fuck the police," because they do stuff like that.

Do I sound too much like the foul-mouthed nun with the whole "You are going to burn in hell, and God is watching?" The guilt thing it's all I've got. That and wit. which usually gets me into trouble. I don't have the strength to be a nun. Oh, I could never be a nun. They don't let you cuss at all, some of them don't seem very happy, and I'm a smartass. I believe that they wouldn't think that most of the stuff I think is funny. It isn't to them. I'd have to borrow those wooden toggles a lot. I don't think they would let me bring any of my old Dominatrix Gear for my punishments. I'm really particular about my underwear. They don't let you choose what you like, and I like a certain kind. I believe in a woman's right to choose. Yeah, that might be an issue. I'm particular about my toothpaste, shampoo, and I like to get high sometimes. Do they let nuns get high? I don't really know. I think I would have a difficult time keeping my fucking mouth shut. If someone was mean or throwing their weight around like Bishop Gomez at the Cathedral in Denver, I would get under his skin for some reason. Hehe. I hope he doesn't hear about this, but if he does, Arch Bishop who is now, "Cardinal," Charles Shapu, his boss thinks I am funny. He likes me, so fuck him if he doesn't like it. I'll go to confession, I'll be fine!

I became a Catholic. Thought I might get married to a Catholic, so I took the classes. I went three days a week and to church on Sundays to get re-confirmed. I was baptized Methodist. My mom said it was okay as long as I was happy with it. It's the same God. I love my mom! Anyways, I got confirmed but ended the relationship with the Catholic guy. When I was going to my classes, Bishop Gomez was one of our speakers and the topic was abortion. He said, "It is always God's will to give life. All abortions are a mortal sin." One girl who was also becoming a Catholic because she was engaged to one, she had to be, we both argued with him. "What about incest and rape?" I'm not going to tell you everything we both said but he didn't like it, so at the break, we both left. I wonder how things turned out for the girl converting for her new husband and their family.

I didn't say I was a perfect Catholic. I also said something funny after mass in front of Charles. He laughed and I told him, "I'm going to call you Chuckles." He laughed again. I asked him, "Is it alright if I choose a female saint, or does it have to be a male saint?" I had asked Bishop Gomez if I could have a male saint. He said, "No, you are a woman! You have to have a female saint." Charles told me right in front of Gomez, "You can choose any saint you want to honey," and gave me a hug. Bishop Gomez looked like he was going to damn me to hell! It reminded me of Pops razzing dad. There was nothing he could do to me. Nothing like a good razzing and most nuns don't like razzing. Those are some of the reasons I wouldn't become a nun. The no razzing rule, is that a good enough reason? I think if any nun hears about this, they would agree. "Jan becoming a nun would be a bad idea. Peace be with you, but no thanks! We are not that hard up for new recruits. Thanks, anyway. Keep it in the pews honey. We are full up here."

I don't like people who are selfish, tacky, flashing around money trying to get attention, full of themselves jack offs; neither does my Mom. They do really stupid things. Like that spazzy egomaniac faggot with the 25 million dollars pink diamond in the middle of his head. I don't know who he is, and I don't care if that little spaz hears about this. He's so starved for attention, it's going to drive him nuts when I don't mention his name! Is he gay with a "pink diamond"? I don't care. I'll just call him spazzy egomaniac! My Mom would have a field day with him! I can just see it. She would say something like, "Son, do you think that's a wise move, a 25 million dollar diamond in the middle of your head? Don't you think that money could be spent more usefully on others? Don't you think of anyone but yourself? Have you heard of habitat for humanity, or the American Negro college fund, or don't you have a fan base that could use some of your money to pay medical bills from Co-vid? Do you know who Martin Luther King junior is? I knew him, and I don't think he would approve of your behavior. When was the last time you were at church? Does your mother know about your behavior?"

That spazzy egomaniac would cry like a baby, rip out that diamond, give it to mom, apologize, and ask for her forgiveness. Mom would say, "Well, that's a start. Now let's work on the rest of you." Mom would straighten him out! She would sell the diamond and give it all to charity, and so would I! Fuck those over-the-top assholes I'm talking about or anyone who is like, "Me, me, me, me." Haven't you ever heard of, "Give unto others." Wow, now I sound really religious. If you are a billionaire, now hear this; if I had a million dollars, I'd give it all away to the needy, blacks, and Latinos. Don't throw your money away, call my bluff! I'll film it, me giving it all away, it's only money. Never going to happen, but nice thought. I can think of a lot of people who could use some help!

The day before I moved to Denver, the engine blew on my car. No joke, I was still going. The engine blew in the middle of the night on the reservation. No lights, it was scary. I remember how hard I started praying. A tow truck driver picked me up, and took me into town! Some people say that prayer doesn't work, but it did for me that night. I got a beater car. I got to Denver. My first apartment at The Leetonia was beautiful. An art deco building off Colfax and Vine, very seedy but all I could afford at that time. I knew I had to have an apartment off a bus route because the beater car wasn't going to last, and it didn't. The apartment was beautiful, marble staircases, rod iron railings, everything trimmed in wood, really pretty. I only had $350 in my pocket. I didn't know anyone and had no job.

In no time, I took three jobs and worked my ass off. I was in Denver for a few months. One day, I was going to work when I noticed a smell. I told John the manager about it. I was collecting my neighbor Dave's mail who was on vacation. I thought he didn't take out his trash. So, the manager said, "You know, this is an old building. I bet a rat died in the walls. I'll call for an exterminator if it gets worse." It didn't make me feel very comfortable, but at least he knows about it and I thought it will get handled.

The next day, it was worse. I used to come home every afternoon and change clothes to go to my next job and I would say hi to Clara. Mrs. Gutierrez, nice woman in her 70s. I'd always ask to help her with her bags, and I wasn't seeing her around much. I didn't want to think about it but I knocked on John's door. "John, I think, maybe, that smell is… and I don't want to think of it, but have you seen Clara lately?" John, shocked, said, "I can't find her! I've known her for 17 years!" Poor baby. John and Clara were good friends, both practicing Catholic and both in the closet in front of their families. They were both gay and always had each other's back. I used to sit and have tea with John when I first moved in and didn't know anyone. John knew I was bisexual and never told a soul, R.I.P. John. It killed me to have to tell him that Clara might be dead, but I had to.

I said, "John, give me the key. I have to go to work. I'll check and then if I am right, you can call the owner and then the police, okay?" He told me, "No, I am not supposed to do that." I said, "I have to go to work, I'll check! Give me the key!" He reluctantly gave me the key. I went up there, the smell was permeating through the door. I took a big breath, opened it about 4 inches, and shut it. Yup, she was very much dead. I told John, "I'm so sorry, you need to call the owner. I'm going to work." When I came home, the smell was so bad! They just took her body away. My sweet friend Eric, this gay guy came down to my apartment, and I answered the door. "Hi Jan! I have something to tell you." I looked at him. "Clara's dead. I know, I told John. I found her." He shook his head. "I met her sister. She came to collect her things, and she said that this is exactly the way she wanted to go, by herself, peacefully." That made me feel much better. When I looked into the apartment, she looked peaceful. She died sitting up. She still had her glasses on, her arm was resting on the chair. I think that's why it was so bad for the building. She died sitting up. Her bodily fluids drained down through the floor and were steeping in from the ceiling below her. They ripped that place apart, and fumigated it twice. I guess, they'll never get that smell out of that apartment completely. I pity the next tenant. R.I.P. Mrs. Guiterez. Well, that was a Welcome to Denver for me! I hope not all my apartments are like this. Clara didn't die from an overdose. She died from natural causes as she had a thyroid problem, and she was about 80 years old.

Speaking of overdose, you can't overdose from T.H.C. or C.B.D. Getting high is a new thing for me, but I only do gummies, T.H.C. and C.B.D. help me relax. I was against it before. I had to educate myself, and I did. I don't need some hippy stoner to tell me about marijuana with a copy of High

Times or whatever that hippy shit is they read. I can't even stand to be next to them at the grocery store. I love organic grocery stores, but some of the hippies who frequently go there, Jesus! The deodorant is this way. The problem is all the stuff they have that's natural sucks, it doesn't work. You know why? They don't test on animals. I'm all for that, but get some Irish Spring or that shit my mother used to wash my mouth with Lava soap. It still makes me gag to think about it. She would use the stuff dad had in the garage next to the kitchen. Easy access, and mom would grab that shit and wouldn't even wash off the grease left on it. Yuck!

Now you know why I behave around my Mom. Moms in her 80s, but she's still in charge! When I first moved to Denver, I took pictures with a bunch of bums and sent them to my racist grandma and said to her, "Look, I have a bunch of new friends in Denver!" My grandma replied, "Well Janny, why do you have so many black friends." She didn't get it. I'm pretty sure that's not what killed her! My grandma lived to be ninety-eight years old, and she was dying from the day she was born. At my grandpa's funeral, when I was eleven, my grandma said to me, "Well, that's your father's plot, and that's where you and your sister will go. We will all be together. That's why we bought all of our plots together." I was eleven and she was telling me I'm going to die, and this is where I will go when I die.

My grandma was a twisted old fuck. Dad's parents were all about looking good and getting the well-earned respect from everyone by having a proper funeral and having all of our family together, which I think is a joke because when we were all together, all they ever did was talk over each other and argue. I can't remember a single time my dad's family ever said, "How are you today? What have you been up to? What do you want to be when you grow up?" Never. They just bitched and complained all the time. I would get letters from grandma and her sister, my aunt Dee-Dee, and they would go on and on about how expensive everything was and how their health was getting bad at the very end of the letter. There was also a Merry Christmas, and I love you along with a check of five dollars in it.

My grandma had money and she would send us five dollars in a check. One year, I framed it as a joke. About a month or so later, she called me, "Janny, didn't you cash your check? The bank said you didn't yet. Don't you need that money?" I couldn't believe it. I said to her, "I am sorry, grandma. I will get right on it." My aunt would send me a thousand dollars for Christmas, but she stopped when I had it out with my dad. I asked too many questions about dad and it made them uncomfortable. I also didn't agree with the comments they would openly make about blacks and any other person who wasn't white. I think they were disappointed in me. To say the least, good! Fuck them! The Williams name ends here! I am the last descendant from our family to pass on that name, and I didn't have kids. My dad and his family would turn in their graves if they knew that! FUCK THAT FAMILY NAME!

I do like to get high at home. I'm not really good in public with it. Not with my mouth. I have a friend who told me she's done more than a hundred mg of T.H.C. in one sitting. I've heard of people who have done more than that. I'm a lightweight, I guess. I can't take more than thirty, and I'm on my face. I do know it has helped a lot of people with a number of medical problems. I did take an anti-nausea drug for my cancer when I was going through my chemo. It had T.H.C. in it. Didn't really work but if someone is suffering and they need marijuana, let them have all they want. Marijuana can't kill you! It should have been legalized a long time ago. I think it could have been if stoner, hippie losers didn't make it look so bad. My ex was always stoned and useless, so I thought all pot smokers were like him. I asked him, "Why don't you quit for one day?" Eric said, "I could if I wanted to. It is not addictive." I asked, "Then why don't you prove it?" He couldn't do it.

Eric was an addict, just like I was a drunk. I also don't compare using marijuana to drinking. They are both a vice! Let's not forget that. But I don't get high and drive ever. You shouldn't ever. I hate these stupid dicks who say, "Oh, I drive better when I am a little high." No you don't, you retard! Get a designated driver. Doesn't matter how old you are. I lived it up in L.A. in the '80s. I hate to say it; nobody was looking out for one another. Now people are a little more aware of situations that could have saved some lives back then. You see a girl who's maybe a little too fucked up, getting into a car late with a stranger, don't look the other way. If you see someone maybe getting a little too drunk or high, say something it might save their life. Or get you killed for trying to help. It's a crapshoot.

CHAPTER FIFTEEN: BLIND DATES, VOLUNTEER

When I first moved to Denver, the fire department came to my building to check the firebox. They couldn't get in, and one of the firemen asked me out. I figured why not! I just went out with a cop, so how bad can this be? This guy's name was Aaron. He was a six-foot-seven white dude who was all about being a fireman. He picked me up, and he said, "Do you like to ice skate?" I said, "Not really. I skated once when I was fourteen, and I was on my ass the whole time." He chuckled. "Well, I play hockey, and if you don't want to skate, you can watch me skate." Wow, that will be fun for me. He couldn't find the skating rink. He ended up asking me if I knew where it was. I told him, "I just moved here." Then, he casually mentioned, "Let's go to my place and watch a movie." We went to his house, and I kept thinking if he was anticipating the idea of sleeping with me. Nope! That was not going to happen.

He started kissing me. At that point, I realized why he couldn't find the rink. This guy was drunk. He wasn't a very good kisser, either. I went home soon. He called me a couple of days later, mentioning, "We are having a get-together at my place with some firemen and women, you should come." I agreed to go. I got there and he didn't put any effort into introducing me. I kind of did that myself. Aaron was already drunk by the time I got there, but I noticed there were some female firefighters there too. I thought, that is great. I can have some women to talk to. Just after a while, Aaron pulled me aside and said, "We don't really like women in the fire department. We just put up with them." I thought, "What a prick!" That boy's club attitude could never win him any points. What a shit thing to say about the people you work with! I hope the women he worked with hear this!

Aaron, his brother, his father, all of the men in his family were firemen. I wonder, were they all arrogant, chauvinistic pigs? I found my way towards the washroom, which was down the hall and couldn't find the light. Some guy tried to help me find it, and we both started laughing because we couldn't find it. Aaron came around the corner, turned on the light and said, "If you want to fuck, do it in your own house." I was shocked. "We are looking for the light switch." He was delirious. "Bullshit! You want to fuck him! Don't do it here." I said to the guy helping me find the light, "Are you kidding me?" He was like, "He's a dick." That's all he said.

I was still shocked. "Is he kidding with this?" The guy said, "I don't think so." I looked at Aaron, called him an asshole and went home. I called his brother and he told me, "Yeah, he gets like that when he's drunk." That was his excuse; he was drunk, that's why he did that. I know there is a lot of alcoholism in police work and among firemen too but is that really an excuse to behave that poorly? That was my first date in Denver.

This incident cleared it for me that I could never be a fireman, too scary. But I do think when they aren't working, they try to pick up chicks a lot. More than cops do, for sure. Why does it take six firemen to go to the market? They also talk about going down in a blaze of glory planning their funeral stuff, which I don't get at all. I can't watch those fireman movies without crying. Mostly because the cast is awesome, but they are heart-wrenching. You know that one with Kurt Russell, Jesus! I balled. I like his Disney work though.

I went on some really bad dates when I first moved to Denver. Mostly, the blind dates. They made me wonder if my friends even liked me or not. Would you fuck this guy? No, why? Throw him to me? I went out with a guy named Mark. He was so uncomfortable being naked he changed his clothes under the covers and wanted the lights off. Wow, was he fun in the sack. Mark came into the club I worked at after we stopped dating. He was an insecure prick who couldn't make any decision without his friends around. He reminded me of fraternity boys who only have confidence when they are all together getting drunk.

Mark was with his friends from work, and he came to my station, sat in my section, and started talking. He told his friends, "She's some waitress I went out with. Watch this! Hey, Jan! I got a new car and it goes fast. My new girlfriend loves it." He was waiting for a reaction for his friends. I laughed. "Cute, really cute," and walked away. Later, I told him. "Well, it is good that you have a new car, hopefully the girl you are going out with now will pay attention to your car instead of you being a bad lay." He had no response to that. He was lucky I didn't say that in front of his friends and tried to embarrass him like he tried on me.

Mark would ask me questions almost anyone could answer, and he was testing me to see if I was smart. He said, "I went out with a lot of pretty girls, and I wanted to see if you were stupid or not." His stupidity had no boundaries, but I chose to let it go. "Really? You have to be kidding," I answered.

The girl he went out with before me put wax on his new car and sent it through a car wash. That fucked up the paint job, which is why he got a new car. I thought, "Whose stupid now, dipshit?" Why don't you give the keys to your new girlfriend and see what she does to it but whatever you do, don't let her see you naked! Turn the lights off! Do you want to know why he wanted the lights off? He was the whitest motherfucker I have ever seen! He glowed in the dark, looking like the Pillsbury dough boy. If you look closely, you could see his aorta.

Next, I went out with a guy who was good-looking and well off! But he used to drink heavily. He is not an ex-boyfriend, just a guy I went out with twice. He wanted to take me to the mountains for dinner. When I got in the car, I could tell he was wasted, so I told him, "I don't feel comfortable going to the mountains for dinner. It might snow and I don't want to get stuck up there," He said, "Would that be so bad?"

"Let's go back to town and we can have dinner there," I told him. He finally agreed and we went back. While we were having dinner, he made a strange comment. He said, "It's nice to see a girl eat and keep skinny. How do you do it? It's kind of sexy to see a woman eat and not get fat." What a shallow piece of shit. I didn't want to go out with him again after this, but he called me later. "Hey, you want to meet for a drink?" I was reluctant, but I still met him.

I didn't think getting in a car with him was a good idea. I may have been a drunk but I'm not stupid. I met him by my old place. When I got there, he was drunk at the bar so I ordered a drink as well. He had three martinis while we were there, and we weren't there long. "Let's go someplace else," he said after a while. That was not happening. I refused. "No, I'm going to walk home to meet my brother." He got the hint. "You think that I had too much to drink, don't you?" I didn't know what to say but the truth. "Yes, I think you had a little too much. I'll walk, it's okay. I'll call you later." I left and never called him.

Then, I went out with a guy named Dana. He had something wrong with one of his eyes, which threw me off. I think, maybe, God gave him a bum eye as punishment because he was a cheating, lying piece of shit. Dana was in a relationship with a woman with a child, and he asked me out behind her back. We went to a concert, and we went back to his house. He was a bad lay and his house was a piece of shit too. He told me, "I just bought it. My house is next to the old Elitch Gardens. They're going to put a golf course there and my house will be worth a lot!" That area is still a shithole and I got the feeling he was a white boy trust funder.

His girlfriend found out, got my number and called me. "Why are you doing this to me? I have a son, and he's with me." I told her, "I didn't know he was cheating on you. I don't ever want to see him again, he's all yours." About a week later, my friends at work said, "Some girl who's pissed off at you came here looking for you." His girlfriend came looking for me. I really didn't need the drama. I called her and cleared it out. "I don't want him! You should drop him. He's a creep, do not trust that asshole." I was honest with her. She could only manage to say a "Thank you." I hope Dana's dick falls off. That poor girl! What a bastard to do that to her not the only guy to ask me out who had a girlfriend or wife, unfortunately.

I used to go fishing in Nebraska with my friends, Pat and Sally. Rest in peace, Pat, you sweetheart. This guy that we went fishing with won't tell you his name, asked me out. We went for lunch near my place. There I figured out why this guy was single. I felt like I should have brought my portfolio and handed him my credit status. He was looking for someone like his mom. It made me think of my ex, and his nightmarish mom. He was very clear about what he wanted from a relationship. It was difficult to keep a straight face most part of the time we had lunch.

After we were done with food, I kept thinking, "What the fuck? Does she looks like the mom in Psycho?" He had a cool dog, Midnight. Really sweet, but now I think his dog may turn into the dog from The Omen if I'm not careful. Kidding, just kidding. He was a nice guy, just not the one for me but he knew exactly what he wanted in a woman. He should go on a dating sight or something to find the woman of his dreams. That way he can see her credit report, get her blood type, her Mother's maiden name, and get her perfect measurements too. Or he should marry his dog, Midnight. They love each other, and he had no complaints about his dog.

My girlfriend Jules set me up with a guy who wanted to suck my toes. I have the ugliest feet. I was a ballerina, so they suck but I don't want them sucked. He was just that kind of guy; he was kind of cheesy but very attractive and successful but it was everything I could do to keep from laughing. Things that were going through my mind was, "Jesus! I usually charge about a hundred dollars an hour for this kind of shit where I am tied up and they lick my feet." I just told him, "I'm not really into that but thanks." Needless to say, he didn't get laid. I couldn't keep a straight face because I wasn't drunk enough, and I'm a fucking drunk. Should have gotten really shitfaced, but I could have made a fool of myself and said something that wouldn't go well like, "Will you stop sucking my toes? Just let me see your cock now, so I know I'm not wasting my time with the toe-sucking thing because if you think you are getting laid with the toe sucking performance, you would be wrong, so let me see your cock. I hope it is better than that toe-sucking thing!" I think that would be a bad ending for any date. He was sweet but again, just not the guy for me.

My friends in Cherry Creek set me up on a date with this guy who lived next to them. He was handsome and rich so we went to a Bronco game. This guy was attractive but slow or something. He didn't talk or anything just sat there and watched the game. I gave him a hug and said goodnight when he dropped me; that was it. He decided to get wasted and call me in the middle of the night over and over again when my sister was visiting. Why is it that all the stupid assholes come over or call me when my sister is visiting? I had to turn off my phone. The next morning, he called again when I turned it back on. I told him, "If you don't stop calling me, I'm going to tell the police where you live and have them arrest you." About a year later, he came into the club I worked at and acted like he didn't know me. He was sitting with some girls, and I said to them, "Don't give him your phone number. Whatever you do, just don't do that. He's a psycho," and walked away. Later some of his friends told me he was in an accident and he had brain damage from a fall. I told them what he did and they said, "He's done that to other people too." Still no excuse boy; oh boy, I have the worst luck sometimes. All dates I had when I first moved to Denver sucked.

This next story is about one of the worst dates I have ever been on. My new friend, who, after this blind date she set me up on, is no longer a friend. She told me this guy was someone who saw me and thought I was cute and wanted to go out with me. I was new in Denver and I thought, why not? I just went on the fireman date. Just how much worse can it get? Blind date, Jesus! I met him at the restaurant out front. It was at Ruth Chris Steak House in downtown Denver about twenty-five years ago. I said, "Hi, I'm Jan." He was on his cell phone, an old flip phone. He replied, "Hi, I am sorry. This is business. I have to take this one of those days, right?" We got seated, and I started noticing this hostess, giving me looks of some sort. My date was kind of an obvious guy. If you didn't notice him, you would notice his cologne. It smelled like he took a bath in Ralph Lauren Polo. Whew!

The waitress came over. She said, "Good evening. May I get you two a drink to start?" She looked at me to take the order, and he interrupted. "Honey look, I need a drink for sure but I'll take it at the bar. You don't mind, do you? This is business," I asked, completely annoyed, "Maybe they can call you back?" He laughed, and went to the bar. The waitress looked at me, "May I get you something?" I said, "Yes, I will have the best white wine you have by the glass. Please. You pick!" I whispered to her, "I might have to down it, depending on how this goes. Do you drink? Get yourself a glass. I work in the business too. I am a chef." She laughed and went to get our drinks mine to the table and his to the bar.

He left me there for about five minutes. It's not long, but when you're alone, it's forever. This was before everyone had a phone so I was sitting alone waiting for him to come back. He came back, slapped his phone shut. All he did was talk about him. He didn't ask me questions like what do you do in your spare time or what Church do you go to? Although he didn't look like the kind of guy who attends Church much, he had on a pinky ring, gold chains, and a kind of flashy silvery suit. I think he was Armenian, not Italian. He looked like something out of Good Fellas. He sat there and talked about himself and nothing else. The waitress came over again, and he told her, "I had a business thing come up, you get it, right? I got to make another call. Just one second." I said, "Well yes, I understand." He looked at the waitress, and then pointing at the menu, he told her, "I'll have this, and this. I'll take another one of these, and bring it to the bar for me. Okay?" Mr. Important! I glanced towards the hostess station and over at the bar. Everyone was watching me and this asshole. It was slow, and they didn't have a lot to do.

The jackass I was with said, "Order whatever you want, sorry. I have to make this call." He went to the bar with his drink. I actually started to feel sorry for the waitress who had to deal with this train wreck of a blind date! "Can I get you anything?" I looked around and a couple of tables by me. They were watching the guy I'm with make a fool out of me! They were looking at me with eyes that were saying, "Why is she putting up with this prick?" I told her, "Let me see your wine list." She showed it to me. I told her, "Okay, order me a Louistre and get yourself a glass of wine too, and take these two bottles to the chefs. We'll go from there." She asked me, "Are you sure?" I said, "Of course, I am." I leaned into her and went, "This is probably the worst blind date, you have ever seen, right?" She was shocked. "A blind date? We just thought it was an asshole boyfriend, and you were his girlfriend or something." Everybody was talking about this date in the whole restaurant! I told the waitress, "I'm going to kill my girlfriend!" She said, "You need any help? I think the whole place would back you up!" We both just started laughing.

The dipshit was at the bar and saw none of this! He was too busy on his phone call to notice, but everyone else did. He finished his call and came back. We started to talk. Tables around us, well three of them, were seeing how this was going to pan out dinner and a movie! Yay! One night only, and we are the stars! He came back. We talked for about five minutes about himself, and he got up! "I hope you don't mind. I have to make another call." I looked around at the people who were watching this shit show, and I went, "Does anybody mind if he makes another call? It's business, you understand?"

The women sitting at the tables around me started to snicker. Let's be real. Women get stuff quicker. It took a little more time for the guys to catch up until their girlfriends said, "Hey honey, watch this! Look over there, right there! Jesus, that bad date over there! How could you miss this? Are you blind? Don't you see it? That guy is an asshole!" The jackass I was with didn't even notice his phone was at his ear, and he didn't care. The waitress looked at me in total disgust with him, "Can I get you anything?" I told her, "Well, yes you can, my dear. This is what I want; order any appetizer, entrée, and dessert to go. Your choice, and two more bottles to the kitchen, another for yourself. Fuck it, I'll have a louistres, again. Do the guys outside in valet want something, go ask, okay?" She said, "Really?" I said, "Absolutely! This asshole can afford it, I'm all alone, and this is the worst date of my life, so why not?" The waitress laughed and made the order for the staff and me.

He came back, and started eating his salad. "Aren't you having anything?" I said, "Mine takes a little longer." Lucky me! He talked with his mouth full. What a treat. Bad manners too. This guy should be having dinner with Madonna! After his salad, he went back to the bar again and didn't ask me if he could go to the bar. He just went. By this time, everyone in the place is watching this disaster date. I'll bet they were taking bets to see how it would end! The people around me were nice, at least I went to the bathroom. I don't think anyone thought I would come back or not. One of the women at a table next to us confronted me in the bathroom. She was a pissed-off grandma whose granddaughter was abused and she came in the bathroom to help me. "Sweetheart, you don't have to take that kind of abuse from him, or anyone. Don't let him behave that way. You're an important person, and he should pay attention to you. You have a voice, young lady. You don't have to let him treat you like that. I had a granddaughter who had the same problem. You know what she did? She almost killed him, took a baseball bat to him, and he deserved it too. She went right for his groin; that's what you're supposed to do. They say, hit them where it hurts. She did!" I had to stop her and explain, "It is just a really bad blind date," and calm her down. We were in there for a good amount of time too, and my date didn't even notice.

My waitress signaled me that my food was ready. When I got out of the bathroom, I went to the hostess stand. I said, "Okay, who won? How long did you think this date would last?" They said, "No, we were betting to see if you'd hit him, or throw a drink in his face." I looked at them, the bartenders, and hostesses, the wait staff, kitchen guys, all of them, and said, "Oh I hit him, just not in the balls!" And I looked at the little old lady who came to my rescue and winked. She laughed. I got my food; I tipped her twenty and told her, "Tell him that I'll call him later."

It actually cost me twenty dollars to go out with him. He called me the next day, pissed off! His bill was almost two thousand dollars. Fuck him! I'll never go on a blind date again. That was my second date in Denver with a man, but lucky me! My ex-girlfriend, Brianna was worse than him by far. At least I didn't have to fuck that guy. Thank God. I used to have a very high tolerance for adults who were spoiled, stupid, self-absorbed, bipolar, whiney, shallow, debutant, barneys wearing, royals, Mormons, Trump-ish, sociopathic, white you must know so-and egomaniacs. I know I left something out. Oh well. Looking back, I should have thrown a drink in his face. Most people would have, but I was thinking like a poker player. Ride it out a little and when they let their guard down, TAKE 'EM! Here is a guy who was underestimating me and was probably thinking, "Who cares how I treat her? It's a blind date. What's she going to do to me, never go out with me again? Please." So I didn't think just a drink in the face was sufficient.

Volunteer work, better than dating. I have always done volunteer stuff, so when I moved to Denver. I went where I could to help. I did face painting at different events. I worked at an elementary school in Five Points. I brought my resume, I didn't know if I would need it or not. Not. The principal took me aside and said, "No gang symbols or rap artist names." I was like, "Really?" He wasn't kidding. With my Mom's experience with underprivileged schools in L.A., I thought it might be a good idea to get some supplies, just in case. I went to The Wizards Chest and bought seventy-five dollars of paints, brushes, party bubbles, and stickers. You name it. It's a good thing that I did. All they had for supplies was a yellow, blue, and red crayon that you wet and draw with. But they didn't work. I was working out then and some of the guys I worked out with were black guys who were Denver cops and they gave me a Denver cop t-shirt to wear as a joke. I wore it to the fair to keep the kids in line. They asked me, "Are you a cop?" I just said, "I am a volunteer." I wasn't worried about the kids. I was the only volunteer that showed up for the whole school to face paint. I was there for four hours. If someone asks you to volunteer, show up!

I called my Mom and told her about my experience. She told me about one of hers. Mom said one of the kids at her school had a mother who was a known prostitute and drug user. She came to school to get her kid high. She slapped one of the teachers across the face, and the police came. I thought wow, I had it pretty easy. I did face painting at four different schools. The last time I volunteered for face painting, I left the supplies, all the paints, brushes, and bubble stickers, all of it. I told them, "You keep it, you need it more than I do. Call me if you need a volunteer." They were happy to have it as they didn't have the school funding for stuff like that. No skin off my nose, but I can go out and buy new stuff if I need to. I also worked with handicapped kids. Among them, there were a lot of kids with Down Syndrome. They were so much fun to work with, not all of them but most of them. They were so happy. Any little accomplishment, and they go nuts. I taught swimming and I had two kids with Down syndrome. I adored them and their moms.

I put together the fishing game and face painting for Halloween one year for the deaf. I was aware that I was losing my hearing. Honestly, I was okay with losing my hearing. Me asking, "What did you just say" works for me. If the people I did volunteer work with, for the deaf, get wind about this little gem, they probably won't want me to volunteer again. I'll call them up. "Hi, it is Jan!" Click. "That's that crazy woman who thinks all white people are racist, no we aren't!" I think their hands would get tired from swearing at me if they saw me again. You get it. They're deaf. They speak with their hands. Oh, Jesus. Anyway, I set everything up at Wash Park – an all-white neighborhood. The guy who was putting the event together thanked me and left me alone. I was supposed to have help. There were two hundred kids. I was all alone. I prayed and God listened. Some little cheerleaders from I don't know where showed up!

Those little girls saved me! Some of them really got into it. I was so impressed. It is wonderful to watch kids help out like that. I wish more kids would like we did growing up. If those little girls remember that day, Halloween, Wash Park, face painting for the deaf, and doing the fishing game: Thank you girls so much for your wonderful help! Any retard can write a check, get up and go buy some old clothes. You didn't mind getting dirty and lending a hand. Karens are like that. They don't cook or clean but they enjoy complaining about it. Lots of excuses. "Oh I would help but I have a pilates class. Well write another check if you want or can I paypal you?" I'm speaking mainly about white women.

Yes, they need more help in depressed neighborhoods. It may be a little scary but if I can do it, why can't other white people as well? I get scared like anyone else. Get over it and go where they need help. Don't be a pussy! This is coming from one of the biggest pussies on the planet who can't watch scary movies without covering her eyes and screaming. So if I can do it, suck it up! Sharing is caring, you selfish motherfuckers and peace be with you. I once volunteered in L.A. at Union Station Downtown. I slipped at the dinner table and said something about it to dad. He went nuts! "I don't ever want you to go down there with those bums again!" We were in the kitchen. We didn't go out where the homeless were. It was an eye-opener for sure, and we did some good. Dad didn't believe in helping anyone who wasn't white because he's a dick. My dad's family only pissed on the poor.

You know what I would love to see? White people going to black churches take that first step. If you don't feel comfortable going alone, take a friend with you. I'll bet nobody will mess with anyone coming or going to Church! They would burn in hell if they did! It's the same God. But don't tell whitey that he's black. Just have a little faith. Call the church and ask to talk to someone if it makes you feel better. Just do what my Mother told me. Don't interrupt, be polite and articulate use your inside voice. Just kidding, be a little open-minded. It might surprise you.

I think if you really want to try a black church, do it. Just go unarmed, no confederate flags. Take a shower, use soap, comb your hair, and look nice. Use your best manners, be polite, but, whatever you do, don't say the first thing that comes to mind. Take a look around you, and better be polite. This isn't Daddy's Club. One little slip of the 'n' word, it's get a rope, Tyrone. White cops don't generally make those calls quickly in those neighborhoods. So this is what I recommend; all of the cops that say we are not like that, we do not discriminate, have them go first to the black churches. Then have them try to fit in and enjoy the services.

Here is an idea: call your black friend you brag about to come with you! Everyone who's white has at least one black friend, right? That's what they tell everyone. If they didn't do anything wrong, why would anyone give them a hard time? They aren't asking for it. Prove it. An honest, decent black man will know if you're being honest or if you're full of shit in about ten seconds. If you have nothing to hide, I dare you. Take the first step, bring your family too. Make it a family event and break through some walls! Try to make a positive change. Attention all white cops, who aren't part of the problem, be a part of the solution. You say you are not a racist, go to an all-black church, and pray together. You have nothing to fear, take the first step! Leave your weapons at home, no guns inside the Church, same rules as Mom's 'no guns or toys at the dinner table'.

Speaking of toys, I did stand up in full bondage gear in Denver once just for shock value long time ago. It was Deacons Grey's idea. He said, "Get 'em right off the bat!"

He dared me. Deacon didn't think I'd do it but when I was dressing in the green room, he said, "You can't go out there naked." I told him, "Come on, David! Why not too much? How about the strap-on, can I use that?" He laughed and said, "NO." Deacon used to be fun. This was coming from a guy who went skydiving just for kicks and a ten-inch strap-on is too much? Really?

There was a bachelorette party in the audience I made her night by giving her a leash and a cock sock. Apart from that, I think I also gave her nipple clamps; I think I can't remember. It was a good show. I wonder if she used any of it. She will never forget her party! The show went well but would have been better with the strap-on. Deacon was holding me back, artistically. I know why he didn't let me use the strap on. It was too small for him because Deacon Grey had the biggest cock on a white man I ever saw. Only once, couldn't handle it twice? Whew! I think that's why he always had that cute little crooked smile like he had a big secret nobody knew about. I think, I'm the only one that called Deacon, David. He called me Janny. I could tell him anything and he wouldn't flinch. I think it's because he's seen it all! I tried to shock him, never worked just made him smile. Rest in peace, David.

I worked at Mel's in Cherry Creek. The owner told us that we can't give customers butter for their bread. He said, "No butter. They can have olive oil." I have to ask you, does anybody like to be told how to eat? No. I told my customers that they weren't supposed to have it but I gave it to them anyway. Mel had one of the most fucked up privileged English families around! The kids wanted to move to the States. They said, "We aren't moving as long as this house is still standing." So they went on vacation without their kids. I think that's why a lot of well-off kids disrespect their parents because they don't pay their kids or give them any attention. They need the attention and love that they are not getting from their parents. So what do they do to get their attention? They act out. Their kids took all of their belongings out of the house and burned it to the ground! I will bet they are related to the queen! The only good thing about working there was the chef, Tylor. He was brilliant. Once I accidentally stabbed myself with the cutting knife for bread all the way to the bone and I showed it to Tylor and he almost fainted. "Oh God someone take her to the hospital now!" It was funny. I told him, "It isn't that big of a deal." Matt, another chef and a top hat Tavern was also great. I can't remember his last name but he got Frois Groas tattooed across his knuckles. I think he worked at Vesta Grill as well. Both of them were wonderful chefs!

I also worked at a restaurant off Larimer Square. I was setting up the patio and this white guy in a Mercedes pulled around the corner, parked in front of a fire hydrant, and halfway into a handicapped zone to run across the street to Starbucks to get his triple soy latte mocha bullshit drink. I looked at him and went, "Really?" with a smile on my face. He glanced towards me and said. "Fuck off." Wow, that's nice. When he went into the Starbucks, right when the door shut, a white van came around the corner, booted his car and ticketed it! It was beautiful; I wanted to make a big bowl of popcorn to watch this movie. He came out, looked at his car and said to me, "Did you see who did this?" I said, "Well no, so I guess I'll go fuck myself, huh?" I said this with a big smile. He followed me into the restaurant, and started yelling at me. I told him, "This is your fault. You parked in front of a hydrant, and halfway into a handicapped spot. What did you think would happen?" He stormed off and left his car there. The stupid son of a bitch left his car! By the end of my shift, it was ticketed two more times and towed. I don't know how much money I made that day but it was the best shift I ever worked there. That was a very fuck whitey moment.

I got a job at a gentlemen's club called, "The Diamond Cabaret." I got hired in the steakhouse. Cliff Young was the owner and he was great, R.I.P. I cocktailed too when Bobby Rifkin owned it; the uniform wasn't bad – a one-piece black leotard thong, back bow tie, and a jacket with tails over your tushy. I've worn less. I heard the money was great but they were taking bets to see how long I'd last. It is a little unnerving at first. You're serving someone a drink while they have tits in their face. Oh, excuse me sir? Basically, it is a circus with tits. But the money was great and I adjusted. I was a stripper for about two years but it wasn't a career goal. I took it as a compliment when someone told me that I don't seem like a stripper. I freely admit it. I never really fit in with that crowd but it was interesting for sure. Chalk it up to experience. I have to say this Bobby Rifkin was a wonderful man. He was a little eccentric but he really cared about his employees. That's hard to come by, especially in the adult entertainment business. Girls would spread rumors about him but I never bought them. Talk about biting the hand that feeds you. He always treated me well. We had a manager who got cancer and Bobby made all of the arrangements to let his family know if they needed anything, just ask; and he meant it. I know he would never do anything like Bill Cosby and Hugh Heffner did to women. I think there are a lot more women who are out there who haven't come forward about Bill Cosby. If you ask any intelligent woman before he went to prison if you think he's guilty or not. I don't think a single one would say "He's innocent" unless they're paid off; and if they take money to do that, I hope you burn in hell. Is that too much? KARMA! That's better.

CHAPTER SIXTEEN: O.K. KAREN

When do you think the name Karen comes to mind? For me, I think of a spoiled skinny white woman who gets everything handed to her. A Karen tells everyone else what's best for them even if they don't want to hear it. A Karen is someone who breaks all the rules but gets away with that because she's white and she only follows rules if they benefit her! A Karen never has time to give unto others but she has all the time for herself. How accurate is this definition? I know there's more, but you get it, right? White privilege! One perfect example of a Karen is my ex-best friend. The girl I mouthed off at on her wedding, where I said, "I give it two years!" Even after that, we remained friends.

I am sure everyone has a "Karen" story to tell, but after you read this, you'll think I'm lying. Nope, I'm telling you everything Karen did and everything she didn't do is the complete truth. Before I go any further I have to tell you this, Karen doesn't go by the name Karen so she can deny that this is about her she goes by a nick name and her nickname isn't "spoiled white girl, lying manipulative cunt" but it should be. After she got divorced the first time, she was about 24 and Karen started to work at a luxury hotel as a concierge. Karen kind of looks like Dakota Fanning, really white! Karen said, "It's a great place to meet rich men." She found one who was 18 years older than her and Jewish.

Karen said to me when they first started dating. "Well, he doesn't look Jewish. He looks Italian, so I can tell everyone he's Italian, not Jewish." I'm pretty sure my Jewish friends would be offended by that. She dated him for a couple of years and they would travel all over the world together. I guess she didn't have a hard time with him being

Jewish for long because she said she was going to convert as he had to marry a Jew. I was surprised to hear that Karen's folks were very religious. I asked her, "Do your parents care if you convert?" Turns out, she didn't ask them if it was okay with them. Karen said she was going to do it no matter what she said, "They have to support me in everything I do. I'm their daughter." I think if I was raised Christian and wanted to convert, I would ask my Mom about how she felt about it. I wouldn't just assume she would be okay with it. I don't know about anyone else, but that's a pretty big decision to make. Karen never asked for permission from her parents for anything, not ever. She got engaged and she was telling me that she wanted more money in the prenup. I asked, "It's not about the money, right? I mean you love him, don't you?" Karen said, "Well, he's worth a lot more than you think. I deserve more than he says I do." From that reaction, I should have known what's to come, but okay, Karen.

Karen came to Durango after she got engaged to show me her wedding ring. It was me and my girlfriend, Nicole. It was a monstrous right; eight and a half-carat sapphire with two three-carat diamonds cut in triangles on each side. She was telling us how they had to get the right jeweler and how much it cost to insure it, and how the stones had to be perfect, only the best of the best. It was kind of like their over-the-top log cabin in Aspen, where they had to have a special crew of guys look for years in the forest for two, thirty-foot long single pieces of wood for handrails that they needed to match for their custom-made staircase.

Karen and her husband bragged about everything they owned. They were surrounded by their expensive and original things, but were the emptiest and shallowest people I had ever met. Karen wasn't exposed to that kind of money before; she was very middle class before she met him. Once, she was going on a yacht with some of his friends, she wore a t-shirt and shorts. This woman didn't even know how to dress. I felt like saying, "It's not a fishing boat on a lake, you idiot." But instead, I said, "These people aren't middle class. Don't be surprised if they snub their nose at you." Another time, she was telling me how her boyfriend bought her a fur coat and diamond jewelry. He told her, "Well now that you have your fur coat and your diamonds, you can dump me, huh?" Then he laughed. Karen thought he was funny. But I sensed some type of major insecurity in him. So I guess he has had his fair share of materialistic girlfriends. I thought they were made for each other.

They eloped in Sweden. Karen called me up later and said, "I have a surprise for you. We are going to have a baby!" I told her, "Karen, why? You don't like kids. Get a nanny and look into schools now if you are thinking of doing this all by yourself. You are nuts. You know you can't do this alone. Get a nanny, Karen!" Sounds like good advice, right? You know what she said to me? "I can't get a nanny because my husband will fuck her." I said to her, "I don't think he would do that, Karen." I thought she was kidding. After a short pause, she said, "Yeah, it's in the pre-nup. He can fuck whoever he wants to, but I can't fuck anyone else or I lose everything but he can go fuck anyone he likes. I don't care, it's only sex." I was a little taken back by that comment but not surprised. Karen always treated sex like it was a big joke. There was no way she could stay faithful.

Karen couldn't keep her legs closed for less than two years in her first marriage. You think a piece of paper will keep her faithful? She was a nymphomaniac! She told me, "He wanted to pass on the family name." That's the worst reason to have a kid. I mean, look at the royals and my dad's family. I guess, they were all backstabbing, racists, self-absorbed assholes who had money, so it was okay that they are dicks because they have the family name. That's what's really important. They thought, "The family name is the most important thing you have to pass on to your kids!" What a load of horse shit.

Karen had the kid and at first everything seemed okay, but I knew it wouldn't last. She called me up out of the blue when I was just getting settled into Denver. She said, "You are right. I can't handle this alone, I tried to kill myself again and it didn't work. I was in the psychiatric ward in the hospital. I need you, Jan. You're the only person who can help me. You are so good with kids, and I'm all alone. My friends came out to see me but they were all gone. It's just my parents, now. I need you to come out here and help me. You are my best friend, you're the only person who can help me!" I knew this would happen. Karen tried to kill herself before. She never went thru with it, Karen does it for attention, but now there's a kid involved. She knew that if she calls, I would never say no to a kid in need.

I said, "How much time do you need, Karen? I'll come out there and help, okay? Don't worry. I'll be there." She told me," Thank you so much, Jan. I knew I could count on you. I really need you. Nobody else can help me but you! Thanks so much!" I don't know many people who would drop everything for a friend and leave their new home to help them but I did. After I tell you what she did, you'll think, "No way! Jan's got to be making this up. No girl can be that selfish." But Karen is. I thought I could trust her. I mean, I was her best friend. I have known her since we were kids, but Karen had other plans for me than just a little help with her kid.

I asked my new boss if I could take a few months off to help a friend who's in trouble. They said that my job would be here when I get back. I asked a friend, Christina, a stripper and comedian to watch my apartment for me. I knew I could count on her. She was one of the few strippers I trusted. If she reads this, thank you sweetie for helping me out! I called my sister, "Karen's in trouble again. She needs my help with her kid. She tried to kill herself again and she needs me." My sister told me, "Don't go. She's using you. She's just looking for attention again. Don't go!" When my sister was telling me not to go help her, she almost cried. She was trying to protect me from her. My sister knew about all of her bullshit, but she was my best friend so I said, "Sis, think about that kid. You know Karen can't handle this by herself."

Next thing I know, I didn't have a car. It only got me to Denver and went cur-clump! I jumped on an airplane and went to Arizona to try to help her. We get in a golf cart to go to her house and she's really skinny, another of her game that I liked to call "The Skinny Game." She used to drop weight for attention too. I said, "Karen, you need to put some weight on. You are really skinny, too skinny." She's all smiles and told me, "Yeah, I know I'll put some weight on. Look, I'll eat this cheerio from this cup. I'm full. Just kidding, I'll put some weight on, don't worry Hehe." Her parents came out to help her and she would drink those "protein" drinks, so it looked like she was trying to gain weight but it was all for show, like anorexic girls who pick at their food to make it look like they are eating. Karen was not a good actress. She was sitting right in front of me, all smiles. There I was, who just quit her new job, had her friend Christina watch her new apartment, and she's smiling like this was fun. Look at me! I'm sick again and everyone is giving me attention. I saw

Karen like this and thought, God I should have listened to my sister.

We got to their massive house that's been photographed with a Ferrari in the garage. You know the type. Her husband had to buy the number one motorcycle they had at Sturges that year. Karen said, "Everyone wanted it but he just had to have it!" Some rich white people are like that. They will buy something just to tell everyone how expensive it is or original it is, and nobody else can have it. They do stuff like that because all they have is their "things," and they have no depth. Karen bragged to me about how they bought the plot next to them for a mere million dollars because they didn't want anyone to build a house there. It would block their beautiful view. God forbid, they donate to the poor or volunteer but they can't lose their view, which is everything that really matters, right?

He parked his perfect bike in his garage and let it collect dust. I don't think people understand how pissed off real riders get when they see a rich white fuck like him on a beautiful bike like that. He doesn't appreciate the time and skill it took to make that bike. He just wants the bragging rights to owning it, the fucker barely knows anything about bikes and is not a skilled rider but hey, he thinks he looks cool.

Karen had a stuffed toad that they used to take everywhere they traveled and would tell people, "This is our little 'Toadle' Isn't he cute? We love him! He goes everywhere with us. He's been all over the world, hasn't he?" She would baby talk to it like a child. Karen thinks doing that will make her more unique, expressive, and interesting like rich people who bring their own silverware to eat with at a restaurant or bring their own wine. Why?

Because it's her favorite kind and she won't eat her dinner without it.

Rich white people have their "special rules." They are just for them to make them feel superior! Ask any waiter, bartender, manager or host at a high-end restaurant. They will tell you how all white rich people are just like that! They are a pain in the ass. They all want something special off the menu, or they expect you to suck up to them because of the "I know the owner" attitude. They treat the staff like peasants! Whenever Karen went out for dinner, and if she didn't get her way, Karen would say, "I'll just take it out of his tip, Hehe." I didn't think that was funny. She used to be a waitress too but now, she was above it.

Karen took me to look at some of her husband's houses. He was into real estate and the contractor said to her, "Are you his daughter?" He wanted to know if her husband or his boss was her father, so Karen told him, "No. I'm his wife" with a big smile on her face; the guy was embarrassed. "I'm so sorry, I didn't know." She smiled harder and said, "That's okay. Everyone does that. I'm used to it. Hehe." Karen enjoyed playing the part of the younger woman. She used to say, "My husband loves it when they do that" Of course her husband loves that. "Look at her! That's my young wife. Isn't she a nice piece of ass!?" Her husband treated her like a whore and she let him. Probably in the pre-nup!

I saw their house before they had their son. It got photographed for some magazine to boost her husband's already inflated ego. My dad did the same thing with his office, got the place photographed to put in a dental magazine so he could say, "That's my office. It's completely original. Nobody else has an office like it!" Their house wasn't made for kids at all, but it looked good, so who cares if the kid hits his head on something sharp, falls down the stairs, or he puts his fork in the light socket. Worse, God forbid, he touches any of their artwork. Karen was showing me her art. "Look at our new Fuller. It was expensive but ours is bigger than our friends. That's from Italy; it's one of a kind."

They were so shallow. I'm surprised that they don't keep price tags on their things to let everyone know how much they think they are worth. They put the kid's room in the guest house next to theirs so the kid won't interrupt them. If you walked into their house, you wouldn't know they had a kid at all. They didn't want the baby to get in the way of their beautiful photographed house. I haven't seen the kid since he was born. He's about two and he's a fucking monster, a complete tyrant! He bites, slaps, and never says 'please' or 'thank you'. I'm not putting up with that shit from any kid! I had him saying 'please' and 'thank you' in two months. Karen saw him do this. She would say, "Oh he never does that for me." I said, "I know. That's why I'm here I guess, right?"

Jesus! The dad decided to throw her a surprise party to show everyone what a good husband he is to his sick wife. He asked me to take Karen to a spa to surprise her. He rented a bunch of rich people to come over and admire his house and artwork, that's it. It was nothing more than him getting attention to look like he gave a damn! It was a joke.

One afternoon, the dad came up to me and said, "Jan, would you leave the house for an hour so I can fuck my wife?" He said this with a big smile on his face, right in front of his kid. I can't imagine how his son will treat women when he grows up with that kind of example. I told him, "Sure. Enjoy your wife. I'll go play with your son." When I came back, I saw him leaving the room with a smile on his face. I went inside the bedroom to see how Karen was. The minute I entered, she said, "Look what he left me on the nightstand." He put a hundred-dollar bill on the nightstand for her, a tip that one offers a hooker. She was smiling. I said, "Are you kidding me? You are right, he's cheap." She chuckled. "He likes doing that. It gets him off, Haha."

When I told Karen I worked at a strip club as a cocktail waitress and was thinking of stripping to get out of debt, she told me "My husband has a friend who owns a strip club and he let me dance for him once. You should do it if you have a nice body." Her husband wanted her to look and behave like a stripper, he encouraged it. I never told people I didn't know I worked as a stripper because of the stigma that goes along with it but he wanted her to be like that in front of his male friends. It was like he was her pimp.

Karen told me she and her hubby used to go to Europe to fuck around with prostitutes for fun. She said, "We don't have sex with them, we just fool around. He really likes it." It was like she was trying to impress me with her 'sex stories' with hookers because she thinks it makes her look 'worldly'. When we were sixteen, we got really drunk and went down on each other like I wasn't fucked up enough about my sexuality, Karen was awful. I thought she was ridiculous, she was so fake and it was all about her. Maybe she should get together with my ex-girlfriend Brianna. They have a lot in common, they're both flat, skinny blonds, and they're both "users" of other people. In addition to that, they're both pathological liars, bad lays, and they both suck cock for money. I know there's more. Oh yeah, they're both cheap, tactless women. I really think they would be perfect together.

When Karen was in college at Santa Cruise, she told me, "Jan, I did this crazy thing. I seduced my professor at school." But is it seduction when a hot young girl with her legs spread says to a man, "Excuse me? Would you like to fuck?" She told me, "I asked him if he wanted to have an affair with one of his students and he said, yes. So I fucked him and he was almost fifty!"

Karen also joined the gay and lesbian club, and she was never bi or gay. I never trusted her enough to tell her I was bi-sexual because everything about sex to Karen was a game. If she knew I was bi, she would have probably asked me to do a three-way and after her pitiful attempt to get me off. Wait, no way! Yuck! What an image. Dead puppies, dead puppies, dead puppies, that's better.

Karen should have become a pornstar. If sex was a weapon, she'd be a Bazooka! In high school, Karen told me she used to sit in class with her legs spread in her cheerleader outfit in front of the male teachers to tease them. When we were kids, sixteen years old, we went to H.O.Y. Help Our Youth for birth control. I was still a virgin but Karen had a boyfriend who she wanted to have sex with, so I went with her and said, "I'll go to the meeting with you." So we had to go to this "sex talk" with the nurses and two girls from my high school were there. Holy shit, they might have thought that I'm not a virgin. I told them, "You guys don't tell anyone at school that I'm here. I'm still a virgin, and she has a boyfriend. I'm just here for moral support, okay?" I made it very clear that I was a virgin. I didn't mind helping her out with this, but I was not going to risk my reputation just so she could get laid.

The girls I went to school with didn't say a word, thank God. I can't remember their names, but they were both nice girls. You know why they kept their mouths shut? They were Latino girls. If they were white girls, my reputation would be ruined because white girls have no loyalty, quoting Tom Segura and Latino girl's rock!

When Karen started to have sex, she played the "I think I may be pregnant" game with me for attention and I gave it to her. "Don't worry. It will be okay, Karen." She would smile and say, "Thanks," but it was all for show. She was never knocked up, anything for attention! Our friend, Craig, asked us together when we were sixteen who was the virgin. I looked at him and said, "I'm a virgin," and he didn't believe me because Karen threw me under the bus and said, "It doesn't matter what everyone thinks, Jan." She didn't want anyone to know she was having sex. That was after I took her to get on the pill and she said to me, "If anyone asks, tell them I'm still a virgin too," so I lied for her. Karen used me to cover for her, that's all she does uses people to cover for her lies it's a pattern for her. She's been doing that bullshit since we were kids.

Karen was sitting at the coffee table at their house and told me, "I'm out of commission right now." I said, "Is it a yeast infection or something?" She said, "No. Herpes comes and goes, no biggie." When she said this to me, I thought she was kidding, so I laughed. Who wouldn't but I asked her, "How did you get it?" She said, "I don't know. I guess he gave it to me or the other way around, doesn't matter. It's no big deal, he just goes and fucks someone else, and when I'm okay, he comes back home and fucks me." I looked at her in awe, but Karen wasn't kidding. She told me this so casually like she told me she had a little cold or something "Yeah, no biggie." Then she said, "It wasn't too bad in the hospital, really."

She said this with a smile on her face, telling me about her stint in the loony bin. Karen enjoyed the attention she got in the hospital. When she was talking about it, it made me think, "They never should have let her out," Because Karen was diagnosed with Bi-polar Disorder. We were in the car and Karen was putting on a little show for me with her husband, "If you just slowed down a little, I wouldn't be like this. We are always going traveling and I'm sick of it. I need to slow down, wha, wha, wha."

So apparently, Karen's problems are her husband's fault. I kept telling her to get help, get a nanny, but she wouldn't do it because her husband would fuck her. That was her excuse for not getting a nanny. She was upset because when they were in Israel, she had to wash the baby's clothes all by herself once and she didn't like it.

Karen said, "My husband didn't get us a maid and I had to wash his clothes all by myself" That's so sad! She got a call from Heather, a girl in our youth group from church, she had a young daughter and she wasn't doing well financially. I asked Karen, "Are you going to help her out? She needs a little money." Karen said, "If I help her with money now, she will think she can ask for it anytime. She is a big girl she can fix her own problems and figure it out for herself." If Heather can fix her own problems, why am I here fixing your problems, Karen? Talk about selfish; if I had any money I would have helped her out, but Karen's living in a multimillion-dollar home with a rock the size of Texas on her hand and she can't help her out a little? Wow! What a selfish cunt. Our Church would work with the needy when I became an adult and moved to Colorado. I still did work with the needy. When Karen became an adult, she never volunteered to help but would tell people, "I go to a Church that helps out so many people." She would take credit for being helpful but didn't, one more lie to add to her list.

Karen had to go to her doctor's appointment, and I told her, "Karen, I should take you. You are on medication." She told me, "No, I'm just going to be two hours. Don't worry, it won't be long. I'll be right back." I said, "No, Karen. You are on medication. It's probably better if I drive. I should take you," She looked at me, smiling and giggling. "I'm fine. I'm leveled out, so you don't have to worry. Look at me, I'm fine. It's only two hours, and I'll be right back. Just watch my son." I asked again, "Are you sure? Maybe I should go with you," She said, trying to look as normal as she could. "No, I'm fine by myself." I looked at her and reluctantly said, "O.K. Karen."

I waited one hour, two hours, three hours, four hours, five hours. She finally called from her car. "Karen, where are you? You said it would be two hours. What happened?" Karen said, "Well, don't be mad. I talked it over with my doctor and we both agreed that I really need to get away from my husband, and work on me. I know this seems spur of the moment but I'm going to my parents in L.A., so watch my son for me, okay?" I couldn't believe it. I said, "Karen, no! You come home right now. I don't know this city and don't have a car or medical emergency, or any contact information on your son. Don't go, what am I going to do with him?" She was super calm. "Well, you have to understand I have to do this for me." I was aghast. "Karen, you're telling me that you're on your way to L.A. right now? Does your husband know about this?" She just said, "Well, I don't want to talk to him." I asked her. "What do I tell him if he calls, Karen?" She told me, "If my husband calls, tell him I went to L.A. to see my parents and I don't want to see him." I was panicking. "No, Karen. You come home right now. You aren't thinking clearly. You said you were leveled out. Please Karen, don't abandon me with your kid. He needs you, don't do this to him." Karen said, "Well, my doctor and I discussed it and we both agree that it's a good idea for me to take some time away from my husband. Don't worry, I'm going to be fine and my son is in good hands with you. Just tell him I love him." Click.

My sister was right, Karen used me to leave her husband, and she knew I wouldn't abandon her son. That's why she called me to help her. My sister is going to be smiling ear to ear when she reads this. Sorry sis, you were right! Karen is a fucking liar! No doctor would say to a patient, "Okay, Karen, you go to L.A. to see your parents. Go make that long drive to L.A. by yourself. It will be good for you even though you're on medication. It doesn't matter, everyone will understand you are bipolar, and it's not your fault. Go take care of yourself. You are more important than your son. Jan will watch your kid and she can tell your husband you left him, so you don't have to talk to him." No doctor in the world would say that to a patient!

I should have known better than to help her because Karen pulled this kind of shit with her first husband too. She would take off and go to Phoenix or Palm Springs because she just wanted a little "alone time" for herself. Bullshit! She was getting away from her husband to fuck around. Karen would come back from her little break and she wouldn't have to answer for anything, except her husband who she dumped. Karen's ex-husband had no idea that she was cheating on him, but I'm not surprised. He wasn't my favorite person, but he didn't deserve to get abused by Karen. She doesn't care who she hurts. He was going to be a doctor and it wasn't enough for her. Can you believe that shit? A doctor's salary wasn't enough for Karen.

The next week, the elderly Jewish grandparents were coming out for a visit and she didn't want to be around for that, but I was there that's why she left when she did, it wasn't spur of the moment. So I stayed with her kid and her husband for two weeks while Karen was in L.A., connecting with herself. I had to stay because her husband didn't know what to do with his own kid. That's how un-involved he was with his son. He had no idea what to do, so I had to stay for the kid's sake. Karen knew I would stay. She set this whole thing up.

Her husband called the house, and she was gone. I told him, "Your wife left you, sorry. She's gone to L.A. to see her parents." He didn't come back to see his son. He went out to L.A. to get her back. They both left me there with their kid with no transportation, no medical info, or emergency contact numbers. I was there for four days by myself with their kid. If they tried that shit and they were a black couple, they would both be arrested and the kid would be put in foster care. White privilege! I was thinking of calling the police but Karen was white, rich, sneaky, and manipulative. I don't know what lies she would make up to get out of any trouble, but the kid needed me. I couldn't just leave him.

Karen orchestrated all of this by herself. She knew exactly what she was doing. This was not a bi-polar moment that Karen was having. "Oh, I must have been off my meds when I did that. I don't remember doing that." Anything for an excuse for her, so she can do whatever she wants, sneaky bitch! When we were sixteen, she worked at a movie theater and she told me she and some of the other white kids used to steal the cash people used to pay for the films and go shopping on it. Karen said, "I don't feel guilty about it. I spend all the money right away, so the manager doesn't get suspicious. We look so innocent. We never got caught." Of course, all the kids who worked at the theater are white kids. Why would anyone suspect a white kid of doing something like that, right? If her parents knew about her stealing, they would say, "Our perfect daughter would never do something like that," and the police would buy it and let her go because she's white. If a black kid did that and got caught, they would wind up in jail. I know how it works. White privilege! White kids get away with shit like that all the time, but black kids don't.

I called her parents and said, "Does Karen need any of her medication or any clothes? She said her trip out there was a spur of the moment, so does she need anything?" Her mom told me, "No. Karen had two bags packed with everything she needs. She's okay, thanks." Spur of the moment? Lies! I knew it.

I also don't buy the whole bi-polar thing. Karen had a degree in psychology with honors from U.C.L.A. She must have known the symptoms, the treatment, and the diagnosis. She never got told the word, no! When she got a white carpet put in her bedroom, I asked her, "Karen, how did you talk your parents into letting you get a white carpet in your room? My mom would never let me have that." She said, "I know neither would the other girl's mothers, so I threw a fit until my mom told me, 'O.K. Karen, whatever you want, honey,' so she let me have it. I always get my way." We went to McDonald's with our Church Youth Group. The advisor said, "Everyone is getting the same thing." It was fine for everyone. Except for Karen, she stood up at the counter, demanded she get her hamburger her way or she wasn't going to eat. The advisors said, "O.K. Karen. Whatever you want, honey. She was at U.C. Santa Cruise and she wanted to transfer to U.C.L.A., so her parents said, "Okay, Karen. Wherever you want to go, honey." Once, she wanted a chinchilla for a pet, so her parents said, “Okay, Karen. Whatever you want as a pet, honey” I wonder what happened to it, I am not sure but her new earmuffs were lovely. Just kidding, but I wouldn’t put it past her! Karen always gets her way and doesn’t like to hear the word “No” from anyone and when she does hear the word no, she runs away and does whatever she wants anyway and never gets punished or in trouble for whatever she’s done wrong. She acts like a child and gets away with it. Now is that being spoiled or being bi-polar? Or maybe they’re the same fucking thing!

When Karen was going to U.C. Santa Cruz, she tried to kill herself and fucked it up. She wasn’t getting enough attention from her boyfriend. She transferred to U.C.L.A. with her ex-husband, got married, and ruined that marriage. I’m sure Karen will get whatever she wants from whoever her next victim boyfriend or husband is. Although, I don’t think she will re-marry. Too much spousal support to lose unless the next guy has more money she can get to. Her friends from her first marriage from college said, “Karen’s a gold digger.” I said to them, “No, she’s not. She really loves him. It’s not about the money.” I feel stupid for backing her up all those years. They were right. She was playing me the whole time, she used me. That’s all Karen does; use people to get whatever she wants, playing the “poor me game.” I was her best friend, I’ll get over it. I’m an adult, but her son. How could a mother do that to her own son? Not okay, Karen.

About two weeks after she went to California, Karen’s husband and I went to California to get her back. I also got to see my sister. She had that “I told you so!” face. I deserved that. We went to some friend’s house with whom we went to church with. I couldn’t imagine the lies she’s been telling them. Karen’s ex-husband was there from her first marriage.

He went to our youth group. I asked him, "How can you stand her?" He said, "She's sick, she needs us."

I couldn't believe it after she made a fool of him? He's feeding into this game, so are the kids we went to church with. This sweet guy, Craig, we went to church with he was friends with her ex-husband. Karen acted like he's her best friend. Karen uses him. Not his fault. Karen will lie to anyone she can to look like a victim! I was watching Karen acting like a crazy person. She was using the whole "I'm on benzos" game. "Look how sick I am." Her eyes were all wide. Karen had green eyes like Regan from The Exorcist, very appropriate. She was playing with someone's kid who's about two going, "You are so much fun. I wish my little boy was here but I can't see him, so I'll play with you instead! Haha." She was throwing him around, asking stupid questions.

"Do you get to pick your clothes for your work or does the hospital pick for you? Hehe." Karen said this to a woman who was a nurse acting like a ten-year-old little girl who doesn't know any better it's an act. My sister saw this and went, "I can't watch this shit show anymore. You can if you want." I said to her, "I'll be right behind you, sis." I sat Karen down and said, "Let's talk, okay Karen?"

I sit her down, "Karen, please tell me you're coming back to Arizona. I stayed when the grandparents were visiting." She can't calm down. It's like she did too much blow or something. The thing was, she was not a good actress. Everyone was there for her and she knew it. Karen couldn't care less; she just wanted an audience for her phony nervous breakdown. As I gazed right into her crazy eyes, Karen said to me, "I knew you would stay with my son, thank you. Look, I got my nails done." I was looking at her like, "What did you say?" She thinks getting her nails done is an important thing? She was blowing kisses to me and smiling really big. Karen continued, "I got a one-bedroom apartment in Pasadena and I bought one of those blow-up mattresses for my son, so if he comes out for a visit, I can put him on that." I was thinking if that's really appropriate for a two-year-old so I guess you can take the white trash out of the girl or can you? Then she said, "I got an attorney and when my divorce is final, don't tell anyone but, I'm going to fuck my therapist, I can't wait. Hehe!" I think by the stunned look on my face and the fact that I wasn't going, "You go for it, Karen! Get laid!" she knew she was in trouble. Karen needed that kind of affirmation from me and she wasn't getting it, so she looked around and whispered, "Are you mad at me or something? I knew my son was in good hands with you," I said, "Yes, he was in good hands with me. I'm going to go to my sister's. You're not going back to Arizona, are you?" She looked around again to make sure everyone sees her playing the victim and said "I can't go back there. It's not good for me, he's so controlling. That place is not a healthy environment for me. You need to understand, I need to be here!" Not a healthy environment for me, she said. It's not good for her, she thinks? Karen never asked me, "How's my son doing or how are the grandparents?" No. She didn't ask me that, but she knows what's not good for her. She's putting on a show for everyone. "Look, everyone. My best friend, Jan, is here. She's not mad at me and she understands that I'm bi-polar, and I can't help all of this." I'm looking at everyone giving Karen all of her well-deserved attention from her pathetic performance, but I couldn't take it anymore, so I left.

I went to my sisters. Karen had set up an apartment and an attorney all for her and it took less than two weeks, but I really think she had been planning this for a long time; she was on her computer a lot. I should have seen what she was doing. Karen got a one-bedroom apartment, so when she starts to date, she can go fuck anyone she wants to and can tell them she doesn't have kids or make up any other lies she wants. Karen can just let the air out of the kid's blow-up mattress and went to town. Her parents would be there to cheer her on because she's their daughter. They have to support her in any decision she made! Those are Karen's rules and her Church friends will be right by her side going, "Hey, look! Karen's doing really well now." Yeah, until Karen "attempts" to kill herself again because she just needs more attention. That's all Karen needs more from everyone, it's never enough. I think one of the reasons she went to L.A. was to get away from her husband, is so she can go fuck anyone she wants without getting caught. Karen was sneaky but not a good actress, and she knew it. She can't fuck around in Arizona, but she won't get caught in L.A.

Two days later, she called me at my sister's. "Jan, my brother died. I really need you!" That was no Joke. Dave was a good guy; he was adopted and he must have had a medical condition they didn't know about. He dropped dead of a heart attack in his early thirties out of the blue. At times like that, water under the bridge. "I'm not mad at you, Karen. Whatever you need, I'm there. It's okay." Karen said, "Thank you. I really can't believe this, can you? So you're not mad at me anymore? Okay, thanks for coming to the funeral. " I reassured her, "Okay, I'll buy a black dress and change my flight. I'll be there." I changed my flight and got a black dress. The day before the funeral, she called me. "Jan, I don't think you should come to the funeral because my parents are kind of mad at you because you said I abandoned my son." I was shocked. "Yes, that's exactly what you did, Karen. You abandoned him with me. I told them the truth." She was whispering on the phone like she didn't want anyone else to hear her and said, "Well, my parents think if you didn't come out to help me, I could have worked out my marriage on my own, and I didn't abandon my son. You were there, he wasn't alone." I said to Karen, "What have you been telling everyone about what's going on?" So now it's my fault her second marriage failed. What a fucking liar.

Now, she was telling everyone, "If Jan didn't come try to help me, I could have worked out my marriage, and I didn't abandon my son. Jan was there." I really shouldn't have been that surprised. Nothing is ever her fault! So now, do you think Karen is a white girl, manipulative, lying, spoiled brat that gets whatever she wants? Or do you think Karen is a white, bi-polar, manipulative, lying, nymphomaniac brat that just needs her meds? Either way, I don't want to be around it. Everything is an excuse or a lie for Karen, and she's never wrong. I think the thing that bothers me most about Karen is that she had a beautiful little boy, and she threw it all away and for what? Money when it comes down to it, that's all she wants. That is what she was all about, money. That and attention. She's a fucking disgrace of a woman.

I hope she doesn't hear about this and try to attempt suicide, again it's getting old, "The boy who cried wolf." I don't think the dad will care about anything I say about him. I'll bet he'll deny even knowing me. I'm sure he doesn't want anyone to know he has herpes and that he's a shit father, but anyone around him will know that anyway! When I got back to Denver, I sent her all our pictures and letters from growing up and wrote her a letter, telling her I didn't think she just had bi-polar disorder. I told her that I thought she had "Munchausen's syndrome," where the mother inflicts pain upon themselves or their kid for attention. I don't think she would hurt her kid unless there was money involved, if she got the right price, who knows?

I asked her if she was going to fight for at least partial custody, and she said, "It would be a waste of 'My' money." Those were Karen's exact words it would be a waste of "my" money. He'll use me being in a mental hospital against me in court, and he will win custody anyway. Why should I lose all of "my" money trying to win a losing battle? I can visit him. She set it all up to "lose custody" of her kid. That's why she played the suicide game again, so the doctors can say Karen must be bi-polar, she can't help her condition. As long as she stays on her meds, she will be fine but I don't think she is stable enough to be a full-time parent she can have visitation rights.

It was all a big game for her. That's all Karen really wanted but honestly, she didn't care if she got to see her son or not. I do know the kid had a price on his head because if she had a kid, she would get more money. "CHA-CHING," and all of her travel expenses were on her ex-husband, so if she went to visit him, she won't lose any money, and if he didn't pay for her to see her son, she could blame him for not getting to be near her sweet little boy like the good mom that she is. Or she could get the opportunity to use her excuse, "I can't travel right now. I'm bi-polar. I need to work on me, just ask my doctor whom I am fucking. I would see him all the time if I could." She will always have an excuse. Well, okay, Karen!

Once, when Karen was talking about her fucked up pre-nup, she said, "If he just invested like I told him, we would be billionaires by now" Karen always wanted more. I don't even think being a billionaire would be enough for her. When I told her I got engaged, she said to me, "Well, if he only makes eighty thousand a year, that is okay but you won't be able to live like we do." I didn't know what to say to that except, "Thanks, Karen. Okay." This was coming from a girl who didn't know the difference between a chardonnay and a cabernet. Karen was unrefined, to say the least. I would rather be middle class and have self-respect than sell out for "Karen status."

My dad's family had money and they were miserable, self-absorbed assholes just like Karen and her husband. They have all the "stuff" money can buy. They can afford almost anything, but the one thing they can't buy is self-respect. I know they have their "yes men" to make them feel superior, so who needs self-respect, right? Both of the parents are fucked up. The dad and I took the kid to the park after Karen left for L.A., he didn't do anything but fish. He paid no attention to his kid. He even called someone to tell them he caught a fish, it was all about him always. He would let the kid sit in his bed with him while he watched violent, scary movies. Sounds like my dad; it's what he wanted to watch. I'm sorry, I think that's wrong to let a kid watch that kind of stuff.

The Dad took the baby to Temple and he threw a fit so he brought him back to me. "He won't behave at the Temple. He's embarrassing me." His two-year-old son made him look bad, oh I feel so bad for the Dad. BOO-HOO If he didn't have a problem keeping his cock in his pocket, he could get a full-time nanny, but his sex life was more important to him than his son. After Karen took off and went to L.A., her Dad told me, "She's never going to do better than me. Soon her looks will go, then what will she have?" For him, she was a "trophy wife." For her, he was a "sugar daddy." They were both using each other and that poor kid got caught in the middle of it. Karen and her ex-husband are nothing more than garbage with a Ferrari in the garage. Put lipstick on a pig, it's still a pig. Get it?

Karen became a Jew for her son. The only thing she gave him was his faith. If she could get any money for it, she'd take it back. When her parents came out for a visit when I was first in Arizona, she went to Church with her parents again. That had to be a slap in the face to her husband. She didn't care who she hurt. Karen was willing to put on any act to get what she wanted, even if it meant lying to God. Nobody can fool God. Or now that she is a Jew, it's okay to lie to God. I don't think my Jewish friends would agree.

When I cooked for Rosh Hashanah, I studied "Mama Leas Jewish kitchen." Great book I had to learn about Jewish Cuisine. I was a SHIKSA; what did I know about kosher cooking? I wanted to be respectful and keep it as kosher as I could. It was lovely, but Karen wasn't happy because the bakery didn't do her bread the way she wanted it. She loved to complain and again, nothing was ever good enough for her.

I watched her pray too. Karen had the prayers down but no feelings behind it. Karen dumped God as easily as she dumped her own kid. I think she would go back to Church or the Temple for one reason only; to find another victim, she can take for his money. We should give a shoot-out to all men with money who attend Church or Temple. If you meet Karen, here is a heads up. Wrap it the fuck up. Karen may have lost her kid, but she'll have herpes forever. I'll bet she gets to keep that in the pre-nup, lucky her.

That poor kid, if he does wind up screwed up, it's a perfect out for both of them. Karen can say, "He raised him and got the nanny, it's his fault." Meanwhile, the dad can say, "Karen has bi-polar disorder, the kid probably has that." It's always someone else's problem. Have you ever watched the movie, The Gentlemen? It's a Guy Richie movie. There's a scene with two very well-off parents blaming society and anything else but themselves for their child's problems. "This has happened to so many of our friends; you mustn't blame yourself, my dear. It isn't your fault, it's a curse." It is their fault that they don't care about their kid, just the family name. That's why the kid's so fucked up. Poor baby, I pray for that kid every day. I can't imagine what the kid's life is like now. Hopefully, he goes to boarding school and doesn't have much to do with Karen or her husband. Better, put him in foster care. That's his best bet. Anything is better than those two as parents. It's so sad that white people with money can't keep it together for one kid, but they expect people to bow down and admire them for being rich. What a joke! My dad's family was like that and look how fucked up my dad was! It doesn't matter how much money you have. A shitty parent is a shitty parent.

Karen ran into my sister a couple of years later at L.A.X. Karen wanted my number. My sister called me and said, "Do you want to talk to her?" I told her, "Hell no! That fucking liar, I'll never trust her again!" I know we are supposed to be very sensitive to people with bi-polar disorder. But take your pill and level out over there. Keep that crazy stuff away from me! Crazy is crazy! I don't care what you want to call it! If they know they need to be medicated and they refuse to take their meds, they are dangerous when they don't. Put them in a padded cell, put them somewhere they can't hurt themselves or anyone else.

Many people use bi-polar as an excuse to act in anyway they want and get away with it. "Oh I wasn't leveled out that day, or I'm still trying to figure out my meds. Sorry, I must have been having a bi-polar panicked moment. I don't remember doing that." There's always an excuse. I'm sure they're not all like Karen but I have had more than one encounter with someone who has it and they are fucking nuts. Take your pills and stay the fuck away from me. I don't trust any of you. To this day, I have yet to meet someone with bi-polar disorder who is not a pathological liar, who spouts off stuff for no reason for attention, unpredictable, manipulative, needy, shallow, untrustworthy, with a Jeckyll and Hyde personality, and has all the excuses in the world.

Karen added bonus to her diagnosis. She plays the suicide game too, yay! I'm sorry I have never met anyone who is bi-polar who didn't carry all of those traits. When you can find someone with bi-polar disorder that's not a complete nut job, I would like to have a cup of tea with them and mellow out. I'm up for that, but I might be a little worried they might do something crazy or violent. They will have an excuse for later. "This tea is nice, but I want my favorite kind of tea or I'm going to try to kill myself and it will be your entire fault!" As they raise their voice and rip their heir out for attention. Well okay, Karen.

I know we have all had our fair share of Karen's but when you have one as bad as I did, you have to share it. I wonder if there are more of you out there who have had a seriously bad encounter with someone with bi-polar disorder. It's like a taboo subject. You can't talk about bi-polar disorder comfortably and you can't make fun of it. That's not true! You can make fun of it if the person has taken their meds. It's a crapshoot; you never know with them. They are so unpredictable. One minute they are the nicest person in the world and the next thing, they hate you and everything in their life that has gone wrong is your fault.

I had friends who introduced me to a girl I didn't know and they told me, "Hey, that girl is Bi-polar." I had to immediately leave because I didn't know if she's taken her meds or not, and I might say something she may not like. I think I may be funny, but it's a 50-50 chance she may have a meltdown and it will be my fault because bi-polar people are never at fault. Karen's never are.

Did you see that bi-polar, stupid, rich, spoiled, blond white woman on "Vice News" during the pandemic? She had "a meltdown." She started to grab masks off the shelves at a market and said it was because she was bi-polar and was seduced by Q and didn't know what she was doing. What a fucking liar!

She was a stupid, spoiled white woman with too much time on her hands and threw a fit for fun just to get attention. Take your fucking meds! This is the same woman who was asked, "You are Jewish but did you know Q is not very supportive of Jews." This stupid bitch said, "I don't pay attention to that stuff." Yeah, I'm sure Hitler said to the troops, "Hey, you guys follow me but pick and choose what works for you." That woman should get together with Karen and see who's better at having an excuse for behaving badly and getting away with it. Karen can say, "I'm bi-polar, it's not my fault that I didn't take my meds. What's your excuse?" They can both laugh and talk about their foolish ex-husbands and how they were only letting them get millions in their pre-nups and how they both think they both deserve more.

They can brag to each other about how they never get in trouble for acting like lunatics because they're both white, bi-polar and privileged, so they get away with it. If a black woman tried that sort of shit she would get beat up, put in jail and disgraced but people like them, bi-polar, white women with money, they walk away with a slap on the wrist. They're never going to say, "Yeah, that was my fault." But they have no problem blaming everyone else for their problems. If white cops show up to a call and it's for a white, bi-polar Karen, even if she is guilty as fuck and has a knife in her hand, they will still try to reason with her because of two reasons; one, she's white and two, a good Karen will try to cry or fuck her way out of the situation. "I'm not on my meds now. I'm sorry I'll put the knife down. I don't think I'm leveled out." And try to look sad and shed a tear or go with the: "Does anyone know how to open this for me?" while she lifts her skirt and winks at them. Yeah, it's all a big game or they just call their daddy to get them out of any trouble. White privilege it's all a white privilege game!

CHAPTER SEVENTEEN: COLORFUL STRIPPERS, DIRTY SUITS

When I got back to work, I was happy to be there. I cocktailed during the day and sometimes at night too during that time, I had to serve some interesting people. The bail bondsmen came in a lot. They were so easy to wait on and good tippers too, very nice guys. Then there were the dirty suits, not much fun to wait on. We called them the dirty suits for the way they talked in front of us. “Hey, you fuck that girl in the ass like I told you to?” Shit like that. I think they talked like that because they had to pay for it. I doubt they would say that to their wives. They were almost all married with kids too and had girlfriends, the strippers at the club. Funny thing, people thought the strippers were getting the coke for the guys, but it was the other way around. They had a lot of skeletons in their closets and their girlfriends had big mouths. This was twenty-five years ago, but I hope some of them hear about this and get a little uncomfortable. Kind of the way I felt when I waited on them. Those guys worked at the Denver Tech Center. Hi fellas!

One guy that sat with the dirty suits was gay. Even though we all knew it, we played along. He went a little overboard trying to look straight. He’d have his tie around his head and his shirt open. Oh yeah baby, whooping it up. But he wouldn’t get a hard-on until the busboy walked by. One of the dirty suits came into another job where I was waiting tables with his wife and kids, and he didn’t see me at first. I said “Hi” to the wife and kids. He looked at me and turned whiter than he already was. I went to the terminal and started to laugh. He came over, and he started to say something. I stopped him and said, "I don't know you from the club, but from now on, no more snapping at me for a drink, and you tip me big. Now go sit down!" He used to snap at me to get my attention, "Hey, a drink over here now!!" That felt so good to do that; order him around for a change. He was one of those assholes that treat waiters like peasants.

You can tell how someone will treat you by the way they treat waiters, animals, and kids. It's true. I knew all about those fuckers, all white guys, of course. They gave me their credit cards, not the smartest men in the world. This isn't New York where the rich men come in through the back door. They weren't very subtle about coming into the club. The club did something very smart the credit card. Their systems wouldn't read Diamond Cabaret on the bank statement when they got the bill because the wives would find out. Their card statement would read, "C.C.C.G.," so the wives wouldn't be suspicious. The bottom line is, the owner Bobby was very smart. R.I.P, Bobby!

I also worked at a porn website, but I don't have the strength to get into it. Pretty funny stuff!

I did work in advertising too. I would pass out business cards at sporting events to the men at the games. I don't know how legal that was. My girlfriend Jules would take me there. We were passing cards out and one woman yelled at me, "My husband had an affair with a stripper!" I said, "I am sorry, but I am not a stripper." She wasn't very happy so she ripped up the card in front of me. Her friends were like, "Hey, take it easy." I looked at her and chuckled. "Well, now I know why your husband had the affair. She's a lot of fun, isn't she?" Her friends laughed their asses off. She looked like she was going to hit me, so I left quickly.

Once I was at a Hawaiian Tropic contest, and before you think I was in it, I wasn't. I was just handing out business cards, and I ran into a guy I went to church with. He wasn't with his wife, but he was with his very young girlfriend. I was in a bikini, but I was okay with it. When he saw me, I smiled and went to say hello. He looked really uncomfortable, I found out why. He was there with his friend's nineteen-year-old daughter; she was his date.

I handed her our cards from the club and said, "We are hiring if you are interested." He looked so mad at me, but there was nothing he could do about it. I know his wife, fuck him. I can't tell you how often I ran into some guy who came to the club outside of work with their wife and kids. I usually am professional, but I have ran into a few men who saw me with their other half, and I made them "sweat it out" in front of their wives. "Oh yeah, you look so familiar. Do I remember you or don't I?" I love to watch them freak out a little. I don't divulge any personal info on men from the club unless they piss me off. After all, they don't make cocktail waitresses or strippers sign non-disclosure agreements, but they probably should. You wouldn't believe some of the stories; I can't get into it all!

I used to get free tickets from season ticket holders from the club. When I started to work at the club, I was dead broke, so I said to the guys who I knew were season holders, "Hey, I'm new in town and I would like to go to a game or two, but I can't afford it. Let me be clear, I am not looking for a date, so if you guys ever have tickets that you aren't going to use, throw them my way," and they did. It was nice. Sometimes when I couldn't use them, I would give them to my neighbors, people at the bank, and market. I have to say, they were good tickets too. My neighbor down the hall said, "Jesus Jan, V.I.P. tickets to the broncos and the packers?

You don't want them?" I was honest. "I got them for free. Just let me borrow a cup of sugar sometimes. Thanks!" I really needed to work so if I could get a shift, I would rather work than go to a game. I got the tickets for free, so I didn't ever charge anyone for them. That wouldn't be right.

The guys I gave the tickets to weren't rich guys and if the guys who gave me the tickets saw someone else in their seats I could just say, "I had to work." This one guy who sat with the dirty suits sometimes gave me tickets and he came in again. "Jan, I've got VIP tickets to the dodgers, you want to go?" I nodded yes! I was waiting on him and his stripper girlfriend, who I didn't like. He said, "Yeah, we are going. It will be fun." Shit! I wanted to go but not with them. Usually he handed me the tickets. I asked, "When is the game?" He told me, "This Sunday."

I said with a sad face on. "Well, I may have to work." Surprisingly, his girlfriend interjected. "No, you don't. I checked the schedule, you're off." I think it's unethical to give someone your schedule but fuck it. I can make something up. "Well, if I have to be honest, when I get to pick up a shift, I do. I need to work, so I may not be able to go." I actually told her the truth, I didn't need to lie. She whispered something in his ears. He turned to me and said, "How much will you make in a shift?" I said, "Well, at least a hundred." He reached into his pocket, pulled out a hundred-dollar bill and said, "Here! Take it, take the day off. You're always working. Treat yourself." He was right. I asked the girlfriend, "You'll be there?" "Yeah, I'll be there." She answered. He said, "Where do I pick you up?" I told him, "I'll meet you there."

I have been followed home twice from the club, only speaking of the incidents that I knew of. It's not funny at all if you think you have been followed. You should always go to the police station or back to the club. I had a guy from the club follow me home and wait outside my apartment once, and it scared the shit out of me.

I get to Coors' field and the girlfriend wasn't there. I asked him, "Where is she?" He told me, "Oh, she couldn't make it. Are we ok?" I felt uncomfortable right off the bat but we were in broad daylight, so I went with it. We started walking towards the VIP section. Honestly, I've been in the VIP at the football, basketball, and baseball game. I'd rather be in the stands. It's more fun, but here we were.

The game was going well. We were about halfway through the game and he left to make a call. Keep in mind that this was twenty-five years ago. He came back after a while. I inquired. "Everything okay that wasn't your wife, was it?" He said, "Oh yeah, very funny." He was smiling. He started to talk. "Jan, you are the most hardworking girl in that place. Everyone loves you and you work so much. You're always doing favors for others, picking up their shifts, and you don't do much for yourself, and I want to help you out." He pulled out an envelope with cash in it, probably five thousand dollars, and set it in front of me.

At that point, I realized that I was being set up. He wanted me to cover for him, the wife was getting suspicious. He said to me, "I know you see this kind of thing all the time, and I always tip you really good, don't I? I give you all those free tickets and I am sure you wouldn't mind helping me out a little like you help the girls you work with. I know you need the money, this will be just like a job on the side, but we won't talk about... you know what I mean." I realized the phone call was probably to the stripper girlfriend and she must have said, "She is always working, she's desperate she has two jobs she really needs the money, she'll do it. Just ask her."

He said to me, "If you need more, let me know. Her number is in the envelope, so if you could just give her a call, maybe today, or tomorrow, that would be great. Her name is Mary, and we are separated. Just let me know when you do." I could feel my blood boiling in my veins. I was so offended. That's what rich white men do. They think people who need money will sell out or take the fall for them because they are rich. Boy oh boy, did he mess with the wrong woman. He wanted me to pretend to his wife and tell her I was his yoga instructor. He wanted me to tell l her that's where he's been, in the gym and not with the stripper girlfriend. This white guy was really in for it. So, I'll tell you what I did. I have never told this to anyone ever!

I did something I'll never do again, but I don't regret it. I looked around and whispered, "Before we go any further, do you want my real name or my badge number?" You should have seen the look on his face, oh God. I continued, "If you ever say one word about this to anyone and fuck up my investigation, I'll arrest you, the girlfriend, and I will tell your wife everything, even about the coke. I'm giving you this one out, but if you show your face at the club ever again, or anyone finds out about this, you are done for good. Understand? I don't have time for this bullshit. Do you hear me?" He nodded his head. I left and left the money. He never came into the club again and the stripper quit. I was labeled a narc, but not just for that.

Two girls were doing blow next to my locker and they got caught and blamed me for it. I wasn't there to make friends; I was there to get out of the debt my ex left me in. I didn't care if those girls liked me or not. I didn't trust any strippers. The first week I was there, the day girls offered me coke. I said, "I can't, I have allergies." It was a crock of shit. They showed it to me, it was shwag! What an insult. I wouldn't put that shit in my coffee, is that sweet and low. How much baby laxative did you put in that? That is what was really going through my mind. It would be like offering Snoop Dogg a joint made with leaves. He'd be insulted. I love Snoop! He just makes you smile, like Dolly Parton. Ahh Dolly. You can't help but smile when you think of them. I wish they would do a Christmas show together. Dolly would sing that Coat of Colors song that makes me cry and Snoop can decorate a pot tree with twinkling lights. Maybe Martha Stewart can cook! I'd watch that show. Snoop and Dolly make everyone happy; maybe the guys from Bong Appetite can help Martha cook. I would definitely watch that show! What fun!

I went out with this guy who was really the jealous type. His nickname was Shadow because he always had a five o'clock shadow. Though he was a really good-looking guy, he was uncomfortable with his height. He never said it but we met eye to eye, and he always wore cowboy boots for the lift. He also had a huge cock that he was fond of and he was a little too unpredictable for me. Once, he was telling me how he got into a fight and wound up in jail, that day he was supposed to come over for dinner and never showed. I called him, and there was no answer. After a while, I got a call. "I got arrested." He came over to tell me about it. I was pissed, so my usual reaction was, "What now?" Because he missed our dinner, I deserved an answer. So he told me this story. "I was at a bar playing pool, and this guy made a snide comment that I didn't like, so I turned the pool stick around and bashed him in the face with it, and I got arrested." I looked at him. "Why did you start a fight? You have been in jail before. Haven't you learned your lesson?" He said, "He shouldn't have pissed me off." I had enough at that point. "You did this to yourself. He didn't do anything wrong. You beat him up just because you didn't like what he said. Jail is where you belong. It's a good thing you didn't call me to bail you out. Who did?" He said, "My brother did."

There were so many weird secrets he had, but the ones I knew about bothered me. He was really hurting when I met him. He followed me to work and watched me work at the club after I told him, "Don't come into the club when I am working. It will throw me off, okay?" I thought I was clear about it. I wasn't joking. Shadow came into the club and just stood there, watching me in the V.I.P. room and he isn't a member. He didn't say a word. I went over to him and said, "What are you doing here? I am working. Please go, okay? So I can concentrate." He looked at me and said, "I am just having a drink. What is the big deal? You can work with me watching you, can't you?" He was really making me uncomfortable and I said, "I could have the security have you leave." He said, "No, you won't. I am not doing anything."

He stood there smoking his cigarette, smiling at me just to fuck with me. This guy was unstable to say the least. God, I understand about trauma, but some people who go through stuff like he did need serious therapy to deal with what he had to deal with. Shadow's dad killed himself and he found him hanging in his house. His dad was suffering from depression and was on Benzos. They kept asking him, "Are you suicidal?" He wasn't until they put him on the meds. So he went off the meds and he killed himself.

Shadow was really calling out for help, but in the worst ways possible. He would deliberately get into trouble and fight. I asked him once, "Do you think maybe you should go seek some therapy for your loss?" He said, "No. Those assholes killed my dad." I came to my house, and after that I stopped returning his calls. He didn't get the hint. He came over and said, "I didn't know where you went and who have you been with." I said, "It's none of your business." He whips out a pen and paper to write down the names of the people I have been with. I said, "Yea, you're not controlling." He said I'm just worried about you. Call me later." I looked down and he had an ankle bracelet on and he wouldn't tell me why he had it. Too many secrets.

I couldn't believe it but I did see him once more. He got a chow puppy and I thought that's good, he needed something to love and that would love him back. We got in the truck and he didn't pick the puppy up and put him in the truck, instead he put the dog on the top of his boot and kicked him into the truck. It took me a while to register what happened. "People are going to think you are abusing the dog if you handle him like that, pick him up. He said, "No. He is a big enough dog. He can get in if I help him like this." I scolded him. "No, you are not helping him. Look, he doesn't have it." I went to put the dog in the car and he yelled at me. "He is a fucking dog. He's got it!" That was it for me. I know he's a man in pain, but I don't have the energy to fix him. I was trying to get my shit together. I don't care if he has a cock made of diamonds. This man was not worth the heartache. I hope he didn't wind up back in jail again. I really cared about him; he really needed professional help.

I met Pandora Peeks, too. She was the stripper in the movie Striptease with Demi Moore. She had watermelon boobs. Apart from her sumptuous beauty, Pandora is a very smart woman. She used to be in banking, no shit. I knew she was going to retire, unlike any other stripper I ever met. This one time, I had the opportunity while nobody was around, I was in the dressing room, and I put her whole cup over my head. I couldn't help it. It went down to the bridge of my nose. I also saw the best cat fight of my life there. Two girls were fighting over money. I was the only person in the dressing room. I was getting dressed and had my pants around my knees when I turned around and saw this girl throwing a lunchbox purse, a metal one, at the girl from about fifteen yards away. She didn't just throw it, she put her back into it like a pitcher during the World Series, and it hit her dead in the face. I fell over laughing. I couldn't get my pants up because I was on the floor laughing my ass off. Then they were going at it, with blood, nails, jewelry, and glitter flying around. Jerry Springer would have loved it.

Some women and men should just not talk. Pretty is all they have and that's okay. I knew a girl who was super-model-beautiful and I had to caddy with her at a golf tournament. In Denver, the guys she was with even commented on the fact that she was pretty but didn't talk or make them laugh at all. She was boring. I made them laugh, and we had fun. She was really nice to look at but don't try to talk to her. It was like pulling teeth. She wasn't stupid either, just had a personality like dry toast.

I went out with this guy Kyle. I went out with him a couple of times. He was always looking in the mirror at himself. Kyle was a very good-looking guy, and he was becoming an attorney. But let me tell you this: Kyle was one of the worst lays of my life next to my ex-girlfriend Brianna. Sex with him was like; I can only imagine it would be like sex with Melanie Trump. He didn't move at all. I wanted to punch him in the face just to get a reaction. He gave me nothing! I think if I put a big mirror in front of him while he fucked me, he might have gotten into it. He was very handsome but really boring. I'd rather be with a guy who's broke but has a personality and a big cock. Come on, be real. If he's funny but broke, he better have a big cock, and if he's old and broke, no that doesn't work if he's old, fuck his cock. He better be loaded. I hope Kyle is a better lawyer than he is a lover. Hopefully, he does nothing but contractual law. That's 90% paperwork. Maybe he can have an office that's got three-way mirrors and a gym, so he can work flex. For some people, looks are all they have. This sounds awful. So here's some advice. If you go out with a pretty person, someone who's really good-looking and they have no personality; they don't laugh, have robotic responses and speak in a monotone voice, fuck them once. If there's nothing there, dump them. Actually, get photographed with them first, then dump them. They aren't like fine wine, they don't get better with age. They just get dusty old and more boring.

I wish we had a class where they could teach pretty people how to let their hair down without looking at it in the mirror and just laugh and be silly. Get dirty and have fun without worrying if you look like you're ready to get your picture taken. You've seen these guys at clubs, gyms, parks, and sporting events. Wherever there's a mirror to glance into, they can't help it. The next time you go out, look for them and laugh. Do it after you read this, it's funny. Just watch.

I got knocked down a couple of times at the club. Once by this drunk guy who pushed me into a table, and I broke my wrist again. Fuck! I had a full section on a Saturday night. I was thinking, I couldn't go to the hospital now, so fuck it. I'm going to finish my shift if it kills me. I was new and they saw me break my wrist at the Fourth of July B.B.Q. I didn't want to be the new girl that wines and cries. I reluctantly told my boss, Dave, "It's not a big deal. I'll go get it fixed later." He was like, "Stop working right now!" I said, "No. I am not walking out on my tips, and it's too busy, no! I'll go get it fixed tomorrow." I just mouthed off to my new boss, and I instantly thought, I hope he doesn't fire me. So, I went the next day to get casted. No biggie! So I worked with a broken wrist for two months with a cast on it. I held my tray with two hands and got a lot of sympathy tips.

I hated girls who complained when they had to work. I was happy to get any shift I could. So what if I got pushed down? Not the end of the world. I got punched in the face by a professional fighter, I can take a hit. She loosened all my front teeth. I had to wear my retainers for a month. My instructor Clarence in class saw it and said, "You okay? Saw you take that hit, nice job!" He pats me on the back. I'm lucky she was holding back. Mercedes, it was her name. She could have really hurt me, but surprisingly, she was really nice too.

I had a bachelorette party at my apartment with twenty strippers. I got cabs for them, so they didn't have to drive. I actually stayed sober for this party, and I'm glad I did after we played "Pin the dick on the guy." And we ate; we all went to a bar after I got everyone lit with blowjob shots. They were getting on the bar, and taking off their clothes. A manager we worked with helped me get some of them back to my place. The bachelorette puked all over his brand new car. I saw her starting to throw up out the door. I opened it up and she tried to wipe it up with her hand, then she wiped her face and hair. She threw up everywhere but the toilet. He was so nice about it. He said, "Well, I was going to get the car detailed anyway." Thank God there was another girl called Jennifer, not the bad one though, who helped me out. We laughed about it. I really liked her.

Jennifer was Mrs. Fitness Colorado. We both had the same idea about stripping; I'm going to do it while I have this body. The bachelorette's hair was all done up. I had to pull bobby pins through her puke to put her to bed. She told me she was hung over for three days. I could only say, "You're welcome." I don't know what she expected she had a drunk throw her party.

I was at work and this new girl, a stripper, had some kind of panic attack on stage. They had to rush her to the hospital. I knew it wasn't a panic attack. It wasn't too busy, but I was worried about her and asked if it was okay to go check up on her. I wanted to make sure that she's okay. They gave me her real name and I found her in the hospital. I said, "Do you remember me from the club?" She was confused. "Yeah, what are you doing here? Am I fired or something?" I reassured her. "Oh no, honey I just wanted to know if you needed anything. I don't know if you have family. Do you want me to call for you or what's going on? I'm not going to say anything, but you're a heroin addict, right?" I cut to the chase. She said, "Yes, I didn't get my methadone today; we were late to the place so I couldn't get it."

I was glad she told me most of the truth. She's an addict. They lie a lot even when you're trying to help, so I still didn't trust her, but she needed help. I asked her, "The boyfriend is an addict too?" She said, "Yeah, we are both trying to quit." I told her, "Okay, listen to me. This is what we are going to do. I'll talk to your nurse and doctor if I have to. I don't think any doctor will really pay attention to specifics with a patient who's a drug addict. So I'll tell them that I am your cousin. They will ask me if I am going to take care of you? That will be a yes, so they'll give you your dose tonight. They'll give me, the responsible adult, the second dose for tomorrow, and I'll get you home safe, okay?" That is exactly how things went. The nurses agreed and let her go with me. I got the second dose for tomorrow. God, I'm good. Not really, though. I was a doctor's kid, so I had the upper hand on how to talk to people in that field and I am white, that's all.

She comes home with me for the night. I didn't lecture her about heroin, I was a drunk myself. Who was I to talk but I did tell her I was a little more than concerned. Her boyfriend came to get her the next day. About a month later, she and her boyfriend got into a bad fight about something I didn't want to get into, in front of the club. They fired her, and I never saw her again.

I tried to get some of the girls I worked with out of that environment by inviting them to some of my kickboxing classes. I guess I should have thought about it a little more. The guys I worked out with after a while said to me, "You have to stop bringing these girls here to work out, we can't concentrate." Yeah, that didn't offend me. I'm just a loaf of bread! Kidding! They treated me like a sister. One by one, they stopped coming or made other plans. I tried. One girl, Michelle, a beautiful girl went with me to class more than once. She had a little drug problem. Michelle got wasted and fell off a second-story balcony and broke a bunch of shit; she's very lucky to be alive. I called her and I asked her if she needed anything. She said, "Yes. Will you go to work, get all of my stuff out, and bring it to me? You're the only person I trust." I asked her this one thing. "Are there any drugs in your locker?" I had to ask. She said, "I don't think so." I still went, grabbed her stuff and got her some groceries because she was on crutches. She thanked me and I did lecture her because she went too far, and she knew it. I did check up on her. I have no idea what happened to her, but I hope she's okay.

I have always tried to keep an eye out for girls from getting into too much trouble. There was this girl who was friends with some of my neighbors. They invited me to go out with them. She was one of those girls, who would have more than two drinks in her and she'd get slutty. Her friends and I were watching her dancing with this guy she's never met. The performance was getting a lot of attention from a police officer standing by the front of the club and he did not look happy. I went over to her, broke it up, and told her, "We have to go, now!" She didn't want to go. I had no choice but to tell her. "You see that cop? He's going to arrest you if we don't go now." She was reluctant, to say the least. Her friends just sat there and laughed at her. I was pushing her fat ass up the stairs and the cop saw us. "You better get her out of here!" I said, "Yes sir! She's going now." She screamed at the cop. "He can't tell me what to do. I'm not that drunk." The cop was pissed at her and I don't blame him. It was his job to arrest drunken mouthy chicks like her, so he started to call for backup, no shit.

I got her outside and there was a cab! Yay! The cabbie wouldn't take her. He would take me but not her. He kept blabbering, "No, no, no. She can no go, you okay but her? No, no! You okay but no her." I looked down the street and I thought, here comes the Calvary with their lights on. I glanced back at the cop, he called them! I had to make a decision, her or me. I got in the cab and went home. She got in trouble, and of course she blamed me.

When I was a stripper, I did it for two years or so. Maybe not that long, I hate that people would make others go there when they clearly don't want to be there. It really is no fun for them! Kathy Saben from Channel Four News, she does the weather, was dragged in the club and she didn't want to be there. I chatted with her a little in the V.I.P. room she was really nice. That's rude to make someone go to those places if it makes them uncomfortable, and you think that's cute? You're a fucking prick to do that. I'm sorry Kathy, you had to go through that and shame on your co-workers for doing that to you. I hope Kathy hears about this, I like her. She does a great job, of course. She may not like anything I say and might get pissed at me for telling everyone she was dragged to a strip club. I hope not, though. I really like her weather reports, but my boyfriend doesn't like her. He calls her, "The Lying Cow Ice Queen," and every time he says that, I defend her. "Shut up! I like her. She's good at her job, Jesus! She doesn't make the weather jackass." We have a really loving relationship. We watch the news first, then Jeopardy and Wheel of Fortune back to back. Yep, I'm that old.

I'm a chef and when I get invited to dinner at friend's house, they usually ask for help. Or they might say, "Can you bring that dish you make?" But this time, they just told me to bring Wine. What a treat! I was running late. I get there and it's a formal sit-down dinner, not family-style and I was underdressed. Fuck me! I didn't know half of the people there. I sit down and we got served. This plate of food was unrecognizable. I started to think they were playing a joke on me. I was late, I was a chef, and underdressed. This had to be a joke.

I said, "Is what I get for being late?" I looked around two guys I knew who were gay were snickering under their breath. I looked at them and said, "You know what this looks like? You see that movie Better Off Dead? With Jon Cusack, you know the plate of food his mom made that slides off the plate when you poke at it? That's what this looks like." The guy who was having the dinner boasted, "It looks great to me." I said, "What? Are you visually impaired?" He looked at a woman at the end of the table who I didn't know. She casually said, “It’s a family dish. You don’t have to eat it if you don’t want to.” I still think their fucking with me. I asked, “What family, the Adams family, the Manson family?” The gay guys were trying not to laugh. I glanced around and nobody had touched the food. The guy having the party said, “She is a comedian, she is just kidding.” I said, “No, I am not. What the hell is this?”

He started to apologize for me to the lady. I realized, “This is not a joke,” but nobody was eating. They’re looking at one another like, I dare you to try it first. I said to the gay guys under my breath, “You don’t want to eat this shit either! Admit it.” They were trying to hold it together. Have you seen Fear Factor? The disgusting crap they make people eat, the plate of food looked exactly like that. There was no way I was eating this and there was no way to back out of this mess gently. I looked at her and said, “Yeah, this was a little joke, gotcha!” And I left. I had to go, I put my foot so far down my throat; I could kiss my own ass.

The guy called later and told me I was kind of rude. I asked him, “What was that food?” He didn’t tell me, so I’m glad I left. That lady was pissed. I told my friend Deacon Grey, a fellow comedian, about what happened at that dinner party, and he laughed. David said, “You should tell that story on stage. Maybe you could do a show with your clothes on for a change.” Deacon would give me a hard time because once I performed half-naked. The audience thought it was funny, why not? I’m too old to do that shit anymore but when you’re young, who cares!

I was going to have a baby shower at my place for a girl I worked with. I didn’t know her very well but she heard I throw great parties. And I did so. She was going to bring her aunt with her to go over the menu with me. Her aunt is

Greek, and I am not. Do I need to say anything more? She walked into my place with a white glove. She didn't have a white glove but she may as well have. I have to be honest, if I go to someone's house, and I smell something, I look around. What can I say? I have some pet peeves! If I see someone's trash overfilling, it bothers me and a full kitty litter box, forget it. Yuck! Worse than that, if I see used condoms in the trash, I go "AHHHH!" That's what that smell is, disgusting. Any sane person can sense that someone has been fucking in this room recently! Clean up before you have guests! Sorry!

I care what people think about my house, that's why I keep it clean. Not just for me, but if someone just shows up, I want it to look nice. The same reason why I don't wear my pajamas to the market or in public anywhere, it's tacky! I wasn't worried about the aunt I kept a very clean home. But some people like to, let's say, intimidate you to get their way. Unfortunately for her aunt, she didn't realize I'm a comedian and I use humor to deflect anything that makes me feel uncomfortable.

We sat down at the dining room table. I made us tea and she was staring at a piece of art I had on the wall. She didn't look happy. I said, "Do you like Salvador Dali?" The picture was Jesus on a cross, Dali's rendition. She demanded, "Take it down." She was doing this in my home. I said, "Well, I can move it somewhere else if you like." She demanded again. "Take it down." I asked again, very politely, "Would you like to look around and see if anything bothers you?" She glared at me and said, "I told you to take it down, why aren't you!" Her niece was looking at me like you should do what she says. So I went over, flipped it, left it hanging upside-down and said, "Is that better?" She got up and left. Her niece said, "I'll call you later." She did call me, and told me, "We are going to have the shower at my aunt's house and you are not invited, sorry." I should have gotten the address to her aunts and sent her the Dali as a baby gift. If I had known it was going to go so poorly, I would have gone the other way, and worn my bondage gear to the door and shown her my goodies. Would be kind of funny, "That's my favorite maple thorp, do you like it? This is my Herbs Ritz, and there is my favorite flogging whip. Have a look at this cock ring, it looks broken. It is this guy who came so hard, he broke the goddamned thing. I have never seen anyone do that, ever! That's my trophy, I love that piece, and maybe I should have it bronzed." I don't think she'd like that. On the other hand, I would love it! That would make a good story for anyone with a Greek aunt in their family. It could work for an Italian, Spanish, Hawaiian, German, and a Chinese aunt. Yeah, the list goes on and on. Some women, mainly old school aunts, are very particular and what they say goes, no matter what. I dare anyone to go home, call their conservative aunt, and try to introduce them to something new easily or at all without a little argument. You know who you are out there. We all have that aunt or your friend does for sure.

Okay, this is funny and kind of gross, but I'm going to tell you anyway because I'm a little bit high and I need to write this down before I doze off. So here you go. My girlfriend had a baby shower for a woman I really didn't know very, but she was really funny and sweet. It was her shower and she had a little rash on her face. I thought I was just sunburn, no biggie. She told us, "Well, I heard that semen masks help your skin if you are pregnant, so I had my husband cum all over my face, and I rubbed it in, and left it for like two minutes. Maybe, I left it on too long." I was trying not to burst into laughter and the comedian in me was yelling, "Jump in! Ask her what he ate!" But I held back. She said, "I think this will be kind of funny, my kids going to see these pictures of my shower and go, 'Mom, why was your face so red? I am going to have to come up with another reason. I can't tell him this is what happens when daddy cums all over my face, that's not good." And she laughed. She was going to be a great mom! What a great sense of humor.

Over the years, I have said some, well, slightly inappropriate comments. In my head, I was just trying to spread laughter by giving people a dose of my humor. But not everyone thinks that I'm funny. I notice a lot of white men and women don't think I'm very funny when everyone else is laughing but them, especially when it is where they work or go to a lot, it makes them uncomfortable. I mostly mouth off to people I don't know, so if it doesn't go well for me, I am out! It doesn't always pan out. "Oh well, live and learn." My brain works so quickly, my mouth needs to learn how to play catch up and it needs to slow down before I open it, OOPSIE!

I was at my friend's house when she had a housewarming party. Julie, or how I liked to call her, Jules, God rest, was a girl I worked with at the Diamond. She was a blast! I went to lunch with her Mom who was visiting from Illinois, and got her tickets for The Phantom of the Opera. She was thrilled what a wonderful person! If she hears about this, I'm so sorry for your loss. I loved your daughter. Jules was one of the girls I did some advertising with for work, she was so funny! Jules was one of the few girls I'd hang out with. I didn't trust many women in the adult entertainment industry. I miss her so much. Jules had one of the most perfect asses I have ever seen on a white woman next to my sister, unlike me with a pancake ass. No booty. I was at her party, and she was busy and didn't have time to go around and introduce me, so I went around and said, "Hi, I'm Jan! What is your name?"

One of those fuckers asked, "Jan like Jan Brady?" I said, "Yep." I walked around him because if he said, "Marsha, Marsha, Marsha," I was going to punch him in the dick. I was trying to be polite, so I walked up to this group of fags at her party and did exactly that. The guys greeted, "Hi, I am Jan. Hi, I am Dave. Hi, I'm Ben. Hi, I am George!" No problem. I went to shake the hand of this one fag, and I said, "Hi there, I am Jan, what is your name?" He looked at me in a very prissy way and went to shake my hand with his wrist turned to the side like he wanted me to kiss it and goes, "HI, I'm Willow," in a really feminine voice. I burst into laughter. Willow? Are you kidding me, really? Maybe it was his delivery but he didn't like that at all! The faggot turned with a big huff and left to go out on the balcony because I was laughing at him and it hurt his wittle fweelings! I started to apologize to his friends, "I am sorry, you caught me off guard. It is a pretty name for a gay boy, oops!"

His friends thought it was funny. I yelled to Jules in the kitchen, "Julie, I just insulted one of your gay boyfriends! Sorry!" She laughed too. Some people can't take a joke or any criticism. I tried to apologize to him but every time I got near him, he'd just roll his eyes and walk away. God, there's the fish who offended me! What did he expect? His name is Willow! I wanted to ask him, "Is that a family name? Did you see the movie, Willow? Is that where you got that name? Do you like midgets as much as I do? Is your last name Twiddledink? It sounds like that would be a good match for Willow. Where is your fairy dust? Do you have a magic wand? Did your mom get a little too many drugs before your delivery? Is that why she named you Willow?" That name warrants a little razzing if you ask me. Hope he hears about this. If he remembers me at her party, Willow, now that's a faggot's name if I ever heard one.

I was at a bar a long time ago, over twenty years or so, and this skinny white guy had on a striped white and red shirt and a navy blue ski cap on. I looked at him and said, "Wait a minute!" I took my friend's glasses, dark-framed Buddy Holly glasses and put them on him and said, "Hey everyone! There is Waldo!" You know from the book, Where Is Waldo? He didn't like it but everyone else did. I apologized, "Just kidding, you look great." He still gave me a dirty look. I couldn't help it and it's not like I told him he looked like a serial killer, just a cartoon. What's the big fucking deal? No sense of humor! I laugh at myself all the time. I'm a dork and white, I just run with it. I try to laugh when someone makes fun of me as long as it's not something rude. I would rather laugh than cry about it. Kill them with kindness and humor, so lighten up faggots, Jesus Christ!

I was working, stripping during the day and these white preppy assholes came in with their stuck-up girlfriends from D. U. Frats to basically offend the girls for fun. The guys were behind their girlfriends, standing up and smoking cigars and the girlfriends were sitting at the long stage. Not a lot of people were there. The girl who got off stage before me was almost in tears. I'm not having that, no way. I looked at the girls and said, "Ok girls, let's all have a good time now, it's just for fun." The girls said, "We are having fun, you're the one working, so get to work." They wouldn't even tip the girls with their dollars. Their boyfriends would put dollars in front of them and brush them off at the dancers. The boyfriends started to laugh and I signaled to Big Wayne. They didn't see it. Big Wayne was six-eight, black, and about four hundred pounds. Honestly, one of the nicest guys you'll ever meet and a go-to guy for sure! They keep mouthing off, "I'm so much prettier than her. God, do you think she even graduated from Junior High? Yeah, she's working her way through college. Hahahaha." Shit like that. They had no idea Wayne was right behind them. I looked at him and went, "This one, this one, this one, this one, all of them now!"

The guys turned around. You know the scene in the movies just before the guy gets killed and he knows he's going to die? They had that look on their faces. I glared at the guys and said, "Yea, he could kill you with his pinky, I've seen him put guys in the hospital, and the morgue. You better do what he says." They said to the girls, "We gotta go, now!" The girls started protesting. "No we don't! They can't throw us out!" The guys went, "Right now, come on." Then they saw Big Wayne. I waved, "Goodbye girls, goodbye!" The D.J. turned it up and we started to sing, "Nananana, nananana, hey, hey, hey goodbye nananana goodbye." Fuck them!

You would know just by looking at these girls that they were bad lays. Did their boyfriends want them to go there to get some pointers? Maybe. I don't know. Most sorority girls are really shallow. They would bicker and say things like, "I won't say yes for less than three carats. If he thinks I'm cooking, he's got another thing coming. Now I don't have to suck his cock anymore. I don't do windows either, haha!" Most of those women get married in Vera Wang to the man of their dreams. It looks good on paper and in photographs but when the pre-nup is finished in five years or less, they end up fucking the pool-boy and getting addicted to heroin. Those guys don't give a fuck about them; they want their trophy wife and something on the side just like dad did. They come to the clubs to do their male bonding; brag about the strippers who won't fuck them unless there's money involved. There is nothing interesting about any of them.

I'm talking about spoiled rich white kids. "Oh my god, we went to a strip club, how daring of us, isn't it?" Nope! You're still boring, cocky, needy, materialistic, and predictable white little fucks. I grew up with some kids like that. They don't have a sense of fear. They should because of their "daddy will take care of it," attitude. It would have been funny if they started something with Big Wayne and one of them ended up in the hospital. How do they explain to those girls' parents, "Where were you when this happened?" I don't think they're seeing the big picture in all of this. What if daddy's a member of The V.I.P. club? It would be worse than they can imagine, if daddy's a member. Don't think daddy will back you up. Because dad has a wife that's going to be like those girls when they grow up; fucking the pool boy and addicted to heroin and I'll bet dads pre-nup said she could fuck around. Good old dad isn't getting any much of anything anymore from his wife, so he goes to the club where dad can blow off some steam. Dad needs the club more than those girls need their reputation. Because with families like theirs, dad comes first! Kids come second if you're lucky. Aaahhhh… is that white privilege, or what!

I gave a table dance for a guy's 90th birthday, I kept it really easy. I thought what if he has a heart attack? Am I going to get fired? Am I going to give him C.P.R. or just have a good cry about it after work? I will pray for him, but at least he went with a smile on his face, I had never seen that before, and I thought I'd seen it all. His nephew brought him there without his mother's permission. His Mom is his grandpa's daughter and they both agreed not to talk about this birthday gift to mom.

They had a blast and then he died. Just kidding! They stayed for about three hours, and the girls loved the grandpa back in the day. He was a looker; he showed us pictures of him in WWII. Boy howdy, he was handsome, just like his grandson. I don't care what anyone says if grandpa wants to go to the strip club, let him go to the strip club! Bring the oxygen and nitros! I'm sure the kid will look back on his life and remember that day as one of his favorite birthdays he ever had. They were celebrating their birthdays together; they were only a couple of days apart. I had some good memories from the club; that was one of them for sure.

CHAPTER EIGHTEEN: PRO ATHLETES, GOLF SUCKS, COVID

During the time I was working at a strip club, one night, the New York Rangers came in. I didn't know who they were, but the girls told me. The Hockey guys are not my cup of tea; the missing teeth and black eyes, not really appealing to me, but some chicks like it. Also, they all dress alike. I can imagine all of them going out together and buying the same black Armani suit. No trace of originality there.

Anyways, they were going to sit in my section and all the strippers would pounce! Now I don't do this normally, but my little brother is a Hockey player and this was his team. Considering that I was a good employee, I decided to break the rules this time. I took a long strip of paper from the terminal and an indelible ink pen. I went over to them and said, "Who's in charge? Who's paying?" It is always good to know who to be extra nice to. I asked the guy in charge, "I have a brother who is a hockey player. Now I have no idea who you are, but you guys are his favorite team, so is it okay if I got all of them to sign this for my brother?" I could sense that he was taken aback. "You don't know who we are? Sure, that's okay."

He was surprised I had no idea who they were, so I looked at the guys and said, "Okay, I'm Jan. I'll be waiting on you." Two of the guys were not paying attention, so I mouthed off to them in French. I spoke a little French. It got their attention instantly. "This is a piece of paper and a pen, you will sign this legibly for my brother who plays hockey. If you do not sign this, you don't get a drink." They all went, "Ooooo." I went around the table and took orders as they signed. One guy didn't sign. So I didn't take his drink order. He was some famous Hockey dude, French. No idea who he was. He had all his teeth.

I came back, served everyone but him. He was visibly offended. "Hey! Where's my drink?" I said, "Are your fingers broken? Everyone signed but you. So you don't get a drink and if you are thinking about going to the bar for a drink, don't. I told the bartender not to serve you, and he likes me, so does my boss. If you want a drink tonight, sign the paper because this guy said to sign it." I was referring to the head hockey guy who was paying, and he just laughed. His teammates joined him as well, the guy paying said, "You better sign it."

So I got him to sign it but I fucked with him all night! I would deliberately serve him an empty glass or a cup of coffee. Honestly, one of the perks of working in that industry is you don't have to watch it if you're a smart ass, sometimes it's funny and other times, you wind up on the floor. "Oops, I thought that was funny." Know your audience.

It's really fun to make fun of guys who have massive egos. The amusement that one feels as an aftermath of hurting a male ego is almost addicting. I mouthed off to so many athletes, just for shits and giggles! I mouthed off to one of the Smiths from the broncos. I can't remember witch one, the one with no sense of humor. But I had fun talking to Tyrone or Tarell Davis or I think it was something like that. Actually, fuck it, I don't know but he was funny. I can't remember half of their names. They thought it was funny when I would wait on them and I didn't know or care who they were.

I met so many of the football guys it's hard to keep them all straight. Sorry, not all of them look alike, but the linebackers do. They are just massive giants with no necks. What can I say? They are fun to fuck with! I do think some of those guys have been hit in the head too many times. I would say something, everyone else would laugh and the linebacker would sit there like Jabba-the Hut on Quaaludes. I was always trying to make everyone laugh a little. I was sitting with of the funniest women I ever met, Christina. She was a comedian, the perfect profession for her. She always made everyone laugh, she was barely five feet tall, but her personality was like Andre the Giant.

She was a hoot and Cinnamon. I swear that was her real name. She was a catholic too and her sisters were all lovely. This woman stands out to me because she was a natural beauty. No plastic surgery, not a lot of make-up, and always in a good mood for the most part. She never got bitchy or complained all the time. You know why? Because she was a black woman with brains, she was there to make money and get the fuck out. Cinnamon didn't do drugs or have a loser boyfriend around. She was just there like I was to make money while you can and get out, and she was one of the nicest and prettiest women there. I don't know if she would remember me, but I adored her.

The same night I pulled the "I want you to sign the autographs for the drinks," I was having a fairly busy night. The Rangers table was one of my last tables and it got interesting. I was finishing up all my tabs and the guy in charge signed the tab, pushed off the stripper that was sitting with him off his chair, and turned around to give me a big bear hug. I was thinking, "I'm pretty sure that stripper would have sucked your dick, but okay." He kissed me on the cheek and handed me his room key. Not the last time that happened, just the first. You know what that was? He wanted what he can't have, that's all that was. There was nothing special about me; I just wasn't going to give it up that easy. He looked at me as a challenge.

I finished my shift and went home. I remembered that key. I lived off Colfax, so I walked down the street and gave it to a bum. I just said, "If you want a hot shower, it's right down the street." I went to give my brother the autographs and I told him, "That guy gave me his room key." He said, "Him?" with shock evident on his face. "I would have slept with him!" I guess it was his idol. If he told me who he was right now, I would have no idea. He might have thought, "Oh, I'm a big famous hockey guy sleep with me!" I don't think so. I don't know who that guy was, but he's famous. I hope he hears this. I would love to ask him, "Did that bum show up at your hotel room to use the shower?" and thanks for the autographs for my brother.

We had a fore warning about some guys who were going to come into the club. They were The Hell's Angels. It was a little shocking. You know why? They were so polite and nice. I had a tray full of drinks and they were like, "Move out of her way, here you go honey." They made everyone move out of our ways just so the girls could serve them without disturbance. That was so sweet, none of us expected it. I asked some of the other waitresses, "Are these guys the fake Hell's Angels? Why are they so polite?" I know we were pleasantly surprised. They tipped everyone, even the girls at the door.

If you meet a Hell's Angel next time, don't judge too harshly but be careful too. My friend worked at a club where they showed up and there was a fight, after the floor looked like a sea of broken glass, so it's hit or miss. The Hell's Angels were good to us! Don't judge a book by its cover! To all the Hell's Angels that tipped us so well that day, thank you! I also know that these guys would occasionally go to funerals of veterans and try to drown out the chanting by revving their engines to all that ridiculous bullshit that the Westboro Baptist Church preach, with their "down with fags" and "God hates America" bullshit! The Hell's Angels who do that are alright by me! They are true blue Americans, show a little respect.

Not to brag, but there was also this one night when The W.W.F. guys came in. I got to put the big belt on. I have a picture of it somewhere too. Those guys like to party! I'm not going to mention any names; it could damage their careers. Jim Norton is a big fan of one of them.

When I got back to work the day, girls abused me. I was doing their check-outs, covering for them when they got too drunk. This was getting old. They were getting really drunk at work. I never drank when I was a cocktail waitress; you're responsible for thousands of dollars in tabs. I was the new girl, and they all got pulled into the V.I.P. room for a little talk from the boss about their drinking without me. They came out, and the manager called me over. "Jan, can I speak with you a bit?" He sat me down and asked me to spy on the girls who were drinking, no shit. I just said, "Okay." But in my head, I was thinking, "No fucking way am I gonna do that!"

I went back to the dressing room and said, "Heads up! They're watching you guys." I warned them. Then they came up with a great idea. "Jan we are going to order shots on our guys tabs and you go get them at the bar and take them back to the dressing room for us and we will take the empty glasses later to the bar and every time you do it we will give you twenty bucks o.k.?" I said, "I don't want to get in trouble." They said, "You won't get caught. You're a good girl." I made so much money off of them at first until they wound up in jail or rehab. Then I told them, "You're always talking about how you are making money at those golf tournaments. I want in!" So, they invited me, and it was like a drunk fest. I was on and off with my drinking for years but I saw more heavy drinking in that club than anywhere I ever worked, and that's coming from a drunk.

I drank a lot in the past, but I never got arrested, or got a D.U.I., but that is pure luck! If you get one D.U.I. that should be enough to learn your lesson. Don't drink and drive again! Two of the girls I worked with had three D.U.I.s. I worked with a bartender who had five. I know a lot of people who have had multiple D.U.I.s. In the restaurant business that I have been in since I was seventeen, there is not a lot of sobriety. So they do their community work and when it's over, they go back to drinking and do it all over again. Learn your fucking lesson!

No sympathy for anyone who doesn't get it after one D.U.I. and decides to walk on the same path of idiocy again. Shame on them! I only had one friend, Brenda who got two D.U.I.s, and it really wasn't her fault but people who have three and four D.U.I.'s, forget it. Ever heard of M.A.D.D. - Mothers Against Drunk Driving? Those women will fuck you up! They are pushing for stiffer penalties for repeat D.U.I. offenders. Think twice before you fuck with those bitches, they are mean business. I wouldn't be surprised if the ladies from M.A.D.D. had little inside skinny on information like where the re-offenders work, where they go to church, who they are dating, where their mom lives, what kind of car he drives, which market he goes to, or where he goes to eat? Yeah, ladies! You have my full permission to pass a bill that gives all the moms and dads who have lost a loved one to drinking and driving all of their personal information with pictures of them too. They should have complete liberty to shout on a bullhorn wherever they go. "This person is a repeat offender with D.U.I convictions, watch out!" Let everyone know who they are. Knock yourselves out! Pass any bill you can to prevent it from happening to any other child.

Anyway, the first golf tournament I worked, they got me stuck in a beer tub. I was setting up and two girls drove by stark naked in a golf cart. "Jan, what's up!" That was at 10:00 am in the morning. By the end of the day, everybody was trashed. There was this guy who everybody was calling with this weird name, I can't remember it, but he had it on the plates on his car. He yelled at me, "Hey, you're the only girl who hasn't shown me her tits, let's see them!" I said, "Nope. You have plenty of tits over there." He jumped out of the cart and came over. "I want to see them! Don't be shy. I won't hurt you, I'll give you a twenty, just for a glance." I said, "Nope, it would take a lot more than a twenty." He boasted. "Why not a hundred?" All of his friends went, "Ooohhh, yeah."

Soon, there was an audience and they were looking at him. His friends were clapping and cheering him on. "Go for it, show him those tits!" I just figured fuck it. I'd tell him the truth then he will leave me alone. "Look, I'm on steroids for my Ashmah, and I have hair around my nipples. I'm embarrassed about it." I wasn't kidding. It's a side effect when you go on anabolic steroids, you get hair where you don't want it and you gain weight. I carried an extra fifteen pounds for years, but lucky me, it went to my tits! He said, "Okay, wow! Not for a hundred. Huh, how about two hundred?" I couldn't believe this guy's balls, but I really needed the money.

I was thinking I'm never going to see this jackass ever again, so I did it. I flashed him and grabbed the cash. He said, "You weren't kidding, hey! You guys, you gotta see this." I was pissed. I said, "Thanks a lot." He shrugged. "I was just kidding, never mind, guys! Don't worry, we all have our little faults." I should have turned on the waterworks, made him give me more money, and feel guilty, but I just wanted him to leave. He gave me an uncomfortable sideways hug and left. I was finishing up. I made five hundred dollars with his money, not bad. I remembered his nickname that he had it on his car plates, so I went out to the parking lot and let the air out of two of his tires, one for each tit. Thanks for the tip!

I did caddy for a really sweet guy from Devron Cherry from the Kansas City Chiefs. I didn't know who he was but he was a good golfer. I told him that I was a chef and he gave me his card. The intention wasn't the usual, "Call me later, baby." That wasn't the case. Instead he said, "If you're in Kansas, there are a lot of great restaurants. Call me if you are in town, my family lives there." What a nice man! No ego, very polite and charming. I wish more professional athletes were like Devron Cherry. He was a gem!

I think John Elway is a foul-mouthed, horse-faced, chain-smoking, arrogant, insensitive asshole! I think we should make buttons that say that. I'd wear one, just not in Denver, the packers would love it. John came into the club after the back-to-back Super Bowls. He sat in my section. Jon's a chain smoker, he was taking quarters, heating them up with his lighter and flicking them to the girls on stage for their tips. He burned one of the girls. My manager had to ask him to stop. You know what he said to him? "Do you know who I am? I was invited here, fuck off." That's the real John Elway, so for those people who worship him, here is a bit of reality on your plate.

If you think I'm making this up, we have Elway on video doing that. One of the security guys saved it for fun, so he can't deny it. From the first glance at him, I didn't like him, so I cut him off. That's my job. I served him a cup of coffee, Jon didn't like it and he told me to go fuck myself. Listen up John, I also pulled a prank on you at a golf game he was at. It was raining and I got out of my golf cart and put K-Y jelly all over his golf clubs. I almost got caught. The guys who worked on the course saw me do it and they let me, because they couldn't stand Elway either. I really wanted to run up from behind him and "Pants" him but I didn't think I could get away with it. He couldn't get a good grip all day; he thought it was the rain! Fuck you, John for all the little kids you won't give your autographs to, you stuck-up prick! I hope this shows up on E.S.P.N. They won't back him up because I met some of them too. I am invisible. If any of them said, "Oh, he's not like that at all. He's really a sweet guy." They would be lying! They know what he's really like. If you want a real comparison to Elway, just watch the movie The Replacements with Keanu Reeves. The quarterback that replaces the quarterback in the movie with the inflated ego, that's Elway. I don't know how his ex dealt with his arrogant ass.

You know what is really funny? I have seen Elway on more than one occasion, and every time I saw him, I mouthed off under my breath, and got away with it because he can't place me. Some people around him heard me say something about him and giggled, but John didn't have a clue. That's funny to me.

I caddied for a lot of golf tournaments. I don't like golf but I went where the money was, this was about twenty years ago. The guys I was going to caddy for told me, "Whatever you do, don't mention O.J. Simpson." That's such a dangerous thing to say to a comedian. "Don't do this!" That's like saying to a drunk, "I have to go to the bathroom. Hold my Long Island ice tea, I'll be right back, don't drink it." What the fuck do you think is going to happen? Of course, they are going to go for it. But they were serious and I didn't know why, but I kept my mouth shut about it.

I do remember telling them, "It's probably a good idea to keep Elway away from me or it's going to be a bad day for him." I got in the cart, and some big black football player slid in and introduced himself. Of course, I didn't recognize him. I knew he had to be famous. We were at a charity event, and Elway was in the front and we were two carts behind him. For those of you who have never been to a golf tournament like this, the most famous person at the events goes first, and that was Elway. There were a lot of famous players there but no swimmers, so I didn't care. I have to say I don't really watch much football. I just don't pay much attention to it.

I was a swimmer, so all I knew was: the quarterback throws the ball, the kicker kicks it, and ten points they score. Woohoo! That's about it for me, the basics. I said to the guy, "So, let me guess. You are a football player, right?" He told me, "I used to play football." I don't recognize him at all. I pushed it more. "Did you play for the Broncos?" He said, "I played in California." I was digging too hard but at that point, it was too late to back off. "Oh, you played for the Rams? My mother loves them. Were you a quarterback?" He replied, "No, I didn't play with the Rams, wasn't a quarterback." He was looking at me like, "Wow, this girl really doesn't know who I am." I started racking my brain to figure out another team in California and I said again with complete confidence, "Oh, the Forty-niners, San Francisco, right?" He shook his head. "Nope, but you are getting closer." The fact that I was struggling was crystal clear on my face and he could see it. I said, "Well, my sister went to Humbolt state, but they're not well known for their football." He laughed and said, "I played in Oakland."

I wished my mouth would play catch up with my brain first before it opened. I spouted out the first thing that came into my head, "Oakland? Isn't that a bad neighborhood? My friend went to Berkley, and she told me never to go there alone. Is that true?" He shrugged and said, "Kind of." I said, "Can we start over? I don't know anything about football." There was a smirk forming on his face. He said, "No shit!" I told him, "I'm a chef." So all day he called me, "CHEF BOY ARE DEE." I cleared my throat and decided to take a different approach instead. "Okay, let's start again! My name is Jan Williams. What's yours again?" He chuckled and said "My name is Marcus Allen. If he was Mark Spits, I would've known who he was.

I said, "Are you famous and are you not the quarterback?" I asked, just to be clear. He said, "Well, I'm kind of famous, but I didn't play quarterback." Honestly, he told me what position he played and it went in one ear and out the next something with the ball, I don't know. I asked him, "Did you ever play against the Rams?" He nodded. "Of course," I said, "Do you have a phone?" He squinted his eyes as if he was trying to contemplate why I was asking that question. "Yes, why?" He reached out into his front pocket and gave me his phone so I called my Mom on his phone. As I was waiting for her to pick up the phone, I started to act like a child who's being lied to and I told him, "My mom knows football, and I am going to ask her who you are, because I think you are full of shit. I have never heard of you at all. So, what was your name again?" He laughed when I asked him what his name was again. He repeated his name once more and that's when I heard my Mom on the line.

Mom, you'll never guess where I am! At a golf tournament! I'm a caddy for this guy who says his name is Marcus Allen. Have you ever heard of him? Of course, you have. Okay, tell me if he's legit." I stretch my arm out and give the phone to him. "Okay, Marcus. Listen to me. My mom doesn't like cussing, I mean it. Don't curse at all!" So I put him on the phone with mom. I thought, if this guy is full of shit and mom doesn't know who he is I'm leaving I'm not getting paid that much and it's hot today but mom knew everything about him. He was very polite. Since mom said he was legit, we went and played golf. I still don't know what she said to him but he was pretty taken back. I hope he hears about this. Thank you Marcus for being nice and polite to my mom. Now I know why they told me, "Don't mention O.J. Simpson." If you don't know, ask a friend later or Google it. I'm not going to get into it none of my business!

I grew up around golf but didn't get into it because it's really, really, really, stupid. Everything about it sucks. What dumbfuck Scotsmen thought of this shit? It wasn't Tiger Woods. He's a disgrace and he really thinks we are stupid enough to believe that lousy, poorly acted bullshit! I am sorry when he got caught fucking around. I mean, are you kidding me? That was so stupid. My grandpas both played, Dad couldn't because of asthma. Again, I just always thought it was really, really, really stupid. I liked Happy Gillmore! That was fun but I still think golf is really, really, really stupid.

There is only this one movie, Tin Cup, a movie I actually thought didn't suck that Kevin starred in. Field Of Dreams was a nice one as well, wonderful movie. But I didn't like

Waterworld at all but I still think golf is really, really, really stupid! I could go the rest of my life without one more golf movie. It's been done! What's next, Golf in Space or Zombie Golf? Sure, why not? Let's dig up Dinah Shore and Arnold Palmer. See what rich white old fucks show up for that tournament. Jesus Christ! If anything, now they're doing rich white guys in space.

In the olden times, when a kid wanted to be an astronaut or a rocket scientist, it was a dream for them to go to outer space. They knew if they wanted that privilege, they would have to go to school, get a degree or a doctorate, and do technical research and have years of experience before they would even get a chance to go to outer space. Now, you just have to be white and have money. Wait, let's let one black guy go up and make it look even sounds like the Mormons. Some greedy little white kid said, "I'm going to throw a fit in front of everyone, if I don't get my way. I want to go to space daddy!" The parents could only say, "Okay Karen!" Some eighteen-year-old little brat got to go to space for the modest price of 28 million dollars. I think they should take another trip to space with the Spazzy Egomaniac with the 25 million dollar pink diamond implanted in his forehead and leave them there. What purpose does either of them serve? I can't think of a single one. "Look at me, I am throwing money away, Yay!" Because now we have U.F.O.s and everyone thinks we are going to be invaded, let's start a human sacrifice to our new friends. If they're going to experiment on humans, give them the ones we don't want, like the kid with a daddy who paid for him to go to outer space and the Spazzy Egomaniac with the pink diamond embedded in his forehead. Hey, we can ask them to take TEKASHI 69 as well. I could go on and on about people I'd like to just leave this planet for the good of others. Someone make a list!

Anyway, I was at one of these stupid golf tournaments and struck up a conversation with one of the kids who worked at the clubhouse in the store that sold clothing and golf crap. I told him how I felt about golf, and he thought it was funny. So, I made him and myself a little fun polo shirt to wear. I went to a shop that does custom shirts and they put a cute little phrase on the lapel in small print that said, "Fuck Golf" over a golf ball with a big smiley face in the middle about the size of a quarter. I don't know why I think it's funny when someone has to get up close to read a stupid pin. The way they kind of squint and try to read it correctly, it just makes me laugh. I don't know why, but maybe because I think it is silly.

Anyway, I wanted to wear the shirt to one of these tournaments as a joke. I went back to the course, and gave one to the kid who worked there. He loved it! We laughed. I started to leave but I was interrupted. Four white guys in their fifties were sitting outside the shop and one of them stopped me. "Hi there, haven't seen you here before." I said, "You probably won't again either." I started to walk around him and he stopped me again. He looked at my shirt and started to laugh. When he could speak, he said, "Her shirt says 'Fuck Golf'. Can you believe that." He thought it was funny.

Now I've done a lot of so-called caddying in my life and some of the caddies are strippers. The men were sitting with an obvious stripper dressed like a golfer. She was wearing her spray tan, a polo shirt with the collar up, long hot pink nails, shorts that make her ass hang out open-toed shoes, not golf shoes. She had her Tiffany's chain around her neck, rings on every other finger, blond frizzy bleached hair, and lots of make-up. God, she looked like my ex-girlfriend, Brianna. Dead puppies. Dead puppies, Dead puppies; that's better.

So little Miss "Debbie Does Golf" leans in and states, "Oh my God, how can you say that? I love golf it's my favorite thing to do. I just love it, don't you guys?" I'm sorry but I couldn't help myself. I looked at her and said, "Yeah Princess, you love golf as much as you like fucking fossils for free." All of the men laughed and threw her under the bus. They didn't say anything in her defense. She glared at me and shrieked, "That's not funny! I have no idea what she talking about," and smiled nervously. I don't think she understood. The more she talked, the deeper she's digging her own hole. She continued, "I play golf everywhere. I bet you don't." I knew what this little bitch was about, she went to play golf with her married boyfriend when the wife doesn't want to travel or suck his cock. So yeah, she's probably seen some nice courses, but she isn't a member.

I asked her, "You worked in the adult entertainment industry, don't you?" The guys went, "Oh, you are busted!" I said to her, "Since you love golf, what is your handicap?" She didn't know. I announced as a matter of fact. "That's what I thought." And I went home and laughed. That woman was definitely out of her element. I love it when people like her say stupid shit. I'm right there to go in for the humor kill, so much fun! I left and I don't know how she was going to get out of that verbal blunder, but I'm sure those guys still got their dicks sucked anyway. Keep it on the pole, Princess!

I went to a B.B.Q. at Wash Park with all my new co-workers from the Diamond, and I fell and broke my wrist. I have a high threshold for pain but I knew I had to get it casted. The problem was that I didn't know the area. I didn't have a car, so I went to my manager, Jason, and tried to tell him gently that I broke my wrist and need a ride to the hospital. He was like my own personal therapist. When I needed advice for anything, I could go to him. I was new in town and he was great, but I didn't want to make a big deal out of my stupid wrist so I told him quietly, "Jason, can I get a ride to the hospital? I don't have a car, and I need to get this casted." He said to me, "You broke your wrist right now when you fell? Why didn't you say something earlier?" I told him, "It's embarrassing. No big deal, I have broken stuff before. You should feel my tailbone." He held me and said, "It's O.K. but I'm not from this area either. Don't worry, we will find the hospital." He paused and then asked me again. "Are you okay?" I mustered up a face with a smile. "I am fine. Really! Let's just get to the hospital. I am not in a lot of pain don't worry."

We went to the Police department off University Boulevard, to find out where the hospital was. I realized that even with all the family and people I knew in the department, I'd never been into a Police station. Not like on T.V. There was one cop in there behind Plexiglas. You know this cop he's a white old fart in his fifties, probably divorced, and should have retired by now but his first ex-wife took him for half. He possibly had a gay son who he disowned. The old man never had a good rim job ever and he's thinking about going postal, because he was invited to a B.B.Q. and he's stuck working in this little uncomfortable box for the fourth of July, so this wasn't this cop's best day. Just a guess.

We went up to him. "Excuse me, I was playing Volleyball, and I think I broke my wrist. Do you know where the hospital is? We aren't from around here and I need to get this casted." He looked at me and said, "You think you broke your wrist, huh? How much have you had to drink today?" I was a little stunned. My boss said, "She is not drunk, she broke her wrist." The cop barked. "Am I talking to you? No. You'll know when I'm talking to you." What a prick. I tried again. "I had a half of a beer about two hours ago, but I'm not tipsy or anything. If I was drunk, this wouldn't hurt so much." I smiled like he might be nice if I'm nice to him. Nope, that didn't work. He looked at me with such annoyance. "Okay, I'll call for the paramedics. If they think you broke something, they'll take you to the hospital. If not, you are going to detox, how does that sound?" I took a glance at my boss and he was looking at this cop like he wanted to punch him in the face because he knew I was really hurt. I said to the cop, "Yes, please call them." The cop barked some more instructions. "Go sit down over there, and wait for them."

We went and sat down. Jason was heaving like he was trying to contain his anger. He said, "That guy's a dick." I was so embarrassed. He was my new boss. I was hoping that he doesn't fire me. I was supposed to work the next four days. I didn't know it then, but Jason stayed with me all night, took me to dinner, and took me home. He put me to bed because I was high as a kite! I didn't have a bad reaction to whatever they gave me. I wish I could remember what it was. Jason, if you hear about this, I love you buddy!

The paramedics showed up in a few minutes. They started talking to the cop. I could hear that peasant of a man say, "She is drunk, but she thinks she broke her wrist. I'm just going to put her in detox, go look at her." They listened to the cop, came over to me. "Does this hurt?" Before I could answer, they bent my wrist back. I heard a snap, and the next thing I know, I'm in the hospital getting casted to my shoulder! I think I blacked out. I never got a bill from those paramedics because they fucked up. That fat old white useless cop should have retired a long time ago. Here I was, thinking that cops are your friends, I was really mistaken. The worst thing about what happened was that the cop could have just said, "The hospital is right down the street, on the right. You can't miss it." Instead, that bastard was just throwing his weight around. He wasn't helping, he was hindering.

Now that I think about it, I guess I shouldn't complain. If I was a black woman in that scenario, what do you think would have happened? That was an all-white neighborhood. If I was black, that fat old white cop would have thrown me in a cell just because he could and wouldn't have even called for the paramedics. White privilege, so if you wonder why white male cops get such a bad reputation, it is because of shit like that. I did realize that daddy doesn't own the cops here. That cop was a dick and didn't have to be like that. He was just too lazy to do a good job; get off his ass and try to help someone who actually needs it.

It is time to talk about CO-VID now. Did anyone else lose their job during CO-VID? I did, but I didn't file for unemployment. I don't think I deserved it. I lived high on the hog for a long time. A lot was handed to me just because my dad had connections and I was white! I have more of a chance to get a job, get a loan get an apartment just because I'm white! My friends and family help me. I'm dead broke, but I get food stamps and Medicare. I'm not trying to feed my kids or make rent, I'm good. It's only money; someone else needs it more than I do. I'm not telling you this so you can go, "Oh she's so selfless and giving." Fuck that. It's just the right thing to do for me. My Mom is not very happy about it. I keep hearing her say, "Why are you putting yourself last? You matter. You need the money too." I think all privileged white people should have a Trading Places moment. Lose everything and work to get it back. It's a humbling experience.

I didn't lose everything, but I'm definitely not as privileged as I was. I'm privileged to have people who care about me and I have my faith. I'm pretty much okay with that. Unfortunately, my car got vandalized, and they took my catalytic converter. A lot of people got ripped off. $2400 to get it fixed so they won't steal it again. I had to pay them to put a metal grate around my converter because they tried to steal it twice! We got it on film, and went to the police. We found out that they used a stolen car with stolen plates, so there was nothing that they could do. Here is a suggestion, if you have to install a camera for your car's safety, make sure you get a picture of their faces or visible tattoos and don't go to the police. Take it to the press, show it on the news, or set a silly Boobie Trap. You can pull a Home Alone. Cover them in glue and feathers, that's the only way to catch them without shooting anybody. Our Trumper neighbor said, "I have an A-K 47 in the garage if you need it." Yeah, no thanks! I think we'll be okay. I don't think that's a fair trade, a car part for a life. No thanks. Some people are a little out of whack! Thank God, he's just a Trumper.

At least we don't have Janice Dickenson as a neighbor. If I saw her come to welcome me to the neighborhood, I'd say to my significant other, "Pack it up! No way in hell I'm not living next to Janice Dickenson. I'd rather live in five points. I don't care if she comes over in a thong and a cowboy hat on, I'll laugh, but if she comes over here with a gun, and a bottle of tequila, I'm gonna fucking shoot her in her kneecaps. The only place she hasn't had plastic surgery. I don't have the energy for that shit, so pack it up and let's go. Not here, not ever. We are moving!" I couldn't make it one day living next to Janice Dickenson. Is she bi-polar? She has everything else why not add that to the list of excuses for her bad behavior! If they write a book about Janice should, it should be called, "It's Not My Fault - By Janice Dickenson, and Co-Written by Karen." Both of them loved to play the blame game. People can give it to friends as a gag gift. "Oh my God, are you kidding? That's so funny! It's never Janice's fault, right? And she's friends with Karen. How appropriate" There's one for the bathroom for sure if anyone runs out of toilet paper, tear out a page, no big loss.

I do like my Trumper neighbor. Though I accidently insulted him, I didn't mean it. His sister was visiting. They were on his porch, and Trump came up. This is pre-CO-VID I told her, "I'm Republican, but I didn't vote for Trump." She looked at him, laughed and said, "He did!" Without thinking, I spewed. "Oh God, don't you feel stupid?" She laughed, and that made me laugh harder. With his mouth upside down, he turned and went inside. I had to ask his sister, "He's a Trumper?" She said, "Big time." Oops! Live and learn. I hope he doesn't get too mad at me for this. He really is a nice guy. I just don't think we should talk politics. Like no religion with my scientology friends and no cock with lesbians.

CHAPTER NINETEEN: NO TECH. GOD LOVES US ALL

Among many other things that you must know about me, one major fact you should be aware of is that I am anti-tech as much as possible. I turned off my computer twelve years ago. The reason was that I was going through identity theft and I didn't want to go through that again, but luck, as always, had something else in store for me. I have had to go through identity theft twice. I got a call in July, "Your social security card has been illegally used to rent a car, and in a drug bust in Texas. Your bank and all of your credit cards have been frozen for the next two years, or until our investigation is finished." No shit! So the movie "Identity Theft" starring Melissa McCarthy and Jason Bateman is very funny, but in reality, it is not so much fun.

Once you go through that, you would be very hesitant to even swipe a key, if you know what I mean. I stayed off the internet because I didn't want this to happen to me again! It sucked. It's not like you get issued a new social security card, get a lawyer, and talk to the government. It's a nightmare going through identity theft; it is like taking too much acid. All you can do is try to stay positive and ride it out! Unfortunately, there's nothing you can do about it.

Some people may say, "It is bad karma on you." I don't think so. I think God has a hell of a sense of humor going, "Don't worry Jan, I got your back. I have challenged you way worse than this you'll be okay, not the end of the world". I have no idea how anyone got all my information, and I don't care. I'm not going to turn into a Karen, and shriek in front of every other person that crosses my path, "Oh help me! My life is over." Nope! Fuck that! Shit happens all the time. I'll deal with it without taking my frustration out on others.

Everyone goes through rough times, so it is best to try to stay optimistic in every situation. At least make an effort. There are people in this country who have lost everything including loved ones, from CO-VID, mass shootings, extreme cold, and heat. The list goes on and on. Who gives a shit about my little problem with identity theft? I consider myself very lucky to be here at all. Every day I count my blessings. In my routine, there is no time for a pity party. Don't we have enough winey white women in the world already? So what if I can't write a check or use my bank for the next two years? Yes, the FBI might have a word with me, but I didn't do anything illegal. Maybe I can't work at all, or try to get a job as they can garnish my wages until they have finished their investigation in two years.

Yeah, I really don't think many people would be able to deal with this once, much less twice. Working with the government is like working with a three-year-old. You need to showcase a lot of patience, but I was with my ex for five years. I think two years with identity theft is nothing compared to babysitting Eric. Thank God for cable, and I can still write.

We have a cable T.V. We get every channel possible, what more do I need? I love music videos. I always enjoy them, even though I can't hear it, I turn the close captioning off. I just want the visuals. I adore J-LO. She is in this video with some guy who is super delicious. He's wearing a white suit in it. I don't know him, but they're up on a roof somewhere. She's wearing a silver suit with chains on the side, boogieing cool. Does it ring a bell?

I also like Billy Eilish, but I can't read or understand a goddamned word she says. She is in this video with another girl who has really neat nails in it. I wish they would slow it down, though. Billy doesn't move her mouth when she speaks or sings, you can just watch her. No complains, though. Here is a great idea. Tell Billy to teach Madonna how to chew with her mouth shut! I also like the one with Rob Snyder in it. I am talking about the "Down, Down, Down" video. It's a take-off of Deuce Bigalow: Male Gigolo. I have no idea what they are saying, but I love the costumes and the humor in it! Well done, Rob. I don't know the name of the artist, but Rob was funny.

Another artist that I love is Cardi B. I enjoy her music video called, "Up." Those dancers are so good, they are right on the money! I don't know any of them but I tell you, there is another J. Lo or Beyonce in that group of women. They are sexy as fuck! I danced for a long time, and I was classically trained so I know the difference. Those women rule! I love the wardrobe with the fringes on the sleeves. Cardi B. has so much confidence, she truly has that "Va- Va-Voom," and that's hard to come by. I wish I could have an ounce of her bad bitch energy. Actually, no way too white, not in a million years. I do think she's wonderful. Cardi B. is a sexy mommy too, congrats!

I also like Lil' Kim when she did Moulin Rouge, fantastic! I'm sure if either of them hears some weenie white lady from L.A. thought their style is wonderful; they would definitely have a good laugh about it. They would both be like, "Who the fuck is that?" They could just say, "Skinny white bitch." They can say, "They all look alike." If you showed them a picture of me, Renée Zellweger, Reese Witherspoon, Clair Danes and Nicole Kidman, all those skinny white bitches, they wouldn't be able to tell us apart.

Yes, we are that fucking boring! But at least we aren't Taylor Swift boring. She is the most boring white woman that exists next to Nancy Regan. Sorry Nancy, you shouldn't have taken your own advice: "Just say no." Nancy could have used a little T.H. C. and a drink or two. Maybe a little toot to lift you up a little if you ask me, Taylor Swift is so boring!! Whispering, waiting, dreaming, hoping, wondering, yawn! She's been singing the same boring shit for the last ten years, except now there's a sweater in it. You want to be interesting, Taylor? Take out the sweater. Replace it with a barbed wire thong. Live it up a little, why don't you Miss boring-vanilla?

Once I had a running toilet and I used Taylor Swift's music to drown out the running sound. That's the only thing her music is good for, running toilets. The only time she was remotely interesting at all was when Kanye West jumped on some award show and grabbed the mic out of her hand and told her she didn't deserve the award. That was great! I hope he goes off his meds, does it again but this time, he punches her in the face. I'd watch that show all day long!

I know he was married to Kim Kardashian. I like her if she does become an attorney, all the best to her. Maybe she can help the people who were incarcerated for marijuana use and get them out. If she does, kudos to Kim! They are all K's; Kim, Kris, and Kloe. I don't know all of them but the dad's now a mom, and he is a "K".

Look, I was in a trans relationship. The whole politically correct stuff with him, her, them, they, it got to be too much for me. I mean, give me a break. I'm bi-sexual, that's my excuse for not getting it right. I guess I'm not gay enough to get it right. That's what T.E.R.F.s will tell you.

I have to ask, do you think Katelyn Jenner is pretty? I think maybe her doctor was a little drunk, or maybe it's the lighting, I don't know, but it looks like she was a really beautiful woman once and someone took her face off and broke it into pieces and went, "Oh shit, how we are going to fix this? Who is good at puzzles?" "Emily, the two-year-old shit shoot kid, she'll do it!"

"Hey Emily, do you want to put this puzzle together for us? Emily would go, "Shit shoot, okay. I'll do it!" Emily started to put it together and you ask her, "Are you done yet, Emily?" And she goes, "Jesus Christ! I'm not fucking finished yet!" She finished it after a while and displayed her work with a proud smile on her face, turning her face from one side to another to make sure the doctor was seeing it right. She would hear, "Not bad for a two-year-old. Good job, Emily." That's what Katelyn Jenner's face looks like. I'm not trying to be mean, but it really looks like someone broke her face up and a small child put it back together. It's not really bad, just a little confusing. I'm sure she has a good personality. Jesus, with that face, she better have a great personality.

I'm sure she has a lot of fans who are going to be mad at me, "She is so brave, how can you say that?" Hey, I'm all for being brave. All I'm saying is Cliff diving is brave, but it scares me. It makes me feel a little uncomfortable. Like when I see Katelyn Jenner's face on the cover of a magazine, just before I open the magazine, I hold my breath a little like just like I do before the cliff-divers jump. I think how bad is this going to get? Will it be a solid landing or should I look away? It's like watching the Discovery Channel, sometimes it's beautiful, and sometimes it's a global nightmare. It depends on how you look at it, some cliff diving is scary if you look at it from a certain angle, just like when you see things from a different perspective, it depends on the lighting. Some profiles look different in the sunlight and then in the dark. If you look sideways, it's better. Does any of that make sense at all? I feel like I'm digging myself a grave, fuck it. "Beauty is in the eye of the beholder." You can't go wrong with that shit.

At least I'm not a total dick like Jim Norton who said, "Katelyn Jenner's face looks like the gypsy from Thinner." That's mean but I'm not going to completely disagree. Little fucker might have a point. Jim Norton likes transgendered women, but I don't think he would fuck Katelyn Jenner unless someone dared him to. He still might have a difficult time keeping a straight face or getting a hard-on. Jim Norton is a little dirty boy, and if he can't keep a hard-on for a trans woman like Katelyn, that's pretty bad, not just for Jim but for anyone belonging to the LGBQT+ community who would try to get him excited and couldn't do it. It could cause emotional damage to both of them, and would require lots of therapy. If he's really desperate he can call Harvey Levin for a rim job. Come on, Harvey will fuck anything that moves but wrap it up; he's a dirty boy too. It could have taken me years to recover from the psychological damage that my ex-girlfriend Brianna inflicted upon me, but thankfully, I have a good sense of humor to get me through that bullshit.

I will never understand the struggles a rrans person goes through. I can't imagine being in the wrong body, that's a different kind of uncomfortable. I didn't want to change my sex parts and do a complete overhaul. I was born a female, no questions about it and I like men and women. "I'm here, I'm bi-sexual. Get used to it. Now I don't want to talk about it anymore now that I'm officially out, I'd like to "not" talk about it. I know Katelyn thinks she's beautiful, and I think it's alright to show off a little. Why not? She spent the majority of her life in the wrong body but maybe, take a step back. There are still others who don't have the benefits of your success. Most trans people can't afford to take the plunge with the best of the best of the best in medical care. We know you are who you want to be, that is great. So how about now you help other trans people with more than a speech, smile, a handshake, and a selfie? Hey, if I can do it, blah blah blah. Don't be all talk. Put together a scholarship for trans people who are athletes, or is that too much to ask of you? Or is it that you don't want to get dirt under your nails?

Katelyn, you're in the spotlight. Use it to your advantage. Don't you have enough pictures of yourself? One picture of her I would like to see where she is not the center of attention! Does Hustler do a trans centerfold? Like cliff diving, that's daring! Is it me or does anyone else think Wendy Williams looks like a Drag queen? Is there something she's not telling me because every time I see her, I look closely to see an Adam's apple scar? Her voice is really low as well. I don't care if she is trans or not, but I'd like to know.

I do think that it's great that people are more understanding of the transgender community and are more accepting of it, but have you seen some of the kids today? I can't tell who's who anymore. It makes me sound so old when I say that but its true! Have you seen Brad and Angelina's kid, the little blond number? Jesus, the kid is going to get the living shit kicked out of him if he's not careful. I hope his dad teaches him how to fight because he's going to need to learn how to fight if he's going to be that "expressive" unless he stays in Hollywood. In the business, he'll be okay but outside that world, he may be in trouble. I can't see him prancing through the middle of Wyoming in

Prada Loafers and a see-through sweater from D.K.N.Y. with ease without a security guard or two. Be as "expressive" as you want, when appropriate.

I wouldn't wear any of my dominatrix gear to mass, don't wear your club clothes to a farmers market unless you're in L.A. Just because there is some T.V. show about trans people doesn't mean everyone in the country is on board with it. I was with my ex, Brianna in Denver, coming home from a club and she got a flat tire. We stopped to fix it, and I said to Brianna, "Do you need help?" She was in a mini skirt of course and said to me, "No, I have got it." I was looking around and people were driving by, watching this poorly dressed drag queen fix her tire. I could see Brianna getting flustered and trying to fix it quickly. I asked her again, "I can help if you need me to do it, I will." She said again, "No, I have it!" Brianna fixed the tire and we got in the car. To lighten up the mood, I said, "Well, that was fun!" She replied, "That's not funny. I broke off a nail." I tried to reassure her. "Well, you have more at home, honey. At least you didn't fuck up your tits." I giggled, Brianna just sneered at me.

I don't think Brianna ever realized how dangerous of a game she was playing with the whole "I'm a whore" look. When we were fixing the tire, guys were calling out at her because she had on a mini skirt that showed her crotch when she was fixing the tire. Brianna was giving them a free show. That's what she wanted, attention. Brianna doesn't care if the attention is negative as long as she gets it, but some of the attention she got was dangerous.

I know this is weird to bring this up but does anyone know what "Q" is? I have tried to figure out what Q is but to no avail. I watched that 3 piece series on Vice News, and I'm still lost. Nobody gave a straight answer. I think I was too distracted to pay attention. I'll tell you why. J.T. Wild is the culprit. Every time he came on, all I wanted to do was to brush his hair. Oh God, his hair is beautiful. You could get lost in it. It's all his fault. All I want for him to do is sit down in front of me, tell me what Q is, turn around, and let me brush his hair. Yummy! Call me J.T. and bring your brush. Hehe. I understand you like "Q" but don't stop doing your own creative stuff. You are so talented, don't limit yourself with your art.

What was more distracting than J.T. Wild? Robert David Steel. You sexy C.I.A. whore! He was one of my mistresses' clients in L.A. I'm sure it's him his demeanor and his body language always bring me back to that time. His "Mr. I am in control all the time" aura is what makes me weak in my knees. Robert David Steel was the best submissive I have ever seen!! He could take a royal beat down like I've never seen before. Not a lot of people can handle it. He didn't like anything dirty, no pee or anything. Most of her clients didn't want that. He had a thick cock! My mistress tried to put a cock ring on him. You know how they work? You put it around the cock and the balls. His cock was so thick; she needed the biggest one she had. There are different sizes, and no, he didn't have big avocado balls either, just a thick cock. He was a trooper. R.I.P.

I worked at Wolfgang Puck's place in Denver. I met Wolfgang in Beverly Hills when I was a kid at Spagos. I didn't like his wife at the time, but I liked him, so I thought that's a good name to have on a résumé. It was hard work: ice bathing, heavy lexis full of stock, making soup in huge tilt skillets, rotate them in the walk-in daily, and everything with a sauce was on you and two other chefs. I worked catering on the side too, didn't sleep much. I went from making the kind of money at the club to making peanuts. They were going to do the chef's performance for "The taste of Colorado." I went just to watch, and they pulled me on stage. They were all drunk and asked me to cook for the cook-off. I said yes. It was my boss, I couldn't say no. All the other chefs were doing small nouveau plates. Theirs were very intricate dishes. I was just thinking, do they know who they are cooking for? This isn't a fine-dining crowd, look around. Jesus. I made a salad and let the audience try the food. I kept asking, "What do you think it needs?" I was having fun. Most of the other chefs were sweating it out.

Guess what? I won the "Taste of Colorado" with a salad! Some of the other chefs were mad and were saying, "She isn't a chef. She didn't go to culinary school like we did. I just had one reply. "Fuck you guys! I beat you, haha!" No, I didn't do that. I was respectful. Some chefs are stuck up and need to have a piece of humble pie. I didn't gloat. All I said was, "Thank you very much" to the audience. We got passes to see Rick Springfield. He was very nice, but I was tired. I didn't expect to cook or be there that long. I wanted to go home, so I gave my V.I.P. passes to some young girls who wanted to meet him and went home.

Some chefs are so stuck-up, like Bobby Flay. He insulted the people in Japan and we almost didn't get to have "Iron Chef" because of that arrogant little prick. I know he's good at what he does, but does he have to be such a cocky asshole? I'd love it if someone just bashed him across the face with a butcher block, kind of the same shit he pulled in Japan; flipping his cutting board and jumping on the counter. We almost didn't have the title and all the blame is on him and his shitty attitude. "Oh I'm Bobby Flay I'm the best." No, you are not, faggot! Americans have a bad reputation for being loud and obnoxious. Don't make it worse by doing stupid shit like that, jackass.

I've cooked in cooking competitions before. I always go into it with ease and it pisses off people when I win or place without trying much. It's kind of like poker to me; I just do it and do it well; I don't put too much thought into it. Honestly, it comes easy to me. It's supposed to be fun. Sometimes people forget that. I don't stress about the small stuff. I also don't have that "I'm number one and you suck 'attitude. I've seen some good winners and some bad winners too. Some people take it too far, like that guy Gordon Ramsey, that English prick. Telling people, "What the fuck is this shit?" If he talked to me like that, I'd call my mom!

My mother hates cussing and if he talked like that in front of her, she would beat the shit out of him emotionally. That English prick wouldn't stand a chance; he has such a bad attitude. What do you bet? He works for the Queen and her fucked up family. Does he talk to the Royals like that? What a great show that would make, watching him throw a hissy fit in front of the Royals. Do you think they would bring back beheadings because I can't see the Queen just giving him a dirty look then letting it go if he said, "Go fuck yourself," to the Queen of England. As much as I rip on the Royals, I know she has a difficult job. You know all about the suffering that goes on in the world, you watch it from your telly. It must be difficult for you to have an American in your family, we are sorry for that. I will pray for you and I'm sorry you lost your hubby. You think she'll buy that? I will pray for her, but I don't think after she gets a load of this, she'll have me over any time soon for tea, even if we are related. You know some weird English history geek is going to look it up. I don't gamble unless I know I will win, so I'll bet anyone I'm distantly related to them. YUCK.

There was this French chef from the cordon blue who came to Denver to give a presentation on frying a duck and a turkey. This arrogant dipshit wanted to do his presentation inside the building. He was told, "You should do the presentation outside." I think everybody, even hillbillies in the backcountry will tell you doing that indoors is, well, the stupidest thing you could possibly do! The stupid French motherfucker set the building on fire. Vie vela France! I'm trying to think of a punishment for arrogant chefs who misbehave? I'm a little high, and all that's coming to mind is the scene from that horror flick "Happy Birthday to Me," where the guy gets skewered with a shish kabob. Well, that would do it Works for me!

I worked at an ice cream shop, which was family-owned. It was small and across the street from a hospital. I got to change the menu, a chef's dream. The white woman who owned the place was a "Born-again Christian." Their so much fun she knew I was a Catholic but still asked me, "Have you accepted Jesus Christ as your savior?" I told her, "I'm a practicing Catholic." She said, "Yes, but have you accepted him as your savior?" I joked. "Well, you can ask my priest if you like." She didn't think that was very funny. I know Margaret Chow has a brother who's a born-again; she dealt with it with humor! Unfortunately, this woman had no sense of humor at all and she was really cheap to boot, very frugal. They did bible study, which she invited me to go to more than once and I turned her down, more than once.

I was in a trans relationship at the time and I slipped. I said "my girlfriend" instead of "boyfriend." I don't exactly remember what I said but it got her attention, and not in a good way. I was on edge with anyone knowing about our relationship. I wasn't out and I was a practicing Catholic and wasn't comfortable talking about my bi-sexual status. I was at the end of my rope with Brianna, my ex-girlfriend and I didn't want her to embarrass me by coming into the ice cream shop in the daylight, not because she was trans. No. It was because anytime Brianna went out she had to have all the attention. My friends who are gay or trans dress and behave appropriately in public, they are fine during the day, but Brianna always looked like she should be standing on the corner of Broadway and Colfax, wearing her mini-skirts, showing off her leg tattoo, smoking a cigarette, and waiting for her next trick to pick her up.

I had to be honest. I told the owner the truth. "My girlfriend is my boyfriend, he is in transition." She looked at me with utter disgust and never looked at me the same again. I had a girlfriend who was trans, obviously man to woman. I told her, "Come in for lunch. I changed the menu. I'll buy you lunch!" She came in when I wasn't working but the owner was there. It didn't go well. I came in the next day, and the owner confronted me. "Jan, some he-she came in here looking for you," I asked, "Who?" She said, "That." She handed me a card with a man's name on it. I didn't know her as a man; I couldn't make the connection. I asked her to describe her, and then I knew who she was talking about. I said, "Oh. Now I know how she is." She didn't like that. She said, "Is 'it' coming back here?" I shrugged my shoulder and mumbled, "Maybe." She huffed and walked away. That's so Christian of her, isn't it?

If I was smart, I would have called in "The cycle sluts of Denver" to come in for lunch. I did stand up for them once at a gay club we went to. They're so much fun! She would have fired me, but it would have been worth it! Her whole restaurant would be covered in glitter! I'll bet she has friends in the West Brow Baptist Church. You know those assholes with the down with fags signs? Yeah, I bet they get along fine and she probably knows David Duke and thinks he's a fine man.

It's amazing how some people think God loves them more because they're straight, white, Mormon, and born-again. Nope. God loves everyone, you holier than thou homophobic dipshit! That bitch will go to Bible, study with a racist, but won't give a friendly hello to a fag! I quit shortly after that. I think Margaret would be proud, I actually think she would have done something really over the top to quit, she's so clever. I hope the born-again gets a hold of this, think she will make the connection and pray for me or do you think she'll be pissed and call the troops from the Bible study to fuck with me? Ooh, I'm so scared! Honestly, I don't think she wants anyone to know a faggot worked for her and didn't become a born-again after working with her. She will fell like a failure because she couldn't save me. The one good thing about working there was this kid, Dusty. She was such a hard worker, and so sweet. She was saving up to buy a car. The kid was sixteen, and I had an old beater that I wasn't using, so I gave it to her. She was thrilled. Her uncle tuned it up for her and she promised me she would never drink or get high and drive. Good kid. I hope life does her right.

I went to the Mormon Church in Durango once. A guy I knew became a Mormon, to get them to back him up, and to keep him out of prison. A woman came up to me and said, "You look lovely but next time you come, would you wear a skirt?" I asked her, "God loves me if I wear a skirt? Thanks for the input." I had on lovely Laura Ashley silk pants. I just didn't wear a skirt. I think she and the ice cream shop owner would make a really good, "God guilt wrestling team" They can judge their non-Christians or non-Mormons harshly until they give in and become a born-again or a Mormon. If it gets really rough, they can call cousin, Walt. He'll have my back. The autistic cousin, Sarah, she can give them advice on how to talk to God. Sarah knows that book cover to cover. She can just refer them to her sister Laura who's got God on her headphones at times. That would be a fun reality show! I think even Joel Olsten would get a kick out of it. I like his sermons; He's not a sleazebag like Swaggart or Baker. He's inspirational, not full of yelling and screaming to get the point across. "God loves everyone!" I hope he doesn't have any big skeletons in his closet. I'd be disappointed if he did.

I'd like to meet Joel, sit down, have some tea, and chew the fat with him someday. I know he's a born-again but he doesn't shove it down your throat. He is accepting of everyone, not like the woman from the ice cream shop. I think Joel is the kind of pastor that you could really feel comfortable talking to in any scenario. I knew a woman Diane, who escaped Jehovah's witness. She was becoming an acupuncturist and I was her last final in her class at the Chinese natural medicine place on York in Denver. She told me her family was very abusive to her and told her, "If you aren't with us, get out." They kicked her out of her house when she was only fourteen because she didn't believe in it, so they banished her. Diane is a beautiful, intelligent, hardworking, funny, sweet, kind, and didn't have a mean bone in her body. She just wanted something else. Those assholes didn't deserve Diane as a daughter! It doesn't matter what your personal religion is. There is something called, "unconditional love." Ever heard of it? That's what kids need. I wish Joel Olsteen was around for her to talk to when she was going through all that. I really think he would have cheered her up! Joel lifts people up with positivity. He doesn't bash them to bits when they don't follow what others would call a "Good Christian lifestyle."

People aren't perfect. We make mistakes all the time. I wish we had more pastors like Joel. It's because of men like him that inspire people to be lifted up towards God, not put down for their mistakes. Some priests and ministers make it a point to "guilt" you in their sermons. What good is that? If those dicks want butts in the pews, they better get more positive! That's what the confession is for. If you're not Catholic, make an appointment. Go meet the dude in charge, sit down with him, and talk it out. That's why we need more positive pastors like Joel. I think it's not your choice of religion that makes you a good person. Think of it as your family name. That's not what makes you a good person. Your actions make you a good person. Having faith, that's what's important. Not where you go to get your faith. What did Dolly Parton's character say in Steel Magnolias? She said, "God don't care where you go to church just as long as you show up!" You said it, Dolly!

CHAPTER TWENTY: EX TRANS NIGHTMARE

My ex-girlfriend Brianna in Denver is a piece of work. I would like to tell you about all the good times we had, but there weren't many of them. Brianna was the worst relationship with a woman I ever had, except she wasn't a woman. I never treated her as anything but a woman. Then when I really got to know her, I found out Brianna's a cunt! Everything is a learning experience, I got to laugh; I figured what the hell? Someday I'll write about this. So here we are, but Brianna hates the truth, so she's not going to like this but after what she put me through, fuck Brianna!

I was at a very low point in my life when I met her. I was drinking a lot, that's my bad excuse for being in a relationship with Brianna. She's a wannabe transgender; more like a split personality, I don't know any other trans people like her. She thinks being a woman means dressing and acting like a complete whore. When I was twenty, I dated a woman in L.A. who used me as her "pretty young girlfriend" and it got old. When I broke it off with her, she said to me, "Your party life is over." I just told her, "I don't need your help to go out. I'm young. I'll figure it out." She didn't like that, but it was the truth. She was about 45 years old, and all of her girlfriends had younger girlfriends. That's where I came in, to fill in the blank. She was never serious about me. I was just "a young pet."

Brianna used me as her "front girlfriend." When I met her, she hadn't come out. She said, "I can't come out or I'll lose my job." Bullshit! She worked from home over the phone and on the internet. Nobody saw her. It was just an excuse. When I first started to go out with her, she kept all of her "Brianna" clothes and make-up at her friend's house, not at her mom's where she would stay during the week. But on the weekends, she went to her friends to change into Brianna until she got a place of her own.

I stayed with her for a few months but she was hiding being a cross-dresser. Brianna said to me, "I'm saving my money for my surgery." but I think Brian/Brianna was staying at his mom's because he was in a financial mess because of his ex-wife. Brian was divorced and I think it went poorly for him. I told Brianna, that I was trying to feel accepted as a bisexual woman. I told her about some of my past with the women I went out with, but she really didn't listen to any of it. I thought she would understand about that but nope. Everything was all about her. Always! There was no way around it.

Brianna had a lot of secrets. The first two months were great. Maybe because I wasn't aware of her true colors by then, I remember there were good times, but it went downhill fast. She dressed like a 1980s prostitute; long nails, frizzy blond hair, open-toed high heels, rings on every finger, and tons of makeup. She kind of looked like a mix between Pamela Anderson [but no tits], Britney Spears, and Peg Bundy, all rolled up into one cheap blond nightmare. Just picture "Mr. Mann" from Scary Movie; she looked just like him. That was Brianna but cheaper. She wore skirts that showed her crotch when she sat down and would play darts in them at Charlie's – a gay bar on Colfax.

Every time she bent down to pick up a dart, people would look, and she loved it. Brianna would drink butter baby shots and text while she was driving drunk and could care less if she got in an accident. I screamed at her to slow down more than once, but she would always say, "I have it." She would drive like a maniac and park wherever she wanted, she just didn't care. Brianna put a Barbie doll on the dash of her car just to get attention. She was so stuck up in an "odd weird" way. That was Brianna, but Brian was very polite, quiet, a Mama's boy, and responsible. Once, I had a seizure at Brianna's place. She called an ambulance and didn't do anything to help but wine to the first responders, "You deal with her. I don't know what her problem is." She knew I was on seizure medication and she didn't give a shit. It was interrupting her painting her toenails. She was literally upset her "painting her nails" got interrupted.

Brianna had a tattoo on her leg of a gecko or a lizard. I asked her about it, and she said, "Those animals only attach themselves to really beautiful things and my legs are so beautiful, they had to attach to me of course. Hehe." Jesus, what an ego! Brianna was always showing off her legs. She thought they were one of her best assets, and she was always tanning. I have seen her throw a fit if the tanning place was closed. She would grab her tube sock and boogie to the tanning beds, so her legs would golden up and look good. Brianna and I were at her Mom's house, and she wasn't the woman I was dating. She was Brian. I saw her mom spotting her thong when he was bent down in jeans.

I told him, "Your mom almost saw your thong, she is going to ask questions." Brian said, "I don't care if she finds out." Bullshit!!! I invited a friend of ours to come to her place and pick me up for lunch. She was trans as well. My friend knocked on the door and Brianna was not in face. He looked through the peephole, and found out that I had invited a friend over. She threw a fit. "Why did you invite her here?" I said, "So what? She hasn't seen you as Brian. She's our friend," With his face upside down, Brian opened the door and explained, "Well, this is what I look like." To say the least, Brian was not a very attractive man.

When I got back after having lunch with my friend, Brianna was furious. She told me "never" to invite anyone over without her permission again. It was one of the many "What the fuck?" moments that I had endured with her. Brianna wasn't just a liar to me, she was to everyone. At her work, with her family she lied to all of her friends. That's why she doesn't have many left. I dated women in L.A., not all of them were perfect. They were all born female, but none of them played the games Brianna did. She was the first trans relationship I have been in, and it will be the last. God, her attitude was so bad. I couldn't keep up with all of her lies. I don't think her friends knew how bad she really was behind their backs. Brianna put down and criticized everyone! I think people who are really insecure do stuff like that, put others down to make themselves feel better. In my opinion, it's pretty weak. Brianna did it all the time to everyone but Brian would never behave that way.

When we first started to go out, I went wherever she wanted to go. One of the places we went to was B.J.s, off Broadway. It was a real dive but kind of fun. Absolutely nothing like the clubs in L.A., not by far! When we first got there, she parked her car in a no parking zone right next to the building. Brianna said, "This is my spot." I asked her, "Do you know the owner? Is that why you get to park there?" She told me, "Well, everyone knows me and that's where I park so they're not allowed to park there." Brianna had her own "Make-believe rules." It was necessary that everyone know about them, or they'd be in trouble! Wow, she really thought she owned the place or acted like it.

She always had Brianna's special table. She would show me off to her friends. It happened before, showing me off, so I went with it for a while. Brianna had one friend who was trans-sexual. I won't tell you her name because I like her and don't know if she's out. She was really nice to me, and I asked her what she looked like as a male because I couldn't picture it. I was being honest. Brianna got pissed at me for even asking. "That's offending. She is who she is, and that's all you need to know." But her friend showed me a picture of him and told me, "I'll show you but don't tell Brianna I showed it to you. I trust you." I said, "Thank you."

I wasn't rude, but Brianna would have a shit if she knew one of her best friends trusted me to see her as him but not Brianna. Oops. Now she knows. I also saw Brianna perform, and she was a bad drag queen with no talent. All she did was walk around and pose poorly. They would play the song, "Don't you wish your girlfriend was hot like me," and she would lip-sync to that. If anyone else dared to use that song to perform, she would say, "Oh my God, that's my song!" and get all upset about it. What a faggot! I would watch the performers and it was fun. I would tip them and clap, cheer them on, but Brianna would tear them to shreds. "Look at her! Why does she even try? She should give it up."

I went out to dinner with some of Brianna's friends when we first started going out. She wouldn't stop showing me off, and it reminded me of the woman I dated back in L.A. It started to get on my nerves. Putting me on exhibition, and feeding off from the attention, that's exactly what she was doing. "Look, everyone! This is my new girlfriend. Isn't she pretty? Tell me you love me. I love you too. Hehe." Going way too far, anything for a show, that's what she lived for.

She was one phony woman. I met her mom down the line. Her name is Jan too. Yeah, that's not weird at all. Anyway, she is a very sweet woman. We went to her Moms house during the day and she always went as Brian. I kept my mouth shut about Brianna because she wasn't out yet she was just waiting for the right moment but there was never a right moment. I was a cover for Brian to his family and for anyone else who Brianna couldn't deal with but, fuck it! I was drunk most of the time.

We went to an all L.G.B.T. event during the day. Brianna only went as Brianna if she was around all L.G.B.T. people. Brianna would say, "I hate that the "T" in L.G.B.T. comes last. We matter! Trans people shouldn't come last!" I told her, "You're not really trans, you haven't had the surgery and you don't live full-time as a woman." I was honest, but that comment really pissed her off. Brian took me to Christmas dinner in Pennsylvania with her family as Brian. Remember when I said that I was her front girlfriend? Yeah. Brian was at another table and I was with his cousin at another table. He was so anti-social he didn't want to talk to anyone. He played on his phone all night, and left the talking up to me.

One of Brian's cousins asked me, "Are you Brian's girlfriend?" I looked at them like, "Really?" So I said, "I guess that's what you want to call me. What do you think?" They awkwardly laughed. "Yeah, that's what we thought." They all knew something was going on. I had really revealing pictures of Brianna and her friend Kelly Joe, half-naked in drag, but I couldn't do that to them. It was Christmas.

Brian was married for two years or so until his ex-wife found sexy pictures of Brian dressed like Brianna. I think he paid her off to keep her quiet about it. He never really told me all of it, and even if he told me something about his ex-wife, I'd still think it was a lie because he lied about everything. I talked to his Grandma and she showed me their wedding photos. I almost didn't recognize him, won't describe what he looked like. His Grandma said to me, "We are so happy Brian is with a nice girl like you." Yeah, how do I tell her that I was just for show? Like when Brian took me shopping, he had me try on clothes he wanted to buy for Brianna, but he didn't want to go out dressed as Brianna during the day. The girls at the shop asked him, "Does your girlfriend know about your cross-dressing?" He said, "Yes. She knows all about it. We love each other." Brian would baby talk trying to look like we are in love. The girls could see this behavior was making me uncomfortable, but Brian didn't care.

Brianna and I went to the Coronation Ball in Denver. Everyone there had a title. "Gay king of Denver," "Gay queen of Denver," and on and on. The running joke was there were more titles in the hotel than in the parking lot. Everyone had a title for something. That was the year Mike and Caris were the King and Queen of the ball. I remember Brianna trying to pretend to cry when Caris won that year, like it really moved her but I didn't buy any of it. Nope. I commented on how beautiful the "Miss Gay Latino" was that year. She was truly beautiful. Brianna just had to jump in with her narcissistic blabber. "She isn't that pretty." What a stuck-up bitch! Anytime I would give a nice comment on someone else's outfit, hair, or make-up, she would snub her nose and cut them all down.

On one of the many unfortunate days that I got to spend with her, we got stuck in a hotel during the ball with friends because of some kind of shooting. The police came and shut down the hotel. We were told to stay in our rooms. Our friends got a room there but Brianna mouthed off to some people involved with the mess because she's drunk and a loud mouth who thinks she can do whatever she wants. I was there, and I saw that attitude. I told her, "Don't do that and make it worse. I will get us out of here." I knew it was going to be a problem if she didn't get out of there. Once again, rescuing someone before they get in trouble is the epic story of my life.

Our friends were nice to let us go to their room when the hotel shut down, but Brianna wasn't happy. I went down to the police in the lobby and I talked to one of the cops. I know how to talk to the police, I grew up with it, so we got to leave and I thanked them. We got in the car and Brianna didn't thank me for my help, she just bitched and complained all the way home. What a miserable woman to be with, don't you think?

Brianna bought me a dress for that year's ball. I tried it on, and I was looking really good. She obviously didn't like it, her jealousy was pretty evident. She always made me dress down, so she got all the attention. Like all gay little boys do! I used to go to clubs with her, but I stopped going because Brianna would openly flirt with men right in front of me. She would dance with a guy and flip her hair like "look how sexy I am." She told me, "I don't want you to come to the clubs with me. You get all jealous." She would say that in front of men she wanted to fuck. "See, that's my girlfriend, she gets jealous." She would put on a little show for them. I think Brianna was getting numbers of men or setting up dates alongside me. It wouldn't surprise me if she had a guy on the side.

Brianna's the gayest "man" I ever met. She used to watch "Zanadu" with Olivia Newton Jon over and over with her sister and dance around. Now that's some gay shit! I know Brianna will hate me saying that but fuck it, I'll say it again. "Brianna's the gayest "man" I ever met." She only pretended to be transgendered. There was nothing straight, bi-sexual, or real about Brianna. She's definitely a "Big Faggot," but I don't know what the fuck she was trying to be! Brianna was the most confusing, rude, loud-mouthed, slutty, obnoxious, conceded, and fake bitch I ever went out with. I could go on and on, trust me, but everything for Brianna was a game or a lie. That was her entire personality, lying and being a slut. I have had my fair share of liars but Brianna takes the cake when it comes to lying, Brianna was almost as bad as Karen!

When I broke up with her, I was invited to go to the Coronation Ball the next year with her ex-friends but Brianna burned so many bridges, she didn't go. I wore a dress that really turned some heads. There was this nice woman who was a dyke. She reminded me of this sweet woman I went out with in L.A., who was butch, and she was great. She didn't hang out with Brianna's friends but I always said hello to them because I'm polite, while Brianna snubbed her nose at them. I didn't realize how many people disliked Brianna until I broke up with her. It looked like she had lost a lot of weight, so I went over to her and said, "Wow, you look great. I know we don't know each other well, but how much weight did you lose? You look so good. I'm Jan, by the way. What's your name?"

She was a little surprised that I was talking to her. She said, "I'm Nancy." I laughed because she's a dyke and joked. "You look like a frank or Bob, but Nancy? I love it." She told me she had lost about twenty pounds, which was great! I told her that I had lost some weight too. "I dumped Brianna." She laughed. "We never understood you two. She's so, you know." Yeah, I know. I was going through a self-loathing period. I said, "I know you look so good. We should take some pictures!" She didn't know I used to model, but the photographer knew it. I asked him to take our pictures. I told her, "Look like you are having your way with me." The first few pictures turned out awful; she was smiling and looked like she got first prize in bingo. I told her, "Look like you have a ten-inch cock and you're giving it to me really hard, no smiling!" We took the picture and her girlfriend was right there. I thought she was going to be mad at us. The picture turned out great, and then her girlfriend wanted one with me too. We had a blast! Best modeling gig ever didn't get paid, but it was fun!

After we took our pictures, some other people wanted to take pictures with me too. I thought, "What the hell? Let's do it." I did with a few people. I'm so glad I got to go without Brianna, everyone was great. Thank you, Nancy! Why can't all lesbians be nice and fun like her? I hope Nancy, Michael, Caris, and the cycle sluts read this. They were all fun and great to me and I'll bet they remember my ex-girlfriend Brianna! Tweet me if you can. I would love to hear from you!

I saw Brianna do something that really bothered me. I came home from work early. Brian was masturbating to pictures of Brianna on her computer. The outfits, the make-up, nails, heels, and everything probably like the ones her ex wife found. But she wasn't in face. He was Brian jerking off to Brianna. I don't know what to make of that. I am still thrown off by that. I asked her if it was porn. I knew what I saw, but I didn't know how to react to something like that. It was unnerving. Brianna said, "No, it isn't porn. You didn't see anything." She looked panicked, like she was going to unravel.

I did come home and Brianna was taking pictures of herself in face dressed up in her favorite outfits. I asked her, "Why are you doing this?" She said with no shame at all, "I look really good in this outfit. I want to remember how sexy I look." I told her, "Brianna, you need to see a therapist if you don't live full time as a woman and are completely out. No doctor will touch you for surgery, and they won't even discuss hormone therapy." She refused to get any help at all. Then I found out she was using illegal hormones over the internet and was surfing for a lot of problematic stuff on the grid.

She also did facial hair removal and that was fine but the enema bag in the shower was never explained to me. Needless to say, when I broke up with her, I got an AIDs test because Brianna was a prostitute. What a bad example she's setting for trans women, but I don't think she cares. She would come home late, drunk and disheveled, but all smiles. I think our friends knew what was going on behind my back, so I got a call from her friends. They told me she was cheating on me. It didn't come as a shock because I knew something was fishy. We stopped being intimate at all. I was determined to stick it out because we had two friends who were going to Trinidad to get their surgical re-assignment surgery; I wanted to be there for that. The longer I was with Brianna, the more difficult it was to keep my smart ass quiet. I slipped a few times at the end of our relationship, it was funny to me. Gotta laugh!

We were going to Trinidad. When I saw her getting dressed, I told her, "Tone it down. This is their first day as a woman, don't let the attention be all about you." I was serious. She didn't tone it down. We were at the hotel, and she wore tight jeans. I saw her putting them on, and she was having a difficult time "adjusting." I couldn't help it, and said, "Brianna, move them to the right. You can still see your ball sack!" She didn't like that. Bitch could never take a joke. I laughed. She told me, "I know you're a comedian, but I take myself very seriously. You can make fun of everyone but me." She said that more than once. "I take myself seriously," but I couldn't keep it together and not smile. Could anyone keep a straight face if that piece of shit Madonna said, "I take myself seriously?" Get the fuck out of here, no way.

When I started to think like a comedian, that's when I started to get mouthy. I did stand up once at a gay club we went to. I couldn't help it. I tore Brianna apart, just like the way she did to all the performers we used to watch. I wanted to see how she'd like it. Nope, she didn't. The Cycle Sluts thought I was funny. I was on my way out of this fucked up relationship, so I figured fuck it. What's she going to do to me? Not fuck me? She's already not doing that. So who cares?

I don't usually talk about my sex life but only when it's really bad, really good, or really fucked up. So I can say this, why not? What is she going to do to me? Brianna was a really bad lay. It was always all about her. She never got me off, not once! Have you ever watched really bad porn, like the kind you watch and you want your money back? The horrible visuals that make you think what a waste of time? She was worse than that. Brianna was like a bad rendition of Waterworld in a cheap wig. I don't think Brianna knew the first thing about pussy. She had no clue and she wanted to have one, you have to be kidding me? She wouldn't know what to do with it. Trust me, I know from experience. She wasn't getting me off in the way she dressed, the way she did her makeup, and the way she acted. She didn't know what to do with her hands, mouth or cock. Brianna was a fucking disaster. What do you think she is going to do with a pussy? I know. Disappoint another lover!

I fucked her with a strap-on, and it still made me want to laugh more than anything. You should have seen her face, her fake smiling, moaning, her baby talking, and her high-pitched giggling. I could hear her giggling in the bathroom once the door was locked and her dildo was gone. She came out all smiles. I asked her, "What was going on in there?" She said, with a sheepish smile on her face, "Nothing, just freshening up." That didn't bother me at all, neither did the way she tried to fuck me. Yuck! Dead puppies, dead puppies, dead puppies; that's better.

If Brianna ever went to California to be a pornstar, oh God! The director would say, "God, who let her in? Get her out of those cheap clothes. Rip off that fucked up wig and get the paint remover. Put her in the back." No matter how they dressed her up, I think she would still get fired for her bad acting and attitude. She would complain about everything! Why don't I have a better parking spot? I want a butter baby shot now! I want my name in the title! She is the perfect example of "Get me more of everything! Me, me, me!" They would throw her off the set. "Go back to Denver, have fun on Colfax. Go suck Mayor Hancock's dick!" Brianna may already have. She would pose on the bed, lay across the bed on her stomach with her butt in the air like she was ready for a good humping but wouldn't give it up for me. She would close her eyes and I can only imagine what she would be dreaming about. She did take all those sexy pictures. I wonder if she has those pictures under the bed, I never looked. She had a wild assortment of pictures of herself, and other stuff. I was not supposed to know about it on her computer. I won't discuss it. Some things are better left unsaid.

Thank God I don't drink anymore. You make really bad choices when you drink. Trust me, if you saw how bad she was sexually, you would understand why you would have to be drunk to fuck Brianna! When I would start to laugh during sex, I'd tell her, "I'm going to cum. Oh right there. You're so sexy. You make me so hot!" The fakest crap you ever heard and saw. Thank God, I didn't fuck her face to face more than once, Yuck! The sad thing was she couldn't tell the difference between laughing and cumming. She bought that fake crap, stupid bitch. I have to thank the academy for that terrible performance. I'm glad she found someone else to fuck. I don't think I could keep that "act" up much longer, and to make matters worse, she had a waterbed. How 70's bad porn can you get? I told you, Waterworld. Yuck!

Brianna let me do her make-up once. I tried to make her look like a woman who wasn't "looking for a date" You get it? But, she said, "You don't do it the way I like it." I thought, "No shit, princess hooker it up!" Sometimes when I'm thinking about something, it just pops out and I'm not sure if I said it out loud until I get a look. Guess how many times I got the look from Brianna and how many times do you think I ignored it? Every fucking time but I guess I said that out loud. Woops. She gave me the look and I ignored it again, so Brianna put her make-up on with a putty knife like she always did. She would look in the mirror, and you could tell she was thinking, "I'm going to get laid tonight!" She was so in love with herself, no wonder she was spanking it to herself. She gets herself off well; I doubt she could get anyone else off. Maybe she could have gotten me off if I paid her like the rest of her "clients".

I asked her, "Brianna, are you going to do the full transition or just the top?" It was an honest question. She kept talking about getting her boob job. She would call it her boobies when she would talk about getting her breasts done. She would "baby talk" like she was a teenage girl asking for something from her daddy. "Daddy, can I get my boobies done?" Brianna said, "Well, I will get it done soon. My friends are way ahead of me. I need to catch up. It's just a piece of skin, I don't need it. I want to be a real woman. You wouldn't understand, it's an internal thing for me." So when I asked her about her plan, I got to know that she thought her surgery was a race to see who gets their work done first. Wow, and now I'm not woman enough to understand how a woman feels? Has she been talking to T.E.R.F.s or what? Either I'm not gay or not woman enough to get it. Great! Brianna was living in a dream world. No way was she ready for surgery. I think that's why she was checking into other options for her surgery in Thailand because nobody in the States would touch her. I got to a point where I was having dreams about ripping off her wig and kicking her in the balls. When you start to have dreams like that, you know it is time to move on!

So we were in Trinidad at the hotel, getting ready to go to the hospital, and Brianna put on her high-heeled sandals, bright pink nail polish, cheap jewelry, her toe-rings on her shitty blond wig, which she said was real hair; it was as fake as her tan. She was wearing a low-cut blouse to show off the fake cleavage she taped together. "Look I'm in a little camisole, don't I look cute?" Then popped her gum in her mouth and she would chew her gum loudly with her mouth open pretending to look like Britney Spears. Off-topic, but I feel sorry for Britney. I hope she gets through her father pushing her around. He's a dick, she was so lucky to have her fans help her through her dad's bullshit. But I think even she would be offended by Brianna's attempt to impersonate her.

We got to the parking lot and Brianna tripped. She picked herself up, and kept walking like nobody saw it. I used to be a good girlfriend. If I had seen her do that a few months ago, I would have gone, "Oh honey didn't see that coming. Did you hurt yourself? Here, let me help you out." Unfortunately, I have had it playing the nice front girlfriend. I looked at her and said, "Why did you wear those shoes? We aren't going to a nightclub!" She had to blow me off, but there were people around. She didn't go out in public during the day much, so she couldn't throw a Brianna fit. That's exactly what she would have done but nothing she could do about it back then. I like a little razzing like my Pops did.

We walked inside the hospital. I went into one of the girls' rooms. They had their surgery on the same day. One of the girl let me see it. She looked great! I couldn't tell she had a dick. I swear to God, it was beautiful. It was a little swollen but looked great. Doctor Marcy Bowers's an amazing doctor, and a complete genius. She came in after a while. I said to Dr. Bowers, "Doctor Bowers, you are so good. She's so happy, thank you." She said, with a charming smile on her face, "Thank you." Then, Brianna walked in. Oh no, Brianna couldn't keep her mouth shut. She was doing the "baby talk" with Dr. Bowers, trying to be cute.

"Oh Marcy, you're so good! I'm Brianna. Everyone knows me. I want my boobies to look just like that. You can do that for me, can't you? We can talk about the rest of it later; you can make me look like that too, right?" Brianna is smiling at her and waiting for a response. Doctor Bowers won't even talk to her. She makes her sick. I apologized for Brianna's bad manners to Dr. Bowers, and I told everyone when we got back to Denver, I was going to leave her. Everyone was supportive of me. I was surprised all of Brianna's friends backed me up. They were her friends first, but she lost a lot of friends when I broke up with her. Brianna got kicked out of a place we went to because her attitude was so bad. She was also really cheap, not just in the way she dressed but the way she treated the waiters. I would tip the waitress behind her back so if the people from B.J.s heard about this, I know it's not there anymore, but sorry for Brianna.

Brianna would do anything for sexual attention. Unfortunately, she wasn't getting any from me. She would play this very dangerous game, where she would get a straight guy drunk enough to think she was a woman and suck their cock in the parking lot of the clubs she went to. When she was done, she would say, "That was fun, but I'm a boy. Couldn't tell, could you?" She got into a few scuffles playing that game. I hope her Mom didn't have to identify her body in face or bail her out of jail for prostitution because that's the road she's going towards.

If Brianna got beaten to death by some straight guy she blew and he got pissed off, it will not be a hate crime. If that happens, it will be Brianna's own undoing. Trans women are trying so hard not to have a bad reputation by dressing and acting like that. Brianna is a disgrace to the entire L.G.B.T. community. I think all her friends knew about Brianna's little sex games in the parking lots. When I broke it off with Brianna, I went back to her place, and she wasn't expecting me. I covered the peephole up to see what she would do. She answered the door, half-dressed in half face. She opened the door as if she was expecting someone else. Her smile was wiped off when she saw me. "Oh, what do you want?" I knew it. There was a picture of a lesbian woman she was going out with. That picture frame used to have our picture in it and she was wearing my blouse in the photo. She stole some of my clothes too. I wonder if she's the new front girlfriend now. I asked her, "Were you going out when we were still together?" She acted like such a liar, as always.

"No. We started going out way after we broke up." When I asked around later, it was evident that she had been cheating on me for months. Not just with another woman, but with men too. Brianna was a whore; she dressed like one, acted like one, and looked like one too. What's the old saying, "If it walks like a duck and talks like a duck and looks like a duck, there you go."

The worst thing Brianna did was at Gay Pride in Denver. I wasn't out, and Brianna knew it. We were right in front of my church, the Cathedral on Colfax. Some of my friends from church saw me and said, "Jan, you coming to mass?" Brianna turned to me and remarked. "You tell them, this is our day" She was smoking a cigarette, wearing a skin-tight dress that almost showed her crouch, and we were up on the steps of my church. People were looking up at her under her dress when they walked by on the sidewalk. It was right before the gay pride parade started.

I was so embarrassed. They were people I knew and go to mass with, so I said, "I'll be right there." I decided to go to mass. As soon as I walked up the stairs to church, Brianna turned around and said, "You don't have to go in there. This is our day." I looked at the people I went to church with and said, "I don't really know her. I think she's drunk." It was the only thing I could come up with, and I was really hurt. When I came out of mass, this really sweet butch girl rescued me, and took me to get a drink. I went on a rant with her. "Brianna is so mean. She did that just to hurt me." When Brian and I went out, I never told anyone about him being Trans but it was okay for her to behave like that in front of the people I go to church with.

She knew I wasn't out, but she did it anyway. What a cunt! Another time, we went to a park for a B.B.Q., and she was sitting on the grass with a mini skirt eating a hot dog, trying to look sexy and she looked like a fool. She wanted everyone to see her panties. "Look at me, again." She became so predictable. I knew when she was going to get obnoxious or throw a fit or do something that I would have to say, "I'm sorry, she did that," on her behalf. Brianna never took responsibility for being mean, rude, or insensitive to anyone. She got off on getting people riled up and mad. It got her off in some weird way. She was so fucked up on so many levels. I would say, "I'm sorry" for her all the time. I think that's why she kept me around that and to cover for her. She was mannerless, even around her friends. She could care less if anyone thought she was a cunt, as long as she could get plenty of cock and attention. Brain would have ever done that. The bottom line is, Brianna wanted Brian dead and Brian/Brianna didn't get along. I have never met a trans person who needed therapy more than Brian/Brianna did.

After I broke up with Brianna, she got a lower back tattoo; a heart with some flowers right above her ass, so everyone knew where to aim. I think we should make up buttons to warn everyone about her; little ones about the size of a quarter, so when you put it on, people have to come up close to read it and go, "Thanks for the warning." The buttons would say, "Warning! Brianna's a lying, cheating whore." I think she would have been much happier if she let me go down on her, but her balls got in the way.

Brianna was the worst example of a trans woman I've ever met. None of my other trans friends played those games; they just wanted to be accepted and feel comfortable with who they were. Brianna makes the transgender community look really bad. That bitch needs a lot of therapy and some truth serum. She doesn't know anything about the truth, not even close. If her cousins hear about this, please get Brian or Brianna help before they get themselves killed. I don't ever want to see Brianna again, but if you are into phony, tactless, cheap, lying whores with bad hair who suck in bed, she's all yours, but wrap it the fuck up. You don't know where she's been, and neither do I.

CHAPTER TWENTY-ONE: MR. NICE GUY, DADDY ISSUES

I was getting burnt out on working in the club, so I took a job as a waitress at a place called "Little Ollie's" in Cherry Creek. Wonderful food! Charlie, the owner, was a sweetie. I met Mr. Nice Guy there. He was about twenty-five, tall, white, and good-looking. He was so nice to me, and he kind of took me under his wing. Honestly, at first, I thought he was gay. He had a belly button ring and liked techno music. I still think he might be hiding something. He liked to go to TRAX 2000, a place my ex-girlfriend frequently visited. I wonder if they ever hooked up. Yuck! He took me to get my hair done by his aunt; we became friends. She was a real sweetheart!

I went to kickboxing class three days a week. I stink; I never had that "Killer instinct." I wanted to learn how to fight because I got tired of defending someone and winding up on the ground. If I see someone in trouble and they need help, if I think I can help, I step in. Sometimes, or let's just say, most of the times, this didn't work out so well for me. I told him, "I work at a nightclub, the tips are great. I'm finally getting ahead financially but the hours are killing me. I need sunlight, I need a change." Shouldn't have said that because all he heard was, "I have money." He was a con artist and I fell for it. I feel stupid to this day. I was just starting to get out of debt and I met this guy. We would go shopping, and I would pay. I didn't notice it because I was having fun. He would say stuff like, "You are so sweet. You're my best friend" Then I got my bank statement. Holy shit! How did that happen? He was really smooth. White men, who are con artists like my dad, they know how to rip people off. But they almost always get caught!

The kid would laugh way too much at his own jokes when nobody else would. He thought he was so charming. He also convinced me to break up with a guy I was dating, prick! He was really nice at first and then he changed. I couldn't tell if he was kidding or serious? He'd say something off, and if it didn't get the response he wanted, he'd say, "You know I'm just kidding, right?" I think looking back on it, he was saying that to cover his ass because he didn't know what he was talking about most of the time.

I don't think this guy knew how ill-informed he was. Okay, I'll just say it, the kid was one stupid motherfucker. I think the kid would take a deaf girl to the opera and a blind girl to see a movie. I'm sure he thinks the earth was once flat too. He was fairly smooth, tall, and good looking, so he had a big ego. Unfortunately, he was a fucking idiot. You ever been around someone who seems almost overconfident or someone who just talks to seem interesting or smart but has no idea what he's talking about? Yep, that was him.

We went to a restaurant together. It was crowded, a drunken guy accidentally spilled a drink down my back, but he clearly didn't mean to. I went to the bathroom to get cleaned up. This kid I was friends with was not a small guy; he was 6'4, about 220. So he had the guy who spilled the drink on me pressed up against the wall, demanding that he apologize to me. The poor guy was shaking. He hesitantly apologized. "I'm so sorry." I told him, "He won't hurt you, he was just kidding." Later, I made it clear to the kid that he went too far. His response was: "Yeah, I got your back." And he looked around like he was my hero after picking on someone half his size. I saw some girls looking at him like "he's a dick" but he didn't care. The kid got off on pushing people around and intimidating people because he was a big guy. I think he did that because he didn't have anything else to impress anyone with.

He liked pushing his weight around, that was a bully move and I don't like bullies! I think the reason he was like that was because he was the fat kid with glasses growing up and his dad didn't give a shit about him. He got teased a lot so now, he's out for revenge. He would put people down and push them around so he can feel better about himself. I was teased too, but that's why I don't do that because I know how much it hurts. He didn't learn a thing. If the kid was in a bad mood, he made sure everyone else was as well. He was moodier than a pregnant woman, but on the flip side, he could be a sweetheart full of compliments. He was so unpredictable!

The kid told me, "If I ever had to go to prison, I'd hook up with the Nazis and the white race guys. They'd have my back." He was right. They would. They would have his back side, front, and any other orifices they can get to watch American History X stupid. The more he talked, the more he sounded like an insecure, cocky, racist jackass, but the thing that really got me was we were on the way to kickboxing class, and he said to me. "You know we are smarter than they are." I asked, "Who?" He explained with a proud look on his face. "We are smarter than blacks. Our craniums hold more knowledge. It's a scientific fact. My dad told me, so it's true. Your dad should have told you about it."

I remember thinking, "Holy shit!" Hitler was a fan of this theory as well. He sounded more and more like my dad when he would say stuff like that. I really was waiting for him to laugh and go, "You know I'm just kidding," like he did all the time, but he was serious. I told him my father was very racist. I never mentioned the Klan stuff to anyone, ever.

That's what white people who are racist do. Test the waters to see how racist they can be around you. That's what he was doing. I told him he was nuts. I walked into the school, and three of the guys we workout with were black. The kid came in when I was lacing up my shoes, and I said, "Why don't you tell them what you just told me in the car?" He didn't say a thing. That racist fuck will spout off that shit to me all day long, but he won't say it to a black man's face? What a pussy!

Here's a little inside news: white, racist men are only really racist when they are on their turf surrounded by their own species in a pack, way out of earshot of a black person. White men are all about, "I'm not like that" to their black friends in public but behind closed doors, totally different story. I would love to see a white racist fuck like that kid talk that way all by himself in front of one black man alone. Give them, let's say, ten minutes. See what happens. All my money is on whoever is still standing after that little chit-chat. I am pretty sure the black guy would fuck him up. Most white men don't give a fuck about your black heritage. They just want to know what you do for a living, where you went to school, what's your family name, and if you are a Republican.

Three guys we worked out with were all black Denver cops. They're going to kill me when they hear about this. Well, maybe not kill but hopefully, they are going to laugh a little. They all had a good sense of humor. You know why black men don't have to hide! They were all honest guys, they told the truth and were pretty funny! They were all good guys, not a racist bone in their bodies! I wish all cops were like them! They had no idea what this kid was really like.

Kenny was on the force. He had one little Achilles heel. He was ticklish, but only if you're a woman. If you try to tickle him and you're a dude, he'd put you in the ground. Kenny is 6'5 and beautiful. He has a body like Mr. Olympian; He used to wear glasses but got the laser eye surgery, so now you can see more of his beautiful face! I never told him this, but if he hears this, I don't care. Kenny is one smoking hot man! I think of him like a brother, so I could never tell him that. It would be too weird.

Bernard Vice cop, he came into class one day and I just laughed. I was thinking, is it Halloween already? I had to ask him because one of the guys we worked out with came into class with his head shaved and no mustache. I asked, "New look?" He smiled and said, "No. It was Halloween, so my son and I got matching grey suits and went as Dr. Evil and Mini-Me. When they opened the door, we did the evil laugh and screamed, Trick or Treat!" I thought that was hilarious, but Bernard was doing a different look for prostitution and drug busts, no candy involved.

He had little dreadlocks along with a goatee. He said, "I'm going to do a Jamaican accent." Bernard is one of the most clean-cut, well-rounded, articulate, honest, and the kindest person you will ever meet. His boss wanted Bernard to look like a degenerate. You have got to be kidding. I asked him to try it on me. The minute he started to talk, I just started to laugh. He was terrible, not believable at all. God bless him for trying. His boss had to be a white guy. What other bright ideas do you think this "white cop" could come up with for the police? I have a good idea. Let's let Mormons do undercover work in five pints. They will fit right in and hey, let's let midget ride scooters on the freeway to give out speeding tickets. Put the Bronco cheerleaders out on Colfax with Brianna for prostitution busts. None of those girls are very pretty, I hope that fucker is retired.

Some people just can't do under-cover work for certain jobs, not that Bernard isn't a good under-cover cop, but how could that idiot think Bernard could play a deadbeat? Who was his boss twenty years ago? Is he still making bad choices somewhere else we need to worry about? Look into that, please. Don't let him have a badge or any authority anymore. He doesn't know how to use it properly. Bernard asked me about the club once. Since he's a vice cop I told him, "Do your own homework, pig. I'm not a snitch." We both laughed. I should have told him about all of Mayor Hancock's dirty secrets. I think he would get a kick out of that information, but I think he already knows about it.

Daymond was on the SWAT team. He was tall and half black. Once, he showed me a picture of his mom, and I swear she could be my mother's sister. She looked just like mom. He had a girlfriend, who I didn't like. She treated him like shit, even when he paid for her boob job and helped with her son but I guess it wasn't enough. I bet her middle name is Karen. I hope her tits fall off! He was too good for her. Anyway, they were all great guys and all deserve the best.

I went to an advanced class, making another addition to my list of absurd decisions. I thought about if I could take an advanced ballet class. But I am an idiot. I can't fight to save my life. I tried, at least. But it's their fault. I really liked them. Anytime I made contact, I'd say, "Oh, are you okay?" I could tell by the looks on their faces after six months of classes, three days a week, they all wanted to say, "Why doesn't she quit? She sucks! But don't tell her. It will hurt her feelings. She will give up eventually."

I did quit eventually. I miss those guys; they were all very good guys to me. They weren't like some cops who are always a cop. They can't just be normal; they're not always on guard. I grew up with that kind of stuff; the white cop attitude. Always on their guard, mainly around blacks and no sense of humor it gets old. I could joke around with them because they had fun personalities. They also let me make fun of them a little too. Usually, I only make fun of cops behind their back. I have done it to their face too, but the only reason I got away with it is because I'm white, white privilege again! They were very nice to me, and didn't know about what was going on with the kid. I don't think they will be mad at me for telling the truth. If they know two things about me, they are; I can't fight, and I'm honest. I can't imagine what the kid will say to them the next time they see him.

The kid had a friend Chad, a tall skinny kid who drank way too much but a sweetie. We went to a middle of the road restaurant. The kid decided to leave without paying the check. They hissed, "Let's go now!" as soon as we were done with the food. I got up and said, "What's going on?" and we ran. I asked them, "You decided to do that? Why?" He reassured me, "You won't get in trouble I do it all the time; don't worry your with me." He told me he used to walk into places like Radio Shack, Home Depot, and Bed Bath and beyond and steal stuff all the time. He told me, "I look so innocent nobody would ever suspect I would steal anything I'd just load up a cart and walk out I never get caught."

I asked him, "How long have you been doing this?" What he said showed how messed up he was in his head. "For years that's how I bought my motorcycle. I'd just return the stuff I stole and get the money for it." The kid lied so much. I don't know how much of it's true, but he tried to scare me, I think. The kid told me, "I was in downtown Denver at night and some black guy came at me, and I beat him to death with a Maglite flashlight." I was waiting for him to say, "I'm kidding," but he didn't. I'm sorry, but that's some twisted shit to say. Am I supposed to be impressed by that? What did he expect my reaction would be? I just said, "That's not funny," and changed the subject. It's like he was trying to impress me by telling me how much he could get away with because he said he's got the family name to fall back on, if he needs it. He reminded me of myself when I was twelve years old. "Daddy will fix it."

Part of me thought, he wasn't just stupid, racist, or cocky. This kid might be a psychopath! I just don't see it. Not like "Buffalo Bill" but, "Yes, please! Invest all your money with me. I'll be in the Bahamas if you need me, psychopath." I don't see him as an investment banker anytime soon. I'll bet that dipshit only got through his last math class in school because he bullied some weakling. "You're going to take this test or I'll kick your ass!" I think that's how he got through college. He was threatening weak kids who were afraid of him. The kid got off on pushing people around, probably picked up that trait from his dad.

Do you know what his dad does? He's a white Denver cop. Like father like son!! What I'd like to know is, how did this guy get a badge? Shouldn't there be some kind of test to see how racist you are before you get that kind of authority? I think there should be one graded by black women because nothing is getting past them!! They have to take the test before they get a badge or a gun, and if they fail, let's treat them like the handicapped kids who visit the police department. Take them on a tour of the department. We can give them a fake badge, a squirt gun, and a whistle. We can give them "time out" for being bad; sit them in the corner and make them watch "Racism videos." After they watch it, they can become the guy in the "cage" that hand out guns and ammo, but they won't be able to be around anyone who's black, or Latino, because they still won't get it! It would take years to get that kind of racism out of your head. I don't think the police department has the funds for all that treatment. Just white male cops will take the test, not all of them, just 75-80%. The kid's dad is one of those cops who say, "I'm not a racist. I have black friends." Yeah, in the department, you should hear him behind their backs, just like my dad. I went to his dad's for Christmas dinner, and the kid has three-year-old step-sisters, very cute, with his "new wife." He only paid attention to the one who had blond hair and blue eyes like him. He said, "We have blond hair and blue eyes. We are more special than everyone!" He sounded like Hitler; his dad must be so proud.

The kid was planning a trip to Europe and he invited me to visit. That's when I realized it was all about money. He sewed a Canadian flag on his bag and said, "I'm going to tell everyone I'm from Canada because they hate Americans there." I asked him, "What do you know about Canada? Where is Quebec?" He didn't know, so he tried to ignore the question. I asked him again. "Sing the Canadian national anthem." He then tried to be smart with me. "Nobody is going to ask me that."

The truth was he had no idea about Canada. Once again, he was going to make up a lie that he could never back up the factless lies that would flow out of his mouth just to get attention were ridiculous! When I was on a train with him in Spain, he got into an argument with a guy about the discrimination against Americans. "I'm an American, I know my rights." That's what he said. Everyone was looking at him like, "That stupid American should go back to his country." He was looking around like he was wronged, I was so embarrassed. The kid argued with a man in Germany about the room, as well. He got into arguments in every country we went to with his "I'm an American" bullshit. Once, we missed a train because he didn't know when it was leaving and lost his pocket knife. Like always, he blamed it on me. Of course, nothing is ever his fault! Then he asked, "Are you having fun? Me too! Hey, can I get some cash. I'm a little short, but I'll pay you back when we get home. You know I will. Thanks." So I took out a thousand dollars from my checking account to help him and he took it. Do you think I got paid back? NOPE!

Before he fell off the deep end, he asked me to find him a girl who he could really like. I set him up with a girl I worked with, Heather. She was tall, beautiful, smart, funny, the whole package. Indeed, a lovely woman. It only took her three dates to figure him out. When I saw her at work, I asked her, "Are you two still going out?" Heather told me as sweetly as she could. "No, I know you are friends with him, but no." I told her about my trip to see him in Europe to reassure her that I could completely understand.

The first day I was there, checking into a hotel in Spain. I was trying to communicate with my English-Spanish dictionary. When I was talking to the woman at the hotel, I wasn't moving fast enough for him and the kid goes, "Doesn't anyone speak English in the fucking country?" He did that right in front of the Spanish woman when we were standing in her own house, in her very own country. He just insulted her without thinking twice. I turned to him and sternly told him. "Don't be rude." I tried to make sense to the woman in front of me. "Mucho Bueno Senorits grasias Bueno." I didn't speak Spanish, but at least I tried.

The lady gave him a dirty look, and we went to our room. The kid had the audacity to have the following sentiments. "You shouldn't even try to speak to them. They don't try to speak English with us." I said, "We are in their country. They shouldn't have to speak English at all!" The next day, I got her a bottle of wine and flowers. I had someone help me write out an apology letter to her. When I started to read it, she stopped me and said in English, "Why are you with this boy? I have a nice boy for you." She was trying to set me up with her son. I told her as nicely as possible. "Thank you, but I'll be okay." That's why people in Spain think Americans are assholes. This happened to me in two different countries. A guy would get to know us at a park or a bar, and after about an hour or two, the kid would get up and when he would leave, the guys would start behind his back. "Are you okay with this guy? He seems a little off. Here is our number if you need it, just in case." That happened twice. Now I know it's not just me getting that vibe.

We were sitting at lunch together in Austria. I glanced at him for a mere second, and he went off. "Why are you staring at me?" He said it loudly enough to make people turn their heads around. I was taken aback, so I apologized quickly. "I'm sorry, I'll look over here if it bothers you." He got up, and walked out. Now people were actually looking at him. He liked the attention he used to get from being upset. People in the restaurant were staring at me. I just sat there for the rest of the time, and they went back to eating. I saw him later, and he was smiling. "Hi there, I forgive you. How was your lunch?" I was thinking, why would he forgive me for anything? I was sitting there, not doing anything and he pounced on me for no reason.

The kid went from being really pissed off to Mr. nice guy in a blink. We were at a club and he came around the corner.

I was dancing, having fun, and he wasn't getting any attention. Out of nowhere, he yelled at me. "Calm down! People are going to think you want to fight me or something." Everyone was having fun, except him. That's why he snapped at me. None of the girls was paying him enough attention. I went over to some guys we met, and they saw him snap at me. That's when they said, "Are you okay with this guy?" and they gave me their number. I mentioned this as well when I was having a conversation with Heather about him.

Heather told me that he whipped out his dick and said, "Don't you like my nice cock? Big, isn't it?" Heather said, "I guess so." What kind of a person does that? If a woman offers you that information like "Wow, I really like your cock," that's one thing, but you don't tell someone, "Don't you like my cock?" She said that he had an average dick and was so insecure about it. He needed to have her tell him his cock was something special to make him feel like he wasn't just an average guy. She also told me he wasn't very good in bed, but that didn't surprise me. I told Heather, "That stupid dick went as superman for Halloween and kept telling everyone, 'look at me, the man of steel!'" She was not surprised. "That makes sense, he's really immature." We talked about it, compared notes, and all of it made so much sense. I didn't see it before; he's bi-polar just like Karen was!!

I just didn't expect it from a man; the unpredictable behavior, Jekyll and Hyde personality, and the sneaky stuff he did, stealing with no remorse and nothing is ever his fault, excuses for everything, always needing attention, the verbal outbursts, the pathological lying, all of it pointed out towards one conclusion, he was bi-polar. Now you understand why I have a difficult time trusting anyone with bi-polar disorder.

All they do is lie to get attention and use people to get what they want. He was exactly like Karen minus the nymphomania. But who knows!

He was on a train with me going to Austria from Germany; He looked at me and said, "I'm going to be in my defensive place. I need some alone time, so I can be alert for anything." It's like he was trying to be something he's not, and I never knew what new personality he was going to be. It didn't make sense at that time, but later on, I got it. He was also doing recreational drugs. He needed to be on drugs, just not the fun ones. He told me he had a special package in my freezer. I found out it was "acid" he was keeping at my place when he was in Europe. The kid said, "That's my secret sauce. Don't let anything happen to it." He did the same thing Eric did with his pot when he hid it in my underwear drawer. So if the police find it, "That's hers!" Or the kid can say, "My dad's a cop," I know that game. I don't know if he was dealing, but it wouldn't surprise me. Out of concern, I called his family to get him help. It was clear that he wasn't just a con-artist. He was sick and really needed help.

When I called his family for help, it backfired at first. He called daddy. "Daddy, she's mean to me." Do you know any twenty-five-year-old man, or let's use the word loosely man, who calls his daddy to help him with a girl who's being mean to him? Pussy! He was pissed at me because I wasn't helping him financially anymore. His dad was a lot like mine, not just a racist asshole, but he also didn't really give a shit about his kid, just the family name. He had his new family to be concerned about. He didn't have time for his kid from his first marriage. His fucked up dad didn't go to the kid's college graduation when he was too busy with his new family stuff. They were coming back from their vacation and it was too much of a stretch to make it back in time to go. I even said to his dad, "Why couldn't you make it back for his graduation? I mean, come on." His dad told me, "Well, his graduation fell on our vacation plans. I'm sure he did fine." What a selfish prick! It's no wonder he has animosity towards his dad. The kid used to bad mouth his own father behind his back but would use his family name to get what he wanted. After he called daddy, he said, "Don't fuck up the family name. I'll pull some strings," and he did.

I get a call from the Denver police department. "Hi, we have a ten-yard restraining order here for you and a harassment charge. We would like to take to you about it. Can you come in?" No shit. I went down there and talked to two female officers. I said to the female officers, "Let's be honest, I wouldn't be sitting with her if his daddy wasn't pulling some strings." I was aware that I was on thin ice doing this. At the end of the day, they worked with him, but I thought maybe they would be honest too, and they were. "Okay, this is a game to them. If you can avoid them, do it. Don't call the police. Here is my number if anything happens." They were on my side; they had seen this kind of shit before; white male cops pushing their weight around. I told them, "You see that family name? It's going to come up a lot if it hasn't already." They both told me, "We will keep an eye out for it."

You wouldn't believe the lies on the statement the kid and his white cop dad made up about me. They said, "She is a dangerous woman who knows people who could have me hurt. She's really violent, and I think she may kill herself over me because she's in love with me." Even the police women didn't buy any of it; they knew they were full of shit. My dad would have "Old schooled" anyone who messed with him or our family. Maybe call a buddy, beat them up, or put a bullet in their foot, just to tell them to fuck off. No paperwork. The lowest level. The harassment charge was dropped but he still has a ten-yard restraining order against me. I had never been in trouble. They knew that the kid wanted the attention. He just did it to try to scare me.

I was a little shaken up. Two weeks later, I was still going to my kickboxing classes, and he stopped. I told the kickboxing owner and teacher, Clarence, a professional fighter, what the kid did. I didn't tell him about the racist stuff though, since he was black. I also didn't tell him about the kid being sexually retarded when he went out with Heather. Although, if I did tell him about it, I'd bet he would laugh, but I think Heather was embarrassed enough. It's a small world. I thought, she may run into one of them and his name could come up. "Oh my God, I went out with that immature sexually dysfunctional, loser!" I was also embarrassed by the fact that I had set him up with her. I still feel bad about it. If she hears about this, I am so sorry, Heather. At least you didn't get ripped off. Just in case, check your safe.

Clarence was friends with the kid and his dad before I met him. The kid told me, "My dad and I have been friends with Clarence for a long time, he would do anything for us." I don't know how much of that was true. I wasn't sure how deep their relationship was either. I was always honest with everyone, even with Clarence, regardless of the fact that I was friends with him. I didn't see the point in lying. Clarence told me later. "I haven't seen either of them but when I do, I'll have a word." I went to class and felt good about telling him what was going on, but I was looking over my shoulder too. That fucker was getting all the attention from daddy he didn't get as a child. It was an opportunity for both of them to get together and have their massive egos grow more.

Them scaring me was a bonding moment between father and son, and that's pretty weak.

About three weeks later, I'm outside class on my motorcycle. I got a Ducati, my mid-life crisis bike. The kid showed up in his new truck that he bragged about, "Yeah, I got a loan for 24,000 dollars, not a lot of people can do that." What a fucking idiot. I told him, "I could have gotten a loan for that much in the first grade if my dad co-signed for it." That's the little spoiled kid in me talking. He said, "Yea, if your dad co sighed for it. I got this all by myself!" Most twenty-five-year-olds could get a loan for that much, probably more.

The kid had no clue about real money and what to do with it. He got out of his truck, and he threatened me outside of class. He looked around to make sure nobody heard him. He was standing at the door of the school. "You better leave if you know what is good for you. You can't say a word to me. I could have you arrested right now if I want. They all know my dad. You better go the ball is in "my" court." He had a big smile on his face when he did this. The kid was using the ten-yard restraining order like a weapon instead of a shield and was warned not to do this by the judge and my lawyer!

I told the judge in court, "He is a liar, and his dad is a cop, so he thinks he is above the law." I don't know if it made any difference, but at least it was on the record, and it wasn't a lie. His dad even had a white male cop friend of his come to court and lie for him. "She has the ability to hurt him." You know they stick together! Can you believe that shit? My dad would have done the same thing with his buddies. Made me think they are Klan. Then Clarence showed up, the kid was all happy. "Oh hi, Clarence." He didn't know I talked to him. Clarence said, "You in my office now!" to the kid. They went into the office and I could barely hear them. He was trying to whisper, that sneaky little fuck. Clarence said to him, "A harassment charge and a restraining order? Are you kidding? She can't fight." The kid said, "Well, she's kind of obsessed with me and the judge said, she was a threat to me, so I got it to keep myself safe. You know my dad and me, so could you tell her to go so I can work out? Since you have been friends with my dad for a long time, will you ask her to leave so I can work out?" Clarence asked him. "How much money do you owe her?" The kid, I'm sure was a little taken back. He didn't know I talked to him. Now, what's he going to do? How many more lies will it take to get out of this? The kid said, "Well, I give her all the money back. It's not that much. Yeah, I'll drop everything, but can you ask her to go? So we can work out? You can call my dad if you want. He will tell you all about her. She isn't as nice as you think. We have been friends for a long time, right? So I know you won't mind asking her to go, so I can work out." And then he really fucked up. "You know legally, she can't be around me and my dad could have her arrested right now if I ask him to" spoiled little shit. "Daddy will fix it" He had the balls to say that to a black man who's been in prison. Clarence wasn't buying any of this. He thundered. "No! You pay her back every dime. Drop the harassment charge and the restraining order. Apologize to her. She told me all about it. Until you do that, get out, and you can tell your dad I said that." He backed me up 100%.

Clarence knew I was telling the truth. Thank God for a good black man! Then he told me, "I was doing his dad a favor, letting his son work out here. His dad asked me to straighten him out because the kid was getting into trouble and he couldn't straiten him out on his own." The kid told me they were friends with him like they were old buddies, another lie! His dad just used Clarence; he wasn't friends with him. The kid was getting into trouble and his cop dad asked him to straighten out his kid for him as a favor to him. "I'm a white cop; every black man wants a white cop on their side." He was using Clarence, just like his kid used me. I guess it runs in the family. He's a typical white guy with a big ego that's more important than his kid. He couldn't spend the time with his own kid to "straighten" him out, who probably just needed a dad who cared. That's probably a big reason why the kid was fucked up. He had a shitty father for sure. Still doesn't mean that it's okay to take advantage of people or rip places off, just because you had a bad dad.

The kid said to me, "I will never get in real trouble. I'm white, and I'm smart. All I have to do is drop my dad's name." Thought it was so funny when he would describe himself as smart. This dumb fuck asked me, "Now that I have been to Europe, can I tell people I'm world-traveled?" I just laughed at him. I asked him just to confirm. "Are you kidding me?" "No, you idiot!" He's so pathetic, using his family name to get his way. I would do that when I was little but he was a grown man, not according to Heather.

I don't think he had much else to impress anyone with except; "My dad's a cop," and whipping out his dick and saying, "Well, don't you like my mediocre white cock?" I'm sure that will work for him as long as the girl is blind and retarded. Wait, that's not nice. A retarded girl would see right past his bullshit and go yell and tell. His best friend, Chad, called me drunk and slurred, "I'm so sorry he did that to you. I love you, and I'm so sorry. Don't hate me." I never returned his call. The kid had Chad write out a false statement about me to give to the police to make him look like a victim. This was falsifying documents to the police, but it was okay for him because his dad's a cop, right! Chad would follow him around like a puppy. Sorry but I don't trust anyone who's his friend. The kid treated his friends like employees at his disposal, and would use them whenever he needed them. I don't want to tell you their names and embarrass them. It's not their fault that he is a bi-polar, con artist with a racist cop dad who doesn't want to be embarrassed either. Too late! I'd like to say this I have five generations of military and police in my family! If you don't want to be embarrassed, tell the truth for a change. But the truth, unfortunately, isn't something that runs your family. My Pops was a cop, he would be discussed with him. Pops would never let me get away with behaving the way his son did. Fuck the family name! If you're a dishonest person who cares what your family name is or if you have a badge! You're a crooked lying racist motherfucker, and so is your son!

I ran into his aunt, who did my hair two years later at a New Year's Eve party. She looked great, and she lost a hundred and fifty pounds! I almost didn't recognize her. I hadn't talked to her because of the restraining order. I followed all of the restraining rules. I didn't know if they were related to the Klan, but the kid was a fan of Hitler. After the shit he told me about his dad, I was a little concerned. I also couldn't talk to his aunt anymore. His aunt was from his mom's family's side, and his dad's side's the one who fucked him up. I can't imagine the lies he had to make up to cover his ass. She knew we were just good friends, or so I thought. She may think I'm the devil. I don't know, but I really liked her as a woman and missed her company. I looked at her and she went, "Oh, Jan!" with a big smile on her face and gave me a big hug. I told her the entire truth. I said, "I'm sorry, I just don't trust him." She told me,

"Neither do I. Not really. There is just something about him." His own aunt knew he was a conman. I threw a party at a restaurant for him when he got back from Europe to welcome him back with his aunt and her sisters. The kid wanted his party to be at one of his favorite restaurants, and he was showing his map with all of his places marked where he went. "Look, this is some girl I fucked in Portugal. She's lucky, right?" they didn't know how much of his trip was paid for with money he got from ripping places off. He was good-looking when he was young, but I saw his dad. His looks aren't going to be much good to him for long. He's going to lose all his hair and probably get fat like when he was a kid. And if he's planning on using his wits and brains to get him what he wants, he's going to be disappointed. I didn't tell his aunt I thought he was bi-polar, but I said he needed therapy, and she thought so too.

The kid's aunt told me that he married a girl I liked. Her name was Janey or something like that. She' was smart, cute, and very nice overall. I met her when they first got to know each other. When we were still friends, we went to have sushi together, and I paid because the kid didn't have any money. The kid told me to "insist" to pay so he wouldn't look bad, but looking back on it, what he was doing was making it look like I was into with him. "Yeah, that's my friend, Jan. She has a crush on me." The kid was always playing little games, but I'm sure she will see through any games he had to play. She was a pretty smart woman. I hope she gets him help. He greatly needs it, along with a lot of medication and love that he never got from his dad. I feel sorry for her to have his dad as an in-law. I remember meeting her and the kid said, "It's okay. She's short, so if we had kids, they wouldn't be too short." I remember him saying that to me about her but he also spewed comments before he met her. They went something like this: "There is a good one to breed with tall pink nipples. I like that. Our kids would be a superior race." Yeah, he's not a closeted Klansman. Who knows, they may be divorced by now. If he is like any other bi-polar patient, he will stop taking his meds because he doesn't think he needs it, and then he's fucked.

I don't think that kid or his dad will give a shit if they hear about this. They do have a ten-yard restraining order but it's not a non-disclosure agreement. I didn't tell you their names, and it was over twenty years ago, but I don't see them coming forward and saying, "I'm the guy who ripped her off, and this is my cop dad, who used to take blacks on ally rides for fun!" My dad had fun stories like that from the good old days too. I have to say, his kid had a big mouth. My father would have bragged with his dad about how they really felt about blacks.

I'm not breaking any of the restraining order rules by telling you this, but if they want the attention because that's what bi-polar people are all about, all they have to do is talk to the female officers. I talked to In the Denver police department. It's all public record, I have nothing to hide. Look it up! Those s stupid fuck ups put it in writing. It's on the record in the family name. I have nothing to hide like those two idiots. The kid lied a lot, but some of it had to be true. I wonder if anyone wouldn't mind looking into his dad's background. I'm sure they would find a lot of questionable arrests from his dad with blacks, and a couple of excessive force charges too. I can't tell you his name; "restraining order." They may be able to lie to a judge and to their fellow white male cop co-workers, but racist crooked people who lie lose their good name eventually. It catches up with you.

You're not going to get much honesty from many white people, but I'm trying. For the record, not all-white male cop kids turn out like that. The kid was bi-polar but still it would have been a lot better for him if his dad wasn't a self-absorbed prick who gave a shit about his kid. But his "New wife" has his full attention. She wears the pants in that family. None of their kids will be as fucked up as his firstborn! When the kid asked if he could keep his furniture in their house when he was in Europe, the new mom said, "Well, you can keep your things here, but 'my' kids may damage them." She didn't give a shit about his stuff or him. She only wanted what's best for her kids. I don't like her, but I don't think she would put up with his dad's crap by doing whatever he wants to and ignoring her kids! I got the impression that she was in charge always. He may have a badge, but she's got his balls in her back pocket.

I hope the guys in the department find out about this and "connect the dots." Figure out who he is and have a good laugh about it. Well, at least the black guys I worked out with; Clarence and the female cops I talked to will. I can see the kid getting a hold of this and telling everyone, "Yeah, that's me she's talking about, but she got it all wrong. I'll tell you what really happened. Maybe I'll write a book too." Anything for attention! The kid is not smart enough to keep his mouth shut because he's bi-polar. I really hope he stays on his meds because I don't think him coming out and saying "that's me." would be good for him or his dad. You both might be in trouble if you do that. That's why it doesn't pay to lie or be stupid enough to put your lies in black and white like you did at the police department when you filled out the restraining order. There were some major mistakes made there. You are both morons. I grew up with stories about cops beating up blacks, and the kid told me some shit that really didn't surprise me. The kid told me, "The police dogs only bite blacks and Mexicans. They don't bite whites unless they are told to." This kid thought that was great to share with me as well as some other shit you wouldn't believe his dad got away with. I don't need to say your name. Your stupid son will do it for you when this comes out. You think you didn't like your son before this? Wait until your co-workers hear about this. Your son wanted attention, here you go. If you spent five minutes of quality time with your son and gave a shit, I wouldn't have gone through all the bullshit your son put me through and you helped him, you dumb fuck. So this is what you get; the truth will set you free! I hope to God that white racist crooked cop is retired by now. You don't think he's a crooked cop? Look at how his son turned out! The kid got that sneaky racist lying bad behavior from good old dad! But I'm sure he will blame society or anything else for his son's bad behavior, just like any other whitey on the planet who doesn't want to look bad. Not all of them, just 75-80% of them.

When we had the "Stanly cup" with the avalanche, I went downtown to a wedding dinner. They were blocking off the streets next to Larimer Square, and I went right up to a SWAT guy in full gear and said, "Can you let me go by? I have a wedding reception to go to." He looked at me like I was nuts and said, "You shouldn't be here. They are going to tear gas. Go down to the 14th Street and you will be safe." I went down the street and walked by a black guy getting pepper-sprayed and the cops looked around and beat the shit out of him, leaving him bleeding on the sidewalk. I ran and called for an ambulance. Looking back, if I was a black woman and tried to ask for help to get out of there, I would probably wind up like that guy in the street, white privilege. That's the kind of stuff white cops brag about to their fellow co-workers. “Hey! I beat the shit out of some black guy during the riots. It was great.” Not all of them, just 75-80% of them. The kid’s dad would have blabbed to his buddies about it with a smile on his face, and so would my dad.

CHAPTER TWENTY-TWO: NUT HOUSE, WHITE PRIVILEGE TRUTH

I've always had a bad reaction to medications, and the credit goes to low tolerance galore. I broke out in hives when I got my appendix out, and I fainted when I got a tetanus shot. Who does that? Me! I got blood poisoning from a cat bite, and the doctor gave me a drug that almost killed me. I had a bladder infection and I let it go a bit, actually a lot. My gynecologist was out of town, so I went to the ghetto, "Planned Parenthood." I had a friend who worked at a planned parenthood and told me some sick stories that would make you cringe, so I wasn't happy to go there. When I got there, I had a nurse take my vitals. I told her, "All I need is a little medication. I get bladder infections all the time. It's no big deal." She said, "No, you are not fine. You have a really high fever and you need to go to the hospital right now!" I was so confused. "You are really over-reacting. I'll be okay." The nurse was adamant. "You either go to the hospital now or I'm calling the paramedics to take you." She was serious. I told her, "I think you are overreacting, but I will go if it makes you feel better." I knew that she won't budge, so I gave in. After all, I did need some medication.

I went to the hospital. They rushed me in, placed ice packs on me and started me on 2 IVs. I guess, I was sick. I have a high threshold for pain, so I might have not realized the severity of my case. I was there for a day or two. I don't know, it's all a blur. I asked if I could go home, and they agreed. So I went home. I guess I drove, but to this day, I don't remember driving home from the hospital. I started to hear and see things that weren't there.

Six months prior to this incident, I was attacked in my home when I was alone. I don't want to talk about the details. I thought I was being attacked, so I called the police. They picked me up and knew I was telling the truth because they called the hospital. "Do you have a patient who could be hallucinating on the medication you gave her?" They said, "Yeah. That may happen. Bring her back here. We will have a look at her." So they took me back. They let me sit in the front of the cop car. I didn't want to look like a criminal. I remember thinking they put me behind the wheel of my car. I was tripping my balls off, and this might have happened? This sounds like malpractice if you ask me, but I was so high, all I wanted to do is cry. This wasn't like dropping acid, that's more fun. On the contrary, this was scary. I had to go back to the same hospital that fucked me up in the first place. This was the third time a doctor had given me medication that I had a severe reaction to, and it almost killed me. My faith in western civilization medicine is deeply bruised, to say the least.

I got checked in, and I still had my armband on from my last visit to the hospital, and I realized they didn't give me a second armband that tells you what I'm allergic to. They skipped that part. They gave me a medication I'm severely allergic to it. I'm really lucky it didn't kill me. That's what was making me go nuts, and I had a really high fever too.

I met my doctor, and he seemed nice. I had an M.R.I., which is really trippy when you are already high as fuck. I talked to a psychologist who had no sense of humor. She was asking me the standard loony questions. She wasn't looking at me or really paying attention to me. It was like someone told her she had to talk to a crazy person, and she didn't want to do it. She was an old lesbian woman and she asked me with no feelings, very monotone, what's it like to be you right now?" I couldn't help it. I said to this woman, "What's it like to be a lesbian woman in comfortable men's shoes? How's that? I don't know what that's like?" I pissed her off. I was trying to make light of a bad situation, not a good idea to piss off a person who can have you locked up and throw away the key, but I was crazy at the time. I watched her through my sheet next to my bed. She slammed her clipboard down right in front of my doctor, who had a good sense of humor. She was so mad! I knew I had to make this funny or I was going to fall apart.

Speaking of funny, I got E-coli poisoning as well. It was so funny. I almost shit myself. Wait, I actually did that. I was pooping blood. Is that bad? I got it when I was on vacation in L.A. visiting my sister, which was such a bummer. When I go on vacation to L.A., I always make a mental note of all the places I want to eat! This ruined my favorite foods from home. Talk about pig-out plans! I even brought my stretchy pants! I'm a chef, so when I have the chance to go to a new place to eat, I go and try it. But when you go home, you know exactly where you're going to go, all the places you can't get the food you like, miss, and crave. Basically, everything that makes your mouth water.

It doesn't have to be five-star. It could be a shithole dive, but if the food is good, you know you're going home to have it for sure. This put a big wrench in my vacation plans, so I went to the hospital; the doctor was Indian, like from India for real, not like Cherokee. I was on the table getting ready for the old "Moon River" up the butt for my rectal exam, and I thought it would be funny to make a little joke to the doctor. I said, "Wouldn't you like to buy me a drink first?" it didn't translate well. The doctor asked with concern, "Would you like a drink of water?" I said, "Nope, but my going rate is a hundred." I didn't even get a smile. He just performed the exam left, came back and said, "You have blood in your stool. How did you get it?" Is he kidding? How the fuck should I know where I got it? Jesus.

When I got E-coli poisoning at that time, it was very easy to get it. You could pick up a drink and get it, just by touching a pencil from someone who has it. It was that easy to get it. The doctor put me on a very limited diet; the first month, I could only have white rice, clear broth, and black tea, the second-month brown rice and dark broth and black tea. I lost twenty-five pounds in a month. I couldn't do it for two months. I looked like a skeleton; the best diet ever! Kidding. It sucked but at least, he didn't give me anything that I was allergic to. Thank God!

Anyway, back at the hospital, one of the nurses who took my vitals said to me, "So are we still hallucinating?" I said, "Oh my God, there's Elvis!" She looked at me with a smile, "Made you look, yes I did." She laughed. Even the doctor who gave me the M.R.I. was giggling with me. I asked the doctor I liked, "That Psychologist didn't have anything nice to say about me, did she?" He said, "Nope, but I thought it was funny." The doctor I liked said, "We are going to get lunch. Do you want anything?" I couldn't help it. The comedian in me came out. "Oh, I know this great place on Alameda. Can we go there?" He looked at me like, huh? I said, "I'm kidding. I know I'm not going anywhere." He laughed and said, "Okay. You can call family if you want to" I asked him, 'Doc, would you please put something in my chart for the other hospital? So the psychologist doesn't think I'm funny." The doctor said, "Sure, honey. I'll put something in there. That's nice."

I don't know what he wrote, but to remind him, I was a smart-ass crazy person about twenty years ago, Thanks doc!!

He was very nice. I wish I could remember all their names or at least one of them. I was so screwed up. It was really hard to concentrate, much less remember any of their names. I had to go to the bathroom, and I thought, why not do it myself since the nurse wasn't around, so I unhooked my I. V., and went to the bathroom. I wasn't in there for very long, and when I got out of there, four security guards were outside my bedroom going. "Patient number thirty-two is missing." They were looking for me. I thought, this is really funny, but I was tired. I wanted to go back to bed. I just stood there and let them sweat it out a bit.

I was right next to the exit. I could have ran or told them, "I thought I was going to another hospital, but I don't think I'm in any condition to drive. Can I get a ride? Shotgun!" and see what their reaction would be. I could've asked, "Do you guys know where the pool is? I need to do some laps," just to fuck with them, but I finally couldn't take it. I went over to them. I was only five feet away and said to them, "Is the patient dangerous?" They all looked around, confused. I said, "Hello. I'm who you are looking for and I am not dangerous or missing. I just had to go to the bathroom."

The guy in charge smiled. I smirked. "You know, I'm going to another hospital, right?" He said, "Yes. Are you going back to bed?" I answered with a sigh, "Yes, I'm really tired." If I wasn't so weak after hearing all this stuff, I would have made it funny, only if I could. There was this one cop, oh God! He was this big white young cop, who said to me, "I have to stay with you from now on." I looked at him and said, "Move over, Tarzan. I'm going to bed. You look a little young to be a cop. Are you old enough to carry that weapon?" He didn't laugh, that was no surprise. My nurse laughed, so did the cop in charge and so did my doctor who I liked, so fuck him with no sense of humor. Go hang out with the psychiatrist. She's a barrel of laughs! I can mouth off to a cop; I'm crazy, so why not? I kept calling him, "Tarzan." I liked fucking with him. What were they going to do, anyway? Fucking cops didn't even arrest me. Why do you think they put Tarzan on this detail? "Go watch this crazy girl. She's fun." They were hazing him because he was new and let the new guys get the "shit jobs" that nobody else wanted. So suck it up, Tarzan. At least I kept it interesting.

I called my brother to get me some clothes. He got me everything but socks and underwear. He didn't want to get into my panty drawer. He thought that it was an invasion of my privacy. How sweet! I love him. This one time, He got a tattoo on his chest and I told him, "Brother, if you don't cry, I'll get one too." That little bastard sucked it up and didn't cry, so I got one too. I was lying on my back, and this guy covered in tattoos and piercings came in. His name was "Sugar Bear." I kid you not, it took him twenty minutes to do my tattoo and it was only the size of a pea; a little heart in a delicate place. Though when I asked him questions like "What about AIDS and infections?" He was very sweet and professional. DON'T JUDGE A BOOK BY ITS COVER!

I'll never get another one. I don't think so, but I'm glad I got one for my brother. Anyway, the E.M.T.'s who were taking me to the nut house were women, and very cute. My brother whispered in my ear, "Sis, introduce me." I said, "I love you bro, but I am in no condition to pimp you out." He smiled. "Sorry sis, habit." Usually, when my cute little brother was around and I was out with the girls, I would always introduce him like, "Hey, everyone! This is my handsome little brother." But during this particular case, I couldn't even tell what day it was much less have the energy to pimp out my brother. He understood. He followed us to the other hospital.

The paramedic was so nice. I asked her, “Is it okay if I sit up? I feel kind of queasy.” She nodded with a sweet smile forming on her face. “Yes.” I felt like telling her more. “I am not a violent person, no matter what that psychologist said. She didn’t have anything nice to say about me, did she?” The girl said, “Nope, but the other doctor was nice.” Thank God. I told her, “I was given a drug that I’m allergic to, and I was hearing and seeing stuff that I can’t explain.” She said, “It’s okay; most people who have your diagnosis are yelling at me, spitting, or trying to hurt me, so you’re fine.” I asked her, “Can you hear that right there?” She told me what I was dreading. “No honey, I can’t.” That’s when I lost it. I started to cry and so did the nice paramedic!

I felt so bad. I have never been so confused and scared. The sweet girl was so nice, she helped me through the hospital, gave me a hug and reassured me, “Don’t worry, honey. You just need to get that drug out of your system, and it will be okay.” I hope she hears about this. I want to tell her, “Thank you so much, you are wonderful!” I was so fucking high it was in Denver. I’m not sure which year I was in, 2001 or 2002? I really wish I could forget all of it like a lot of other stuff I’d like to forget. The details on all of it are still fuzzy. To that sweet paramedic and the nurse at the hospital please tweet me so I can thank you for your wonderful help!

I also called my friend, Jon Nielson. He came to the hospital, and boy oh boy did I need him. Jon can always make me laugh. We used to drive down Cherry Creek with the top down in his Porsche. I’d put on a string bikini, and Jon with his beautiful grey hair, would play Ludacris Hoes in Area Codes, just to watch the reactions of all the stuck-up white people lose their shit! “Oh My God, look at that dirty old man with that young girl!” We loved it! We both have a sick sense of humor; it's a little twisted for some people, but Jon Nielson is fucking hilarious! He called me from Vegas, "Hey Janny, I'm getting my dick sucked by a hooker." It didn't faze me at all. "Great, Jon! Call me after you cum! Wrap it up!"

We have a very open and honest relationship. He's so much fun to hang out with. He knows my whole family. We went to his office party that had a Hawaiian theme and Jon, with his beautiful grey hair, I dressed him up like a tourist and me in a two-piece string bikini got out of his Porche and all of his male co-workers went nuts! "Wow look at Jon," I went to them to say hello and all of their wives were looking at me like, "What a whore, who's that girl with Jon?" I said hello to his male friends. "Hi guys, I'm Jan. I'm with Jon," They all said hello with big smiles on their faces and then I went to say hello to the wives. All I was wearing was a bikini and really high sandals and a see-through sarong. I said hi to one woman who I'm sure worked the pole once too, and she was smiling and said, "Hi, are you "Friends" with Jon," I said, "Yea Jon and I are old friends; he knows my entire family." They looked at me like, "She's a hooker, she's lying." One of the women said, "What do you do for a living?" Do you think for one second I'm going to give those women any ammo to shoot at me when I tell them "I'm a stripper?" Hell No!! I said, "I'm a professional chef. I work with Wolfgang Puck."

They all thought I was lying but I said, "I know never to trust a skinny chef, but I've been a chef for twenty years." They were taken back, but some of them still didn't believe me. I looked at the woman I thought used to strip and said "What do you do?" She said, "I don't work anymore," I said, "I get it," and winked at her. She smiled and I went to talk to Jon and said, "Can I stay here with you guys?" He said,

"Yes" so we hung out for the rest of the party and had a blast! Jon and I babysat my hairdresser's son, Christian. He looked like a little Q-tip for my friend Michael Eastman, the best stylist in Denver. We used to party in the nineties hard! Now, we are both sober and have quite normal lives. We were really lucky but some of our friends weren't! The kid loved Jon, me too but John had that thing" like my mom. Kids are just drawn to him. He's so loveable but don't fuck with him. He's tough; don't let the grey hair fool you. He will knock you out if he has to. He was there for me, and I really needed him because I really thought I had lost my mind. I was scared to death, trying to hold it together, and I knew I wasn't going anywhere, but if nothing else, Jon could cheer me up.

I got to the nut ward, it's a locked ward; you can't leave. They took my bag, and Nurse Ratchet placed three pages in front of me. "Sign here, here and here." I couldn't read it. The print was so small, and with my eyes flittering, I was hearing all that stuff. It was really hard to concentrate. I said to her, "Will you please read this to me? I can't read this. I can't sign anything unless I can read it." She looked at the security guard, and then started talking in a baby voice. "These are admittance forms, you need to sign them." I was confused as hell, but I was still holding on to some sense. I said, "I'm sorry, but I can't." Nurse Ratchet said, "Are we going to have a problem with you?" I said, "Yes, I guess you are if you try to make me sign something that I can't read."

I knew there were different parts of the nut ward, and I didn't want to be put in a straitjacket and locked in a padded cell. I tried to clear myself. "I am not trying to be difficult, I just can't read this." She rolled her eyes and Mr. Sensitive Hippie Ponytail therapist walked inside. There is a reason why I'm not a big fan of hippies. Anyways, he was trying to make friends with me and gain my trust, but if this asshole smells like patchouli, I am going to slap him.

I was tripping balls, and all I wanted was for it all to stop. I was really on edge and felt like I was going to snap. I have never been a violent person but fear might make a person do things they could never imagine. What I was going through was really scary and confusing. I didn't know how I would react one second to the next. To say the least, I was utterly terrified.

Mr. Sensitive Hippie Ponytail therapist tried to come over to me gently. "Hi. I'm not going to hurt you. I just need to take your vitals, okay?" He was wearing a pair of Birkenstocks, a Hawaiian shirt, to make the patients feel cheery, open, with a wife-beater under it, he was wearing hiking shorts, and that stupid hippie jewelry, that has real meaningful spiritual meaning to it. Let me tell you all about it, bullshit!

He was coming at me like he was approaching a wild animal; with ease, small steps, and his hands out. I looked at Nurse Ratchet, she looked at him like, "You take her. I don't want anything to do with her." I said to him, "Fine, let's go." I went with him. When he started to take my vitals, a little crowd was gathering to talk about me, the problem patient who won't sign her admittance forms. He said, "Wow! Your blood pressure is really high and you have a fever too." I looked at him, not smiling, and I said, "No shit! I know all of this. Tell me something I don't know." He got up, went to the little crowd of nurses and security, talked to them and came back. I asked him, "Can I go lay down now? I'm really tired." Mr. Sensitive Hippie Ponytail therapist said, "Just a minute." They called out for meds. I am not taking anything but all the other nuts were lining up for their drugs.

Mr. Sensitive Hippie Ponytail therapist pushed me to the front of the line in front of all the lunatics waiting for their meds. This dick was going to get me beat up by these nuts, who are giving me dirty looks because I get to go first. I went to the front of the line. There was a little "candy striper trainee" giving me drugs. She was looking at her senior nurse to watch her do this. "Okay, these are your drugs. I mean your meds. I need you to take them here." She smiled like she was doing a good job. I looked at her and said, "What is this?"

She gazed back at her boss for help, and the candy striper said, "Well, your doctor prescribed them to you." She was smiling, pushing the meds and water towards me. I asked her, "Can you get me a P.D.R. so we can look it up?" The junior nurse was visibly panicking now, looking at her boss, and realizing that she was never trained for this. Her boss said, "We don't have one in this section of the hospital." That was one of the worst lies or cop-outs I had ever heard. I told her, "Drugs given to me by a doctor in a hospital is the reason why I am here. I have a low tolerance to drugs. So what the hell is this that you're giving me?"

There were about five people around me who were trying to get me to take these drugs and the nuts in line, trying to get their meds were pissed that it's taking so long and I was being difficult. The head nurse said, "Your doctor will be here in about two hours." I told her, "Great! I'll be right there." I pushed the drugs back to the scared-to-death candy striper and sat down in the front room where I got to see the loonies come and go. Now, I'm an aggravated problem patient who won't sign her admittance forms and won't take her meds. I was just waiting for a shot in the neck with a needle from behind. No way am I taking any drugs. That was all I was thinking. I'm crazy, not stupid! I was hearing all kinds of stuff, and it was really hard to concentrate. I couldn't believe where I was. Like how did that even happen?

I sat down and tried not to cry while I was waiting for the doctor to come. This nightmare of a woman came in white and pretty, looking for any attention she could get from anyone. She was trying to cry, but no tears were leaving her eyes. She was looking around for a response from anyone. She looked at me and I gave her a look like, "I'm not buying it, princess." She was off the rails; she made sure everyone knew she was there. This nut job went back to get her drugs, pushed herself right up to the nurses' station in the most overdramatic way possible. She's been there before. This woman got her meds; some of the nurses knew her. Two hours later, she came out spick and span. Extremely happy people were visiting her, getting her presents. "Oh, thanks for coming. I really appreciate it." She was really enjoying herself. She was bi-polar, just like Karen! I told the staff, "Don't put me in the same room as her." Instead, they put me in a room with Princess Valume Sorority girl. She reminded me of a cross between Tori Spelling and Lindsey Lohan, a really bad combination but fat and more winey. You ever want to punch a white girl in the face? Of course you have. I didn't until I met her. NUF-SAID! It was really hard for me to keep my mouth shut when I saw what was going on in that place, but I tried to keep it together and not make waves. It was okay until the last day I was there.

My doctor came in and went to the nurses to talk to them. Then comes over to me, "Hello, I'm your doctor." He looked like a cheesy used car salesman with over-whitened capped teeth. He said, "I hear you're not taking your medication." I told him, "No. I can't take anything until I know if I'm going to have a bad reaction to it like this one." When I was saying this to him, you had no idea how hard it was to concentrate. I was hearing and seeing things that were scaring the shit out of me. I couldn't stop it. I think it would be what you would call, "A bad trip!" He said, "I understand, and I will explain it all to you." He signaled to the nurses, this poor girl who was training looked really overwhelmed. I felt so sorry for her. She came over reluctantly, handed the meds to the doctor. He gave her an annoyed look – the usual "Put it in front of the patient, stupid."

I could tell this doctor is an arrogant prick. I feel sorry for the staff that had to work with that asshole. I wish I could remember his name. This poor girl put the meds and the water in front of me reluctantly and rushed back to the nurses' station. She kept looking at me now and then. I guess I wasn't paying enough attention before. I look over, and there's a crowd of people watching this little "Days of our narcissistic lives show." The doctor said, "Well, Barbra. I'll explain this to you." I said, "Um, excuse me? Did you just call me Barbra??" The doctor confirmed. "Yes, Barbra Williams." He nodded as he glanced at his clipboard. "Barbra Williams, that's you." No, I can't be this fucked up. Did he just call me Barbra?

I said, "Sorry to tell you Doc, but my name is Jan. Not Barbra Williams. Look it up." He looked down. "Honest mistake! They gave me the wrong information for a different patient. I'll be right back." He was trying to blame his incompetence on the nurses because he's a fucking privileged, male, white doctor, who would never admit his fault. My dad would have done that kind of thing. The doctor went to the nurses' station, bitched like a little girl, and came back with a completely different set of pills. "Here you go, Jan." He was smiling. I looked at him, pulled out one of his pens and a piece of paper. When I reached across the table for his pen, the security guards straightened up a bit and it made him really nervous too. I told him, "You are going to write out in bold print every medication you have prescribed to me, and I am going to call my mom, who has a P.D.R. at home. She will look up everything and she will know what I am allergic to because you don't."

I called my mom to look up the medication for me to take, but I was so whacked out of my mind that I couldn't remember her phone number. I had to look it up. Mom has had the same number for twenty-five years, that's how bad I was. "Mom, you'll never guess where I am." I told her I was drugged by a doctor and they wanted to give me more. She was so mad. "You put that doctor on the phone right now. Goddamn it!" My mom not only cussed, she took the Lord's name in vain. I handed the phone to the doctor. "Yeah, my mom wanted to talk to you." I'm holding the phone to him, and everybody's watching!

The doctor looked around, backed away with his hands up, and said, "I'm sorry. I don't know if that's your mother and I don't think that's a good idea." He was putting on a little performance for the people he worked with. He mumbled as low as he could while looking at me like basically, "I'm not liable." I gave him a warning glance and said, "It really isn't a good idea to piss off my mom. I warned you." He just left. That "all-up-his-own-ass" doctor left it up to the nurses to deal with me, the aggravated problematic patient who won't sign the admittance forms and won't take her meds. Yeah, I'm fun. I had to. I just had to ride it out. I only took the medication my mom said was okay, and drank a lot of water to get that shit out of my system.

I refused to go to the group. I didn't need to hear those people's problems, no offense. I just wanted to get some sleep and have everything to turn off. One of the therapists told me, "If you don't go to group, you can't go outside for a smoke break." I told her, "I don't smoke. Oh and I'm not allergic to everything, either. That's why I'm here. You should check your records. Oh wait, you don't do that." I said that right to her face. She just walked away. I could have gone up to the nurses' station and asked for the medication for Barbra Williams. I would have gotten them with no problem. That place was so ill-run, I feel sorry for long-term patients who can't leave.

A sweet girl came in the last day I was there. All the noises and stuff I was seeing were shutting off, thank God. The poor girl had been repeatedly raped over the years by her stepfather and his son. She couldn't take it and tried to kill herself. That's why she was there. Whoever just dropped her off at the nut house was an asshole. She was sitting all by herself surrounded by loonies. Jesus. She's scared to death. Poor girl was left all alone, so I talked to her. She said, "That therapist wants me to talk in group, but I really don't want to." She was referring to Mr. you know who of course. I told her, "I don't usually go to group, but I'll go with you and if he picks on you, I'll get him to stop. Don't worry. I will just really embarrass him if I have to."

We went into group. The first thing he does is point her to talk. I knew that hippie fucker was going to do that. Prick! I said, "I don't think she wants to talk. Would you ask someone else, please?" We are in a room with about forty people in it and he wanted her to open up in front of everyone? What a cock. He looked at me and said, "Well, opening up would really help her." When I looked at her, tears were streaming down her face, and she was frozen. I said as politely as I could. "No. She really doesn't want to talk. Ask someone else, please." I was trying to be as nice as possible. He looked over at the other five therapists in there, and they weren't doing anything. He cleared his throat and tried to speak again. "Well…" I stopped him right there. "Goddamn it she doesn't want to open up! Leave her alone." He wasn't expecting this. "Okay, we don't have to get violent."

I couldn't help it anymore. "This isn't violent, you hippie dick! But I'll show you violent if you don't leave her alone." He got it. "Okay, calm down. Does anyone else want the floor?" So he left her alone. I was getting the fuck out of there and I kind of didn't give a shit what any of them thought of me. I got her to talk to a female therapist after the group meeting. Poor baby, I hope she's alright. She will always be in my prayers.

I had another little encounter when all the shit turned off! There was this woman, an elderly one, who was there. She and I talked because I refused to go to group, and I didn't want to sit in the T.V. room with the schizophrenically-drug-induced guy who looked like Kurt Cobain. He was constantly talking to himself, which was kind of funny for about two or three minutes. Then, it got annoying. Most loonies don't really have a good sense of humor, and I couldn't go to my room. My roommate, this white girl, a princess Valume, was having a crisis intervention or something with her sorority sisters. Princess Valume was there because her rich husband was giving her enough attention, so it's his fault she would drink and pop pills. Poor baby boo-fucking hoo! KAREN!

Her shit was everywhere. She was a sorority pig with guests. I think she was used to having someone clean up after her she is having a little "Pow wow" with the gals, right when I was trying to sleep. I was lying there and there were four women in the room trying to give her words of encouragement and cheer her up. "When you get out of here, we can have a girl's day. We can bleach our asses too! That's a new thing, right? We can put it on your husband's card. If he doesn't pay attention to you, he will to his credit card statement. Haha." Go Cappa, Omega, Zeda, Alpha bullshit or whatever the girls' sorority's names are. My mom was in an all-girl's Christian sorority. If you wanted to be in, you had to be a virgin, no joke. These girls were annoying, not like the women my mother would associate with and they were saying some really ridiculous stuff. "We can go to Mexico again, and you can have virgin daiquiris."

I was trying not to hear anything. These bitches were annoying times ten. They were showing each other their wedding ring, talking about when she gets out, they're going to go out and introduce her to alcohol and then she's back where she started. Those women are not her friends if they do that. I couldn't help myself but say, "Hey, princess! Take the girls club outside. I'm mad, and I get violent when I get mad." They immediately left. I'm sure they said something to the nurse about me. "That girl said she was going to get violent with us." I really think if things get tough with those sorority white girls, they throw you under the bus. I went to school with girls like them; white, pretty, spoiled, future Karens! Not all of them, just 75-80% of them.

It's one thing to visit a nut-ward for a day to see your friend who's having a hard time, but if Princess Valume needed bail money or financial help with her divorce, I'll bet their phone would have a bad connection that day she'd call for help from a faithful sorority sister. "I don't get it. We all bleached our assholes together. Why won't they return my calls?" The princess would wonder. I'll tell you why: there is no such thing as white girl loyalty!

When I finally got some sleep, I woke up and I knew they said something to the nurse about me. She was there and asked me, "Everything alright?" I said, "Yes, finally got some sleep. Do you want some juice?" The nurse replied with, "No thanks. I'm okay." I doubt the nurse even paid attention to them when they complained about me. They have had their fair share of whiny Karens. I know Princess Valume will never forget her time in the hospital; her friends were always calling her, all hours of the day and night. They were giving her the whole, "Don't worry. It's not your fault. It will get better." The bitch was always on her phone. I wanted to flush it down the toilet while she slept, but I never got the chance. When I think of those girls and their response to anyone who made fun of sorority girls or thought they're a joke when they'd say, "You're jealous. You want to be just like us." When they said stuff like that, I think Ted Bundy hit the wrong sorority girls over the head. "Hey, Ted! You missed a couple over here! Jesus!"

Anyway, this elderly woman was waiting for her son-in-law and her daughter. He wanted her to sign some papers; she was uncomfortable and didn't even know why she was there. Her son-in-law said he needed them signed as soon as he got there because he was in a hurry, and she didn't get a chance to talk to her attorney. He's on his way right now. I asked her what they were for. She said, "My estate." I knew what this fucking guy was up to. He put this woman who had Moderate Alzheimer's in this nut house to get her away from her attorney, so he could trick her into signing something she didn't understand. People who steal from the elderly should be burned at the stake!

I told this sweet woman, "Don't worry. I'm with Loyd and Evrett." I realized later how it sounded like a red-neck firm I just made up! "I'm a legal assistant. I'll find out what he wants you to sign." She said, "Thanks so much!" I was trying to put this poor woman at ease. She didn't know what was going on at all. I hid my hospital armband in my shirt. I was already dressed to leave. I tried to put her at ease by comforting her with the best reassuring words I could muster up at that point. She's in a nut house for God's sake, and she didn't know where she was. I just didn't want her to be taken advantage of.

We sat and chatted for an hour. My best friend, Jon, was on his way to get me out, so I was feeling good! All the noises stopped. Things were back to almost normal. I still had a fever on and off, but I was better. This prick came in with her daughter. I said, "Hello." That douchebag ignored me completely. He started to open his briefcase right away and took out some legal documents. So I introduced myself. "Hi! May I see those?" He asked with an arrogant, smug face. "Who are you?" I lied. "I'm an attorney. Her lawyer asked me to be here."

He started to put his papers back in his briefcase, and he looked so guilty. "She has Alzheimer's. She doesn't know what she's saying." Really? I pulled him aside and had a little "Talk" with him. At times like this, I wish I had a 357 magnum like dad did. I said, "Look, I'm not going to file charges against you for elderly abuse or insurance fraud but I will do something else you won't like. My associate is on his way right now." He looked at me like I was some dumb skirt. His eyes were screaming, "What are you going to do to me?" I said, "David, you live in Castle Rock with two kids, and your wife is Sally. You're a real estate broker and you drive a Range Rover, right?" His mom told me all about him. The guy was frozen and I said, "I'm not a lawyer. Mess with her again, and I'll have your legs broken." Right when I said that, Jon walked in!!! His timing couldn't have been more perfect! What is he going to do to me? Have me committed or arrested? All the police will do is laugh at him for being tricked by a crazy person. I could've just used the excuse bi-polar Karens use all the time. "I was on medication. I don't remember doing that."

I looked over his shoulder. Jon took one look at him, sneered, and the guy looked like he was going to just about shit. That bastard won't fuck with her again. He gathered up his stuff and it turned out to be a quick meeting with grandma and he left. I gave a heads up to the ill-informed staff. "Hey, listen up! This guy is trying to take advantage of her." I don't even think they cared. That place was run so poorly. No wonder why we have a problem with people who are nuts! All they wanted to do to the patients was give them drugs. I didn't get the feeling that any of those patients were really getting the one-on-one psychological care they needed. I was in the loony bin for two days. I was supposed to see my personal doctor for one hour a day. I saw him fifteen minutes in two days, and he couldn't remember my name. That was my personal experience. Some other people may have had a better experience in a nut ward. I just didn't care for it. The food sucked too.

Now, it was time to get the fuck out of dodge. The doctor came in. I told my friend, "Jon, play along. I'm getting out of this shithole today!" He just smiled and said, "You got it." When the doctor walked in, he saw Jon standing behind me. He asked, "Is this your dad?" That is the worst thing he could say. Jon has grey hair, but he is not old enough to be my dad. That's a sure way to get punched in the face by Jon! I said, "No, he's not my dad. I am ready to go now, so we need those release forms so I can go home." The doctor mentioned rather casually, "Well, you didn't sign the admittance forms and I'm not sure you're ready to go." I had enough. "Look, doc. You tried to give me medication for a different patient." He stopped me and mumbled under his breath, "Well, that was an honest mistake from the nurses." What a dick!

I said, "Look, if you don't get me out of here now, you are going to buy me my next house. Guess who he is now." He thought Jon was my lawyer. All the color almost drained from his face. He told me to hold on and got the admittance forms and discharge forms. Jon picked them up and started crossing shit out on it. The doctor tried to interrupt. "You can't do that." Jon looked at him and said, "Do you want to buy me a house too?" That shut the doctor up. I loved it! They gave me back my backpack, gave me a bag full of drugs which I flushed when I got home. Mom got mad at me for flushing the drugs down the toilet because she said it was bad for the environment. I can't win.

I got home from the nut house and there was a get-well-soon card from the police department. They even checked up on me. I found out later the police were there three times. They told me to go back to bed. I didn't remember all of that. They gave me "First class" treatment. I sat up front in the police car. I didn't want to feel like a criminal, and I didn't even have to mention my dad's name. They did all that for me because I was white and for no other reason. If I was a black woman in that scenario, the police would have cuffed me, stripped me, beat me up, locked me up and thrown away the key. There were no black patients in the nut ward, none! They don't get the option to get mental help. They just get beat up, thrown in jail, or killed. That was the worst case of white privilege I have ever experienced!!!

White people will say, "Oh, she is so ungrateful. How can she be so rude to the police that helped her?" No, I'm grateful, I just wish white male cops would give the same courtesy to blacks, and they don't. It was twenty years ago, but who was the dipshit cop who told me to go back to bed? I had seizures, and I could have died. Or are they going to cover that up too? It's on record somewhere. Everything I'm telling you is the truth. I was treated with respect and compassion by the police, and that shows they can be compassionate and helpful when they want to be. My Pops was a cop in the thirties, and my little adopted brother is a cop too. He's very upset with how people treat white male cops because he's not like that at all!

Cops like my brother and others who don't behave that way, are being persecuted because of cops who behave badly. He doesn't deserve to be dumped on because of other cops who do rotten shit and he has to pay for it. It isn't fair, but life isn't fair all the time. Is it? Don't believe me? Just ask a black man about fair and unfair. They live it daily.

White people just see how blacks get treated on T.V. mostly "White news." So make sure you sugarcoat it for Middle America white viewers. They didn't show us anything about "Martial Law" during the riots in '92 because they were protecting their families with white cops who made sure there was no crime in white neighborhoods. There was no favoritism, right? Bullshit! I saw first-hand how much we get favored. White people haven't scratched the surface of what black people go through, not just getting pulled over or walking down the street. A black person has to be unconscious or bleeding out to get medical attention and if they are having "a mental health issue," they don't go to the hospital like I did. They don't have that option. Instead, cops just kill them. I saw whites get privilege when I got my appendix out when I was eleven years old and when I was in my thirties in the loony bin. The special privilege whites get has been going on forever, not just in L.A. but in Denver too.

Aurora isn't any better. It's a bigger city, more room to sweep dirt under the rug if you get my drift. Don't believe me? Ask Eliza McClaims's parents. I bet they would agree. That's what triggered those memories of his death. I don't know why I never met him or his family. I don't even know where they go to church, but for some reason, it made me think of dad in '92 during the riots, with the white cops in L.A. Nobody was held responsible because they are all white. They get to slide like always. That beautiful boy died, and none of those cops got in trouble, much less went to prison. I think all of those cops and the E.M.T. s involved with his death should be held accountable. I don't understand what's wrong with us? How are we letting this get so out of hand?

White people need to take a look back at the interaction they have had with the police where they were nice to you because you were white or because you were polite? George Floyd was polite. Look what happened to him. I really think if we didn't get George Floyd's and Eliza's murders on film, they wouldn't get any justice. The cop that killed George Floyd, he went to prison, but what about the other cops? I don't believe in de-funding the police, but we need to be more on top of the excessive force used on blacks. I think we can all agree on that. After the many killings and beatings of blacks, a wise black man said, "Now that white people have seen the many killings and beatings of black men, maybe white people can start to be more compassionate to us and treat us as well as they treat their dogs." The words were not exactly this, but along those lines, sad but pretty accurate.

If the Los Angeles, Denver and Aurora police departments don't want the reputation of harassing, offending, and utter blatant discrimination when it comes to blacks and Latinos, then they should stop doing it. Don't judge a book by its cover. Don't any of you go to church, or why didn't your mother tell you that? We all need to be more honest and truthful; don't lie, cheat, or steal. We all know that, but we need to be more accepting of one another. That's a start. We can all work on it at our own speed as long as you don't ride the breaks. Everyone will tell you that it is bad. Just chug along and do your best, but remember this: God hates a straggler. Some white people have a lot of catching up to do. Someday we can get there, hopefully, while I'm still alive to see it.

What I want everyone by the end of this book is to tweet their opinion on what I wrote. I don't know much about tweeting, though. I got really turned off by it because of Trump's lousy tweets. I just want to hear from my old friends, and none of the assholes that ripped me off and abused me. I'm not worried about them. Karma will get them in the end tenfold. I know I have been taken advantage of in the past, but I also drank a lot in the past too. I don't give a shit about my identity theft with a stranger, but when it's from a friend or partner, that's when it really hurts.

If I said anything that made you upset, I'm not interested in babysitting you again, Karen. So cry to someone who buys your load of horseshit. The other people who want to take a shot at me, I can take a hit and I'm not going to apologize for anything. I said, if you don't like it too bad! If any of you don't believe what I wrote, look it up! There are records of everything I'm telling you, call my bluff! Find out who the white cop was who knew my dad and let me go when he pulled me over in front of his office, he was a clan member in L.A., 1984. He looked like Dennis the menace. Probably Hitler youth!

What about Darrel Gate's bullshit with martial law that happened in '92 during the riots in L.A.? Someone knows more about it than I do. I don't know how they are going to cover that all up, but honestly, this may not even get their attention. Where is the record of the black girl who got turned away at my doctor's office by security? She went to L.A. County hospital when I went to a private hospital? Who were the white cops that didn't arrest me when I was tripping balls on medication and took me to the hospital? They even sent me a get-well card but wait? Don't they do that for everyone? Who were the white cops that let me get away with drinking and driving when I crashed my car in front of my parent's house? Who were the white cops who let me get my friends home when Ted got pulled over after our school dance in Pasadena when I told them my dad was a cop? I'd like to know the white cops at Disney Land who let those white girls go when they got caught shoplifting!?

Yeah, no favoritism at all! Bullshit! It's all white privilege! It's all in black and white and on the record! I love it when the black and whites put it in black and white because they can't turn that camera off! I should have had a camera for the riots when I saw that black guy get pepper-sprayed and beat up. I feel stupid not getting the card from the white cop who asked me if I was okay when that black guy was broken down on the side of the road. If that's not nuts, I don't even know what is.

I would remember what he looks like. I'll bet his picture is at the Aurora police department! The list goes on and on, with white cops showing favoritism to whites. We all see it all the time; we just don't usually talk about it. I think maybe we should. Is there anyone else out there who has some stories about white cops giving whites special treatment or are we going to keep covering that up? I hope the cops I knew in Durango don't connect the dots to this and realize who the cop that I mentioned was. It was a blind date, but I'm sure he's not going to be very happy about this when he remembers that call on his police radio in his car on our date when I didn't tell him it was my ex., who got pulled over. Sorry, I'm not a snitch! If you don't want to go through all that trouble of doing your homework and looking into the facts in black and white, just call Marcus Allen. Ask him if I'm lying. I doubt he would forget a caddy that put him on the phone with their mom! I would like to hear from those other women who got abused by Robert in 1989, the guy who fired me for not sleeping with him. Well ladies, I think he's caught! If Rich Little gets a hold of this, I would like to know if he is still alive? If yes, this is for you. I hope your dick falls off you, dirty old fuck!

My publicist is going to make me do the social media thing, but I'm not happy about it because I think social media is a cesspool. I guess I'll figure it out. So to all the Klans out there, if you're not too busy fucking your sister or burning a cross on someone's lawn, go have someone read this to you because my book has a lot of big words in it, you may not get all of it. I'll bet they'll say, "Jan's dad was one of us. Jan's a race trader. We need more pure white kids. How could she do this to us?" Don't worry. Before I got cancer, I saved my eggs – my pure white eggs. Yep, I gave them to a lovely infertile black couple so they can start a family.

When I told them about my dad's genes, I gave them full permission to drown it at birth if it pops out hailing Hitler, and they were pretty cool about it. So now with the social media, I have to do, I guess. It will be difficult to ignore my likes and dislikes. Honestly, I still don't give a shit about it. If you have something meaningful to say, I will read it and will try to respond? I'm glad I got all, well not all, but most of this out. I would like to hear from some of the other comedians who knew David/ Deacon Grey and I hope Willie Aimes reads this, as well. You are so sweet, and I would love to see you again! This time I will try not to wet my pants when I meet you. Hehe.

I have to give a shoot-out to my mom. I know you are going to read this. I'm sorry for so much and that I cursed, but I know you will always love me. You are the best mother a girl could ever have. I apologize for being such a difficult kid. I didn't write this for attention or fame. I just wanted to tell the truth and make you think, laugh, and pray a little too. The last part is for my sister. Hehe. I'm still a little concerned about how this will all be taken. I don't have the privilege of being well off anymore and the only "connections" I have is to God. If anyone comes after me, I guess I'm just going to pray a lot and try to stay incognito. Yeah, like that will work.

I may need some backup down the line. Let me know if you can lend a hand if I need it. I'll make you dinner as a thank you. I'm broke, but it's not the end of the world. It's the thought that counts, right? Fuck it! If you really want to help me out, buy a million copies of my book! Haha. If nothing else, it will make a good gag book. Then we will pass them out at Trump Rallies. They would make great stocking stuffers for the Boogaloos moms. I have a great idea, go to the Los Angeles gun club, do the "gunman's" handshake with a middle-aged white guy, and say, "Here is a book you'll really like. You're in it," and see what their reaction is! I would really get a kick out of that but I don't have the balls to do it. You shouldn't either, unless you're a white guy. Once again, white privilege. I hope you get something out of reading this. Hope it opens some eyes a little, and peace be with you.

Printed in the USA
CPSIA information can be obtained
at www.ICGtesting.com
LVHW010906061023
760263LV00037B/655

9 781088 047163